Nation Building, State Building, and Economic Development

Nation Building, State Building, and Economic Development

Case Studies and Comparisons

S.C.M. Paine, Editor

M.E.Sharpe
Armonk, New York
London, England

Library of Congress Cataloging-in-Publication Data

Nation building, state building, and economic development : case studies and comparisons /
S.C.M. Paine, editor.
  p. cm.
 Includes bibliographical references and index.
 ISBN: 978-0-7656-2244-0 (cloth : alk. paper)—ISBN: 978-0-7656-2245-7 (pbk.: alk. paper)
 1. Nation-building—Case studies. 2. Economic development—Political aspects—Case studies.
 3. Developing countries—Politics and government—Case studies. I. Paine, S.C.M., 1957–

JZ6300.N385 2009
338.9009172'4—dc22   2009003212

Printed in the United States of America

The paper used in this publication meets the minimum requirements of
American National Standard for Information Sciences
Permanence of Paper for Printed Library Materials,
ANSI Z 39.48-1984.

∞

| CW (c) | 10 | 9 | 8 | 7 | 6 | 5 | 4 | 3 | 2 | 1 |
| CW (p) | 10 | 9 | 8 | 7 | 6 | 5 | 4 | 3 | 2 | 1 |

Contents

List of Maps and Table

Maps

Table

Acknowledgments

Historians, more so than specialists in the social sciences, tend to be literate in the languages relevant to their geographic focus. Yet they rarely write for those outside their field. More often than not Americans rely for their understanding of foreign countries on those lacking literacy in the language of the country in question. Americans would be very skeptical of anyone without fluency in English claiming expertise about their country. Yet many highly educated Americans rely on precisely such linguistically constrained people to understand the world beyond their borders. If the United States were not a world power, this situation might be more humorous.

I do not profess any expertise on more than a few other countries, and even concerning these countries, I do not pretend to possess anything close to perfect understanding. So, I have tried to assemble experts on a variety countries, chosen by criteria explained in the Introduction, to see what conclusions and inferences can be made about a trinity of problems—nation building, state building, and economic development—on the basis of country-specific expertise, as opposed to expertise about the theories or methodologies of any particular academic discipline such as political science, economics, or sociology. I do not pretend that this approach will provide the definitive answers that have so long eluded others. Rather, I intend this book to make a serious contribution to the discussion concerning what is required for impoverished countries to become more prosperous.

It is my pleasure to acknowledge the assistance of many and to absolve all of any shortcomings that remain. The Earhart Foundation very generously helped to fund a year in Australia, where I edited the essays contained in this volume. The contributors brought to my attention useful terminology from a variety of fields and, in some cases, of their own creation: Martin McCauley and Kirk Beattie emphasized the distinction between state and nation building; Martin McCauley pointed out the difference between a nation and a nationality; Amy Blitz offered the term *contested state*, Hank Nelson provided the terms *incomplete state* and *alternate state*; Deitmar Rothermund highlighted the term *steel frame* in reference to the state; and Philip Robins and Kirk Beattie emphasized the *rentier state*.

Kay Adamson, Kirk Beattie, Robert Cribb, Alexander Macfie, and Hank Nelson all carefully read the introductory and concluding chapters to make numerous helpful comments. Bruce Elleman and Colin Jackson provided extremely helpful comments on the concluding chapter. Martin McCauley and Colin Jackson both forwarded useful reading lists. Heidi Lane suggested Jordan as the paired chapter for Israel. Alice Juda located key statistical information, while Robin Lima secured books through inter-library loan. At M.E. Sharpe, I am grateful for the expert assistance of Patricia Kolb, Makiko Parsons, Ana Erlić, Susannah Driver-Barstow, and Sandy Koppen. Patricia Kolb offered numerous helpful suggestions for the introductory and concluding chapters. Finally, the support of John H. Maurer, John P. LeDonne, and Yu Minling was essential for the completion of this project.

I will make my own expertise clear at the onset. I am an historian. As a graduate student, my major field was Russian history and my minor field was Chinese history. The dissertation that became my first book examined the history of the modern border between these two countries, covering the 1858 to 1924 period. My study of Sino-Russian relations convinced me of the importance of understanding Japan as well. To make a long story short, I have spent over eight of the last twenty-three years living abroad; one year in China, two and a half years in Taiwan, three years in Japan, one year in Russia, and one year in Australia. My research has relied on primary and secondary sources in Chinese, Japanese, Russian, French, German, and Spanish, which brings me to my undergraduate major in the equivalent of Latin American Studies. As an undergraduate, I conducted a summer of research in Peru, where I unwittingly traveled through areas where the Shining Path was busily laying the groundwork for the brutal insurgency it launched two years later.

Although trained as an Asianist, I am a professor in the Strategy & Policy Department of the U.S. Naval War College, where half of my colleagues are officers from all services of the U.S. armed forces and where the other half are civilians, equally divided between those with doctorates in history and in political science. Students at the college earn a Master of Arts degree in National Security and Strategic Studies. Teaching at the Naval War College has made me keenly aware of the interaction between civil and military institutions, and the importance of crafting an integrative national strategy in order to achieve national objectives.

I would like to make clear that thoughts and opinions expressed in this volume are those of the author of each chapter and are not necessarily those of the U.S. government, the U.S. Department of Defense, the U.S. Navy Department, or the U.S. Naval War College.

Finally, I would like to dedicate this book to my mother, Henrietta R.C. Paine, who emphasized the vital importance of nation building during my childhood. Many of my early memories of her concern her participation in the civil rights marches of the 1960s that contributed to making our nation more complete with the inclusion of African Americans in the American dream.

Nation Building, State Building, and Economic Development

Introduction

S.C.M. PAINE

Why do some countries prosper, while others languish? Over the years, any number of explanations have been advanced, including geography, natural endowments, population growth, culture, property rights, political organization, governmental policy, economic organization, macroeconomic policies, and so forth. In the absence of definitive data, the debate goes on. Many studies reason deductively from hypotheses, but testing the hypotheses often requires accurate and comprehensive economic, political, or social data generally unavailable for any but the most economically developed and open societies. Less fortunate countries lack the data or manipulate what data they do have. Such limitations lead some analysts predisposed to mathematical solutions to test just one factor. Others, the synthesizers, look to multiple interacting factors.

The current work takes an inductive approach. It examines a set of case studies written by country specialists to ask: what general observations concerning nation building, state building, and economic development can be derived from the actual historical experience of their country of expertise? Like the deductive approach, this method is also incomplete, but has been undertaken in anticipation that an examination of an important problem from a different angle might provide useful insights.

The Intuitive and the Counterintuitive

In 1961 Massachusetts Institute of Technology brought together experts on economic development. They rated Iran, Iraq, Pakistan, and Burma as "transitional societies" on the path to economic development and ahead of the bottom tier of so-called neo-traditional societies. Above these two categories, they ranked India, Brazil, the Philippines, and Taiwan as "actively modernizing societies."[1] The intervening half century has reshuffled the deck. Burma and Pakistan teeter on the edge of becoming failed states. The Philippines has stagnated, while Taiwan has taken off, and Brazil and India are belatedly on the march. Despite the great expertise of the many authors of the MIT study, their 1961 classifications did not stand the test of time.

Intuitively, one might think that dictatorship would be a key inhibitor to

3

economic development, while democracy would be a key facilitator; that aggressive foreign military intervention, a lethal national security threat imposing high military budgets, or explosive population growth would be key inhibitors; and that high literacy levels, a broad land distribution, and a substantial resource endowment would be additional facilitators. Intuitively, one might assume that prosperity requires a strong state and a strong state requires a strong nation, so that the natural progression would be strong nation to strong state to strong economy.

The case studies in this book do not bear out the conventional wisdom. Dictatorial early South Korean governments laid the economic foundations for that country's current prosperity. Although Papua New Guinea has remained democratic since independence, it has among the world's highest crime and poverty rates; and when the Congo became democratic, civil war ensued. The two greatest success stories, South Korea and Israel, have prospered despite the existential threat posed by their immediate neighbors, while foreign military intervention has not been universally pernicious. U.S. military intervention in the Dominican Republic brought investment in infrastructure, public health facilities, and education that benefited Dominicans after U.S. soldiers returned home. Likewise, U.S. intervention in the Korean War saved South Korea from annihilation, and massive U.S. financial aid thereafter benefited the entire South Korean population and facilitated subsequent economic development.

Countries with the most rapid population growth have not necessarily done poorly, while those whose population has grown slowly have not necessarily done well. Of the case studies examined, Israel and Jordan experienced by far the largest percentage population growth since 1950, yet Israelis are rich by international standards and Jordanian standards of living have continued to rise. Meanwhile the collapse of Russian birthrates since 1950 is not a sign of prosperity. In the paired cases of the Dominican Republic and Haiti, the Dominican population rose more rapidly, yet Dominicans remain much more prosperous than Haitians. (See the table, "Statistics for the Case Studies," in the concluding chapter on page 294.)

Although much of Latin America has very high literacy levels, prosperity remains elusive. The Philippines has both high literacy and strong democratic traditions, but not prosperity. Haiti has long had a very equal land distribution, but the act of redistribution undermined the plantation economy that had made Haiti the wealthiest part of Latin America in the late eighteenth century. Some countries with the richest resource endowments remain among the most dysfunctional—Congolese, Gabonese, and Russian economic achievements fall far short of what their resource endowments might seem to promise—while countries with virtually no natural resources have thrived—South Korea and Israel, to name two.

Some of the economic nonperformers have strong nations (North Korea and Haiti), and a subset has a strong state too (North Korea), while some top performers have incomplete nations (Israel vis-à-vis its Palestinian minority). Therefore the relationship among nation building, state building, and economic development is not linear. Yet the three seem interlinked in that most wealthy countries seem strong in all three categories.

If the data do not support intuition, what do they suggest? High illiteracy and gross environmental degradation are important inhibitors to prosperity, but South Korea rapidly overcame both. Other inhibitors include a capital-intensive resource endowment more conducive to funding dictatorial rule than to promoting even economic development; a subordination of domestic to foreign policy, leading to a diversion of precious resources to a grand foreign policy agenda; and an internal leadership deficit, meaning that no matter how generous the foreign aid, it went to waste. Poverty correlated with populations locked in zero-sum conflicts that precluded basic nation building; with governments wedded to highly ideological agendas; and with leaders focused single-mindedly on politics as plunder.

The Analytical Framework

This volume employs case studies and inductive reasoning, with one country per chapter. Each chapter begins with an abstract summarizing its findings. All contributors have already published at least one book on their country of expertise and read the language of that country.[2] The more senior contributors have extensive publications. The case studies fall into three categories corresponding to the three parts of this work. Part I focuses on colonization as one route to nation and state building. These cases include: India, the crown jewel of the British Empire; Algeria, which went beyond a colony to become a constitutionally integral part of France; the Philippines, the U.S. attempt at colonial development; and Manchuria, which Japan transformed into the most industrialized part of Asia outside the home islands.

Part II turns to the nationalist reactions against imperialism. These cases focus on charismatic leaders who transformed their countries. These were not new countries but polities of long standing. They include: Soviet Russia, Turkey under Mustafa Kemal Atatürk, China under Mao Zedong, and Egypt under Gamal 'Abd al-Nasser. All were originally empires or influential polities of long standing that had once dominated their respective regions but more recently had fallen into decline. Conscious state and nation building by a key leader marked an attempt at both transformation and restoration.

Part III is composed of paired cases, in which ostensibly similar environments yielded different outcomes. Gross national income per capita (GNIPC) has been used as a simple, but nevertheless telling, measure of these differences.[3] The paired cases are: Haiti ($560 GNIPC) and the Dominican Republic ($3,550 GNIPC), which share an island; Jordan ($2,850 GNIPC) and Israel ($21,900 GNIPC), which both were once parts of the British Mandate of Palestine; North Korea ($935 GNIPC or less), the most industrialized part of the Korean Peninsula under Japan, and South Korea ($19,690 GNIPC), one of the Four Asian Tigers; and the Republic of the Congo ($1,540 GNIPC) (not the People's Republic of the Congo, formerly Zaire, a much larger country) and neighboring Gabon ($6,670

GNIPC), whose citizens have among the highest per capita incomes in Africa; Papua New Guinea ($850 GNIPC) and Indonesia ($1,650 GNIPC), both parts of the same island chain.

All authors based their essays on a common set of analytical questions, but not all questions applied to each case. The list of questions was divided into two parts. The first set concerned the environment in which state and nation building take place. The environment constitutes the combined constraints and opportunities that face policy makers. The second set of questions concerned the choices made within this environment and an evaluation of the choices. The case studies outline the policy objectives of the state and nation builders, describe the strategies employed to achieve these objectives, and evaluate the effectiveness of the strategies to achieve their intended outcomes.

Questions Regarding The Environment for National Construction

Security environment: Was the country at peace or war? Now? Recently? Typically? Are its neighbors friends or foes? What are their relative strengths? Has the country been an object of third-party intervention?

Economic environment: What is the country's resource endowment? Is that endowment broad or focused on just a few items? How valuable are the resources? What is the infrastructure endowment? Likewise, is it broad or focused? Who owns the country's wealth: the state or private individuals? What is the distribution of the wealth? What is the general level of poverty? Who is educated: just elites, certain social or ethnic groups, or the general population?

Political environment: What is the institutional endowment? What are the nature and strength of legal, political, and economic institutions? How stable are these institutions? Is the locus of power a charismatic leader; an economic, political, or social elite; or the general adult population? Does the country have a sense of nation based on antiquity? Does the country sit at the core or the periphery of a civilization? Does it have a sense of nation based on ethnic homogeneity? What is the burden of the past? Are the core values of major social groups religious or secular? Do these values emphasize the individual or the group? Are they acquisitive or nonacquisitive, tolerant or intolerant? Is the typical method of conflict resolution a zero-sum winner-take-all solution or a compromise where everyone gets something?

Questions Regarding the Choices Made in This Environment

The strategy: What strategy did leaders pursue? Was the catalyst for change internal or external, voluntary or coercive, reactive or proactive, elite or popular? Was the strategy determined by intent or by default? What were the goals of the strategy: survival, wealth, military power, development of the civilian economy? Were they driven by ideology or religion? What expertise was employed for drafting the strategy: a politicized party platform or apolitical technocratic advice? Did the strategy focus on the public or private sector, politics or economics, internal issues or foreign foes?

An evaluation of the strategy: Did the chosen strategy produce its intended results? Was there a significant improvement in per capita income? How rapidly did reforms take place? Were the benefits of change concentrated within an elite or dispersed throughout the population? Likewise, were the costs of the strategy concentrated on a few or dispersed among many? Which was greater: the costs or the benefits of the strategy, its risks or its rewards? Were there missed opportunities and better roads not taken?

The Terminology

Before proceeding, it is important to get the terminology straight. Some nations are not states (the Kurds); some states are not nations (the former Russian empire); and only a few are nation-states (Iceland).[4] The terms *state, nation, nationality, nation building, state building,* and *economic development* are used variously. In this work, they will be used in a particular way.

According to Max Weber's famous definition, "a state is that human community which (successfully) lays claim to the *monopoly of legitimate physical violence within a certain territory.* . . . [T]he state is a relationship of *rule (Herrschaft)* by human beings over other human beings, and one that rests on the legitimate use of violence (that is, violence that is held to be legitimate)."[5]

The term *nation* has two distinct usages, which confuse discussions of nation building. People use the word *nation* to signify a place or a people. The first meaning refers to a country with a sovereign government. The second definition refers to a community of people usually with a shared language, religion, culture, and territory. A third term, *nationality,* also refers to a community of people with a shared language, religion, and culture, but not a fixed territory. In practice, the many gradations between second-definition *nation* and *nationality* are hard to delimit precisely. Perhaps the two concepts should be looked at as poles on a continuum of human experience.

In this work, *nation building* will be used to mean the development and strengthening of a shared set of overarching values and an overarching common identity among the inhabitants of a country with a sovereign government. In other words, it puts people before place. This population can encompass one or multiple nations in the second-definition meaning of *nation.* This shared identity and these shared values form foundations conducive to the development of legitimate state institutions. When people cannot agree on a national identity, domestic unrest and even civil war often ensue.

State building refers to the creation and strengthening of the civil and military institutions that comprise a government. Highly industrialized countries have a wide array of such institutions, which go beyond the military and the three branches of government to include economic, educational, public health, public works, police, welfare, and many other types of institutions. Ideally, the activities of these institutions are generally considered to be legitimate by the vast majority of the population, whose overarching common values include the type of government they share. Resilient state institutions are a function of a strong underlying sense of community. This community can be composed of one nation (second definition) or many, but most must share an overarching set of common values in order to produce legitimate state institutions. Thus, the legitimacy of state institutions is often a function of the prior success of nation building, the source of the shared values that allow a government to operate according to accepted norms. However, nation building can also be a function of the prior success of state building when disparate nations (second definition) come to consider state institutions legitimate. Under these circumstances, a growing sense of legitimacy concerning state institutions can serve a homogenizing function conducive to nation building.

The term *economic development* follows a layperson's, not a specialist's, usage. Economic prosperity is construed as an end and economic development as a means to achieve it, on the logic that most people, the poor in particular, care deeply about their standard of living. For the least affluent, income fluctuations translate into the ability or inability to buy life-sustaining necessities. Prosperity has been measured crudely but simply through calculations of per capita national income.

Economic development and economic growth do not occur when the legitimacy of state institutions is under siege, for example during a civil war or during endemic unrest. Economic development requires investment; investment requires stability; and stability requires strong state institutions. However, strong state institutions do not guarantee growth or prosperity, as North Korea so painfully demonstrates. Likewise, democracy does not guarantee economic progress let alone development, as the case of Papua New Guinea shows, nor does dictatorship preclude it, as South Korea made clear during the 1970s and 1980s.

It is also important to distinguish *building* from *rebuilding* or *reconstruction*. The United States did not engage in nation or state building in Germany and Japan after World War II. Both had strong national identities that survived the war. Both also had strong prewar political and economic institutional legacies to fall back on. Instead, the United States engaged in the reconstruction of state institutions and of the economy. Although the United States replaced Japan's Meiji Constitution with the MacArthur Constitution and, in doing so, changed the institutional structures of Japan, both the pre- and postwar structures fell within westernized parliamentary traditions. Germany and Japan rebuilt rapidly after the war because they already possessed the expertise to re-create what had been bombed flat and had long experience administering complex organizations of all kinds.

It is far more difficult and time-consuming to build the expertise and habits of mind to create such institutions and infrastructure the first time around. The process of reconstruction tends to be far less divisive than the act of creation. Old institutions and old habits tend to have a legitimacy conferred by time and tradition. If such institutions worked in the past, people often accept that they will work in the future. People also have a mental image of the future based on the familiar past, and many may share the same mental images. Thus, re-creation can leverage the legitimacy conferred by tradition, and the expertise and experience acquired in the past, in order to rebuild rapidly and with comparatively little controversy.

Creation, however, presupposes a choice among alternatives, none of which has been vetted in the past or can be imagined in high resolution. Alternatives presuppose a debate, but a debate without incontrovertible evidence relies on conjecture and value preferences. In order to build the new, citizens often must acquire new skills and organize themselves differently. This takes time and requires stability to proceed. Yet unresolvable political debates over major issues tend to grow, not subside, over time, particularly when basic economic needs remain unmet—the general condition in poor countries. In weakly institutionalized countries, such debates can lead to debilitating instability that derails both building and development. Without an institutional "steel frame" such debates can escalate into violence, insurgency, and civil war. For these reasons, although reconstruction can take place within one generation, even rapid state building and economic development generally take two to three generations. Both state building and economic development require stability, which, in such situations, tends to be in short supply.

The above time estimate is a best-case scenario based on the world's few success stories: Meiji Japan, South Korea, Taiwan, and Singapore. Note that all four have cultures that emphasize education, hard work, authority, and family. Note that two are former Japanese colonies, which Japan had forced to implement its own successful model for economic development. Note also that three possessed ancient national identities and so did not require any nation building with or without Japan. Singapore alone constructed a national identity from scratch out of the combined concepts of multiculturalism, meritocracy, and citizenship.[6]

Further general observations and conclusions will be presented in the final chapter, following the three groups of case studies.

Notes

1. Max F. Millikan and Donald L.M. Blackmer, eds. *The Emerging Nations: Their Growth and United States Policy,* Center for International Studies, MIT (Boston: Little, Brown, 1961), 134, 137, 140.

2. The only exception is the essay on Algeria. That author reads French, the language of most scholarly publications pertaining to Algeria.

3. World Bank, "GNI Per Capita 2007, Atlas Method and PPP," World Development Indicators Database, http://siteresources.worldbank.org/DATASTATISTICS/Resources/GNIPC.pdf, accessed 22 December 2008.

4. I have lifted much of the wording for this sentence from an e-mail from my colleague Karl Walling, sent to me on 15 February 2007; I am grateful to Martin McCauley for recommending Hugh Seton-Watson's excellent book, *Nations and States: An Enquiry into the Origins of Nations and the Politics of Nationalism* (Boulder, CO: Westview Press, 1977), which lays out the difference between state and nation very clearly on page 1.

5. Italics in the original. Max Weber, "The Profession and Vocation of Politics," in *Weber: Political Writings*, Peter Lassman and Ronald Speirs, eds. (Cambridge: Cambridge University Press, 1994), 310–11.

6. Michael Hill and Lian Kwen Fee, *The Politics of Nation Building and Citizenship in Singapore* (London: Routledge, 1995), 31, 39, 107.

Part I

Imperial State Building:
La Mission Civilisatrice

1

Nation Building in India Under British Rule

DIETMAR ROTHERMUND

Abstract: *This case study analyzes the unintentional aspects of British rule that turned out to contribute to nation and state building in India. It discusses the bureaucratic "steel frame" holding India together, the imposition of a legal system amalgamating British and Hindu legal traditions, the introduction of a new universe of discourse with the spread of British education, and the alternating current of national agitation and British constitutional reforms. At independence, the Indian personnel of Britain's Indian Civil Service became the nucleus of the Indian Administrative Service, which provided administrative continuity during the change of governments. The independence movement contributed to nation building, as Indian nationalists tried to create a shared identity capable of unifying India after the British departure. Finally, the chapter deals with the traumatic experience of territoriality caused by the partition of India and the emergence of an independent democratic republic under the leadership of Jawaharlal Nehru, a passionate parliamentarian.*

The British Challenge and the Indian Response

The British did not conquer India in order to build an Indian nation. On the contrary, most of the British posted in India never conceived of India as a nation and referred to it as "congeries of nations" which could never be united. They also used the old imperial strategy of divide and rule. And yet, they contributed unwittingly to nation building by their very presence. They imposed a more or less uniform institutional framework of governance on India so as to control it. But even more important was the challenge they provided to the Indians by demonstrating what a nation could do whose power was derived from social cohesion and efficient organization. In the eighteenth century, when the East India Company gained territorial control of large parts of India, there were about 6 million British people. The former Mughal empire had approximately 150 million inhabitants. It was a confrontation like that between David and Goliath. The match was even more uneven, because the number of British men sent to India was very small. The British did not invade; they hired Indian soldiers to conquer India for them and paid them with the money of Indian

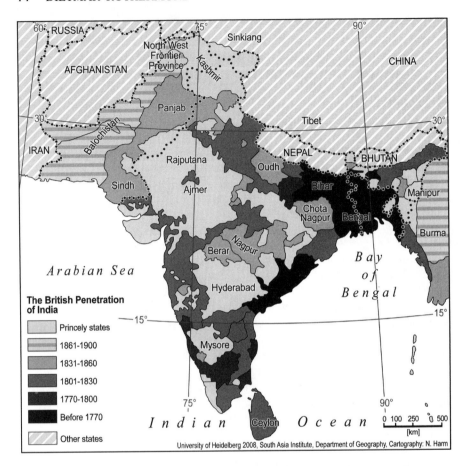

The British Penetration of India

Princely states
1861-1900
1831-1860
1801-1830
1770-1800
Before 1770
Other states

University of Heidelberg 2008, South Asia Institute, Department of Geography, Cartography: N. Harm

taxpayers. The Great Mughals had based their central power on a monetized land revenue. When the British gained control of the rich province of Bengal, they could use its revenue for financing their further operations in India.

British military strength was not based on superior weapons. All weapons used in those times were easily available to Indian rulers too. But the British introduced modern methods of infantry warfare, which consisted of making soldiers fire well-timed volleys at the enemy's cavalry with a devastating effect.[1] Traditional Indian musketeers were skillful marksmen, but they were not used to concerted attacks. A few British drill sergeants sufficed to teach them the new methods of warfare. The British were also better military paymasters than their Indian adversaries. Indian military heroes were often inept as far as financial matters were concerned. They might win a battle and then be unable to pay their troops, who promptly deserted. Officers in the service of a company of traders calculated their military ventures more carefully.

British military leaders in India also had other important characteristics that distinguished them from their adversaries. As members of a bourgeois nation, they never succumbed to the feudal temptation to become independent warlords after a victorious campaign. Warren Hastings, the first governor-general and the founder of the British empire in India, even humbly submitted to his recall and his impeachment by the British Parliament.[2] He was accused of conquering large parts of India "illegally." Although the Parliament impeached him, it never considered restoring those territories to their Indian rulers.

Another source of British strength was naval power, which had been neglected by Indian rulers. The most powerful local rulers were land based and did not care for maritime affairs. The smaller rulers, who controlled individual seaports, benefited from customs duties and welcomed traders of all nations. They never thought of trying to control or oppress traders, since they knew that maritime trade could easily shift to other ports. The despotic regime of the monsoon shielded India against maritime invaders, as their supply lines would be cut each year. This made Indian rulers complacent as far as control of their maritime periphery was concerned.

Only the perceptive young ruler of Maharashtra, Madhav Rao, remarked, in 1767, that the British had encircled India with a ring of naval power.[3] By that time it was too late, even if Indian rulers had stopped their internecine warfare and had turned their attention to naval defense. The British had the best ships of the world at their disposal. In the 1660s the East India Company had closed its own dockyard and had adopted the very modern method of leasing rather than owning ships. Private ship owners then competed with each other to offer state-of-the-art ships to the company.[4] These ships sailed very fast and were heavily armed. They were the pride of the British nation, and their captains were expert navigators who earned high salaries. National efficiency was clearly demonstrated by the performance of this impressive mercantile fleet. High freight charges imposed a strict discipline on its operations. Timetables had to be closely watched, as each day lost at sea meant a loss of much money. Capitalism subjected the British even at this early stage to its rigorous rules.

The Indians noticed the challenge posed by the British nation very slowly. Therefore their response took a long time. They were not confronted with a large foreign occupation army, which might have provoked immediate resistance. The British gradually usurped and transformed Indian institutions. After the decline of the Mughal empire, the commercialization of power had increased in India.[5] Some Indian rulers mortgaged their states to merchants who organized the collection of their revenues and managed their treasury. In this context the activities of the East India Company were not unusual. This company could adjust much more easily to Indian conditions than an administration manned by royal officers of a foreign power would have done. The servants of the East India Company could play many roles. Initially they were hired as commercial employees only. Their salaries were meager, and they had to pay a large deposit when beginning their career. It was taken for granted that they would enrich themselves in India. The deposit would be forfeited only if they hurt the company's interest by their machinations. If they served the company well, they could quickly rise to high positions.

The career of Robert Clive provides striking evidence of this flexible pattern of company rule.[6] He went to India as a teenager and was first employed as a "writer," or clerk, in the company's office in Madras. In 1751 he emerged as a military hero in a war waged by the company against Indian rulers. He valiantly defended the fortress of Arcot against an Indian army. He then returned to his commercial line and made a fortune. He retired at an early age and campaigned for a seat in the British Parliament. He lost much money in the election campaign and did not win a seat. So he returned to India, after having procured the patent of a lieutenant colonel. He was sent from Madras to Calcutta, commanding troops of the East India Company. The Nawab of Bengal had taken action against the British settlement there because it had been fortified by the British, who had defied his orders. Clive defeated the Nawab in 1757 and established British rule over this fertile province, becoming its first British governor. The Battle of Plassey, which Clive won, was a mere skirmish. His success was due to bribery rather than to military valor as the Nawab's general deserted to join forces with Clive. (The traitor's name, Mir Jafar, is still a synonym for treachery in India.) There was no parallel to Mir Jafar's behavior among the British. Clive was cunning and devious, and he lined his pockets with Indian money, but he faithfully served the British cause.

When the East India Company became a territorial ruler, the methods of Clive and his contemporaries had to be changed. The commercial servants of the company became "civil servants" who earned high salaries, which were supposed to prevent them from succumbing to corruption. The company established a special college at Haileybury, in England, where the candidates for the civil service were trained. They followed regular careers, starting as a district officer and ending as a secretary to government or even as a member of the governor's council. They were freely transferable and were expected to cope with any assigned task. Indians had earlier been ruled by military commanders, who employed scribes to do the administrative work for them. Now they were to be ruled by British scribes.

Administration: The Bureaucratic "Steel Frame"

The comparison of the British civil service in India with a "steel frame" that kept the country together was made by Prime Minister Lloyd George in 1922. It was not an expression of imperial bravado, but rather a desperate plea at a time when the star of the empire was sinking. Lloyd George wanted to attract to this service young British men who were no longer certain whether they could look forward to a lifetime career in India. After India had gained independence in 1947, the powerful home minister, Vallabhbhai Patel, used similar words in order to defend the maintenance of the "steel frame," now manned by Indians. Addressing the Constituent Assembly, he asserted that the country had to be kept together by a "ring of service."[7] His arguments were accepted. There was a change in name only: the old

Indian Civil Service (ICS) became the new Indian Administrative Service (IAS). The rules of the service remained the same; it was centrally recruited and was under the jurisdiction of the central home ministry. The terms of service were enshrined in a special section of the Indian constitution.[8] The officers of this service could be freely transferred. They usually started their career in a district, and would then rise to higher positions in the respective state government or could be deputed to a central ministry. They could also be put in charge of a large public sector enterprise. As "generalists" they were supposed to be able to cope with any task assigned.

Vallabhbhai Patel was a staunch nationalist and a close associate of Mahatma Gandhi. He could be expected to hate the civil service, whose members had jailed so many nationalists in the course of the freedom movement. In fact, the members of the service feared that Patel might take revenge, disband the service, and even prosecute individual members for what they had done under British rule. Instead Patel surprised them by wholeheartedly opting for the "ring of service"—and they did keep the country together. This was a striking instance of adopting a British legacy and using it in the interest of state building. Patel's decision was prudent. The Indian national leadership had not attained power in a violent revolution but in a "transfer of power" by the departing British. It was thus advisable not to cast aside one of the main instruments of the power transferred by the British.

The exigencies of the Second World War greatly enhanced the British administrative legacy.[9] Before the war the British-Indian government was powerful but small. It consisted of a few departments that determined rules and regulations but had hardly any executive functions. This changed dramatically during the war, when two million Indian soldiers served in the British Indian army. They had to be equipped, and Indian industries were geared to the British war effort. These industries remained in private hands but the procurement was managed according to a cost-plus rule. The bureaucrats calculated the cost of production and added a margin of profit (usually 10 percent).

Another task faced by the British-Indian government was the accumulation of buffer stocks of grain so as to prevent speculative hoarding and an inflationary increase of prices. Initially this was attempted by imposing price controls, but this encouraged a booming black market. Only a massive accumulation of buffer stocks would enable the government to dominate the market.[10] Procurement and storage of such stocks required a new institution. It still exists as the Food Corporation of India and nowadays stores huge buffer stocks. British India was turned into an interventionist state with a vengeance, and the instruments required for this were bequeathed to independent India. This creation of an interventionist state could be regarded as another instance of the unintended consequences of British rule over India, which contributed to the process of state building. Jawaharlal Nehru knew this very well. He praised the state that he had inherited as a school of the Indian nation.

Another British legacy akin to the inherited state was the colonial legal system, which had slowly evolved over a long period of time. Many old British acts are still on the Indian statute book. Hardly any questions are raised when they are applied today. Only very rarely do they emerge into the limelight of public debate. A recent instance is the application of the draconian Land Acquisition Act of 1894 for the establishment of Special Economic Zones.[11] In general Indians are proud of the rule of law, but occasionally it is necessary to examine the root of laws that have existed for a long time.

Jurisdiction: The Imposition of a Legal System

Even before the British began to build up their civil service system in India, they imposed a new legal system on the territory that they controlled. Having been entrusted in 1765 by the Great Mughal with the Diwani of Bengal, meaning the right to collect the revenue of Bengal, they were also responsible for the Diwani Adalat jurisdiction, meaning the courts dealing with civil law and land questions. This was a kind of customary law that was a mixture of Muslim and Hindu law. It permitted a great deal of judicial discretion, which was soon exercised by inexperienced British district officers.

Parallel to this jurisdiction was that of the Supreme Court of Calcutta, which was originally restricted to the legal affairs of Europeans settled in the territory controlled by the British. The judges of this court were legal luminaries appointed by the British crown. The brightest among them was Sir William Jones, who arrived in Calcutta in 1784.[12] He was not only a brilliant legal scholar but also a great Orientalist who knew Arabic and Persian well and became a master of Sanskrit in India. In a letter written in 1787, he already referred to the similarities of Sanskrit, Greek, and Latin, foreshadowing the subsequent discoveries of comparative philology. Soon after his arrival in India, he founded the Asiatic Society in 1784 and started the project of the codification of Hindu law with the help of Indian pandits (Hindu scholars).

Having a Hindu law code was of immediate practical importance; British judges, who had to decide cases involving matters of inheritance and the like, could simply refer to this code. This codification was a revolutionary initiative and upset Indian traditions. Earlier the Brahmins, as interpreters of Hindu law, could adapt it to different circumstances. The published code put an end to this power of interpretation and also to its inherent flexibility. But it universalized the codified law and made it applicable throughout British India. In a way this was also a contribution to nation building. Jones had not conceived of it in this way. To him, a genius of the Age of Enlightenment, codification was simply a matter of the advancement of knowledge.

British courts were spreading in India like wildfire in the late eighteenth century. Providing this new type of jurisdiction was not an altruistic measure; it yielded substantial revenue from court fees, which far surpassed the cost of maintaining the courts. At the same time it helped to enhance the legitimacy of British rule. Indian litigants flocked to these courts, deserting their own judicial institutions. Litigants who could afford to pay the best lawyer were almost sure to win their case before such a court. Becoming a lawyer assured educated Indians of a lucrative career. At a later stage they could even aspire to a position as a judge in a high court, because the British also followed the rule "from the bar to the bench" in India. They selected judges from the ranks of the best lawyers, who would feel honored by being addressed as "Mr. Justice" and so would gladly forgo a higher income as a lawyer. Indian Bar Associations, which were established even in small district towns, served as focal points of an emerging civil society. They also became the breeding ground for Indian nationalism. Almost all the leaders of the Indian freedom movement were lawyers. But this happened only at a later stage. At the time when the British began establishing courts in India, they certainly had not thought of the unintended consequences of their policy.

Education: A New Universe of Discourse

A similar story of unintended consequences can be told about the spread of British education in India. In the early nineteenth century, the provincial governments established only very few government colleges, but those were soon followed by colleges established by different Christian missions. In 1835 the Law Member of the Governor General's Council, Lord Macaulay, announced the aims of British educational policy in India.[13] Unlike Sir William Jones, he was not in sympathy with Oriental scholarship and despised Indian languages and literatures. To him only English education was acceptable. He wanted to convert educated Indians into perfect gentlemen. Strangely enough, Macaulay's policy was even supported by Raja Radhakanta Deb, the great Sanskrit scholar. Of course, Deb did not share Macaulay's views with regard to Indian languages and literatures, but he thought of "jobs for the boys." He knew that only an English education would secure a career for Indians under British rule. This was a realistic assessment, and Indians were soon employed in great numbers as subaltern bureaucrats. Colleges proliferated, and their syllabi and curricula were copied from those of British colleges. The works of William Shakespeare and the philosophy of John Stuart Mill were read eagerly by Indian students. Some of them even surpassed the British civil servants in their intimate knowledge of English literature and their command of the English language.

Unwittingly the British provided the Indians with a new nationwide universe of discourse and with ideas that could be easily turned against them. Indians who read John Stuart Mill's work *On Liberty* could not help assessing their own position under foreign rule in terms of this liberal philosophy.[14] Dadabhai Naoroji's famous book, *Poverty and Un-British Rule in India,* showed this impact of British ideas on Indian nationalists very clearly. Assessed in term of British ideals, British rule in India was "Un-British." The new type of education introduced under colonial rule also led to the rise of a lively Indian press. Many newspapers were published in Indian languages. Indian journalists created a new prose, whereas earlier Indian literature was written in verse and was devoted mostly to poetic themes. The novel, as a new genre, captured the attention of Indian readers. The new prose style enriched many Indian languages. College graduates who did not get a government job often became translators who rendered English publications in Indian languages. The new universe of discourse was thus extended beyond the narrow circle of those who knew English well. Among the unintended consequences of British rule in India, this was perhaps the most important one. It had an immediate relevance for nation building.

Agitation: The Rise of the Freedom Movement

Indian nationalism arose among those who shared the new universe of discourse.[15] This nationalism followed two different lines. One school of thought considered British rule as a necessary precondition for Indian nation building. Its adherents were the liberal constitutionalists who later on were called "moderates." The other school consisted of national revolutionaries who claimed that India had always been a nation and only needed to break the shackles of foreign rule to come into its own again. The "moderates" called them "extremists." In order to justify their claim of an "eternal Indian nation," the national revolutionaries had to delve into a "useful past" which corresponded to their aspirations.

They could turn to the findings of Indologists, whose discipline had progressed enormously after its early beginnings in the days of Sir William Jones. The German Indologist Max Mueller, who taught at Oxford, was a friend of many Indian nationalists.[16] He did not hesitate to support their cause publicly. Mahatma Gandhi later stated that he had learned much about Hinduism from Mueller.[17] Gandhi was a devout Hindu, and therefore this statement seems to be rather strange. What could he learn from Max Mueller about his own religion? It was "Hinduism" as a general concept of nationwide relevance that Mueller portrayed and that inspired Gandhi like so many other Indian nationalists.

Even before Gandhi, Indian nationalists had produced a new ideology: Neo-Hinduism. It highlighted elements in the Indian tradition that supported national solidarity, such as the Vedanta philosophy, which proclaimed that the human soul and the universe are one and that self-realization leads to a recognition of this unity. The divisive nature of the caste system did not fit this vision and was rejected by nationalists espousing the new ideology. Neo-Hinduism, however, could not inspire the Indian Muslims. On the contrary, they had to reject its inclusiveness, which was incompatible with Islam.

Mahatma Gandhi tried to arrive at an "overlapping consensus" of Hindus and Muslims in the arena of agitation against injustice and colonial rule. The American philosopher John Rawls, who coined the term *overlapping consensus*, has stressed that this consensus can be achieved only if those who are striving for it do not appeal to "comprehensive doctrines" such as religious beliefs. In his famous work *The Theory of Justice,* Rawls devoted a chapter to the right of resistance.[18] A reference to Gandhi and his satyagraha (his philosophy of nonviolent resistance) is conspicuous by its absence in this chapter. Rawls must have known about Gandhi, but he obviously thought of him as a religious leader wedded to a "comprehensive doctrine." This is why Rawls did not refer to him. In fact, Gandhi had achieved an "overlapping consensus" in his first agitational campaigns in South Africa, which were jointly supported by Hindus and Muslims.

Gandhi returned to India during the First World War, when political agitation was ruled out under emergency laws. He could conduct some local campaigns only of a "non-political" nature. Only after the end of the war could he win over the Indian National Congress for his nationwide noncooperation campaign. He had announced the principle of noncooperation with the British colonial rulers in his manifesto *Hind Swaraj* in 1909. In this he had argued that the British had not won India by the sword but that the Indians had handed it over to them and that the Indians still kept the British in India by cooperating with them. In 1920 this Gandhian message found an enthusiastic response among Indian Muslims, who resented the terms imposed on the defeated Turkish caliph by the victorious British. A so-called Khilafat movement (1919–24) to protect the Ottoman empire in the aftermath of World War I spread like wildfire in India, and Gandhi supported it because he was glad to find a cause on which an "overlapping consensus" could be based.

He did not realize that this cause was subject to the volatility of the Pan-Islamic sentiments of the Indian Muslims. When the Turks themselves abolished the office of the caliph in 1924, the cause was lost and the "overlapping consensus" disappeared. In fact, many Indian Muslims then turned their attention to communal organizations and spurned any cooperation with the Hindus. With the benefit of hindsight one can state that Gandhi made a mistake by opting for the Khilafat movement.[19] Mohammed Ali Jinnah, the leader of the Muslim League, who had been a secular rather than a communal politician, had rejected Gandhi's agitational politics and had been marginalized by him. Jinnah considered the Khilafat movement to be reactionary and had not supported it. But when the Muslims were disappointed by its demise, they turned to Jinnah, who then emerged as a communal politician with a vengeance. The first steps toward partition were taken at that time although nobody was thinking in terms of partition as yet.

In 1922 Gandhi terminated his noncooperation movement when it threatened to disintegrate in sporadic violence. While the movement had not reached its immediate goal, it had produced a large number of enthusiastic volunteers who remained full-time politicians. Gandhi was a great fund-raiser and managed to support them. When taking over the leadership of the Indian National Congress, he reorganized it. The boundaries of Provincial Congress Committees (PCCs) were redrawn along linguistic lines, because Gandhi wished Indians to conduct their political debates in their respective mother tongues rather than in English.[20] He also saw to it that the PCCs recruited more members in rural areas. This prepared the ground for rallying the Indian peasants in the next round of national agitation in the 1930s.

The Indian peasantry, particularly the richer strata, originally had no reason to side with the nationalists. In the course of the late nineteenth century, the British had passed many tenancy laws benefiting these strata of the peasantry. In this way the British had hoped to find a new social base for their colonial rule. In the course of the constitutional reforms of the 1930s the British had enfranchised 10 percent of the Indian people and had seen to it that the dominant strata of the peasantry got the vote. The colonial rulers hoped that they would vote for pro-British agrarian parties rather than for the rebellious Congress Party. But the impact of the Great Depression spoiled this plan.

Grain prices were halved within a few months in 1930 and 1931, but the peasants still had to pay the old rates of land revenue or rent. Moreover, most peasants were indebted and the moneylenders charged the same usurious interest rates as before or even foreclosed mortgages in order to recover their capital. British monetary policy added to the plight of the peasantry. By maintaining an overvalued currency so as to prevent a "flight from the rupee," the British appreciated the amount of rural debt and made the burden of the peasants unbearable.[21] This drove the peasants into the arms of the Congress Party, which was well prepared to rally them to the cause of nationalism. Since the moneylenders pounced on the peasants, the British tried to control their activities by special legislation. This did not relieve the peasants very much, but made the disgruntled moneylenders also flock to the Congress Party. When elections were held from 1936 to 1937 under the new Government of India Act of 1935, the Congress Party captured seven out of the nine provinces of British India. These were the Hindu-majority provinces; the two Muslim-majority provinces, Panjab and Bengal, were won by regional parties and not by Jinnah's Muslim League.

The new constitution provided for "provincial autonomy" and the Congress Party formed provincial ministries. These ministries resigned at the beginning of the Second World War, because the British refused to announce what they would do about India at the end of that war. Winston Churchill, the great imperialist, could not be expected to support Indian nationalism. Instead he encouraged his friend Jinnah, who emerged as a great leader during the war while the Congress leadership languished in jail. The provincial governments of the Panjab and Bengal did not resign. They remained in office throughout the war and supported the British war effort. Led by local politicians, these governments did not feel that they had to take orders from Jinnah, whose Muslim League did not play an important role in their provinces. They agreed that Jinnah could pose as a "national" spokesman for them as long as he refrained from interfering with their provincial affairs.[22]

In order to enhance his "national" position, Jinnah sponsored the famous Lahore Resolution of the Muslim League of 1940, which became known as the Pakistan Resolution, although the word *Pakistan* was not used in it. The term had been coined by Rahmat Ali in 1933. Jinnah had rejected the Pakistan idea at that time, because he was then primarily a leader of the Muslims in the Hindu-majority provinces, to whom *Pakistan* did not apply. In 1940 he still avoided the word but opted for its substance, announcing his two-nation theory according to which Hindus and

Muslims are two nations "by any definition of the term."[23] He added this because he knew that it would be difficult to define his "Muslim nation" in territorial terms, as millions of Muslims lived in the Hindu-majority provinces and were bound to remain there. In subsequent years, he kept his cards close to his chest and never revealed his plans for the territorial demarcation of Pakistan. He hoped that it would at least include the whole of the Panjab and the whole of Bengal, although this would have been incompatible with his two-nation theory, as substantial parts of the East Panjab and of West Bengal were Hindu-majority areas.

During the war, Indian nationalism could not find expression in agitational movements. When Gandhi announced a Quit India movement in 1942 demanding immediate independence, the British nipped it in the bud. Gandhi and all other Congress leaders were jailed once more. Because Gandhi could not give any direction to the movement, it led to the spontaneous August Revolution of the younger generation.[24] These revolutionaries attacked district headquarters, destroyed railway tracks, and committed other acts of sabotage. But the British knew how to deal with such activities, and by the end of August they were once more in full control of the country. Gandhi was released from prison in 1944 ahead of the other Congress leaders. By then the British knew that they would win the war.

Gandhi was old and could not start an agitational campaign all alone. He had a round of talks with Jinnah in order to call Jinnah's bluff by asking him to spell out his plans for Pakistan. He conceded Pakistan to Jinnah in these talks but hoped that Jinnah would have to admit the absurdity of carving out Pakistan from British India. Jinnah skillfully avoided all concrete details. Finally Gandhi proposed that before partition a treaty should be concluded between the two successor states of British India that would assure their peaceful coexistence.[25] To this Jinnah replied that such a treaty could be concluded only after partition, because otherwise the contracting partners would not exist. Gandhi could not controvert this argument and withdrew. Henceforth he avoided any further talks with Jinnah; he must have realized that in matters of constitutional law he could not match Jinnah's legal acumen. By the end of the war, partition seemed to be inevitable unless the British government took a bold step by announcing a road map for granting independence to India and fixing a date for the transfer of power.

Partition: The Traumatic Experience of Territoriality

In the summer of 1945, Winston Churchill's war cabinet resigned and elections were held. To everybody's surprise the Labour Party won and Clement Attlee became prime minister. He was familiar with India, as he had chaired the Indian Committee of the war cabinet. He could have taken a bold step immediately, the more so as India had emerged from the war as a creditor to Great Britain and thus the crucial problem of India's national debt, which had been debated before the war, did not exist any longer.[26] But Attlee missed his chance and the future of India remained uncertain. In August 1945 President Harry Truman decided to have the atom bomb dropped on Japan. Gandhi was shocked and would have liked to condemn this inhuman act. But he kept quiet and even sent a letter to the *Times* in London, stating that he had not said anything about the atom bomb.[27] He felt that he had to refrain from criticizing Truman in the interest of the Indian freedom movement. He feared that the United States and Great Britain might jointly suppress this movement armed with the terrible weapon to which no resistance was possible. Gandhi's nonviolent campaigns had always been aimed at an adversary who could be faced and challenged. The bomb made him feel helpless, and he did not dare to think of further agitations at this stage.

Instead of providing a road map for India's independence, Attlee ordered that elections should be held in India in the winter of 1945 to 1946. The results of the provincial elections strengthened Jinnah's position. The Congress Party again captured the seven Hindu-majority provinces, but this time the Muslim League did much better in the Muslim-majority provinces and the regional parties declined. The demand for Pakistan became more insistent. In March 1946 a Cabinet Mission was sent to India, consisting of three members of the British cabinet. Again an opportunity was missed to make a statement concerning India's independence. Therefore the mandate of the Cabinet Mission was not clear. It could only make recommendations that were not binding and could be rejected. Jinnah derived great political strength from his veto power.[28] Finally the viceroy, Lord Wavell, dared to defy him and appointed Jawaharlal Nehru as interim prime minister of India in August 1946. After some initial opposition, the Muslim League joined Nehru's cabinet but obstructed its work.

Attlee then cut the Gordian knot and appointed Lord Mountbatten as the last viceroy in March 1947. Mountbatten had a clear mandate to prepare India for independence. A date for the transfer of power was set for August 1948. After assessing the situation in India, Mountbatten asked for an earlier date: August 1947. He was afraid that by August 1948 not much power would be left that could be transferred. The British Parliament quickly passed an Independence of India Act based on the Government of India Act of 1935.

The final problem was how to respond to the demand for Pakistan. Mountbatten, after obtaining the consent of the political parties in India, sent a plan, suitably called "Plan Balkan," to London, where it was revised in an unexpected manner. Instead of burdening the British with the odious task of partition, the new plan suggested that independence would be granted to the provinces of British India and the princely states. These units could then decide which kind of states they wished to form. Mountbatten showed this plan to Nehru, who became furious when he saw it. Nehru's reaction surprised Mountbatten. But Nehru saw clearly that this plan could indeed lead to an irreversible balkanization of India.[29] With no central government left, the newly independent units might prefer to go it alone. A partition at the hands of the departing British was to be preferred. Mountbatten revised the plan accordingly, and even Gandhi acquiesced to it although he had earlier referred to partition as the "vivisection of India."

With partition the Indian leaders had to face the problem of territoriality for the first time. The freedom movement had been aimed at independence from British rule; it was not inspired by any territorial quest. In the beginning of the twentieth century, India's great poet, Rabindranath Tagore, had coined a term for territoriality: *rashtratantra*.[30] He had argued that Western nations were obsessed with it, but that India was free from this obsession. Jinnah had introduced this "obsession" by staking a claim for Pakistan, but till the eve of partition he had not discussed the actual boundaries of that state. Mountbatten then asked Jinnah to nominate an impartial person who would demarcate these boundaries. Jinnah opted for a British judge who had no prior knowledge of India.[31] This judge then looked at the census data of the districts of the Panjab and of Bengal, and separated the Hindu-majority districts from these Muslim-majority provinces. Jinnah called this a "moth-eaten" Pakistan, but he could not object to the criteria, which were formulated according to his two-nation theory.[32]

Of course, this partition could not solve the problem of the large Muslim diaspora which remained in India, nor were the princely states included in the terms of reference of the judge who partitioned India. This is why Kashmir later on remained in India although Muslims were in a majority in this princely state. India accepted partition, but it could never accept the two-nation theory, as one-third of the Muslims of the subcontinent continued to live in India. Mountbatten realized that the traumatic experience of territorial division might cause great unrest. Therefore he decided to grant independence to India and Pakistan first and announce the new boundaries only afterward. He perhaps hoped that the joy of independence would benumb the people so that they would not feel the pain of "vivisection." In this he was mistaken. As soon as the details of the partition were revealed, hordes of refugees stormed across the new borders and there was much bloodshed.

In territorial terms, the two new states had different problems. India was riddled with hundreds of princely states, which all became independent in their own right. But as India inherited a strong central government, it was able to incorporate these princely states with a mixture of generosity and coercion. Pakistan included very few princely states, but faced the territorial absurdity of two wings, which were more than one thousand miles apart. Islam was the only common denominator of these two wings. West Pakistan then behaved like a colonial power and imposed its control over East Pakistan, which finally seceded in 1971 to become the independent nation of Bangladesh. This was the only revision of the colonial territorial legacy in any colony throughout the world. Everywhere else this legacy has been preserved although many colonial boundaries were of a rather arbitrary character.

In 1948 Mahatma Gandhi became the most prominent victim of the partition. He did not grasp the full meaning of partition immediately. When he was told that it would also mean the division of the British Indian Army, he could not believe it. But when he saw that this would be a logical consequence of territorial partition, he predicted that the two armies would fight each other—which they soon did. Then the problem of dividing the financial assets of British India also came up. Being at war with Pakistan, the independent Government of India was reluctant to transfer to Pakistan 550 million rupees, which would fill the enemy's war chest. Gandhi pleaded for fairness and started his last great fast in order to persuade the Indian government to part with this money.[33] Hindu nationalists regarded this as high treason and one of them assassinated him on 31 January 1948.

The Republic of India: A Democratic Government

The Father of the Nation was gone, but his heir, Jawaharlal Nehru, now guided the country and saw to it that India would be a democratic nation-state. The two men had often differed in their judgment of current affairs and their visions for the future of India. But Nehru had never parted company with Gandhi because he knew that Gandhi was in touch with the Indian people and understood them much better than he could ever do. On the other hand, Gandhi appreciated Nehru's sincerity and his devotion to the cause of the Indian nation.

Unlike Jinnah, who became governor-general of Pakistan and thus continued the viceregal tradition, Nehru remained prime minister of India. Under the viceroys there had been no prime minister until Lord Wavell appointed Nehru as interim prime minister at the tail end of British rule. The constitution of independent India contained only a very laconic reference to the office of the prime minister.[34] All powers were vested in the president of India, but it was presumed that he would act on the advice of the prime minister and there was a provision that this advice could not be inquired into by a court of law. These rather rudimentary provisions were the foundation of parliamentary democracy in India. It was obviously assumed that the conventions of the unwritten British constitution would also be valid in India. But these conventions had to be established in India—and this was Nehru's great contribution to democratic nation building. He was an enthusiastic parliamentarian. He usually attended all of the sessions of Parliament and frequently participated in the debates.

Nehru's contribution to India's political life was crucial, but he could also rely on the Congress Party, which was a powerful political machine. No other state that emerged from the wave of decolonization sweeping Asia and Africa from 1947 to 1960 inherited such a national party. The discipline and cohesion of this party was to a large extent due to Mahatma Gandhi, whose followers were still active in the first two decades after independence. Most of them had spent many years in jail during the freedom movement and had proven their worth in this way. Gandhi, however, had never conceived of the Congress as a party; he saw in it a national forum that had achieved its aim with independence and should be disbanded, making way for ordinary political parties.[35] This wish, which he expressed shortly before his death, was disregarded by his followers, who preserved the Congress Party as his heritage. For several decades this party would rule India at the center and in almost all states. Thereafter regional parties emerged, which challenged its dominance.

The regional parties were a product of Indian federalism, which had been introduced by the British in the 1930s in the interest of the devolution of power. In this way the colonial rulers had hoped to retain central power while relegating Indian politics to the provincial arena. Nehru hated federalism for this reason, but he retained it after independence. In fact, it has served India well. It provided a democratic framework for regional political aspirations which could have threatened a unitary national state. But even after making headway in various Indian states, regional parties for a long time remained underrepresented in the central parliament. They did not get the number of seats corresponding to the votes they had received.

In recent years this has changed. The two national parties, the Congress Party and the Bharatiya Janata Party (BJP), get about a quarter of the votes each, the various regional parties win almost 50 percent of the national vote, and the seats in the central parliament now reflect this more or less accurately.[36] Strangely enough, the election results under a majority election system thus approximate the results that would prevail under a system of proportional representation. Such results have led to the emergence of national coalitions headed by one of the national parties and supported by regional fellow travelers.

Coalition building requires the shrewd tactics of forging alliances. These tactics can contribute to nation building in a fragmented society, as the recent success of Mayawati Naina Kumari, the chief minister of Uttar Pradesh, has shown.[37] Mayawati is the leader of the Bahujan Samaj Party (BSP) representing the Dalits (Untouchables), who account for about 20 percent of the population of this huge state. The BSP is the main rival of the Samajwadi Party (SP), which represents the so-called Other Backward Castes (OBC) and also used to attract a large part of the Muslim vote. Muslims have a share of about 17 percent of the population of Uttar Pradesh. The Brahmins, with 10 percent of the population, are also of some importance in this state. They and the members of other high castes (Rajputs, Banias, and the like) used to support the BJP, which also managed to get some OBC support. Mayawati was sure of the complete loyalty of her Dalits and could therefore afford to cultivate the Brahmins and the Muslims so as to defeat the SP government and to marginalize the BJP. In political terms, the hierarchy of the caste system has been completely overturned in this way.

As the caste system, which is based on the assumption of permanent inequality, is incompatible with national solidarity, it must be overcome. Many Indian social reformers, Gandhi in particular, have tried their best to do so, but their efforts have not been very successful. The shifts of power in the political arena of a vibrant democracy may accomplish what social reformers have failed to bring about. Democratic nation building has very special features in India, but it seems to be rather successful.

The British legacy, which is of great importance for India, is due to the unintended consequences of colonial rule. The structure of the British-Indian state was built so as to keep India under imperial control, but in due course this state served as the foundation of a modern democratic nation. The building of that nation progressed in a long freedom struggle against the British. Without this struggle India would not have gained the political maturity that enabled it to become one of the premier powers of the postwar world.

Notes

1. Hermann Kulke and Dietmar Rothermund, *A History of India,* 4th ed. (London: Routledge, 2004), 229.

2. Peter Marshall, *The Impeachment of Warren Hastings* (London: Oxford University Press, 1965).

3. Kulke and Rothermund, *History of India,* 235.

4. Ibid., 222.

5. Ibid., 227.

6. Ibid., 231–33.

7. *Constituent Assembly Debates,* vol. 10 (New Delhi, 1946–1950), 51.

8. *The Constitution of India,* articles 308–23.

9. Dietmar Rothermund, *An Economic History of India,* 2nd ed. (London: Routledge, 1993), 115–17.

10. Henry Knight, *Food Administration in India, 1939–1947* (Stanford, CA: Stanford University Press, 1954).

11. Dietmar Rothermund, *India: The Rise of an Asian Giant* (New Haven, CT, and London: Yale University Press, 2008), 84–85.

12. S.N. Mukherjee, *Sir William Jones: A Study of Eighteenth Century British Attitudes to India* (Cambridge: Cambridge University Press, 1968).

13. Kulke and Rothermund, *History of India,* 254–55.

14. Lynn Zastoupil, *John Stuart Mill and India* (Stanford, CA: Stanford University Press, 1994).

15. Kulke and Rothermund, *History of India,* 286–87.

16. Dietmar Rothermund, *The German Intellectual Quest for India* (New Delhi: Manohar, 1986), 47–49.

17. Ibid., 57.

18. John Rawls, *A Theory of Justice* (Cambridge, MA: Belknap Press, 1971).

19. Dietmar Rothermund, *Mahatma Gandhi: An Essay in Political Biography* (New Delhi: Manohar, 1991), 35–36.

20. Ibid., 37.

21. Dietmar Rothermund, *India in the Great Depression, 1929–1939* (New Delhi: Manohar, 1992).

22. Ayesha Jalal, *The Sole Spokesman: Jinnah, the Muslim League and the Demand for Pakistan* (Cambridge: Cambridge University Press, 1994).

23. Kulke and Rothermund, *History of India,* 315.

24. Ibid., 310.

25. Ibid., 316.

26. Ibid., 317.

27. Rothermund, *Mahatma Gandhi,* 107.

28. Stanley Wolpert, *Jinnah of Pakistan* (New York: Oxford University Press, 1984), 288.

29. Kulke and Rothermund, *History of India,* 322.

30. Dietmar Rothermund, "Rabindranath Tagore und seine weltweite Friedensmission," in *Globale Lebensläufe. Menschen als Akteure im weltgeschichtlichen Geschehen,* ed. Bernd Hausberger (Vienna: Mandelbaum, 2006), 198.

31. Wolpert, *Jinnah,* 332.
32. Kulke and Rothermund, *History of India,* 320.
33. Rothermund, *Mahatma Gandhi,* 127.
34. *The Constitution of India,* article 74 (1).
35. Rothermund, *Mahatma Gandhi,* 129–30.
36. Rothermund, *India: The Rise of an Asian Giant,* 26.
37. Ibid., 173.

2

France in Algeria: The Heritage of Violence

Kay Adamson

Abstract: *This case study examines the French legacy of economic centralization, army dominance, and political violence in Algeria. Just as nineteenth- and twentieth-century France experienced political and economic instability involving difficult transitions from one regime to another, so has postindependence Algeria. The development of the oil industry has reinforced this trend. France faced stiff opposition to its rule, which it imposed through its army. Postindependence leaders have all had military backgrounds or close ties to the army. Given the tightly controlled elections and the deepening ethnic divisions between Algeria's Arab and Berber-Tamazight citizens, political legitimacy remains tied to the thinning ranks of those who fought during the bitter war for independence. Successions are destabilizing and often violent. Because Algeria was an integral part of France during the colonial period and was administered through institutions in Paris, France left only a faint institutional imprint, although there was a strong intellectual influence.*

France's legacy to postindependence Algeria reflected the various ambivalences that had characterized the colonial project over its 132-year history. On the one hand, France had invested in transportation infrastructure, but the war for independence (1954–1962) severely damaged it. There was an education infrastructure, but it was modeled on its French counterpart and unevenly spread. The French legacy also reflected the 173 years of domestic struggles since the 1789 French Revolution over the creation of a state and an economy that would be "modern" and also retain the Enlightenment ideals that had inspired the revolution. Strategies to realize these ideals had changed over the years to reflect the different political priorities of successive republics, empires, monarchs, and presidents. Each left its own imprint on colonial Algeria. There were, however, two continuities—the central role of the state in economic affairs and the central role of the military in state affairs.

Colonization in the Pursuit of National Prestige

The spontaneous development of an inequality among states in the nineteenth century, and their differing levels of industrialization and political institutionalization, allowed colonization to take place and flourish. While economic explanations of colonization are common, this discussion generally occurs independently of discussions of the relationship between economic development and political structures. Likewise, examinations of the impact of nationalism on colonialism have also skirted the subject of economics.[1]

Although the French Revolution translated and transformed the term *democracy* to encompass the different meanings of nation, people, and *patrie,* two nations emerged during the eighteenth century: an elite that had lost its place to England and a nonelite motivated by promises of equality.[2] France then moved toward a modern economy, but one in which the state extended economic privileges. French ambivalence toward economic matters—support for strong state intervention in the economy on the one hand and support for private enterprise on the other—both predate the revolution and then sustained afterward by these social divisions.[3] Changes in France's political makeup in the nineteenth century influenced not only its own economic development but also its plans to develop the economy of its colony, Algeria.[4]

French policy makers viewed the colonization of Algeria as part of their strategy to overcome France's perceived economic inadequacies by spurring economic growth and expanding the empire. This goal was important as a proof that France remained a global power despite the upheavals following the French Revolution and as the means for France to catch up with its principal global rival, England. France sought to emulate the European expansion over the North American continent, where France had initially played a key role. French citizens lauded the expansion of European civilization across the Americas as indicated in the 1830s by various visits to the United States by key political and economic figures such as Alexis de Tocqueville, the author of *Democracy in America,* and Michel Chevalier, who supported European expansion in Africa.[5]

In 1830 Charles X undertook the initial conquest of Algeria for the more immediate concerns of royal prestige and survival of the Bourbon dynasty. The dynasty had been restored after the fall of Napoleon, but remained in difficult straits. Charles X desperately needed a foreign success, and the initial invasion of Algeria was an attempt to quell pirates operating off the Algerian coast. Louis-Philippe's coup d'état of 1830 deposing Charles gave the conquest of Algeria a new purpose, namely to provide the physical terrain for the development of French capitalism. French interests moved inland to the conquest of territory.

The French made two miscalculations. First, they grossly underestimated the strength and organizational capacity of the likely resistance to their colonial designs. They failed to understand that if the Ottoman navy and its corsair mercenaries could dominate the Mediterranean sea lanes, then the Ottomans were a credible power that could produce a creditable local resistance.[6] Second, they overestimated the willingness of the post-Revolution French citizen to emigrate and staff the colonial enterprise. The first miscalculation reflected the attitudes that characterized the great histories of the time written by public figures such as François Guizot[7] and

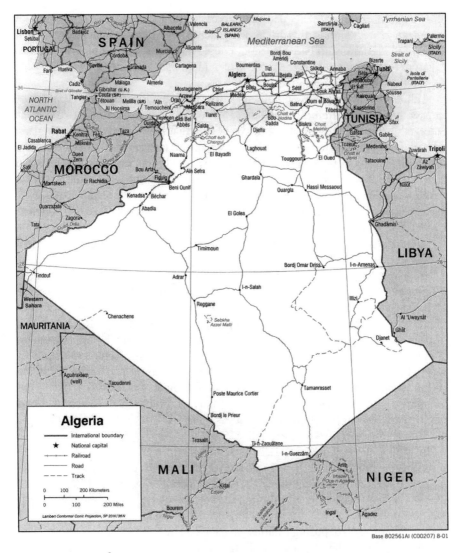

Base 802561AI (C00207) 8-01

Augustin Thierry[8] extolling French achievements, while the second reflected the postrevolutionary settlement in France creating legal and constitutional arrangements largely unaffected by the defeat of Napoleon Bonaparte at Waterloo. These arrangements included political and religious freedoms so that the French citizen had few incentives to emigrate. Furthermore, the French economy, on the whole, grew during the nineteenth century, thus providing enough internal opportunities for migrant labor. Only in the latter half of the century did environmental problems in agriculture, and more especially in viticulture, render emigration economically attractive. The other major temporary push for emigration came from the defeat by

Prussia in 1871 that resulted in the loss of the departments of Alsace and Lorraine, creating a displaced and therefore mobile population.

The Military as the Agent and the *Colon* as the Beneficiary of Colonialism

The Bonapartist settlement of the first decade of the nineteenth century gave an important role to the military in French affairs. This military infrastructure significantly influenced the organization of the colonial state.[9] The dominant role of the army in Algeria's governance survived four changes of regime: Charles X, a Bourbon monarch, began the conquest but fell in 1830 to a populist revolution that brought Louis-Philippe of Orléans to the throne. The Orléanist monarchy succumbed to the 1848 Revolution that established the Second Republic (1848–52) with the election of Louis-Napoleon Bonaparte as its president in December. It then fell to a coup d'état that installed the Second Empire (1852–70) with Louis-Napoleon Bonaparte as its emperor. However, his confrontation with Bismarck's Germany in the Franco-Prussian War (1870–71) led to his own overthrow, by a popular uprising that also created the Paris Commune and the beginning of the Third Republic (1870–1940), which fell during World War II.

The Third Republic transformed Algeria from a colony into an integral part of France. The three departments of Algiers, Oran, and Constantine became French departments. This change was important for Algerians of French extraction, known as the *colons,* because they gained the right to vote in French elections and be represented in the French Assembly in Paris. Muslim Algerians, however, remained unrepresented.

The importance of the French army in Algeria is evident in a number of different ways. Until the advent of the Third Republic, the army was the most significant force in Algeria. There was a constant exchange of military personnel between Algeria and France. For example, Marshal Thomas Bugeaud had been governor-general of Algeria (1841–47) when he was recalled to Paris in 1847 to lead the Orléanist government's resistance to the popular revolution of 1848, while another governor-general, Patrice de Mac-Mahon, would be elected in 1873 as the first president of the Third Republic.

If Algeria's governor-generals were military officers, they were supported in the countryside by the *Bureaux arabes* (Arab Offices). These played a dual role. As the field representatives of the army's Department of Arab Affairs, they were responsible for both the pacification and administration of the rural areas until 1871. They were also responsible for collecting intelligence broadly defined. Some officers used their spare time in scientific observation of the countryside, recording its natural environment as well as the manners and customs of the rural population.[10]

During the Second Empire (1852–70), Napoleon III visited Algeria in 1860 and 1865 and his regime attempted to improve the position of Muslims with its passage of two pieces of legislation, the Senate decrees of 1863 and 1865 (or

Senatus-Consulte, meaning legislation promulgated by the emperor but ratified by the Senate). However, neither decree had much positive effect in practice. A major revolt in 1864 followed the Senate decree of 1863, while the innovative step by the 1865 Senate decree to separate citizenship and nationality was paired with the requirement for Muslim applicants to renounce their religion for a successful citizenship application. This meant that relatively few Muslims applied. Both measures also excluded Algeria's native Jewish population, something that was remedied in October 1870 by an act of collective naturalization sponsored by the lawyer Adolphe Crémieux, who was active in the founding of the *Alliance Israélite* in 1860. The practical exclusion of Muslim Algerians from administering Algeria continued until 1946 and the post–World War II reforms.

In addition to the refugees from Alsace and Lorraine in 1871, population growth in France as well as problems within the rural economy meant that emigration began to occur. It was also accompanied by a substantial emigration from the southern region of Spain, where both economic and political conditions at the end of the nineteenth century had produced a dispossessed rural population. These emigrants formed a majority of the *colon* population in the department of Oran.

In Algeria, the role of the army began to decline after the establishment in 1870 of the Third Republic, which eliminated the Arab Offices. The growth in civilian power did not necessarily bring much benefit for Muslim Algerians, as it responded to the *colon* voice, which alone had direct representation in the Paris Assembly. The *colons* used their exclusive voice in Paris to block any attempts at political reform that might have favored Algeria's Muslims.

The Independence Movement

Growing segments of Algeria's Muslim community began demanding greater rights in the 1890s. Yet under the Jonnart Law of 1919 that expanded the franchise, less than half a million Muslims could vote. North African Star (*Etoile Nord-africain*), established in 1926, became the first political group to demand independence. It called for civil rights, universal suffrage, land redistribution, and education through Arabic schools, and its membership included Communists. France banned the party in 1929. Also in the 1920s, an Islamic reform movement took root on a platform calling for the implementation of the Quran and the Sunna. In 1933 France repressed this movement by banning its members from addressing state-supported mosques.

The Great Depression caused great hardship. In 1936, the Algerian Communist Party at the first Algerian Muslim Congress in Algiers promulgated a comprehensive Charter of Demands for civil and economic rights for Muslims. These demands gave rise to France's Viollette Plan to extend French citizenship to a Muslim elite, but Algeria's *colons* ensured that the plan was stillborn. Throughout Algeria's colonial history, its *colon* minority remained uncompromising in its exclusion of Muslims from the political and economic life of Algeria.

World War II, however, catalyzed a reconfiguration of political forces toward independence. The fall of France to Nazi Germany severely weakened French authority over Algeria, and in 1943, after the Allies deposed the Vichy regime in Algeria, Muslim leaders were able to present the free-French colonial government with the *Manifesto of the Algerian People,* demanding legal equality for Muslims. The government responded with the reforms of 1944 based on the failed Viollette Plan. They granted French citizenship to Muslim university graduates, officers, professionals, and elected representatives, but this meant only 60,000 persons.

On V-E Day (8 May 1945) a series of demonstrations by Algerians combining victory celebrations for the Nazi defeat with calls for independence turned violent in Sétif and the surrounding region. Official estimates of European deaths varied between 88 and 103. France responded with a bombing campaign, ground warfare, and civil repression. Estimates of Muslim deaths vary from an initial official tally of 1,500 to the Algerian figure of 45,000.[11] Thereafter, groups supporting independence rapidly grew, fueled also by the overall failure of French government attempts to offer a measure of representation to Muslim Algerians. These attempts included the establishment by the 17 August 1945 Ordonnance of a second electoral college, giving Muslims rights of representation at the National Assembly, a proposed constitution, and Prime Minister Paul Ramadier's compromise, which retained Algeria as a group of French departments administered by a governor-general but with an independent budget.[12] Ramadier, a leader of the Socialist Party, was nominated in January 1947 to chair the council responsible for drawing up the postwar French constitution. In 1947, France gave Algeria a legislature of 120 members, but divided into two electoral colleges of equal size, one representing the small *colon* and assimilated Muslim population, and the second representing the other 90 percent of the population. Rules requiring a two-thirds majority vote gave the *colons* veto power, which meant the ability to retain the status quo. Accusations of French intervention in the elections of 1948 and 1951 further undermined French legitimacy and contributed to preparations for a revolutionary war.[13]

From 1954 to 1962 Algerians fought a bitter war for independence, the costs of which included the demise of the Fourth Republic (1946–58) when the wartime resistance leader General Charles de Gaulle took power, becoming president and establishing the Fifth Republic (1959–present). In 1957 France had 415,000 troops deployed at a cost of 300 million francs per year.[14] The war was notorious for brutality, epitomized by the 1957 Algiers campaign of Brigadier General Jacques Massu and immortalized in Gillo Pontecorvo's 1966 film *The Battle of Algiers.* Opposition to the war in France grew. In Algeria, the European population was divided. Meanwhile the brutality of the military campaign meant that while the Muslim population might be divided internally, it was united externally in demanding independence. In one last attempt to prevent Algeria from becoming Algerian, a group of four senior French commanders (Maurice Challe, Edmond Jouhaud, Raoul Salan, and André Zeller) led a military putsch in April 1961 that attacked Gaullists, left-wing opponents of the war, and Algerians. Salan's capitulation ended the rebellion quickly, but it still added considerably to the death toll.[15] It also contributed to the overall climate of fear and insecurity, which precipitated the departure of 1.45 million *colons* and pro-French Muslims.[16] Although de Gaulle had been recalled to maintain a French Algeria, he soon recognized its impossibility and agreed to peace talks with the leaders of the National Liberation Front (*Front de Libération nationale* or FLN) that produced the Evian Agreement of 19 March 1962 for France's withdrawal.[17]

Violence and Political Instability

Algeria's birth was painful, framed by a struggle against a colonial power that was reluctant to leave until the very last moment and whose exit was accompanied not only by the kind of violence that today would be classified as "terrorist" but also by three major population movements. The most familiar of these involved the one million colonial settlers, French citizens by virtue of their residence in Algeria, but of mixed ethnic and national origin. The resettlement of some of these former settlers in Corsica laid the basis of the Corsican independence movement. A second movement involved the majority of Algeria's native Jewish population; and a third, rather more notorious given its circumstances, was that of the *harki* or Algerian Muslims who had been members of either the French army or one of the police services. The Algerian nationalists considered them to be traitors, and several massacres caused senior French army officers to organize their evacuation.[18]

Algeria's long and bitter war for independence involved atrocities by all participating parties. However, it was not until the publication in 2001 of the memoirs of a former French army commander, General Paul Aussaresses, admitting human rights abuses including torture, that there was official recognition by the French state of a dirty war in Algeria.[19] In some respects, it should not be surprising that the war entailed such abuses, as there were nineteenth-century precedents. These included the asphyxiation in a cave in 1845 of 500 men, women, and children of the Oulad Riah by French military forces led by Generals Aimable Pélissier and Jacques Achille Le Roy de Saint-Arnaud.[20] There had also been various policies, from the time of Marshal Thomas Bugeaud in the 1840s, that aimed at rural resettlement. During the independence struggle, the French army used this tactic against the FLN to resettle the rural population into policed, secure encampments (*regroupement*).[21]

The war for independence was just the latest phase of years of violence. France conquered Algeria only after a decade-and-a-half-long war. Between 1832 and 1844 'Abd al-Qadir led a revolt against French rule; he was captured in 1847 after the French employed a scorched-earth military strategy. Thereafter, *colons* expropriated the fertile coastal plain under the protection of the French army, displacing the local Muslim population. Resistance continued for the duration of French rule. The al-Muqrani revolt entailed 200,000 anti-French forces in the Kabyle region from 1870 to 1871 and the deaths of some 2,500 *colons*. The new Paris government nominated Vice-Admiral Louis Henri de Gueydon as governor-general to crush al-Muqrani's revolt. This he did by using a combination of executions, the levy of indemnities, and land sequestrations, which were immediately made available to the refugees from Alsace and Lorraine.[22]

There was one notable Algerian-perpetrated assassination during the independence struggle itself, that of Ramdane Abbane, an important theorist of the FLN and the key intellectual figure at the 1956 Soumman Congress, convened to discuss FLN strategy. He fell victim to an internal FLN power struggle in 1957.[23] (The other main organizer of the congress, Belkacem Krim, was assassinated in 1970.) An internal civil war followed the eight-year war for independence from France; together these wars took the lives of hundreds of thousands of Algerians and perhaps as many as one million.

Leading figures in the independence struggle disagreed over goals. These disagreements and ensuing violence were already evident during the presidency (1962–65) of Ahmed Ben Bella, who briefly imprisoned Mohammed Boudiaf for his criticism of the postindependence conduct of elections as well as Mohammed Ben Youssef Khider. Boudiaf, who founded the Party of the Socialist Revolution, went into exile in Morocco, and did not return to Algeria until asked to be president in 1992 after the resignation of President Chadli Bendjedid (president 1978–92). However, his return and assumption of the presidency lasted only 106 days before he was assassinated. While Boudiaf survived his self-imposed exile in Morocco, others did not, including Khider, who had been the FLN's treasurer and was assassinated in Madrid in 1967. Because of his assassination, the Algerian government took until 1979 to obtain the FLN's war treasury.[24] Another notable assassination was that of Belkacem Krim, who had been one of the historic chiefs, meaning a signatory of the November 1954 declaration of intent and later founder of the Democratic Movement for the Algerian Revolution (*Mouvement démocratique pour la Révolution algérienne*). He was an opponent of both President Ben Bella and his successor, Houari Boumediene (1965–78). Krim was found strangled in Frankfurt in 1970.[25] These assassinations indicated that the apparent political stability under President Boumediene—the former defense minister who came to the presidency in a coup against Ben Bella in 1965 and remained until his death in 1978—actually masked a continuing conflict over ends among leading figures of the independence struggle.

In an interview between the late Algerian sociologist Abdelmalek Sayad[26] and Hassan Arfaoui in 1996, Sayad attributed the endemic violence in Algeria to the brutality of the struggle for independence that had created an environment in which violence was acceptable, which in turn made the violent struggle of the 1990s acceptable. The car bombs of the 1990s were not new. In 1962 just before the end of Algeria's struggle for independence, two car bombs were exploded in Algiers and Oran respectively.[27]

The consequences of this painful birth are still very evident. Political stability remains elusive. A sense of discontent with the outcome of the independence struggle was particularly acute in the Kabyle region where Algeria's Berber minority lives. Kabyle became the scene of several revolts against central power in these early years of independence. Among the leaders was Hocine Aït Ahmed, one of the founding members of the FLN, but who also had founded the Socialist Forces Front (*Front des Forces Socialistes* or FFS) in 1963.[28] Aït Ahmed was imprisoned by President Ahmed Ben Bella and condemned to death but granted clemency. He escaped from prison in 1966 and remained in exile until 1989.[29]

Language and Ethnicity: The Berbers of Kabylia

Events in Kabylia raised the question of national borders. Kabylia, which lies in western modern Algeria, was the last substantive area to be colonized. Because of existing population pressures, the region became the focus of the early migrations to France. Migrants of Kabyle origin were to be found working in coalfields of northern France in the early part of the twentieth century. As a result, they were among the first Algerians to become politicized. They were members of trade unions and formed the core of Algeria's first significant political movement, the North African Star of Messali Hadj.[30]

Between the end of World War II and the outbreak of the independence struggle in 1954, Kabylia became an important center of opposition to colonial rule, certainly in part influenced by the shock of the massacres that took place at Sétif, Kherrata, and Guelma on V-E Day in 1945.[31] While actual numbers of dead are disputed, the fact that during victory celebrations for the end of World War II the participation and sacrifice of many Muslim Algerians could be so easily forgotten profoundly shocked many people. During the independence struggle, Kabylia became the site of murderous struggles not only between the French military and the Algerian insurgents but also within the independence movement. Kabyle leaders became prominent in the liberation movement, giving rise to several high-profile assassinations, including that of Ramdane Abbane.

When the state under Boumediene chose Arabic as the national language in 1962, it did not choose Arabic as spoken in Algeria. This had a divisive effect not only on the Arabic-speaking community, many of whom lacked the education to speak the official language chosen by the government, but also on the non-Arabic speaking areas. Most importantly this choice ignored Tamazight, the principal non-Arabic language spoken by the Berber population of Kabylia.

A reemphasis on Arabic allowed Algeria to align with the Arabo-Muslim world of the Eastern Mediterranean including the Egypt of President Nasser. However, looking eastward downplayed the significance of Algeria's complex ethnic composition and, in particular, the place in it of the Berber regions. The change in language entailed the switch on the state radio and television channels from French to Arabic. As the Kabyle singer Idir pointed out, this decision immediately excluded people like his mother, living in rural Kabylia, leaving them without a voice in the country for whose independence they had also fought.[32] He chose the name Idir, which means "it/he lives," in order to express the enduring importance of his Kabyle identity.

Despite the logic behind the adoption of Arabic, it created a simmering resentment that periodically boiled over into open conflict. Discontent in the Kabyle region reemerged in 1980. Often called the Berber or Tizi-Ouzou Spring, this period reflected concerns about a Berber identity and a Berber culture that were linked to the Berber language movement.[33] Beginning in March of 2001, resistance to the national state once again erupted in Kabylia. Whereas the terms *Berber Spring* and *Tizi-Ouzou Spring*[34] had an embedded optimism, this was absent in the 2001–2 unrest. The repression that followed became known as the Black Spring (*Printemps Noir*). Even the recognition by President Abdelaziz Bouteflika (1999–present) of Tamazight as a national language in October 2001 did not eliminate this conflict, which resumed in March of 2002 with further arrests of militants and the boycott of the legislative elections in May by the two principal representative parties in the region, the Rally for Culture and Democracy (*Rassemblement pour la Culture et la Démocratie* or RCD) and Hocine Aït Ahmed's Socialist Forces Front. The Algerian League for the Defense of the Rights of Man (LADDH), in a report published in April 2002, recorded eighty-three deaths for the months of April, May, and June 2001 that were directly attributable to the protests, and further deaths during March and April 2002.

Centralized Economic Management

After independence, the FLN pursued state-sponsored solutions to economic development, emphasizing industry over agriculture. The FLN, like most twentieth-century independence movements, traces its intellectual roots back in a more or less continuous line to the ideologies of socialism and communism and their associated political parties, the 1917 Russian Revolution, the writings of Karl Marx and Friedrich Engels and subsequently Lenin, and to the political manifestation of their ideas in the regular meetings called Internationals. The ideas, the writings, and the regular meetings that formed the backbone of nineteenth-century socialism and twentieth-century communism also gave birth to sympathetic parties in virtually every country of the globe and proved particularly attractive to colonial subjects, who were normally denied access to political decision making in their native countries. The projects for which Marx and Engels were the inspiration seemed to present a way forward to combat the inequalities that had accompanied nineteenth-century industrialization in the form known as industrial capitalism with its global expansion, more commonly referred to as imperialism.

Under France, the *colons* not only dominated the rural economy but also expropriated the best lands. During the colonial period, Algeria had been self-sufficient in food, but the *colons* had derived most of the profits, particularly from agricultural exports such as wine. With the exodus of foreign managers and skilled labor following independence, the agricultural sector collapsed and never recovered. The flight of the colonial settlers exacerbated rural dislocation because it left vacated land but not the resources to farm it. In some cases this ensured that the vacated lands could not be farmed immediately. At the same time, the mass departures of the colonial settlers also left vacant previously European-dominated urban space. It was far easier for rural migrants to occupy such urban space than to attempt to take land in the countryside.

Postindependence, the resettlement camps represented another element of rural dislocation and disconnection from the land that nineteenth-century expropriations had left to be resolved. The implementation of a new land resettlement policy turned out to be more difficult than the original population movements off the land.[35] While the seizures of land under the auspices of self-management (*autogestion*) that occurred with independence were attractive at a political level, their benefits for many of the old seasonal agricultural workers were less evident.[36] The collectivization of agriculture in the 1970s further reduced agricultural productivity.

Even if the successor Algerian state might have been inclined to focus on agriculture, several developments post 1962 made this unlikely. In keeping with France's centralized approach and also in keeping with the Soviet economic model favored by the independence generation, President Ben Bella promoted centralized socialistic economic planning in pursuit of economic self-sufficiency, not trade or a vibrant consumer economy. Independence did not affect all economic actors equally—oil companies such as SN Repal and CFP (*Compagnie française de pétrole*) did not leave; rather, small- to medium-sized employers made up the exodus of Europeans. The crucial event was the June 1965 coup d'état by the head of the Algerian military, Houari Boumediene.[37] In the years until his death in 1978, it was primarily his vision for postindependence Algeria that dominated both politics and economics. He launched a succession of multiyear economic plans, which, in keeping with the Soviet economic model, emphasized heavy over light industry, meaning the neglect of consumer goods. He also nationalized the oil industry.

In the 1960s, technological advances made Algerian oil and gas reserves economically viable to exploit. A focus on energy as opposed to agricultural development offered the government more immediate as well as higher returns. Ben Bella chose the organizational framework of the national state corporation in the form of the umbrella oil and gas company, Sonatrach. The company then became an important political player in the allocation of government investment funds, particularly under the leadership of Sidahmed Ghozali, but its emphasis on the energy sector did not necessarily benefit the long-term development of the Algerian economy.[38] Sonatrach had enormous technical importance in Algeria's development plans both in internal politics and in the economic strategy advocated by the French economist Gérard Destanne de Bernis.[39] French technical advisers such as de Bernis, who followed the economic theories of François Perroux, remained important for the development of the energy sector.[40] As an indication of the continuing dominance of oil and now natural gas in Algeria's economy, in 2005 they constituted 98 percent of Algeria's exports and were expected to retain this position until 2030, with the balance between them shifting in favor of gas.[41]

Not only did Algeria suffer from continuing political instability but the oil sector came to have a pernicious effect on economic development.[42] It turns out that estimates of the secondary employment generated by the oil sector were exaggerated. In other words, the "industrializing industries" thesis of de Bernis was overly optimistic.[43] Furthermore, governments like the Algerian, despite the rent obtained from oil and gas, still could not finance the exploration phase and, as a result, remained heavily dependent upon foreign companies such as British Petroleum to ensure oil supplies. The advantages of oil exploitation have not accrued to the population at large even though leading figures within Sonatrach, such as Sidahmed Ghozali (president), Sidahmed Boukadji (director of finance), and Nordine Aït Laouissine (director of exports and executive vice president) became major players in political and economic life generally.[44] The problem of making oil resources work for the national government is not unique to Algeria but evident in oil company dealings with post-Soviet states such as Kazakhstan, Russia itself, and even the Gulf states. This has sometimes been referred to as the "curse of oil," reflecting resource-rich but labor-poor economies.[45] In Algeria, state dominance of the oil sector and oil sector dominance of the Algerian economy fit the prior French colonial model of export dominance of the economy and *colon* dominance of the export sector. The majority of Algerians have been left out of the economic benefits in both cases.

Political Legitimacy and the Paternalistic State

Likewise, the majority of Algerians remain excluded from the colonial and postcolonial political system. France did not leave a democratic legacy in Algeria whereby elections served as the primary source of political legitimacy. Postindependence elections have not been conducted fairly, so legitimacy has come from participation in the war for national liberation, whose desirability and success are a rare source of public consensus. Algeria has yet to elect a leader who did not participate in the original struggle for independence that ended forty-five years ago. As a result, the generational transition from those who fought for independence to those born later has yet to take place, and the independence struggle, despite its temporal distance, continues to dominate domestic politics. The language and the aspirations of the independence movement, embracing a radical collectivist ideal, framed the postindependence environment and yet remained at odds with the postindependence economic decisions, which oscillated between state control and liberal economic expansionism. This caused tensions between the political and the economic spheres and a succession of legitimacy crises for the postindependence governments.[46]

In many respects, the return of Abdelaziz Bouteflika to the center of the political stage in 1998, following the surprise resignation of Algeria's first elected president, Liamine Zéroual (1994–99), after he called for early presidential elections in 1999, was curious. Given Bouteflika's close association with Algeria's second president, Houari Boumediene, who took power in an army coup d'état, the Bouteflika period evokes a certain ambivalence as it disrupted legitimate politics but brought about political and economic stability. However, a closer look suggests that the army's decision to ask Bouteflika to take up the presidency reflected the problematic nature of the political system of postindependence Algeria. By 1998, the ranks of those who had participated in the war of liberation had thinned. Bouteflika, as one of the youngest, having been just seventeen years old in 1954, becomes a less surprising choice. Nevertheless, by 1998 he was sixty-one and in 2001 required medical treatment at the French military hospital of Val-de-Grâce.[47]

This raises the difficult question of succession or transition from the generation of the liberation struggle to a new political generation. Although Bouteflika has now been elected twice to the presidency, in the election in 2004 other candidates withdrew at the last moment, while his own nomination as candidate back in 1998 and 1999 came at the behest of the state's powerbrokers, the military. However, the balance in the struggle with the army may be shifting in Bouteflika's favor, as the army is apparently withdrawing from political affairs. This development has been symbolized by the publication of a law to amend the number of state holidays including the 19 June anniversary holiday celebrating the takeover by Boumediene.[48]

As the independence generation inevitably passes from the scene, Islamic groups intend to make Islam the source of political legitimacy. Although the military has been a significant powerbroker in the past, the Islamist parties seek to become the powerbrokers of the future. Islam is potentially equally influential over both military and civil political contenders. Nevertheless, in Algeria, Islam has been primarily a force in civil politics via political parties. These parties see and use religion much in the same way that nationalist parties in Europe used religion as a resource in the power struggles of the nineteenth century.

The postindependence Algerian state is paternalistic. Increasing support for the Islamist movements has reinforced this tendency. Islamist movements seek to retain those elements of the paternalistic state that globalization has made difficult to sustain, such as the provision of social welfare, housing, and education.[49] There is a strong link between Islamist parties and the provision of social welfare. In the 1980s, the Islamic Salvation Front (*Front Islamique du Salut* or FIS) grew rapidly because it offered to the marginalized urban dweller elements of a social welfare system which the state could no longer supply. The decline of oil prices in 1986 hit the Algerian economy hard. By 1988 there were bread riots. Unemployment rates were high, consumer goods and even necessities were unavailable. This failure of centralized planning to provide basic necessities led to economic and political liberalization, which in turn led to the overwhelming electoral defeat of the FLN at the hands of the Islamic Salvation Front in 1991. The FLN responded by dissolving the parliament in 1992. Violent demonstrations, martial law, and the banning of the FIS followed in close succession. The welfare crisis in Algeria continued with the different regimes of the 1990s and 2000s unable to provide basic housing for large segments of the urban population.

Bouteflika's election in 1999 led to a short-lived deal with his different opponents including the Islamists. The resumption of the civil war was partly linked to a change in the leadership of the Armed Islamic Group (*Groupe Islamique Armé* or GIA) in April 2002, but it also involved the other major Islamist grouping, the Salafist Group for Predication and Combat (*Groupe Salafiste pour la Prédication et le Combat* or GSPC) and a new organization, Al-Qaeda's wing in north Africa that claimed responsibility for a suicide car bombing in September 2007 and for the car bombing of the United Nations headquarters in December 2007. The resumption of the Islamist-inspired conflict has resulted in over 600 deaths since the beginning of 2002.

This murderous civil war has echoes of the independence struggle, as have the claims by the former army officer Habib Souaïdia in his book *The Dirty War*[50] that many of the attacks in the 1990s on civilians attributed to the Islamists had in fact been perpetrated by the security forces. When the book first appeared, its accusations of army involvement in massacres were repudiated. However, President Bouteflika appointed Farouk Ksentini to investigate the claims and Ksentini concluded that Algerian security force members were responsible for the disappearance of some 6,000 civilians. During the independence struggle, similar crimes were attributed to the French army.

As under France, the military has played a key role in postindependence politics. Whether this is in the process of changing remains to be seen. All Algerian presidents except the most recent have had military backgrounds. Ahmed Ben Bella served as a career soldier in the French army. Houari Boumediene was chief of staff of the FLN's military wing and defense minister under Ben Bella. His successor, Chadli Bendjedid, served as a career officer, and Boumediene's defense minister. During the civil war of the 1990s a succession of military leaders held power. And although Algeria's current president, Adbelaziz Bouteflika, has always been a civilian, the military brokered his succession to the presidency. Algerian postindependence governments have followed in the French colonial tradition of using the military as a substitute for strong civil institutions to impose their will.

The French did create civil institutions of government, but because Algeria was an integral part of France with formal representation of the *colons* in the central government in Paris, when Algeria became independent much of the government structure disappeared with the French. French exclusion of virtually all of the native population from governance greatly limited the French contribution to state building in Algeria. This was very different from British colonization of the Americas, India, Australia, and New Zealand, where Britain relied heavily on the local population to staff colonial institutions, particularly at the local level. As a result, British institutional influence endured long after the independence of these colonies.

Most of the Algerian population remains both politically and economically excluded as it was under France. Postindependence governments have retained the French tradition of centralized rule and state direction of economic affairs. For many years, Algerian leaders gravitated to Soviet economic models including the collectivization of agriculture and the nationalization of industry. Algerian economic policies also echoed those of both the early Turkish state of Mustafa Kemal (Atatürk) and Gamal 'Abd al-Nasser's Egypt, where many of the leading nationalist players found refuge during the independence struggle. On the other hand, unlike in Turkey and Egypt, Algerian leaders, beginning with Boumediene, attempted to incorporate a carefully nurtured Islamic project in the hopes of bolstering the legitimacy of the state. But the Islamic movement assumed a life of its own. When the Algerian government failed to deliver prosperity or provide the social welfare benefits expected of a paternalistic state, this contributed to a state legitimacy crisis.

Notes

1. Since 1983, when Ernest Gellner and Benedict Anderson first published their studies of the role of nationalism in the development of political structures in Europe, few have focused on the relationship between economic and political structures. One exception is Liah Greenfield, who has explored connections between the attitudes concerning capitalism and differences in European nation building. Examples of both types of study are: Benedict Anderson, *Imagined Communities* (London: Verso Books, 1983, revised edition 1991 and new edition 2006); Ernest Gellner, *Nations and Nationalism* (Oxford: Basil Blackwell, 1983); Liah Greenfield, *Nationalism: Five Roads to Modernity* (London: Harvard University Press, 1992); Liah Greenfield, *The Spirit of Capitalism: Nationalism and Economic Growth* (Cambridge, MA: Harvard University Press, 2001); Albert O. Hirschman, *Essays in Trespassing: Economics to Politics and Beyond* (Cambridge: Cambridge University Press, 1981); François Perroux, *Dialogue des monopoles et des nations* (Grenoble: Presses Universitaires de Grenoble, 1982); Samir Amin, *L'Accumulation à l'échelle mondiale* (Paris and Dakar: Éditions Anthropos and IFAN, 1970); Samir Amin, *Le développement inégal* (Paris: Editions de Minuit, 1973).

2. Greenfield, *Nationalism,* 178, 185.

3. Greenfield, *Spirit of Capitalism,* 134–40.

4. Kay Adamson, *Political and Economic Thought and Practice in Nineteenth-Century France and the Colonization of Algeria* (Lewiston, NY: Edwin Mellen Press, 2002), 171–88.

5. Alexis de Tocqueville, *Democracy in America,* trans. Henry Reeve (1835, 1840; reprint, Ware, Herts.: Wordsworth Editions, 1998), 10–12; Alexis de Tocqueville, *De la colonie en Algérie* (Bruxelles: Editions Complexe, 1988), esp. the introduction, "Tocqueville et la doctrine colonial," by Tzvetan Todorov, 11–15; Jean Walch, *Michel Chevalier: Economiste–Saint-Simonian, 1806–1879* (Paris: Librairie Philosophique J. Vrin, 1975), 113–257.

6. Linda Colley, *Captives: Britain, Empire and the World, 1600–1850* (London: Jonathan Cape, 2002). Part One: Mediterranean—Captives and Constraints, 23–134, gives a picture of the nature of this wealth and power.

7. François Guizot, *Memoirs of a Minister of State from the Year 1840* (London: Richard Bentley, 1864), 266.

8. Augustin Thierry (1795–1856) had been secretary to Claude-Henri Saint-Simon (1760–1825), whose adherents were influential players in Algeria. Their role in Algeria is

discussed in Adamson, *Political and Economic Thought,* 107–49; however, Thierry also wrote widely on the history of France, as in, for example, *Récits des temps mérovingiens: précédés de considerations sur l'histoire de France,* 3rd ed. (Paris: Furne, 1846).

9. Raoul Girardet, *La société militaire de 1815 à nos jours* (Paris: Librairie Académique Perrin, 1998). Girardet lectured at the Institute for Political Studies as well as at the French military academy of Saint-Cyr and has written extensively on the role of the military in French affairs since the beginning of the nineteenth century. He has also written about the colonial idea in French political life and the particularities of French nationalism. Raoul Girardet, *L'Idée coloniale en France de 1871 à 1962* (Paris: La Table Ronde, 1972).

10. Adamson, *Political and Economic Thought,* 229–30; Patricia M.E. Lorcin, *Imperial Identities: Stereotyping Prejudice and Race in Colonial Algeria* (London and New York: I.B. Tauris, 1995), 79–85.

11. Boucif Mekhaled, *Chroniques d'un massacre, 8 mai 1945: Sétif, Guelma, Kherrata* (Paris: Syros/Au nom de la Mémoire, 1995). For estimates of the number of victims, see pages 204–9.

12. Guy Pervillé, *Pour une histoire de la guerre d'Algérie 1954–1962* (Paris: Editions A. et J. Picard, 2002), 55–56; René Rémond, *Le siècle dernier 1918–2002* (Paris: Librairie Arthème Fayard, 2003), 391.

13. Ted Morgan, *My Battle of Algiers* (New York: Smithsonian Books, 2005), 18.

14. Anthony Clayton, *The Wars of French Decolonization* (London: Longman, 1994), 120.

15. Rémi Kauffer, *OAS: Histoire de la guerre franco-française* (Paris: Editions du Seuil, 2002); Alain-Gérard Slama, *La guerre d'Algérie: Histoire d'une déchirure* (Paris: Gallimard, 1996), 107–9.

16. Jean-Jacques Jordi, *1962: L'arrivé des Pieds-Noirs* (Paris: Editions Autrement, 1965), 134–38.

17. Rédha Malek, *L'Algérie à Evian: Histoire des négociations secrètes 1956–1962* (Paris: Editions du Seuil, 1995), Annexe IV: 313–65. Malek was one of the Algerian negotiators and a major figure in subsequent governments.

18. Jean-Jacques Jordi and Mohand Hamoumou, *Les harkis, une mémoire enfouie* (Paris: Editions Autrement, 1999), 39–49.

19. Général Paul Aussaresses, *Services Spéciaux: Algérie 1955–1957* (Paris: Perrin, 2001).

20. Adamson, *Political and Economic Thought,* 46.

21. Michel Rocard, *Rapport sur les camps de regroupement et autres textes sur la guerre d'Algérie* (Paris: Librairie Arthème Fayard/Mille et une Nuit, 2003), 103–53.

22. Pierre Montagnon, *La conquête de l'Algérie: Les germes de la discorde, 1830–1871* (Paris: Pygmalion/Gérard Watelet, 1986), 401–9; Louis Rinn, *Histoire de l'insurrection de 1871 en Algérie* (Algiers: Adolphe Jourdan, 1891), 648; Morgan, *My Battle of Algiers,* 7–8.

23. Pervillé, *Pour une histoire de la guerre d'Algérie,* 147–53; Mohammed Harbi and Gilbert Meynier, *Le FLN: Documents et histoire 1954–1962* (Paris: Libraire Arthème Fayard, 2004), 263–83.

24. Yves Marc Ajchenbaum, ed., *La guerre d'Algérie 1954–1962* (Paris: Librio in conjunction with Le Monde, 2003), 116.

25. Ibid., 116–17.

26. Abdelmalek Sayad (1933–1998) was a sociologist of Kabyle origin who wrote extensively on Algerian migration to France. He was a close collaborator of the French sociologist Pierre Bourdieu, from the period that Bourdieu spent in Algeria during the Algerian War of Independence. He joined Bourdieu in France after Algerian independence. For a more detailed discussion of Sayad's work, see Kay Adamson, "Emigration-Immigration: Abdel-

malek Sayad's Sociology of Migration," in Nabil Boudraa and Joseph Krause, eds., *North African Mosaic: A Cultural Re-appraisal of Ethnic and Religious Minorities* (Newcastle upon Tyne, UK: Cambridge Scholars Press, 2007), 119–34.

27. Mike Davis, *Buda's Wagon: A Brief History of the Car Bomb* (London: Verso Books, 2007), 5.

28. Hugh Roberts, *The Battlefield Algeria 1988–2002: Studies in a Broken Polity* (London: Verso Books, 2003), 117.

29. Hocine Aït Ahmed, *Mémoires d'un combattant: L'esprit d'indépendance 1942–1952* (Paris: Sylvie Messinger, 1983); this is Aït-Ahmed's personal reminiscence of the events in the lead-up to the launch of the independence struggle.

30. Adamson, *Algeria,* 187; Mohammed Harbi, *Aux origines du FLN: Le populisme révolutionnaire en Algérie* (Paris: Christian Bourgois, 1975), 12–59, provides a detailed chronology of events from 1937 to 1954.

31. Mekhaled, *Chroniques d'un massacre,* 115–59.

32. *Le Monde,* 14 August 2002.

33. Roberts, *Battlefield,* 140.

34. Tizi-Ouzou is a town in Kabylia where the government banned a speech in April 1980 that sparked the protest movement pressuring it to cease repressing the Berber language and culture.

35. Pierre Bourdieu and Abdelmalek Sayad, *Le Déracinement: La Crise de l'agriculture traditionnelle en Algérie* (Paris: Editions de Minuit, 1964), 99–115.

36. These seizures were viewed positively by Europe's radical socialist left. For a good example of this kind of sympathetic analysis, see Ian Clegg, *Workers' Self-Management in Algeria* (London: Penguin Press, 1971). The book is a detailed study of the extent to which *autogestion* or self-management followed an established socialist tradition.

37. Although he retained this name during his presidency, it was originally his *nom de guerre.* His actual name was Mohammed Boukharouba (Harbi and Meynier, *Le FLN,* 884).

38. Ali Aïssaoui, *Algeria: The Political Economy of Oil and Gas* (Oxford: Oxford University Press for the Oxford Institute for Energy Studies, 2001), 277–93.

39. Gérard Destanne de Bernis, "L'Algérie à la recherche de son indépendance: nationalisation et industrialisation," in *L'Afrique de l'indépendance politique à l'indépendance économique,* ed. J.D. Esseks (Paris: François Maspero/Presses Universitaires de Grenoble, 1975), 19–61.

40. Gérard Destanne de Bernis, "Industries industrialisantes et contenu d'une politique d'intégration régionale," *Economie appliquée* 3–4 (1966), 415–73, outlines the economic theory behind postindependence economic policy in Algeria.

41. *Le Monde,* 7 October 2007 quoting from *World Energy Outlook* 2005.

42. The positive potential role for the oil sector in economic development has come under increasing scrutiny both in general works such as Lal and Myint but also in specialist studies of Algeria's oil and gas industry, as for example Aïssaoui. Deepak Lal and Hla Myint, *The Political Economy of Poverty, Equity and Growth* (Oxford: Clarendon Press, 1996); Aïssaoui, *Algeria,* 277–93.

43. De Bernis, "Industries industrialisantes," 415–73.

44. Kay Adamson, *Algeria: A Study in Competing Ideologies* (London: Cassell [now Continuum], 1988), 140, 171.

45. Lal and Myint, *The Political Economy of Poverty,* 196–200, 209, 396.

46. Jürgen Habermas, *Legitimation Crisis* (Cambridge: Polity Press, 1988). This is an application of Habermas's model, 24–31.

47. Raphaëlle Bacqué, *Le Monde,* 22 August 2007.

48. *L'Expression* Edition Online, 16 February 2005 (www.lexpressiondz.com).

49. Allcock used the term *paternalist state* to describe the Yugoslav state. I have suggested that it is a descriptor that can be transferred to the Algerian situation. John Allcock,

Explaining Yugoslavia (London: Hurst, 2000), 433–34; Kay Adamson, "Political Contexts and Economic Policy in Algeria: Some Theoretical Considerations and Problems," in Ahmed Aghrout and Redha M. Bougherira, eds., *Algeria in Transition: Reforms and Development Prospects* (London and New York: RoutledgeCurzon Studies in Middle Eastern Politics, 2004), 9–34.

50. Habib Souaïdia, *La sale guerre: Le témoinage d'un ancien officer des forces spéciales de l'armée algérienne* (Paris: Editions La Découverte, 2001); *Financial Times,* 4 January 2005; Pierre Vidal-Naquet, *Les crimes de l'armée française: Algérie 1954–1962* (1975; reprint, Paris: Editions La Découverte/Poche, 2001). A similar point is made by Général Paul Aussaresses, *Services Spéciaux: Algérie 1955–1957* (Paris: Perrin, 2001), 31–39, in respect of Philippeville (Skikda) in 1955. See also Gillo Pontecorvo's 1966 film, *The Battle of Algiers.*

3

The Philippines: The Contested State

AMY BLITZ

Abstract: *This case study charts the influence of a succession of colonial powers over the Philippines. First came the Spanish, who established a highly concentrated pattern of land tenure that channeled wealth to a narrow elite, while creating an ongoing source of revolutionary opposition. Next came the United States, which overthrew Spain in 1898, but soon after faced war with a mass-based Filipino opposition. To stabilize the country, the United States used a combination of military and democratic strategies, developing Filipino educational, legislative, police, health care, as well as military institutions. Nevertheless, revolutionary opposition, particularly among the peasantry, persisted for decades and eventually spiraled into the Huk Rebellion after World War II. The Japanese wartime occupation caused much destruction but left little lasting imprint. Post-war U.S. aid to prevent a growing Communist revolution strengthened Philippine military institutions at the expense of its civil institutions, particularly under the long dictatorship of Ferdinand Marcos. Still, the revolutionary movement grew, with leftists and moderates allying. As the situation veered toward revolution, the United States pressed Marcos to restore democratic institutions. When this failed, Filipinos took to the streets to force Marcos from power, and, in what would later become an awkward alliance with the military, they succeeded.*

The Philippines have been under the colonial rule of not just one but three countries: Spain, Japan, and the United States. Two profoundly affected the course of Philippine history. Spain left a lasting legacy in the concentrated pattern of land tenure and the predominance of Roman Catholicism. The United States left an equally lasting legacy of strong, democratic and military institutions as well as high literacy rates. The combination of highly inequitable land distribution, a profound popular faith in democracy, and massive foreign aid allocated by members of the elite to the military in order to maintain their predominance have made the Philippines a chronically contested state, where regime changes have resulted from a recurring pattern of destabilizing competition among revolutionary, democratic, and authoritarian forces.

Spanish Colonization

In 1521 the explorer Ferdinand Magellan claimed the Philippines for Spain, but Spain did not make it a formal colony until 1571. While native resistance persisted, there was no centralized threat to Spanish rule, so military requirements were relatively small. With few colonists and little to attract them to the countryside, the Spanish focused their attention on Manila, using its port as a center for ship repair, shipbuilding, and trade. Manila quickly became an *entrepôt* for the galleon trade, with Mexican silver exchanged for luxury goods such as silk and porcelain from China and spices from the Moluccas. These goods were then brought, via Mexico, to European markets.

Spain required all rural adult male Filipinos to pay tribute, essentially a tax, under an *encomienda* system. The *encomienda* (or land grant) system preserved the Spanish monarchy's ownership of colonial land, but granted colonists the right to collect tribute from the inhabitants of the land. The colonial *encomiendas* were not hereditary beyond the third or fourth generation, when they reverted to the monarchy. With little incentive to develop the long-term profitability of the *encomiendas* and with much incentive to maximize short-term gains, *encomenderos* (or tribute collectors) frequently abused their privileges. The institution was abolished throughout the Spanish Empire except in the Philippines, where it remained for lack of alternate resources to support the local government.[1]

While conflicts among tribal groups predated the Spanish conquest, the *encomiendas* intensified them. Some collaborated with the Spanish for personal profit, while taking bribes from villagers seeking to avoid Spain's labor conscription. Out of this early colonial policy emerged Filipino *caciques,* native chiefs serving as local bosses carrying out Spanish colonial rule. They were responsible for collecting tribute and administering colonial policies. In return, they were exempt from paying tribute and from providing forced labor.

The Catholic Church deeply influenced the course of Philippine history. The land expansion drives of the friars made religious corporations the largest landowners by the end of Spanish rule. These drives encompassed several modes of acquisition, including land grants from the Spanish Crown, the official owner of all lands in the colony; purchases of land from the colonial government; donations and bequests from religious Filipinos; purchases from natives, typically at very low rates; foreclosure of lands mortgaged by natives to the friars; and outright landgrabbing.[2]

As increasing numbers of native producers lost their land, feudal sharecropping arrangements became the predominant pattern of agricultural production. The produce of the land was then appropriated as a fixed share of the harvest, as tribute, or as a forcible purchase by the state at government-set prices.[3] The friars became monopolists over the internal trade of their districts and were often powerful enough to fix produce prices. Religious corporations and other church organizations participated in the galleon trade.[4]

The French occupation of Spain from 1808 through 1814, during the Napoleonic Wars, temporarily severed Spanish links with the outside. This cut the flow of Spanish friars to the Philippines and Filipino priests filled the vacancies. The war also cut the economic ties between the Philippines and Latin America. By 1811

50

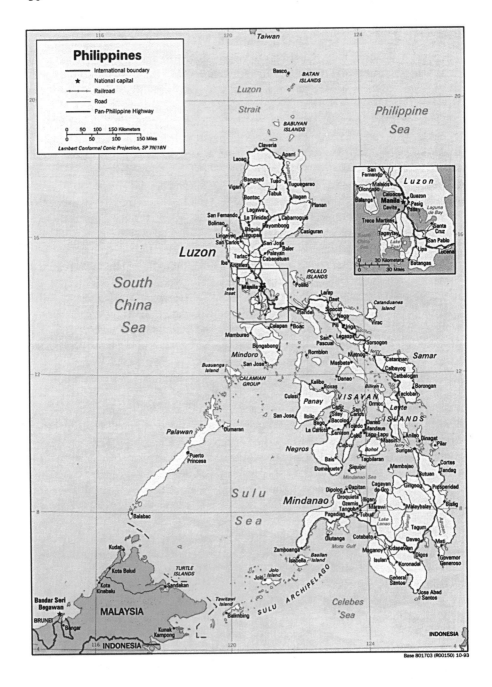

Base B01703 (R00150) 10-93

the last galleon had left Manila, ending centuries of trade between Spain's Asian colony and its counterparts in the Americas.[5]

After the Napoleonic Wars, it was Spain's eventual undoing to encourage solidarity between elite and poor Filipinos, and between Filipinos and those of Spanish blood born in the Philippines, known as Creoles. Spain did so by extending restrictive policies to them all, regardless of class or background. Such restrictions not only fed agitation against Spain; they also gave formerly divided groups a common enemy and a new sense of Filipino nationalism, which strengthened by the mid-1890s when two opposition movements joined forces to oust Spain.

The first emerged in 1892, when a group of elite Filipinos, who came to be known as "*ilustrados*" or "enlightened ones," formed the Filipino League (*Liga Filipina*) under the leadership of José Rizal.[6] Although Rizal pledged allegiance to Spain, arguing only for reforms while rejecting the radicalism of the other opposition movement, the Katipunan, which demanded independence, he was executed for treason in 1896. Rizal became an instant martyr and symbol for both the moderate and revolutionary opposition. Spain's unwillingness to distinguish between moderate and radical reformers created the rationale for an alliance between the *ilustrados* and the Katipunan.

The concentrated land tenure established under Spain created a social elite of landed families that endured long after the Spanish departed. Likewise, Philippine vulnerability to external changes, such as changing trade rules dictated by Spain or European wars that cut it off from trade, has been another enduring pattern.

U.S. Colonization

In 1898 an insurrection against Spain broke out in Cuba, long a hotbed of revolutionary activity and a matter of concern to U.S. policy makers. After a heated debate between U.S. isolationists and interventionists, the United States intervened on the side of the Cuban revolutionaries to oust Spain. Soon afterward, under the guise of containing the potential threat from Spain, the United States expanded the war to the Philippines, where outmoded Spanish ships were anchored. U.S. naval forces sailed into Manila harbor and quickly routed the Spanish forces, in what became known as "the splendid little war."

A less "splendid" war of U.S. conquest followed, leaving as many as half a million Filipinos dead while aggravating a long-standing tension within the United States between isolationists and interventionists.[7] Hostilities in the Philippines escalated when the United States and Spain excluded the Filipinos from the peace negotiations. War broke out between U.S. forces and the Filipino nationalists in 1899. American forces inflicted terrible casualties on the troops of the Katipunan leader, Emilio Aguinaldo.[8] Nevertheless, Aguinaldo continued to control the main island of Luzon and maintained a favorable force ratio of about two Filipino soldiers to every one American.[9] U.S. soldiers soon learned that they could win battles but could not hold territory.

Aguinaldo tried to balance the moderate and the revolutionary as well as the elite and the peasant factions of his movement; but the United States better understood, or at least better capitalized on, what Spain had not. The economic and social differences among the Filipinos created schisms, which, if exploited, could seriously weaken the revolutionary movement. By working with the *ilustrados*, the United States drove a wedge into Aguinaldo's organization, isolating the moderates from the revolutionaries. Aguinaldo soon faced a growing political challenge as many defected from his ranks.[10]

In all, 126,000 Americans took part in the war at a cost of $600 million, with a toll of 4,234 dead, 2,818 wounded, and thousands succumbing to disease. The war generated substantial domestic conflict in the United States as well, presaging more recent domestic conflicts over wars in Vietnam and Iraq. For Filipinos, the toll was much greater, with deaths estimated between 200,000 and 600,000, the rice harvest reduced to one-quarter normal levels, vast areas of the countryside in ruin, and rule by another colonial power.[11]

The United States tried to balance soft-line and military tactics to win the "hearts and minds" of Filipinos. Soft-line tactics included a program inaugurated in 1903 for young Filipinos to study in America, launching, in the process, Filipino migration to the United States. By 1909 the United States had increased the number of elementary schools in the Philippines threefold to roughly 4,000, doubled the number of students to 400,000, and tripled the size of the native teaching corps to 8,000. These figures are misleading given the high truancy rates and minimal education of the teachers, who mostly had not gone past the sixth grade. The United States increasingly emphasized vocational training, stressing secondary education for the select few and primary education for the masses.[12] Nevertheless, this focus on education left an enduring positive legacy: Filipino literacy rates are high compared to other countries at the same per capita income level.

In other moves, the currency was stabilized by fixing it to the U.S. dollar, which reassured foreign bankers and merchants. A succession of U.S. governors brought the American government and private investment to infrastructural development projects. They also raised Philippine taxes to cover the costs of building networks of roads and shipping lines as well as wharves and warehouses, all needed to stimulate interisland and foreign trade.[13]

In 1902 the U.S. Congress passed the Cooper, or Organic, Act. This formally established U.S. colonial rule in the Philippines with provisions for a bicameral legislature comprised of a Filipino-majority assembly of elected representatives in the lower chamber, an American-dominated commission, and an American governor with veto power in the upper chamber. The U.S. president, subject to congressional approval, appointed the commission and the governor. The Cooper Act prevented U.S. investors from buying the vast tracts necessary for efficient sugar production by limiting individuals to purchases of 40 acres and U.S. corporations to 2,500 acres.[14]

The limitations on land ownership inhibited both American economic intervention and the commercialization of Philippine agriculture. In so doing, it allayed the fears of American farmers, who worried about foreign competition.[15] Meanwhile, Filipino elites were allowed unlimited access to the newly released church lands, which the United States had purchased from the Vatican in 1903. This further increased the concentration of Philippine wealth and power.

Far from addressing the roots of social unrest, which centered on the unequal land tenure patterns, U.S. policies deepened such economic inequalities. Though statistics on such key economic indicators as the distribution of land or the amount of land devoted to cash versus food crops are unavailable for the period, a fact-finding survey conducted years later, in 1936, found the vast majority of rural Filipinos living in dire poverty, deprived of civil and political rights, and with no formal right to vote due to property requirements.[16] The land tenure question remained a festering source of peasant anger and revolution.

The Cooper Act also established duty-free trade between the United States and the Philippines. As a result, Philippine land devoted to export production increased at the expense of food production.[17] Foreign commerce jumped between 1908 and 1910, quadrupling in dollar terms from 1908 to 1926. Yet the economic dependence of the Philippines on the United States also greatly increased. In 1908, exports to the United States accounted for 32 percent of total Philippine exports. This figure more than doubled, to 73 percent, by 1926, while imports from America nearly tripled, from 17 percent in 1908 to 60 percent in 1926.[18]

Preparation for Independence

The first U.S. governor was federal circuit judge (and later U.S. president) William Howard Taft, who had headed the Taft Commission, which established the new civil colonial institutions. He recommended eventual self-rule for Filipinos following a period of democratic tutelage under the United States. In 1906, the United States lifted a ban on pro-independence political parties and allowed Filipinos in 1907 to elect a legislative body. The body, however, functioned under the U.S.-appointed American governor, who retained veto powers. Suffrage was restricted to landowners, taxpayers, and the literate,[19] meaning just 3 percent of the population.[20] Several opposition cliques fused together to form the Nationalist Party (*Partido Nacionalista*), which favored independence. The party captured fifty-eight of the eighty legislative seats and dominated Philippine politics for decades to come.

Representatives from the legislature—one appointed by the U.S. governor and the other by the Philippine assembly—held seats as resident commissioners in the U.S. House of Representatives, where they could speak, but not vote. Until 1916, one of these representatives was Manuel Quezon, who used his time in the United States to study the workings of the American system and to establish himself as the eventual leader of an independent Philippines.[21]

In the Philippines, elected Filipinos increasingly resented the governor's veto powers, which they argued made the Filipino assembly less a legislative body than a debating society. They also resented the large numbers of Americans in government posts even though the number of Filipino officials had grown to roughly 6,000 by 1913.[22]

U.S. debates on the political future of the Philippines split along partisan lines, with Republicans generally supporting continued U.S. colonialism and Democrats generally favoring independence. While the Democrats sought to protect small U.S. farmers by keeping their Philippine competitors outside tariff walls, the Republicans sought to protect the interests of U.S. industrialists and agricultural refiners, notably the Sugar Trust, by retaining the Philippines as a colony and Philippine goods within tariff walls. A similar schism centered on strategy during the U.S. colonial period, with hard-liners focused on military solutions to ongoing conflicts with Filipinos and soft-liners focused on socioeconomic and democratic solutions. For example, in 1901 hard-liners created the Philippine Insular Police, later known as the Philippine Constabulary. Meanwhile soft-liners established public institutions to manage health, education, economic development, political change, and other issues of central concern to the masses of Filipinos.

By 1916, after years of intense debate over Philippine policy, President Woodrow Wilson signed into law the Jones Act, which acknowledged Philippine sovereignty and established provisions for a gradual transfer of power. The act revoked the veto power of the governor and gave Filipinos a majority in the appointive commission, which until then had been controlled by Americans. Because Filipinos already held a majority, by law, in the elected legislature, they now predominated in both the upper and lower houses.[23] Americans serving in the Philippine government shrank from about 3,000 to about 600, while the number of Filipinos increased to more than 13,000.[24]

Although the Jones Act allowed for eventual Philippine independence, it also allowed American military forces to remain for twenty more years, until 1936. By 1917 these forces included a small naval station at Subic Bay and an army fort at Clark Field, originally funded by the U.S. Congress. In 1934 President Franklin D. Roosevelt agreed to transfer U.S. Army property to the Filipinos after independence, with the disposition of naval bases to be settled through negotiations.[25] Unlike his Republican presidential predecessors, who viewed the colony as a strategic and economic boon to the United States, Roosevelt, like his Democratic predecessors, viewed the colony as a drain on U.S. resources, now more needed than ever at home due to the Great Depression.[26]

In 1934, in preparation for independence, a Philippine convention assembled to draft a constitution. The convention called for a separation of executive and legislative powers, as well as regular elections for a unicameral legislature and a president with extensive veto powers far greater than his American counterpart had. A U.S.-appointed high commissioner would help manage a ten-year transition to self-rule. Suffrage was also extended to men and women over the age of twenty-one, though continued linguistic and property restrictions kept the proportion of eligible voters to less than 14 percent of adults.

Quezon returned from the United States to participate in the convention and soon leveraged his U.S. connections to run for president. The peasantry, however, resisted forcefully. Although World War I had created a huge global demand for raw materials that had enriched the islands,[27] the sharp drop in postwar prices soon shattered the Philippine economy, betraying its lopsided, export-based dependence on the United States, similar to its earlier dependence on Spain. While sugar and coconut barons had grown rich, rice farmers and other basic-foodstuff growers had fallen further and further behind, leading to a resurgence of revolutionary activity among the peasantry during the 1920s and 1930s.

Just after President Roosevelt approved the new constitution in early 1935, but two weeks prior to a Filipino plebiscite on the proposed constitutional changes, peasants in central Luzon called the *Sakdalistas*, or "strikers," revolted. They opposed the proposed changes as well as Quezon's bid for the presidency. They stormed municipal offices, constabulary barracks, and police stations on May Day 1935. A bloody battle ensued, killing about sixty, with eighty more casualties and 500 arrests. The Sakdalistas were quickly subdued, and, by September, Quezon was elected commonwealth president. The Sakdalista uprising was nevertheless better organized and more ideologically grounded than any previous peasant uprising and tapped a reserve of peasant anger, which deepened when the worldwide depression undermined the profitability of Filipino agricultural exports.[28]

President Quezon soon requested the services of General Douglas MacArthur, the head of the U.S. Army's Philippine Department since 1928, to help create a Philippine military.[29] Working with his assistant (and future U.S. president) Dwight Eisenhower, MacArthur used the Swiss military model to create an army of citizen-soldiers.

Japanese Colonization

Then international events again intervened. As Japan expanded its war in China in the 1930s, the Philippines requested immediate independence in order to remain neutral in the brewing conflict between Japan and the United States. The United States refused, but could offer no reinforcements when Japan invaded in 1941. Hundreds of thousands of Philippine civilians perished in the ensuing war.[30]

Beyond the terrible human carnage of the war, the main impact of the Japanese period of colonization was to delay Philippine independence. Although legislative elections had been held earlier in 1941, the body had not yet met when Japan invaded. Upon the occupation of Manila, the Japanese declared martial law in 1942 and then dissolved all political parties.

Just as many Filipinos had cooperated with the Spanish and the Americans, many cooperated with the Japanese. Japanese collaborators included many in the U.S.-trained Philippine military, who quickly changed sides when one colonial power gave way to another. Many from the economic elite, particularly those of Spanish descent, also defected to the Japanese, surviving the loss of U.S. markets by profiting from trade with Japan instead.[31] Even the pro-independence leader, Aguinaldo, heeded the Japanese call for Asian nationalism and made common cause with them.

The Japanese also cultivated the Sakdalista leader, Benigno Ramos, who had established in 1939 a militant pro-Japanese organization, comprised largely of former Sakdalistas. During the war, this organization was subsumed into the Kalibapi, a consortium of organizations created in order to replace political parties.[32] The Japanese designated Stanley Laurel president of a pro-Japanese provisional regime run by Filipinos, while the former Nationalist Party campaign manager, Benigno Aquino—the father-in-law of future President Corazon Aquino—became director-general of the Kalibapi.[33]

Other Filipinos, however, worked closely with the United States, maintaining a shadow commonwealth regime during the war, with Quezon remaining president. Still other Filipinos waged effective guerrilla operations against the Japanese, including loyal U.S.-trained troops, the Chinese in Manila with support from Chinese nationals,[34] as well as revolutionaries.

The Philippine Communist Party (*Partido Komunista ng Pilipinas* or PKP) declared itself ready to cooperate with all political groups in order to form a unified front against Japan. In March 1942, the PKP and the Socialist Party of the Philippines established the National Army Against Japan (*Hukbong Bayan Laban sa Hapon*). This group became known as the *Huks* and was a particularly potent anti-Japanese guerrilla force.[35] Comprised largely of poor sharecroppers and landless farm workers from central Luzon, the Huks built upon the earlier revolutionary movements as well as labor and peasant unions. Except for the military commander, a socialist with peasant roots named Luis Taruc, however, the Huk leaders were mainly urban intellectuals with links to the PKP.

The Huks launched a broad-based revolutionary campaign in the countryside, attempting to form an underground government in alliance with other guerrilla units and to lay the foundation for radical postwar social reforms. In the meantime, the Huks remained loyal to the commonwealth government and expected a role in a postwar administration, with which they intended to promote land tenure and labor relations reforms.[36]

Then the shock came. After the war, far from rewarding the Huks, U.S. forces ordered them disarmed and arrested several leaders, including Taruc. Mass protests and more arrests followed. The Huks, now unarmed, faced retribution by powerful landlords, many of whom had fled the countryside during the war and now began to return, much to the resentment of the peasant population, which had remained to defend the country against Japan. Huk leaders remained open to nonmilitary tactics and participated in elections. In July 1945, Communists and Socialists, peasant unions and other leftist groups, joined to form the Democratic Alliance, in preparation for legislative elections scheduled for 1946.[37] Meanwhile, the Philippine armed forces relayed concerns to the U.S. Army of feared repercussions following the withdrawal of U.S. forces.[38]

In the period around the conclusion of the war, the U.S. military under the command of General MacArthur, together with his associates in the Philippines, including many former Japanese collaborators, gained control of Philippine politics. In the process, MacArthur revived the long-standing competition between U.S. military and political colonialists.[39] MacArthur promoted his friend Manuel Roxas and the Liberal Party, swiftly exonerating Roxas in April 1945 of all charges of wartime collaboration. America's new drive to contain communism, together with the momentum building behind Roxas, displaced earlier pledges to punish war criminals. In August 1945, MacArthur freed 5,000 collaborators.

Roxas won a narrow victory against the Nationalist Party, taking just 54 percent of the nearly three million votes cast. The Liberal Party also took over the legislature. Although all six of the Huks who ran for office won seats, in April 1946 President Roxas replaced them with his own supporters, a move that intensified peasant anger.

Independence, Interdependence, and Insurgency

On 4 July 1946, despite World War II, the Japanese occupation, and the onset of the Cold War, the United States kept its earlier promises and granted the Philippines independence. The growing Huk uprising and its Cold War context, however, compromised the political transition from the start.

In the countryside, local authorities interpreted the expulsion of the Huks from the legislature as a signal to subdue the Huks without mercy. They arrested or killed Huks and their supporters in droves. Now the Huks changed their name to the People's Liberation Army (*Hukbong Mapalayang Bayan*), relinquished all hopes of a political solution, and dug up their World War II arms. The Huk message of agrarian reform, national sovereignty, and opposition to U.S. bases rapidly gained popularity, and full-scale civil war broke out in Central Luzon.[40]

The 1949 elections, which excluded the Huks, were the most corrupt to date on both sides. An official study later estimated that at least one-fifth of the ballots had been fraudulent, largely in favor of Elpidio Quirino.[41] Still Quirino won by just a narrow margin over Stanley Laurel, the Japanese-collaborator and Quirino's bitterly anti-U.S. opponent. Quirino shifted the tax burden to the poor and responded so brutally to the Huks that the Huk leader, Taruc, later claimed, "We couldn't have had a better recruiter."[42] U.S. officials grew concerned that Congress would refuse to continue supporting such an administration. Amid nationalist insurgencies in Indochina and Indonesia as well as civil war in China, the United States worried that Quirino might fuel, not quell, revolution. By 1950 the Philippine government had run through more than $1 billion in U.S. aid granted in the first four years of independence; yet the economy remained as weak as it had been at the end of the war. Half of Philippine dollar earnings came from the U.S. Treasury, while the other half came from exports, primarily of copra, the raw material for coconut oil, whose price was grossly inflated and likely to fall.[43]

During the Cold War, the growing importance of U.S. military bases in the

Philippines created a strong, shared interest between the two governments to eliminate the Huk insurgency. Under U.S. pressure, Ramon Magsaysay, a veteran of the anti-Japanese guerrilla forces and member of the Philippine legislature since 1946, became the new secretary of national defense in late 1950.[44] Using U.S. assistance, Magsaysay supplemented military strategies aimed at the Huks with political and economic ones.

During the period from fiscal years 1949 to 1952, U.S. economic aid totaled $584.2 million while U.S. military aid totaled $80.2 million. Magsaysay worked in close cooperation with a former advertising executive, U.S. Air Force Lieutenant Colonel Edward Lansdale, whose office eventually became subsumed into the U.S. Central Intelligence Agency (CIA). On the economic front, Lansdale sought to undercut Huk promises of land reform by helping Magsaysay establish credit banks, clinics, and agrarian courts, though these were soon dominated by local landed elites. Lansdale also sought to isolate the Huks from their bases of support, offering land on public tracts on the southernmost island of Mindanao, far from Central Luzon and the home to Filipino Muslims. To ensure that the homesteaders would not spread the rebellion to Mindanao, loyal ex-soldiers and civilians were to be stationed in the resettlement communities.

The program was an economic disappointment but a political success. Six years later, the land grants had benefited about 5,000 people, though only a fourth of these were actually Huks. The majority were Magsaysay's allies.[45] Although the Huks tried to publicize these facts, the peasants nevertheless came to think of Magsaysay as their patron.[46]

Magsaysay also used the military for infrastructure projects, education, medical care, and legal services in rural areas. In the process, he broadened the role of the armed forces in the countryside.[47] He put the constabulary, a particularly ineffectual and corrupt organization, under the command of the chief of staff of the armed forces and reduced it from 17,000 men in 1950 to 7,100 by the end of 1952.[48] He then purged the army of its most corrupt officers while nearly doubling its size, to 56,000, by 1952.[49] Lansdale also launched a psychological warfare campaign against the Huks with "talking" graves, meaning deaths staged to resemble the work of Filipino folk creatures.

While such tactics contributed to Huk losses, the Huks also erred in concentrating all of their forces in Central Luzon, which made retreat and reorganization difficult. They erred further in concentrating their urban forces, the central nervous system of the campaign, in a Manila complex. In October 1950, military forces swept through the poorly defended Huk base in Manila and captured reams of documents, weapons, money, and 105 suspected Huks including six leaders. The raid was a devastating blow.[50]

Lansdale did not restrict his activities to the Huk insurgency, but intervened in electoral politics as well. In the 1951 legislative elections, Lansdale impeded the movements by plane of the ballot-stuffing supporters of President Quirino. A record four million voters ignored Huk calls for a boycott, participating in the relatively honest balloting.[51] The Huks underestimated the Filipino faith in democratic processes, a legacy of the American colonial era.[52] The CIA and U.S. corporations helped finance Magsaysay's presidential campaign.[53] As a warning of U.S. intentions, a group of American warships arrived off Manila just before the elections, while American military advisers supervised the voting.

Magsaysay buried Quirino in a two-to-one victory in the heaviest voting since independence, earning Lansdale the sobriquet "Landslide" and notoriety as the model for the character Alden Pyle in Graham Greene's novel *The Quiet American*.[54] Magsaysay quickly earned political capital, however, when, in 1954, the senior Huk leader Luis Taruc surrendered.[55]

The United States spent half a billion dollars in economic and military aid on the Huk conflict between 1951 and 1955. The Philippines used much of what was left, after siphoning by Quirino and others, to acquire an arsenal of modern weapons and aircraft, all expressly targeted under the 1951 Mutual Defense Treaty at internal "threats" to security, primarily peasants who remained yoked to the grossly unequal land tenure system.[56]

The Suspension of Democracy Under Ferdinand Marcos

Enter President Ferdinand Marcos in 1965. Like Magsaysay, Marcos held the defense portfolio for the first thirteen months of his term and used this to secure the military's loyalty. Upon his election to the presidency in 1965, he launched the largest reshuffling in the history of the Philippine military, replacing most of the top echelon with family or friends from Ilocos Norte.[57] Marcos used U.S. aid to bring the military back into civic action projects on an unprecedented scale, particularly in the construction of feeder roads linking rural communities with towns and cities.[58] Marcos also distributed much of the U.S. money and construction contracts to a network of supporters who, unlike the traditional elites, had primary loyalty to Marcos. While the military did establish health, education, legal, and other community service projects, it also emerged as a highly politicized counterinsurgency force.

By November 1969, Marcos ran for reelection in what was widely considered to be the most corrupt presidential election to date, leading to mass protests that escalated into riots. Only with the deployment of a U.S. marine detachment was order restored. In the countryside, remnants of the Huk rebellion and widespread popular anger at Marcos coalesced into a Maoist movement known as the New People's Army (NPA).

As the two-term limit for presidents loomed, Marcos used a government-choreographed armed attack on the defense minister as a pretext to declare martial law on 23 September 1972. He blamed the NPA and other Communist organizations for the attack[59] and then used martial law to arrest the political opposition, abolish the legislature, prohibit mass activities, outlaw political parties, suspend civil and political rights, and impose a curfew, leaving the military as the primary instrument of the national government outside of the presidency.

By treating moderates as revolutionaries, as the Spaniards had mistakenly done, Marcos actually helped recruit many to the revolutionary movement. From 1969, when the New People's Army formed, through 1985, it expanded from a few hundred to roughly 16,000 regulars, a million active supporters, and a broader base under the leftist umbrella group, the National Democratic Front (NDF), estimated at ten million nationwide, or about 20 percent of the population.[60] The movement sought removal of the U.S. bases, improved human rights, and a restructuring of the Philippine economy, entailing land reform and restrictions on U.S. investments.[61] The left's strength was greatest in the countryside, where roughly 70 percent of Filipinos lived and about 80 percent of the land belonged to only 20 percent of the population.[62] Support grew in tandem with human rights violations by the military. From 1977 to 1985, over 21,000 people were arrested for political reasons, and from 1975 to 1985, over 700 disappeared and more than 2,400 were killed or, in the disturbing lexicon of war, "salvaged."[63]

Nevertheless, Marcos retained U.S. backing for the next fourteen years of his regime, arguing essentially that he had to destroy democracy in order to save it.[64] When Marcos learned that the U.S. bases in the Philippines housed nuclear weapons, a fact that Philippine presidents had long suspected but had not known for certain, he used this trump card over and over again to secure U.S. aid and other support. Upon the declaration of martial law, the U.S. nearly tripled its military aid, from $18.4 million in 1972 to $50.4 million in 1973, while economic aid rose as well, from $111.8 million in 1972 to $124 million in 1973. U.S. economic and military aid totaled close to $2 billion for the period from 1972 to the end of the Marcos era in 1986. Though U.S. officials were loath to describe any linkage between the aid and the bases, privately, successive administrations understood the aid to be a form of strategic rent.[65]

Marcos more than tripled the size of the Philippine military, still explicitly designed for internal security, from 62,000 in 1972 to 200,000 by the end of his regime,[66] and increased the military's annual budget from $82 million in 1972 to $1 billion by 1980.[67] Meanwhile, the Marcoses continued to amass a fortune estimated at close to $100 million, a fortune made all the more controversial since neither husband nor wife came from wealth.[68]

Silenced at home, exiled opposition leaders such as Benigno Aquino, Jr. mobilized U.S. opposition to Marcos, particularly among the roughly one million Filipinos in the United States and the even larger Filipino-American community. Following Watergate and the revolutions in Indochina, Iran, and Nicaragua despite massive U.S. military intervention, segments of the U.S. foreign policy establishment became receptive to such opposition figures, and a growing human rights lobby gained a toehold in Congress and in the State Department.

The Restoration of Democracy

Although only a few undid democracy in 1972, it took the ingenuity, courage, and commitment of many, working for years in the Philippines and in the United

States, to reestablish it. Far from silencing opposition, the repression fueled both revolutionary and moderate opposition, particularly after the 1983 assassination of Benigno Aquino, Jr. on the Manila airport tarmac. Many held Marcos personally responsible. Aquino, like Rizal before him, achieved instant martyrdom. The church, business, military, political, and other sectors of the established oligarchy began defecting from Marcos in droves.

The political crisis spurred an economic crisis, which fed the political crisis in a vicious cycle. Investor confidence plummeted, leading to massive capital flight estimated at more than $10 billion[69] and a downward spiral in the economy.[70] Evidence surfaced in late 1983 that the Philippine Central Bank had been falsifying estimates of its foreign debt and reserves in order to cover the Marcos regime's mismanagement. Foreign banks refused to renew short-term credit; real GNP fell by 7.1 percent in 1984; and unemployment reached 25 percent.[71]

Eighty-five percent of registered voters participated in the legislative elections of May 1984, signaling an abiding faith in democratic processes.[72] Despite fraud and violence, the opposition won 59 of the 183 eligible seats, nearly double the predicted 30 seats.[73] When U.S. policy makers concluded that a failure to reform would mean the loss of the bases in five to ten years, they began secretly channeling funds to Radio Veritas, a Catholic radio station, which quickly became the voice of the moderate opposition.[74]

In 1985 the U.S. Congress began holding hearings on the Philippines, linking, by May, aid to Marcos with his efforts to rebuild democracy. In November 1985, Marcos, in an attempt to comply, called for "snap" presidential elections in early 1986. When all twenty-six accused in the Aquino assassination were acquitted, Aquino's widow, Corazon, announced her candidacy.[75] Cardinal Sin, as a leader of the Catholic Church, then helped to unite the moderates behind Aquino, in the presidential slot, and Laurel, in the vice-presidential slot. This was a critical achievement, since a split opposition would have allowed a Marcos win.[76]

State Department analysts noted a spectacular voter participation rate and estimated that Aquino had won 60 to 70 percent of the vote.[77] President Ronald Reagan initially indicated his continuing support for Marcos, but gradually changed his position amid mounting evidence of fraud.[78] When the Marcos-controlled National Assembly formally declared him the victor, the opposition members walked out in protest. A hundred bishops then condemned Marcos, while over one million Aquino supporters rallied near a statue of Rizal, invoking an earlier era of resistance. Soon afterward Defense Minister Juan Ponce Enrile and General Fidel Ramos mutinied in the Manila military base called Camp Aguinaldo, invoking yet another resistance hero. The Marcoses soon fled by a U.S. helicopter to Clark Air Base on their way to exile in Hawaii.[79]

Although Corazon Aquino became president, the conditions of the transition required an uneasy alliance with Ramos and Enrile, who had been among her husband's tormentors. This undermined her ability to consolidate the democratization process, with recurrent coup attempts by a still-politicized military. During her tenure, which ended in 1992, she oversaw the return of the Subic Bay and Clark air bases to the Philippines, when the base agreements expired in September 1991, ending the century-long U.S. interlude. Events beyond her control determined the outcome of the base negotiations. In June 1991 Mount Pinatubo erupted, burying Clark Air Base in a foot of rain-sodden ash. The cost to restore the air base would have been enormous. Meanwhile, the demise of the Soviet Union in 1991 marked the end of the Cold War, reducing the strategic importance of the U.S. bases in the Philippines.

Political stability has remained elusive since the U.S. departure. Successive Philippine administrations have fallen prey to well-founded accusations of corruption. The military remains an important force in politics—indeed General Fidel Ramos succeeded Aquino as president in 1992—but elections have been held with regularity, making the Marcos era the exception, not the rule.

During the colonial period, U.S. goals emphasized the creation of strong civil institutions, especially democratic ones. The United States has left a colonial legacy that includes a strong faith in democracy and comprehensive democratic institutions as well as a strong military. The United States greatly aided Philippine state and nation building, but it created stronger military than civil institutions. Perhaps this is not surprising given that the U.S. vehicle for colonization was its own military and a significant part of its aid after independence was military aid. This military aid focused not on external threats but on internal ones, which erupt periodically in response to the deep political, social, and economic inequality, rooted in the land tenure patterns established under Spain.

The United States also provided significant economic aid after independence, which successive Philippine presidents used to shore up the continued economic dominance of the social elite, the great landholding families. The Philippines has never overcome the highly skewed land tenure established under Spain. This deep social divide remains a formidable barrier to nation building and helps explain the enduring political instability. Economic development, even after four decades of significant U.S. economic aid, also remains elusive. The social elite established under Spain did not use the post–World War II economic aid nearly as effectively as did the South Koreans and Taiwanese, whose standards of living rose from levels comparable to that of the Philippines to those of developed countries by the end of the twentieth century.

Notes

1. This essay is based on doctoral research for my first book, Amy Blitz, *The Contested State: American Foreign Policy and Regime Change in the Philippines* (Lanham, MD: Rowman and Littlefield, 2000). See also Rene Ofreneo, *Capitalism in Philippine Agriculture* (Quezon City: Foundation for Nationalist Studies, 1980), 3–13.

2. Renato Constantino, *The Philippines: A Past Revisited* (Quezon City: Tala, 1975), 74.

3. Rene Ofreneo, *Capitalism in Philippine Agriculture*, 3–13.

4. Renato Constantino, *The Philippines*, 58, 75.

5. Raymond Carr, *Spain: 1808–1975* (New York: Oxford University Press, 1982), 257–306; Stanley Karnow, *In Our Image: America's Empire in the Philippines* (New York: Random House, 1989), 57–77.

6. Renato Constantino, *The Philippines*, 150–172; Stanley Karnow, *In Our Image*, 67–77.

7. Stanley Karnow, *In Our Image*, 78–80; Jerald Combs, *The History of American Foreign Policy* (New York: Alfred A. Knopf, 1986), 155–56.

8. Brian McAllister Linn, *The U.S. Army and Counterinsurgency in the Philippine War, 1899–1902* (Chapel Hill: University of North Carolina Press, 1989), 12; Sand-30 (pseud.), "Trench, Parapet, or 'the Open,'" *Journal of the Military Service Institution* 31 (July 1902), 471–86.

9. Stanley Karnow, *In Our Image*, 185.

10. Renato Constantino, *The Philippines*, 244–46; Brian McAllister Linn, *The U.S. Army and Counterinsurgency in the Philippine War*, 163–70.

11. Renato Constantino, *The Philippines*, 247, 251; Stanley Karnow, *In Our Image*, 194.

12. Morgan Gates, *Schoolbooks and Krags* (Westport, CT: Greenwood Press, 1973), 136–69; Stanley Karnow, *In Our Image*, 205–7; H.W. Brands, *Bound to Empire* (New York: Oxford University Press, 1992), 71.

13. Lewis E. Gleeck Jr., *The American Governors-General and High Commissioners in the Philippines* (Quezon City: New Day, 1986).

14. H.W. Brands, *Bound to Empire*, 99; Luzviminda Bartolome and Jonathan Fast, *Conspiracy for Empire: Big Business, Corruption and the Politics of Imperialism in America, 1876–1907* (Quezon City: Foundation for Nationalist Studies, 1985), 262–63.

15. Renato Constantino, *The Philippines*, 303–5.

16. Rene Ofreneo, *Capitalism in Philippine Agriculture*, 24.

17. Ibid., 15–16.

18. H.W. Brands, *Bound to Empire*, 98.

19. *The Election Law* (Manila: Manila Bureau of Printing, 1907), National Archives, The Philippine Archives Collection, College Park, MD.

20. H.W. Brands, *Bound to Empire*, 98.

21. Ibid., 60–84, 106; Stanley Karnow, *In Our Image*, 227–56; and Charles Farkas, "Partido Federal: The Policy of Attraction," *Bulletin of the American Historical Collection*, Manila (October–December 1978), 33–37.

22. Stanley Karnow, *In Our Image*, 244–45.

23. H.W. Brands, *Bound to Empire*, 109.

24. Stanley Karnow, *In Our Image*, 245.

25. Ibid., 330.

26. H.W. Brands, *Bound to Empire*, 163.

27. Stanley Karnow, *In Our Image*, 245–46, 225–26.

28. Renato Constantino, *The Philippines*, 373–80; Stanley Karnow, *In Our Image*, 273–74.

29. H.W. Brands, *Bound to Empire*, 166; Stanley Karnow, *In Our Image*, 258–76.

30. Stanley Karnow, *In Our Image*, 302–5.

31. Theodore Friend, *Between Two Empires* (New Haven: Yale University Press, 1965); Renato Constantino and Letizia Renato, *The Philippines: The Continuing Past* (Quezon City: The Foundation for Nationalist Studies, 1978), 52–83.

32. Renato Constantino and Letizia Renato, *The Philippines*, 10–11.

33. Ibid., 52–83; H.W. Brands, *Bound to Empire*, 198–204; Theodore Friend, *Between Two Empires*.

34. Renato Constantino and Letizia Renato, *The Philippines*, 27–83, 146.

35. For an excellent account of the history of the Huk rebellion, see Benedict Kerkvliet,

The Huk Rebellion (Berkeley: University of California Press, 1977); see also Eduardo Lachica, *Huk* (Manila: Solidaridad Publishing House, 1971).

36. Renato Constantino and Letizia Renato, *The Philippines*, 155.

37. Ibid., 155; Eduardo Lachica, *Huk*, 103–17; Benedict Kerkvliet, *The Huk Rebellion*.

38. Military Intelligence Section, U.S. Army Pacific Command, Secret Intelligence Report No. 109–1357, 22 December 1945, National Security Archive, George Washington University, Washington, DC.

39. Renato Constantino and Letizia Renato, *The Philippines*, 157.

40. Eduardo Lachica, *Huk*, 118–36.

41. H.W. Brands, *Bound to Empire*, 235.

42. Stanley Karnow, *In Our Image*, 345; Benedict Kerkvliet, *The Huk Rebellion*, 159.

43. H.W. Brands, *Bound to Empire*, 234–35.

44. Stanley Karnow, *In Our Image*, 346–48.

45. The Fact-Finding Commission, *The Final Report, Pursuant to R.A. No. 6832* (Manila: Bookmark, 1990), 32; Stephen Shalom, *The United States and the Philippines* (Philadelphia: Institute for the Study of Human Issues, 1981), 79–80.

46. Personal field research, 1984–86.

47. The Fact-Finding Commission, *The Final Report, Pursuant to R.A. No. 6832*.

48. U.S. Department of the Army General Staff, *Intelligence Research Report: The Philippine Constabulary,* Project No. 7557, December 15, 1952, 1–2, National Archives, "The Philippines Archive Collection," College Park, MD.

49. Stanley Karnow, *In Our Image*, 350.

50. Renato Constantino and Letizia Renato, *The Philippines,* 236–37.

51. Stanley Karnow, *In Our Image*, 351.

52. Renato Constantino and Letizia Renato, *The Philippines*, 248–50.

53. Stanley Karnow, *In Our Image*, 352; H.W. Brands, *Bound to Empire*, 253.

54. CIA, OCI No. 1026, 20 November 1953, National Archives, The Philippine Archives Collection, College Park, MD; H.W. Brands, *Bound to Empire*, 254.

55. Renato Constantino and Letizia Renato, *The Philippines*, 248–57; interview with Manuel Manahan, October 1983.

56. Stanley Karnow, *In Our Image*, 350.

57. The Fact-Finding Commission, *The Final Report, Pursuant to R.A. No. 6832*.

58. Ibid., 40–41.

59. Staff report prepared for the U.S. Senate Committee on Foreign Relations, *Korea and the Philippines: November 1972*, Committee Print, 93rd Congress, 1st Session, 18 February 1973, National Security Archives, The Philippines: The Marcos Years, George Washington University, Washington, DC.

60. Compiled from Ibon Data Bank, *Ibon Facts and Figures*, vols. 7–8, (Manila: Ibon Data Bank Philippines, 1984–85).

61. Interviews in the Philippine countryside with peasants and NPA organizers, May 1984 to February 1986. For accounts of the NPA, see Gregg R. Jones, *Red Revolution* (Boulder, CO: Westview Press, 1989); William Chapman, *Inside the Philippine Revolution* (New York: W.W. Norton, 1987); Richard Kessler, *Rebellion and Repression in the Philippines* (New Haven: Yale University Press, 1989).

62. Ibon Primer Series, *The Philippine Financial System* (Manila: Ibon Databank Philippines, 1983).

63. Richard Kessler, *Rebellion and Repression in the Philippines*, 137.

64. "The Philippines Tries One-Man Democracy," secret report from INR, distributed 1 November 1972, National Security Archives, The Philippines: The Marcos Years, George Washington University, Washington, DC.

65. "Overseas Loans and Grants, 1961–1988," Special Report Prepared for the House

Foreign Affairs Committee, Office of Statistics and Reports, Bureau for Program and Policy Coordination, Agency for International Development, National Security Archives, The Philippines: The Marcos Years, George Washington University, Washington, DC; H.W. Brands, *Bound to Empire*; William E. Berry, *U.S. Bases in the Philippines* (Boulder, CO: Westview, 1989).

66. The Fact-Finding Commission, *The Final Report, Pursuant to R.A. No. 6832*.

67. Raymond Bonner, *Waltzing with a Dictator* (New York: Vintage Books, 1988), 364.

68. Gerald Sussman, David O'Connor, and Charles W. Lindsey, "The Philippines, 1984: The Political Economy of a Dying Dictatorship," *Philippine Research Bulletin*, Friends of the Filipino People, Durham, NC (summer 1984), in Daniel B. Schirmer and Stephen Rosskam Shalom, eds., *The Philippines Reader* (Boston: South End Press, 1987); Ibon Data Bank, *Ibon Facts and Figures*, vols. 7–8; Belinda Aquino, ed., *Cronies and Enemies*, Philippine Studies Occasional Paper No. 5, Philippine Studies Program, Center for Asian and Pacific Studies (Honolulu: University of Hawaii, 1982). Note that she is no relation to Benigno Aquino Jr.

69. Lewis Simons, *Worth Dying For* (New York: William Morrow, 1987), 172.

70. U.S. Embassy in Manila to the State Department, Secret Cable No. 23099, 6 September 1983, National Security Archives, The Philippines: The Marcos Years, George Washington University, Washington, DC.

71. George P. Shultz, *Turmoil and Triumph: My Years as Secretary of State* (New York: Charles Scribner's Sons, 1993), 16, 611.

72. Richard G. Lugar, *Letters to the Next President* (New York: Simon & Schuster, 1988).

73. Frederick Z. Brown and Carl Ford, "The Current Situation in the Philippines," Committee on Foreign Relations Report to Congress, September 1984, p. 7, National Security Archives, The Philippines: The Marcos Years, George Washington University, Washington, DC.

74. Interviews with Walden Bello and an Asia Foundation officer, November 1993; interviews with priests conducted by Raymond Bonner, *Waltzing with a Dictator*, 524.

75. George P. Shultz, *Turmoil and Triumph*, 615; Unclassified Cable No. 337854, 3 November 1985, National Security Archives, The Philippines: The Marcos Years, George Washington University, Washington, DC; from U.S. Ambassador Stephen Bosworth to the U.S. State Department, Secret Cable No. 39432, 18 December 1985, ibid.

76. Interview with D.H. Sawyer staff conducted by Raymond Bonner, *Waltzing with a Dictator*, 522; Stanley Karnow, *In Our Image*, 412; interview with a confidential source from the firm D.H. Sawyer, May 1993.

77. Richard G. Lugar, *Letters to the Next President*, 131, on number of voters; Secret Cable No. 041479, 10 February 1986, National Security Archives, The Philippines: The Marcos Years, George Washington University, Washington, DC; interview with Stephen Bosworth, March 1989.

78. Stanley Karnow, *In Our Image*, 414; Amy Blitz, "The Press and Foreign Policy: A Case Study of *New York Times* Coverage of the Philippines, 1985–1986," unpublished M.A. thesis, 1990, Massachusetts Institute of Technology, Cambridge, MA; Unclassified Cable No. 049446, 15 February 1986, National Security Archives, The Philippines: The Marcos Years, George Washington University, Washington, DC.

79. Confidential Cable No. 05363, 16 February 1986, National Security Archives, The Philippines: The Marcos Years, George Washington University, Washington, DC; Confidential Cable No. 05323, 15 February 1986, and Confidential Cable No. 05362, 16 February 1986, ibid.; interview with Fidel Ramos and Radio Veritas broadcasts, February 1986.

4

Japanese Puppet-State Building in Manchukuo

S.C.M. Paine

Abstract: *This case study of the Japanese colonization of Manchuria in the first half of the twentieth century shows enormous economic achievements at the cost of enduring Chinese hostility over the brutal methods employed. Japan failed to create a sense of nationhood among Manchuria's diverse population of Han Chinese, Manchus, Mongols, Koreans, and Japanese. In an attempt to leverage cultural differences, Japan created segregated worlds that could not coalesce into a nation. Although it established an elaborate system of state institutions, the fiction of Manchu imperial rule and the reality of Kwantung Army dominance meant that the state institutions disappeared along with the Japanese Army upon its defeat in World War II. However, Japan did create an enduring transportation and communication infrastructure as well as a comprehensive heavy industrial base of mining, metallurgy, and machine tools that transformed Manchuria into the most industrialized part of Asia outside the Japanese home islands.*[1]

In 1931 Japan invaded all of Manchuria, an area with twice its territory and one-third its population, to found the state of Manchukuo, which remained in existence until Japan's defeat in World War II.[2] In these years of escalating warfare, first against China in the Second Sino-Japanese War (1931–45) and then against the Allies in the War of the Pacific (1941–45), Japan transformed Manchuria into the most industrialized part of Asia outside of its home islands, out-producing even Shanghai and the Yangzi River valley cities, long the heart of China's modern economy.[3] Japan used a state capitalist model for economic development that it had applied with great success to itself and then to its island of Hokkaido during the Meiji Restoration (1868–1912). Japan made concerted efforts at nation building, state building, and economic development in Manchuria in order to restore its own domestic economy, ravaged by the Great Depression, to contain Soviet expansion in Asia, to transform Manchurians from foes into allies, and to provide the aura of an independent country.[4]

Modernization and Westernization

At the height of European imperialism, Imperial Japan transformed itself from a traditional shogunate into a modern power with a full array of westernized civil and military institutions. When Britain and France defeated China during the Opium Wars (1840–42, 1856–60) and the U.S. Navy came calling on Japan in 1854 with similar demands for a westernized trading and diplomatic regime, Japan responded by sending numerous fact-finding missions to Russia, Western Europe, and the United States. Although Japanese leaders had initially favored armed resistance (the strategy pursued by China), after long trips abroad they concluded resistance would be futile because Japan was technologically and militarily inferior to the imperial powers.

Instead the Japanese chose a combination of modernization and selective westernization in order to protect their country's national security. Unlike Chinese leaders, who concluded that China should modernize its military, meaning acquiring state-of-the-art weapons, Japanese leaders understood that the ability to produce and develop state-of-the-art technology (modernization) rested on a broad organizational base of both military and civil institutions (westernization). They chose a domestic policy of state building and economic development followed by a foreign policy of wars to contain Russian expansion in northeast Asia, where Japan intended to create its own empire. Because the great powers of the day were all empires, Japanese leaders saw their transformation into an imperial power as the antidote to Western imperialism.

The domestic program took one generation to complete. During this phase, Japan westernized a whole array of institutions: In 1869, a year after the restoration government seized control, the elimination of the feudal domains, long fracturing Japan, overturned the internal distribution of power. In 1872 elementary education became compulsory in recognition that modernization required an educated citizenry. In 1878 military westernization entailed the creation of the Army General Staff to coordinate military planning. In 1882 the westernization of financial and legal institutions began with the creation of the Bank of Japan and the promulgation of a westernized criminal code. In 1885 Japanese leaders created a cabinet subordinate to a prime minister. In 1886 Tokyo Imperial University became the center of higher westernized learning. In 1887 a new civil service examination system began testing westernized subjects. In 1889 Japanese leaders promulgated a constitution, and in 1890 they convened the first Diet, reorganized the judicial system, and introduced a westernized code of civil procedure. Thus, between 1868 and 1890 Japan completed a far-reaching westernization program.

Although these reforms became known as the Meiji Reforms, in deference to the ruling Emperor Meiji (r. 1868–1912), in reality, a group of middle- and low-ranking samurai dominated the new government after a brief civil war in which the last Tokugawa shogun stepped down. During the domestic phase of Japan's grand strategy, the government carefully avoided foreign wars so as not to derail

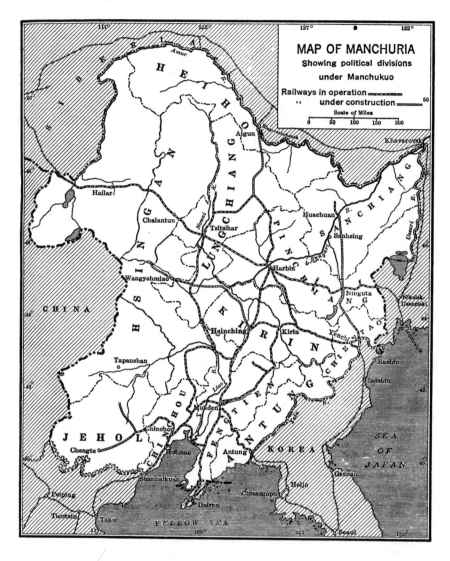

MAP OF MANCHURIA
Showing political divisions
under Manchukuo
Railways in operation ══════
   ˌˌ   under construction ══════
Scale of Miles
0   50   100   150   200

the reforms. In contrast, China became entangled in one conflict after another so that little modernization let alone westernization occurred.

Westernization entailed the sacrifice of many venerated traditions, such as the replacement of the long-privileged samurai, or warrior, caste with a conscript army, and the emphasis on Western subjects of study at the expense of topics associated with Japanese culture. Such reforms were extremely unpopular, since the general population resented being forced to change the way they had lived for generations.

The reforms did not become widely accepted until a generation later, when foreign policy successes against China and Russia at the turn of the twentieth century vindicated the sacrifices of the reform program for an increasingly nationalistic public. Victory in the First Sino-Japanese War (1894–95) transformed Japan into the dominant regional power at China's expense. Victory in the Russo-Japanese War (1904–5) transformed Japan into a great power, a status that it has retained to the present despite its defeat in World War II.[5]

The Japanese were immensely proud of these achievements. Within two generations they had transformed their country from an object of imperialism to a perpetrator. They had defeated the two greatest land empires of the day and had allied in 1902 with the prevailing superpower, Britain, in the latter's only long-term alliance between the Napoleonic Wars and World War I.[6] Japanese leaders believed that their model for national security through modernization and westernization could benefit others, particularly their many impoverished and unstable neighbors.

Japan was the only developing country in the nineteenth century to embrace as a national security strategy comprehensive westernization—not of its culture but of its political, military, legal, economic, and educational institutions. It westernized in order to modernize while preserving its culture, and it modernized in order to ward off foreign imperialism.

Colonial Antecedents

Japan applied the many lessons of its own westernization and modernization to its colonies. This began with Hokkaido, the sparsely populated, historical homeland of the Ainu people and northernmost main island of Japan. The Japanese focused on Hokkaido because of Russian expansion through the Aleutian Islands on to California and down the Kuril Islands toward Japan.[7] Both to preempt Russia and to mitigate Japan's shortage of arable land, the Japanese government established the Hokkaido Colonization Office in 1869. It encouraged former samurai, relieved of their privileged status and stipends in the 1870s, to emigrate to Hokkaido. Colonist-militiamen were to settle in strategic hamlets. Government investments focused on the development of coal mining, railway lines, forestry, and agriculture. Fine railway systems and the rapid development of heavy industry became the hallmarks of Japanese imperialism. Japan also engaged in city planning and the spread of education. These efforts were sufficiently successful that the Colonization Office closed in 1882.

Thus, Japan had a certain amount of expertise when it won Taiwan in the First Sino-Japanese War and proceeded to visit the Meiji reform package on Taiwan. Again Japan focused on the development of infrastructure and resource extraction, which in Taiwan meant agriculture. Japan created modern ports in Keelung in the north, Kaohsiung in the south, and a railway and improved road system in between. It invested in hydroelectric power, greatly improved public health and sanitation, spread modern practices in agriculture, created a modern banking system, and imposed an effective police system under an all-powerful governor-general. Taiwan

became a major supplier to Japan of rice, sugar, and camphor, and developed a
food-processing industry.[8]

In Korea, Japan also imposed centralized government institutions under an all-
powerful governor-general and a staff of Japanese military officers, who tolerated
no dissent. As in Hokkaido and Taiwan, the Japanese government encouraged
Japanese immigration, made massive investments in infrastructure and resource
development, put together a modern banking system, created an array of modern
enterprises, and established a nationwide educational system to inculcate Japanese
values. Prior to the Japanese takeover of Korea in 1910, the country was noted for
its poverty and the government for its corruption and dysfunctionality.[9] Japan laid
the foundations for industrialization and modernization but at the price of intense
Korean hostility to foreign domination and particularly to the execution and im-
prisonment of those who resisted, most notably their murdered queen.[10]

Victory in the Russo-Japanese War won Japan Russia's southern Manchurian
railway concessions connecting Changchun (later renamed Hsinching) in central
Manchuria with the commercial port of Dalian and the naval base at Lüshun (Port
Arthur), both on the Liaodong Peninsula in southern Manchuria. This railway line
became known as the South Manchurian Railway and the concession area, the
Kwantung lease. The railway company became a quasi government and massive
umbrella organization for the development of all resources in the lease area, most
notably coal and iron mines. Japan's army in Manchuria, the Kwantung Army
(Kantō Army) was the power behind the railway company.

As in Hokkaido and Korea, the government encouraged Japanese immigration.[11] Japan invested massively in the Kwantung lease area, developing a wide
array of business, government, economic, educational, and other institutions. Again
the railway was central to Japanese plans for resource extraction and economic
growth, and for troop deployments to quell local resistance and repel foreign invasion. Endemic unrest in China from the fall of the Qing dynasty in 1911 onward
threatened these massive investments.

The Communist revolution in Russia in 1917 and Great Depression in 1929
heightened these security problems. Japanese leaders considered China vulnerable to communism, an anathema in their eyes. When the Western protectionist
response to the Great Depression suddenly deprived export-dependent Japan of its
main markets, Japanese leaders considered the invasion of Manchuria in 1931 as
the best solution to these escalating national security and economic concerns. If the
West would not trade, Japan would turn to autarky, which required an empire of
sufficient size for economic self-sufficiency. Manchuria would serve this purpose
and also as a bulwark against Communist expansion by Russia into Asia. The invasion of Manchuria marked the beginning of the Second Sino-Japanese War, which
progressed in phases: the pacification of Manchuria (1931–33), the North China
War (1933–35), the invasion of coastal and Yangzi River valley China (1937–39),
and the Ichigo Offensive through south central China (1944). The war ended with
the Soviet invasion of Manchuria and the U.S. atomic bombing of Japan (1945).

Nation Building

The Japanese tried to construct a nation in Manchuria out of Qing dynasty antecedents. The Qing or Manchu dynasty (1644–1911) was China's last dynasty. The Manchus had conquered the last Han Chinese dynasty, the Ming (1368–1644), to install Manchu minority rule. Their own overthrow left the Manchus despised outcasts until the Japanese found a use for them in their ancestral homelands.

According to Japanese scholars, the Qing dynasty coined the term *Manchuria* in the seventeenth century. The founding Qing emperor, Nurhaci (r. 1616–26) used it to distinguish the Manchu homelands from the Qing empire.[12] According to this line of thinking, Manchuria was not an integral part of China. General Ishiwara Kanji, the mastermind of the invasion of Manchuria, then took the argument a step further: "In comparison to the Han race, the Manchu people are more closely related to the great Japanese race."[13]

The Japanese attempted to create a state around the person of the last Manchu emperor, Henry Puyi, rescued from obscurity in Tianjin and enthroned in Hsinching (Xinjing), meaning "new capital," the new name for Changchun.[14] The Japanese argued that Manchuria had regained its independence under the rule of the Manchus. Its ethnic composition, however, no longer supported a Manchu dynasty. Years of Han Chinese immigration had transformed the ethnic map so that the Manchus had become a minority in their own lands. By the 1930s, the Tungus tribes, of which the Manchus were one, lived primarily in the inhospitable far north, the Mongols of Inner Mongolia in the west, the Koreans along the Korean border in the east, and the Han in the south.[15] In 1935 just 16.2 percent of the Manchukuo population was Manchu, 2.4 percent Mongol, 2.1 percent Korean, and 0.3 percent Japanese, leaving 79 percent Chinese.[16] The Japanese referred to these groups as the five races of Manchukuo, a framework that unwittingly emphasized division, not unity.

Initially Japanese officials referred to northeast Asia as Manchuro-Mongolia but eventually they opted for a Manchurian, not a Mongol, state.[17] Having the deposed Manchu emperor in tow probably predisposed this decision. Yet the Mongols occupied over one-third of Manchukuo's territory, disliked the Chinese, and saw Japan as a potential counterweight to China, making a case for Inner Mongolian statehood; but the Mongol population was tiny.[18] Mongols had long sought independence because of the unrelenting encroachments on their pasturelands and their nomadic way of life by Han Chinese engaged in settled agriculture. When faced with the choice of continued Chinese domination or something new, the Mongols chose the something new, which was Manchukuo.[19]

Because the Mongols were generally friendly to Japanese and remained nomadic, they fell under separate administration. The Japanese wanted the Mongols to continue producing beef cattle, dairy cows, and wool. Separate administration also reflected the strategic location of the Inner Mongol homelands as a buffer zone between the industrial heart of Manchukuo and the Soviet satellite, the People's Republic of Mongolia (formerly Outer Mongolia). The Inner Mongolian lands of

Hulunbuir became Hsingan (Xing'an) Province, where the Battle of Nomonhan (1939) erupted between Japan and the Soviet Union.

Much of the Han Chinese population in Manchuria consisted of temporary residents trying to earn some money before returning home. On average, Han laborers earned three-quarters of the wages of Koreans, and less than one-third those of the Japanese. Han women earned one-tenth the salary of Japanese men. Korean women earned about one-third what Japanese men did, slightly more than Han men.[20] Prior to the Great Depression two-thirds of Chinese laborers remained in Manchuria; after the Japanese invasion the retention rate plummeted.[21]

Japan tried to create an overarching ideology to bind the new nation. When Puyi formally assumed the throne on 9 March 1932, he proclaimed the Princely Way of Enlightened Rule and emphasized Confucian Ethics and Benevolence as the country's unifying ideology. The ideology was intended to compete with the democracy of the West, the communism of the Soviet Union, and the Three People's Principles of China.[22] Japanese leaders emphasized the connection between the Manchukuo and Japanese emperors. Later, the Japanese emphasized the East Asian Co-Prosperity Zone to forge an imperial identity among Japan's subject peoples. They used the Manchukuo educational system to spread a common language, a common base of knowledge, and a common culture—all Japanese, but the attempt foundered on an insufficiency of Japanese-language instructors. Japan also established Concordia Societies throughout Manchukuo under the banners of a "princely paradise," "harmony among the five races," and Confucianism. By 1944 there were over four million members and 5,000 branches.[23]

Japan aggressively promoted immigration as a means of border defense against the Soviet Union.[24] It launched a twenty-year plan to settle five million Japanese in Manchukuo, mainly in strategic hamlets along the border. Although Japan did not come close to meeting immigration targets, the program created tensions. Since the immigrants rarely opened new lands, they generally expropriated fields from Han Chinese owners.[25] When the Han refused to sell at the prices offered and then resorted to armed resistance, the Japanese responded with brutality, clearing entire districts of any Han population, killing many in the process.[26]

Japan's investment in immigration was massive, with separate companies for Japanese and Korean immigrants, and four-year training and support programs. Immigrants fell into two categories: mainstay and ordinary. Those constituting the mainstay or nucleus, comprising about 15 percent of the total, were discharged soldiers who formed advance parties. Later ordinary immigrants followed under the guidance of the mainstay group.[27] These Japanese settlements were separate from the general population and received preferential treatment. For example, in 1940 Japanese got at least double the grain ration of the rest of the urban Manchukuo population.[28]

No shared sense of nation emerged from these initiatives. The Japanese remained a privileged minority. Mongols and Koreans fell under separate administrative structures. The activities of the Kwantung Army were far too numerous, visible, and coercive to leave any doubt that it, not the Manchu emperor, was in charge.[29] The Manchus wanted their dynasty back, the Mongols and Koreans each wanted independence of ancestral lands overlapping with Manchukuo, the Han wanted local or national Han Chinese rule, and the Japanese wanted to dominate them all. Japan never built a nation in Manchuria. Given these competing interests, it is not surprising that Japan failed to transform the five races of Manchuria into one people with a shared sense of nation bound to the territory of Manchukuo.

State Building

Even if Japan did not create a nation, it did create a state, albeit one of short duration. The Kwantung Army first focused on the establishment of public order, long absent in Manchuria. It did so through a succession of police and military institutions.[30] In April 1932, it unified the Manchurian land and naval forces, and created a national police force, but the Manchukuo Army suffered persistent desertion and depended heavily on Japanese personnel.[31] Initially the police force and army cooperated but operated separately. As the army became increasingly involved in maintaining public order, it absorbed the police.[32]

In January 1934, the Japanese resurrected the *baojia* system, China's traditional method of local control through collective responsibility, that Japan had employed with great effect in Taiwan. The Japanese divided the Manchurian Han population into a pyramid of groups of ten: every ten household heads elected a leader, ten such leaders elected their leader, and so on to create four tiers that together produced a 10,000-family unit. If anything went wrong within the unit, potentially all paid. Law enforcement and militia organizations followed the baojia system, and all able-bodied men between the ages of eighteen and forty were required to serve.[33] The Mongols and Koreans, however, were not submitted to this system, which was considered a relic of Han culture not applicable to other races.[34]

The Japanese relied on a variety of strategies to impose order: the baojia system, occupation by the Kwantung army, ground operations, self-defense units, strategic hamlets, various police organizations, weapons confiscation, public education (propaganda), and the fingerprinting and census of the population. They greatly improved communications and transportation, which facilitated military and police operations. Likewise, they tried to take opium production from the hands of the opposition, who used it to finance their activities. Manchukuo authorities used opium monopoly revenues to feed state coffers instead. Opium addiction was pervasive, with half a million registered addicts in 1942.[35]

By the end of 1933, Japan had virtually eliminated warlord and bandit opposition, by 1938 the Communist insurgency had fled across the Soviet frontier, and by early 1941 the Korean insurgency had largely been eliminated. Border incidents with the Soviet Union, however, remained endemic, although greatly reduced after the Nazi invasion caused a reorientation of Soviet priorities in 1941.[36] Throughout the Manchukuo period, Japan maintained a large army of occupation. The Kwantung

Army increased in size from 10,000 men at the time of the invasion to 60,000 in 1933; 80,000 in 1936; 700,000 in 1941; and 780,000 in 1945.[37]

Japan also created an elaborate government structure consisting of the imperial family and associates, organizations under the central administrative institutions, and government ministries. The government had four branches: the legislative, the administrative, the judicial, and the investigatory. This mirrored China's government minus the examination branch, mandated in the model devised by the founding father of the Republic of China, Sun Yat-sen. In 1937 Japan dispensed with the investigatory branch as redundant with the Kwantung Army's activities.[38] A complete reorganization of local administration in December 1934 entailed the establishment governmental institutions at the provincial, county, village, and street levels, ending decades of governmental paralysis in Manchuria.[39] Legal reforms in 1934 replaced the Chinese legal system with one conforming to Japanese practices.[40] In early 1937, Manchukuo introduced new criminal, civil, and commercial laws again based on Japanese models.[41]

In the early years, the institutions associated with the imperial family were headed mainly by Manchurians of both Manchu and Han extraction, but in later years each chairman had a vice-chairman, who was generally Japanese. Likewise, although Manchurians headed the ministries, their immediate subordinate was usually a Japanese. As the number and complexity of government institutions grew, so did the Japanese dominance over them.[42] Although a Manchurian held the office of chief executive, the real locus of power was the Japanese-headed General Affairs Office, which resembled Japan's cabinet in function.[43] Although Han Chinese manned many parts of the new bureaucracy, police force, and army, Japanese nationals held virtually all senior positions.[44]

As the Kwantung Army lacked sufficient personnel to staff an entire government, Manchukuo also employed many former personnel of the South Manchurian Railway and several hundred senior civilian Japanese government officials on temporary postings to provide crucial expertise.[45] Several groups of Manchurians took government positions: those who had suffered under Manchurian warlord rule, those who had studied in Japan or had close relations with the Japanese, and Qing loyalists who hoped for a revival of the dynasty. Initially local notables populated the Manchukuo government, but over time appointments increasingly gravitated toward those with expertise, pro-Japanese sentiments, and fluency in Japanese. The proportion of Japanese local officials rose from 29 percent at the end of 1934 to 65 percent in the spring of 1940. Likewise, the proportion of Japanese provincial officials rose from nearly one-third in 1934 to nearly two-thirds in 1940.[46] By 1940 Japanese dominated the government institutions concerning security, the maintenance of order, the economy, and the infrastructure, accounting for three-quarters of the personnel.[47]

Ostensibly this government came under the authority of the emperor of Manchukuo, the bespectacled Henry Puyi, now outfitted in stunning imperial regalia and the reign title of *Datong,* meaning "utopia."[48] Upon his enthronement as the emperor of Manchukuo in 1934, his reign title changed to *Kangde,* meaning "abundant virtue." In reality Japan ruled, not as it constitutionally should have, through its prime minister and his cabinet in Tokyo, but through the Kwantung Army.[49] Manchukuo was not supposed to be a colony either, but an independent country allied with Japan. Both the emperor of Japan, the "emperor of the heavens," and the emperor of Manchukuo, the "emperor of the emperors," reigned but did not usually rule. They served as powerful symbols of national unity at least in Japan, and, the Japanese hoped, also in Manchukuo. Regardless of the flowcharts on paper outlining the structure of the Manchukuo government, in practice the chain of command ran from the Kwantung Army to the Assembly of the Legislative Yuan to the Office of the Councilors and only then to the emperor of Manchukuo, who obligingly made any required public pronouncements.[50]

Elaborate government structures required funding. In 1932 the government assumed responsibility for the collection of maritime tariffs and the salt monopoly, and unified customs and tax collection. In November of that year it established a monopoly on the opium trade.[51] Tax collection offices dispersed throughout Manchukuo greatly increased revenues.[52] For the Kwantung Army, the main sources of income were customs revenues, the salt tax, and the opium monopoly.[53]

On 15 March 1932, Japan reduced Manchuria's fifteen circulating currencies and 136 types of bank notes to two major currencies, one for domestic use and the other, a gold-backed convertible currency, for trade. The latter was eliminated in 1935 after the domestic currency became convertible into yen. Previously, three to six currencies had circulated in each city. By mid-1935 virtually all the old currencies had been converted, ending decades of financial anarchy and currency debasement.[54]

On 11 June 1932 the Kwantung Army established the Central Bank of Manchukuo. The bank set monetary policy and created a stable credit system. It also gave Japan control over much of the Manchukuo economy because general banking constituted only a fraction of the expropriated banks' business. Previously banks bought and sold, and produced and invested in, Manchuria's principal commodities and industries: soybeans, cereals, petroleum products, flour milling, sugar, brewing, shipping, power generation, textiles, forestry, and mining. These banks handled over half of the soybean crop, Manchuria's primary export. Nationalization of these banks included all of their subsidiary enterprises, which were then separated from banking and put under Japanese management.[55] Therefore, banking reform constituted a massive expropriation of Chinese assets. In 1936 Japan established the Manchurian Industrial Enterprise Bank in order to provide investment capital to develop heavy industry. By 1945 this bank provided nearly all loans to mining and nearly three-quarters of all loans to construction and industry.[56]

Improved revenue collection helped finance a building spree particularly in the new capital, but also in Fengtian (Mukden), Harbin, Tumen, and Mudanjiang,[57] where Japanese planners created carefully organized boulevards, logical traffic patterns, spacious central parks, Shinto shrines, and a proliferation of large government buildings in the Asian totalitarian style. These planned cities served as architectural symbols of authority and the new order.[58]

When Japan lost World War II and the invading Soviet army put Japan's civil and military personnel into prisoner-of-war camps, from which few returned, this elaborate state structure disappeared with them. The impressive buildings remained but the institutions vanished. The Japanese left behind a political vacuum that the belligerents in the ensuing final phase of the Chinese Civil War (1945–49) strove to fill. Manchuria became the decisive theater in that war because of the economic prize left behind by Japan.

Economic Development

In contrast to nation building, where the Japanese failed, and state building, where their achievements were ephemeral, their economic development program was remarkably successful. Prior to the Japanese invasion, large-scale industry did not exist outside the foreign concession areas in Manchuria. There were just a few large match, textile, and brick factories built in the final years of warlord administration.[59] As Japanese investments poured into Manchuria after 1931, the Japanese home economy showed signs of recovery in contrast to the economies of the West, where the high unemployment rates of the Great Depression lingered.[60] Japanese zaibatsu (large financial and business conglomerates) established extensive operations. Okura had the oldest large investments. Mitsui and Mitsubishi then became key players during the Manchukuo period.[61]

Japan invested massively in Manchukuo, on the order of at least 100 million yen per annum and often a multiple of that, meaning that Manchukuo ran huge trade deficits with Japan. Included in the Japanese investment statistics and in Manchukuo's service deficit were the costs incurred by the Kwantung Army, which provided the "service" of armed occupation. Japan footed the occupation bill until 1941, when the war with the United States meant that Manchuria had to bear these costs and Japan turned from resource development to resource extraction. This helps to explain the implosion of the Manchukuo economy from the outbreak of global war forward.[62] Nevertheless, even if one removes the occupation costs, Japan still made massive investments and the Manchurian economy developed rapidly despite China's long civil war and Japan's rapidly escalating regional war.

Initially Japanese investments focused on infrastructure development. In 1933 Japan nationalized the Chinese-owned railways, subsuming into the South Manchurian Railway 1,864 kilometers of Chinese-owned tracks or about one-third of the total railway mileage in Manchuria. In 1935 the acquisition of the Chinese Eastern Railway from the Soviet Union added another 1,700 kilometers of track or about another third of the Manchurian total. This put Japan in control of all railways in Manchuria. Between 1933 and 1945, Japan added 6,354 kilometers of new track, almost doubling the pre-invasion railway system to 11,004 kilometers. Japanese investments produced an equally impressive expansion of the road system, adding 14,482 kilometers between 1932 and 1939.[63]

Japan expropriated a fragmented railway system. The Russians had built their railways to a wide gauge to integrate their track into the Russian, not the Chinese, system, while the formerly Chinese-owned railways were undercapitalized, possessing inadequate numbers of locomotives and cars per kilometer. There were also few links connecting the three systems. Japanese investments solved these problems. On 18 June 1937, Japan finished standardizing the tracks to the Chinese gauge to create a unified transportation grid.[64]

Japan then focused investments on resource development, particularly in the areas of energy, mining, and heavy industry.[65] It made major investments in electric power generation. Whereas Manchuria had the capacity to generate 221,800 kilowatts of electricity in 1931, this rose to 2,081,000 kilowatts in 1944. In 1931 it produced 542,960,000 kilowatt hours of electricity and 4,247,200,000 kilowatt hours in 1942. Japan built numerous factories for textiles, metallurgy, machine tools, brick making, chemicals, food processing, gas, building materials, and publishing.[66] Between 1934 and 1938, 210 machine tool factories opened; in 1939, 144 additional machine tool factories opened; and in 1940, 283 more. By 1944 Manchukuo had become an important center of shipbuilding, constructing 1,825 vessels with a total tonnage of 264,058.[67]

Investments in mining grew by nearly seventy times between 1936 and 1943, the peak year for mineral extraction. Manchuria had a rich resource endowment in iron, lead, aluminum, coal, magnesite, shale oil, limestone, dolomite, silica, gold, and talc.[68] Japan established the Manchurian Heavy Industry Company as an umbrella organization to develop a wide variety of mining and heavy industrial enterprises.[69] In August 1935, mineral extraction became a Manchukuo monopoly.[70] Japan developed extensive coal, copper, lead, zinc, antimony, sulfur, iron ore, chrome, manganese, tungsten, molybdenite, mercury, and graphite mines as well as shale oil fields.[71]

Production statistics rose rapidly. Mining production in 1941 was 2.45 times the output for 1930. Other figures for the same two years show electricity production up 6.98 times and pig iron production up 3.5 times. Chemical and machine tool production quadrupled between 1937 and 1943. By 1943 Manchuria produced 49.5 percent of all Chinese coal, 78.2 percent of its electricity, 87.7 percent of its pig iron, 93 percent of its steel, and 66 percent of its concrete. Whereas industry had accounted for 29.4 percent of the Manchurian economy in 1931, it grew to 59 percent in 1943. In 1940 just 4.7 percent of factories employed more than 100 persons, but their employees constituted 53.8 percent of Manchuria's industrial labor force and produced 61 percent of its industrial output.[72]

On the eve of the 1937 escalation of the Second Sino-Japanese War, Manchukuo launched its first five-year plan (1937–41), which soon required major revisions as a result of the escalation. Manchukuo met less than half of the production targets of the original plan, let alone of the revised plan. Both plans set ambitious targets—for instance, a tripling of pig iron production in the original plan and a quintupling in the revised plan. Nevertheless, Manchukuo doubled the output in many categories.[73] Japan completed this economic transformation in just fifteen years under extremely difficult wartime conditions.

The benefits of the industrialization accrued to Japan. While 54 percent of investments went to industry and manufacturing, 30 percent to transportation and communications, and 11 percent to immigration, a mere 5 percent went to agriculture.[74] Yet in 1943 agriculture employed 70 percent of the Manchukuo population. Agricultural production corrected for inflation increased just 10 percent between 1937 and 1943. Soybeans remained the main cash crop. Consumer good output stagnated, meaning that the general standard of living did not necessarily improve. Processed-food production, for instance, plummeted by nearly half between 1937 and 1943.[75] Prior to the Japanese occupation, the Chinese had developed numerous small-scale food processing enterprises producing soya oil, flour, and distilled sorghum; they had also invested in the textile industry and the production of silk thread.[76] These consumer industries atrophied under Japanese domination.

The Economic Legacy

Defeat in World War II cost Japan its empire. The residents of Manchukuo never became a nation. Instead, Manchuria became the central front in the ensuing final stage of the long Chinese Civil War and, at that war's end, reverted to the three northeastern provinces of Heilongjiang in the north, Jilin in the middle, and Liaoning in the south, plus Jehol farther south. The Manchukuo state apparatus disappeared and the Soviet Union did much to undo Japan's economic legacy. The Soviet Union declared Manchurian industry as its "prize of war," even though its participation in the Asian theater had lasted just over a week and the country it was expropriating was not Japan but China, by far the greatest victim of Japanese aggression. According to the Pauley Report, completed just after the war, the United States estimated that the Soviet Union's "prize of war" constituted an $895 million loss to Manchurian industry and, with the damages from the Soviet occupation, totaled $2 billion, an extraordinary sum for the time. Japanese figures indicated that the $895 million calculation should have been revised upward to $1.2 billion. The Soviet Union took 83 percent of Manchukuo's electricity generation equipment, 86 percent of its mining equipment, 82 percent of its cement production equipment, and so on.

Nevertheless, these items constituted but a fraction of Japanese investments. The extensive railway grid remained, as did the many mines that Japan had developed at such cost.[77] The Japanese, like colonial powers elsewhere, left an extensive economic legacy in the infrastructure, buildings, and industry that remained after their departure. Just as the Europeans rebuilt rapidly after the devastation of World War II, so did the Chinese Communists in Manchuria and the Korean Communists in North Korea, who inherited the centers of Japanese investments in northeast Asia.

Manchurian industry was essential for Mao Zedong's plans to win the Chinese Civil War and to industrialize thereafter.

Japanese economic achievements were most important as a model for what was possible. After World War II, many East Asian countries followed the Meiji model for economic development, which relies on state initiatives to build infrastructure and to promote export industries, nowadays focusing on high-tech consumer goods. Whereas in the colonial period these exports went to Japan, they now go to the world. The Meiji model, unlike the Communist model for economic development, left wide latitude for private enterprise, both large and small. Often the largest companies worked hand in hand with the government. In this sense Japan leveraged state planning and private initiatives, permitting a broad spectrum of economic activities.

During the Meiji Reform period in the nineteenth century, Japan demonstrated the ability of a resource-poor country to become a great power within two generations. This required a combination of careful government planning and private initiatives. During the Second Sino-Japanese War, Japan transformed Manchuria, an area exceeding the combined area of Germany and France, into an economic powerhouse. In the second half of the twentieth century, Japan demonstrated the ability of a country utterly devastated by war to become a great economic power within one generation. It is no coincidence that Japan's primary former colonies, Korea and Taiwan, developed so rapidly in the postwar period. State building in South Korea and Taiwan depended on local efforts, but their rapid economic development greatly benefited from the extensive physical infrastructure left behind by Japan as well as from the Meiji model for national development.

Although many of Japan's neighbors continue to despise it for its numerous wartime atrocities, the East Asian countries that became wealthy in the twentieth century all emulated its economic model. This is especially true of China under Deng Xiaoping, who followed the Meiji model with such great economic success. Many in Asia focus on Japan's horrific military history of invasion, coercion, overextension, and brutality, which were its misguided solution to the Great Depression, the Chinese Civil War, and the spread of communism in Asia. Japan also left a positive but unrecognized economic legacy that has helped hundreds of millions of Asians to rise out of poverty.

Notes

1. The thoughts and opinions expressed in this chapter are those of the author and are not necessarily those of the U.S. government, the U.S. Navy Department of Defense, the U.S. Navy Department, or the U.S. Naval War College. All chapter and article titles are rendered in English only, while book titles are rendered both in the original Japanese and in English translation.

2. Japanese Foreign Ministry (hereafter JFM), J.1.2.0–J15, vol. 2, 満州日々新聞社 (Manchuria-Japan Daily Newspaper Co.), Dalian, 1937, 6–7.

3. A.M. Ledovsky, *The USSR, the USA, and the People's Revolution in China*, trans. Nadezhda Burova (Moscow: Progress, 1982), 102.

4. I am particularly grateful to two authors in this volume, Martin McCauley and Kirk Beattie, who have emphasized the distinction between nation and state building.

5. S.C.M. Paine, *The Sino-Japanese War of 1894–1895* (New York: Cambridge University Press, 2003).

6. S.C.M. Paine, *Imperial Rivals: China, Russia, and Their Disputed Frontier* (Armonk, NY: M.E. Sharpe, 1996), 219–25.

7. George Alexander Lensen, *The Russian Push Toward Japan* (Princeton, NJ: Princeton University Press, 1959).

8. Harry J. Lamley, "Taiwan under Japanese Rule," in *Taiwan,* expanded edition, ed. Murray A. Rubinstein (Armonk, NY: M.E. Sharpe, 2007), 209–14, 222–27, 237.

9. Paine, *Sino-Japanese War*, 34–44.

10. Carter J. Eckert, et al. *Korea Old and New* (Seoul: Harvard University Press, 1990), 269–73, 309–13.

11. JFM, J.1.2.0–J15, vol. 3, 業務概要, Manchurian Development Co., Dec. 1944, pp. 1–2; ibid. vol. 2, 満州日々新聞社 (Manchuria-Japan Daily Newspaper Co.), Dalian, 1937, 10–12.

12. 満州中央銀行史研究会 (Manchurian Central Bank Historical Research Committee), ed. 満州中央銀行史 (History of the Manchurian Central Bank) (Tokyo: 東洋経済新報社, 1988), 1–2; 塚瀬進 (Tsukase Susumu), 満州国「民族協和」の実像 (Manchukuo "Racial Harmony" in Reality) (Tokyo: 吉川弘文館, 1998), 14.

13. Cited in 金安泰 (Jin Antai)," "Manchurian Incident and U.S. Foreign Policy," 史学集刊 (1983), 12 no. 3, 73.

14. JFM, A.1.1.0–21, vol. 4, from Consul General Hayashi to Foreign Minister Shidehara, 12 November 1931, 490.

15. Tsukase, Manchukuo, 12.

16. 塚瀬進 (Tsukase Susumu), 中国近代東北経済史研究 (Research on the Modern Economic History of Northeast China) (Tokyo: 東方書店, 1993), 37–38.

17. JFM, A.1.1.0–21, vol. 4, from Consul General Morishima to Foreign Minister Yoshizawa, 12–13 February 1932, 688–89.

18. 幕内光雄 (Maku-uchi Mitsuo), 満州国警察外史 (Unofficial History of the Manchukuo Police) (Tokyo: 三一書房, 1996), 109, 111.

19. JFM, A.1.1.0–21, vol. 1, 19 September 1931, from Kwantung Army chief of staff to vice chief of staff, 5–6 October 1931, 771.

20. 松村高夫 (Matsumura Takao), "The Formation and Development of Immigration and Labor Policies after the Creation of Manchukuo" in 日本帝国主義下の満州 (Manchuria under Japanese Imperialism), 満州史研究会 (Manchurian History Research Committee), ed. (Tokyo: 御茶の水書房, 1972), 289, 295, 301.

21. 田中恒次郎 (Tanaka Jirō), "Anti-Manchukuo and Anti-Japanese Movements" in 日本帝国主義の満州支配 (Manchuria under Japanese Imperialism), eds. 小林英夫 (Kobayashi Hideo) and 浅田喬夫 (Asada Kyōji) (Tokyo: 時潮社, 1986), 380.

22. Tsukase, Manchukuo, 67–68.

23. Maku-uchi, Unofficial History, 74–77, 81, 83–84, 199; 風間秀人 (Kazama Hideto), "Management of Rural Administration" in Kobayashi and Asada, Manchuria under Japanese Imperialism, 279.

24. JFM, J.1.2.0–J2–23 本邦移民関係雑件　満州国ノ部,満州開拓政策基本要綱案 (General Plan for the Colonization Policy for Manchuria), July 1939, 2.

25. Maku-uchi, Unofficial History, 202–6, 210, 215–16, 222–23.

26. JFM, J.1.2.0–J2–23, Charles Bishop Kinney, "Comment on the Alleged Han Massacre," *The Peiping Chronicle* 28 December 1934?, pp. 1–3.

27. JFM, J.1.2.0–J15, 満州拓殖会社関係一件, vol. 2, 満州日々新聞社 (Manchuria-Japan Daily Newspaper Co.), Dalian, 1937, 18, 24, 30, 34–37, 52, 56–57.

28. Maku-uchi, Unofficial History, 159.

29. JFM, A.1.1.0–21, vol. 4, from Consul General Morishima to Foreign Minister Yoshizawa, 12–13 February 1932, 688–89.

30. Maku-uchi, Unofficial History, 87–92.

31. Kobayashi, "Creation and Collapse of 'Manchukuo,'" in Kobayashi and Asada, *Manchuria under Japanese Imperialism*, 33; 満州国軍刊行委員会 (Manchukuo Army Publication Committee), 満州国軍 (Manchukuo Army) (Tokyo: 正光印刷株式会社, 1970), 216, 927–50.

32. 飯島満 (Iijima Mitsuru), "Establishment and Collapse of the 'Combined Army-Police' in Manchukuo" 駿台史学 108 (December 1999), 46, 49, 55.

33. 古屋哲夫 (Furuya Tetsuo), "Creation of 'Manchukuo,'" in 山本有造 (Yamamoto Yūzō), ed.,「満洲国」の研究 (Research on "Manchukuo") (Tokyo: 緑陰書房, 1995), 74–76; Maku-uchi, Unofficial History, 110–17.

34. JFM, D.2.1.2–4–2, from Chifeng, Jehol Consul Kiyono Kyōtarō to special plenipotentiary to Manchukuo Minami Jirō, 16 April 1935.

35. Maku-uchi, Unofficial History, 99, 102–3.

36. Ibid., 141, 147, 174–81.

37. 吉田裕 (Yoshida Yutaka), "Military Rule (1) during the Manchurian Incident" in Kobayashi and Asada, Manchuria under Japanese Imperialism, 106; 吉田裕 (Yoshida Yutaka) and 纐纈厚 (Kōketsu Atsushi), "Military Operations, Combat, and the Supply of the Japanese Military" in 十五年戦争史 (History of the Fifteen Year War), vol. 3, ed. 藤原彰 (Fujiwara Akira) et al. (Tokyo: 青木書店 1989), 106.

38. Tsukase, Manchukuo, 31.

39. Furuya, "Creation of 'Manchukuo,'" 60, 62.

40. Ibid., 32–33.

41. 副島昭一(Soejima Shōichi), "Abolition of Privileges concerning Political Control and Extraterritoriality in 'Manchukuo'" in Yamamoto, Research on "Manchukuo," 135, 148.

42. China, Central Archives (中央档案馆), comp., 伪满洲国的统治与内幕 (Inside Story and Rulers of the Puppet State of Manchukuo) (Beijing: 中华书局, 2000), 793–810.

43. Tsukase, Manchukuo, 28–30.

44. Furuya, "Creation of 'Manchukuo,'" 70; 山室信 (Yamamuro Shinichi), "Discussion of the Evolution of Rule in 'Manchukuo'" in ibid., 113–16.

45. JFM, K.4.1.0–1–4, vol. 1, 満州国日系官吏及職員調査 (Survey of Japanese Government Officials and Staff in Manchukuo), 7 June 1934; JFM, A.6.2.0–2–13, 満州国政況関係雑纂：日系官吏名簿 (Miscellaneous Papers on the Manchukuo Political Situation: Register of Japanese Civil Servants) 1 April 1938; Tsukase, Manchukuo, 37.

46. Tsukase, Manchukuo, 41–42, 45.

47. Ibid., 43.

48. 張芳杰 (Zhang Fangjie), ed. 遠東漢英大辭典 (Far East Chinese-English Dictionary) (Taipei: 遠東圖書公司印行, 1996), 271.

49. Yamamuro, Discussion of the Evolution of Rule in "Manchukuo," in Furuya, Creation of "Manchukuo," 94, 111.

50. Tsukase, Manchukuo, 31.

51. Furuya, Creation of "Manchukuo," 60, 62; Kobayashi, "Creation and Collapse of 'Manchukuo,'" 33.

52. JFM, E.1.3.1–5–2, 合機密第178号, 9 March 1937.

53. 臼井勝美 (Usui Katsumi), 日中外交史研究 (Research on Sino-Japanese Diplomatic History) (Tokyo: 吉川弘文館, 1998), 63.

54. 西村成雄 (Nishimura Shigeo), "Japanese Government's Recognition of the Republic of China and Zhang Xueliang's Sovereignty" in Yamamoto, Research on "Manchukuo," 21; 安富歩 (Yasutomi Ayumu), "Economic Development of 'Manchukuo' and Domestic Capital Flows" in ibid., 239, 246–47; Japan, Defense Research Institute, 059/M/6384, 満洲年鑑 (Manchuria Yearbook) (Dalian: 満州文化協会, 1933), 152–57; 満史会 (Manchurian History Committee), ed. 満州開発四十年史 (Forty-Year History of Manchurian Development), vol. 2 (Tokyo: 小泉印刷株式会社, 1964), 853; 小林英夫 (Kobayashi Hideo), "Course of the

Reforms of the Manchurian Financial System" in Manchurian History Research Committee, Manchuria under Japanese Imperialism, 169.

55. JFM, E.2.3.2–12–1, vol. 2, "Central Bank of Manchou and Appendix of Laws Pertaining Thereto," Hsinking, the Central Bank of Manchou, 1934, 1–4, 10–11.

56. Manchurian Central Bank, History of the Manchurian Central Bank, 48, 118–20.

57. 西沢泰彦 (Nishizawa Yasuhiko), "'Manchukuo's' Construction Industry" in Yamamoto, Research on "Manchukuo," 407–9; Manchurian History Committee, Forty-Year History of Manchuria Development, vol. 2, 351.

58. Ibid., 437.

59. Nishimura, Japanese Government's Recognition, 23.

60. 佐藤和夫 (Satō Kazuo), "Microeconomics and Macroeconomics of Interwar Japan" in 戦間期の日本経済分析 (An Analysis of the Interwar Japanese Economy), 中村隆英 (Nakamura Takafusa), ed. (Tokyo: 山田出版社, 1981), 9; Tuvia Blumenthal, "Interwar Japanese Economy" in ibid., 43–45.

61. 原朗 (Hara Akira), "Manchurian Economic Controls Policy in the 1930s" in Manchurian History Research Committee, Manchuria under Japanese Imperialism, 55.

62. 山本有造 (Yamamoto Yūzō), "Development of Foreign Economic Relations Surrounding 'Manchukuo'" in Yamamoto, Research on "Manchukuo," 195–96, 198, 215–16.

63. Ibid., 219; Nishizawa, "'Manchukuo's' Construction Industry," 388–90, 392, 405, 407: Manchurian History Committee, Forty-Year History of Manchuria Development, vol. 1, 357.

64. Nishizawa, "'Manchukuo's' Construction Industry," 395–96.

65. Yamamoto, "Development of Foreign Economic Relations," 217.

66. Manchurian History Committee, Forty-Year History of Manchuria Development, vol. 1, 537–39, 646, 722, 876.

67. Kobayashi, "Creation and Collapse of 'Manchukuo,'" 82, 87.

68. 東北財経委員会調査統計處 (Northeast Financial Committee, Statistical Survey Department), ed., 旧満州経済統計資料 (Northeast Financial Data for the Puppet Manchukuo Period) (1949; reprint, Tokyo: 柏書株式会社, 1991), 164.

69. Manchurian Central Bank, History of the Manchurian Central Bank, 111.

70. Yamamuro, "Discussion of the Evolution of Rule," 114–19.

71. Japan, Defense Research Institute, 059/M/205, 満州鉱工年鑑 (Manchurian Mining and Manufacturing Yearbook), 1944, 107–67.

72. Northeast Financial Committee, Manchuria Financial Data, 5, 36.

73. Hara, Manchurian Economic Controls Policy, 73.

74. 君島和彦 (Kimishima Kazuhiko), "Development of the Management of Mining and Manufacturing" in Kobayashi and Asada, Manchuria under Japanese Imperialism, 600.

75. Northeast Financial Committee, Northeast Financial Data, 6, 36, 299.

76. Tsukase, Modern Economic History, 36.

77. アジヤ経済研究所 (Asia Economic Research Bureau), 中国東北地方経済に関する調査研究報告書 (Research Report on the Survey concerning the Economy of Manchuria, China) (Tokyo: 産業研究所, 1986), 26, 35–36, 53.

Part II

The Anticolonial Reaction:
The Rejuvenation of Old Polities

5

State and Nation Building in the Soviet Union Under Vladimir Lenin and Joseph Stalin

MARTIN MCCAULEY

Abstract: *This case study shows how national integration was hindered by the Soviet decision to make nations and nationalities the basis for the many republics forming the Union of Soviet Socialist Republics (USSR) or Soviet Union. When the strong center disappeared in 1991, the Soviet empire fractured along these national lines. This study describes the political and economic model developed by Lenin and Stalin that so influenced economic and political development throughout the world. Lenin created the original one-party state in which a vanguard political party oversaw a social revolution. He fostered worker management of enterprises and assumed a confluence of state, worker, and nationality interests that would mean that both nationalities and the state would ultimately wither away. Stalin greatly centralized power through the collectivization of agriculture, the nationalization of industry and commerce, the development of five-year economic plans, and the introduction of forced-draft industrialization that transferred agricultural resources to industry. This had the unintended consequence of creating a state based on patronage, which in turn fed corruption and constrained economic development. Stalin's reliance on terror to impose his will contributed to these problems.*

Russia has never been a nation-state but has always been an empire. In the Soviet period, the Communists relied on ideology, Great Russian primacy, and military force to create a Communist state and economy out of the scattered pieces of Imperial Russia. Lenin provided the theoretical foundations for the state and the Communist Party. Stalin then created a unitary state out of a welter of nations and nationalities. Through a process of trial and error Lenin began to develop an economic model, which Stalin then made comprehensive through irreversible nationalization and collectivization in combination with forced-draft industrialization.

Vladimir Lenin and the Theoretical Foundations for State Building

According to Karl Marx and Friedrich Engels in *The Manifesto of the Communist Party* (1848), the dictatorship of the proletariat would follow the overthrow of the

86

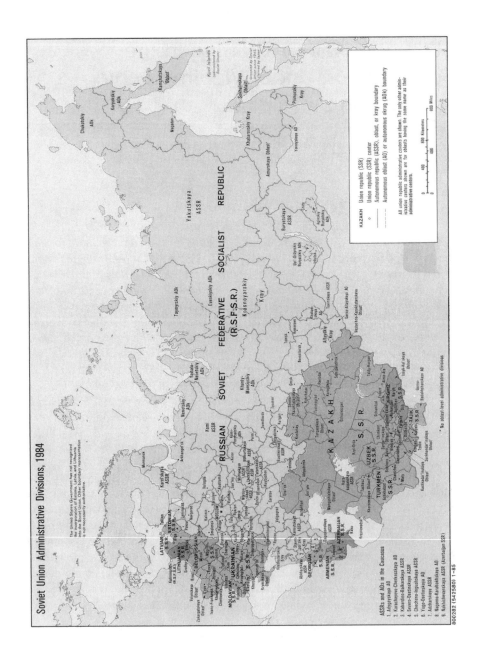

Soviet Union Administrative Divisions, 1984

The United States Government has not recognized the incorporation of Estonia, Latvia, and Lithuania into the Soviet Union. Other boundary representation is not necessarily authoritative.

KAZAKH   Union republic (SSR)
   ○   Union republic (SSR) center
────   Autonomous republic (ASSR), oblast, or kray boundary
─ ─ ─ ─   Autonomous oblast (AO) or autonomous okrug (AOk) boundary

All union republic administrative centers are shown. The only other administrative centers shown are for oblasts having the same name as their administrative centers.

0   200   400   600 Miles
0   200 400 600 800 Kilometers

* No oblast-level administrative divisions

ASSRs and AOs in the Caucasus
1. Adygeyskaya AO
2. Karachayevo-Cherkesskaya AO
3. Kabardino-Balkarskaya ASSR
4. Severo-Osetinskaya ASSR
5. Checheno-Ingushskaya ASSR
6. Yugo-Osetinskaya AO
7. Abkhazskaya ASSR
8. Nagorno-Karabakhskaya AO
9. Nakhichevanskaya ASSR (Azerbaijan SSR)

800282 (545580) 1-85

bourgeoisie by the working class. The instrument for the implementation of this dictatorship would be the state. This stage would last until the new Communist society had come into existence. Until then the state would not be "free," that is to say, totally subordinate to society. Marx savagely attacked those socialists whose goal was a "free" state. From his perspective, the state had eventually to be swept away. Why did the proletariat need the state after the revolution?

Engels, in *Anti-Dühring* (1875), argued that its sole raison d'être was to "suppress violently opponents"[1] of the new order. The proletarian state would only be a transitory phenomenon. Engels wrote of the *"absterben"* of the state. *Absterben* can be translated as either "withering way" or "dying out." The former envisages a gradual process, whereas the latter suggests a more rapid demise. Lenin always understood *absterben* to mean "withering away."

In the *Critique of the Gotha Programme* (1875), Marx stated that Communist society would be attained in two stages: the lower (socialism) and the higher (communism). During the lower stage, immediately after the proletarian revolution, private ownership of the means of production, distribution, and exchange would be abolished. However, there would still be inequality. A person's rewards would be commensurate with his or her input into society. There would be a contradiction between mental and physical labor. Contradictions and inequalities would only disappear during the higher phase of communism, when objective needs of all would be met.[2] Significantly, Engels regarded as mistaken the views of the French Blanquists, who envisaged the establishment of workers' rule by a highly disciplined vanguard. Hence Marx and Engels were aware of the danger of an emerging ruling elite, which could claim, in theory, the right to exercise power in the name of the proletariat.

Lenin's major contribution to the development of Marxism was the concept of the revolutionary party, sketched out in *What Is to Be Done?* (1902). The miniscule size of the Russian working class, its low cultural level, and its fragmented nature doomed it to languish in the quagmire of "trade union consciousness."[3] It was, therefore, unaware of the revolutionary role it could play. This role could be revealed to it only by a (self-appointed) elite from outside the working class. A disciplined party of professional, full-time revolutionaries was needed to guide and mold the minds and actions of workers to fulfill their grand mission, predetermined by history, to take power from the bourgeoisie. This vanguard was to keep its distance from the working class so as not to be "contaminated" by infiltrators or non-Marxist ideologies. In other words, it was to lead the working class, not be led by it.

In *The State and Revolution* (1917), Lenin turned his attention to the type of state that would emerge after the revolution. The bourgeois state had to be totally destroyed so a different form of state would take its place. For the first time in history, a majority would oppress a minority. The guided democracy in the workers' state would be enjoyed only by workers, while the "exploiting classes" would be politically excluded during the phase of the dictatorship of the proletariat. This transition period would last only as long as it took to overcome the former "oppressors." Lenin thought that during this period democracy would reach a level never before attained in human history. During this phase "armed workers" would resist and defeat the violent reaction of the "exploiters" fighting to defend their property. Lenin conceived of the national economy as a postal system. Orders would be transmitted from one worker to another, with management unnecessary as workers possessed almost all the skills to run enterprises and the economy. (Here Lenin revealed his failure to grasp the role of management. He never bothered to study how a modern industrial enterprise functioned.)

The new state bureaucracy would consist mainly of workers, who would be elected directly by the population. As officials would not enjoy any privileges or better salaries than other workers, they would not develop into an interest group with their own agenda. Communes would run local affairs. Ordinary people would be capable of solving any emerging problems. Lenin conceived of the communes uniting and agreeing to "voluntary centralism." A highly disciplined Communist Party would manage the state in pursuit of common interests and tasks. Lenin did not conceive of a conflict of interests emerging between the vanguard and the base; therefore, coercion would be unnecessary.

According to Lenin, the lower stage, socialism, would last as long as the dicta-torship of the proletariat. The higher stage would see the end of the dictatorship, and the state would wither away. Under socialism there would be inequality as everyone would be compensated according to their contribution to the building of the new order. Under communism there would be no dictatorship (as capitalists and exploiters had been eliminated), no classes, and no state. The differences between mental and physical labor would also vanish. Communism would be born only when a new type of person—selfless, highly disciplined, and moral—emerged. Lenin did not touch upon the role of the Communist Party during the lower stage, socialism, and the higher stage, communism.

In January 1918, three months after taking power, Lenin began to revise his ideas. He dropped all discussion of communism and concentrated exclusively on socialism. He began writing about the transition phase from capitalism to social-ism and ridiculed those who believed that society could leap from capitalism into socialism. Soviet Russia was only at the beginning of this "difficult" and long process, whose success required the support of the world proletariat.[4]

With the economy in chaos in May and June of 1918, the clearly demonstrated weakness of the workers' state forced another rethink. Lenin tried to enlist "bour-geois specialists" with the expertise to run industry and the surplus-producing peas-ants in his struggle to build a new Russia. The antagonism between the bourgeoisie and the working class was downplayed. Now the main enemy of the revolution was not the bourgeoisie but the "petty bourgeoisie" and its "anarchic" tendencies. Lenin directed his ire against traders operating within a market framework. The "educated" bourgeoisie should be recruited as allies and those who refused to co-operate repressed.[5] The construction of socialism, in Lenin's eyes, depended on the formation of large-scale industrial production units. Since workers did not possess the technical, organizational, or managerial skills necessary to promote this process, he expected the "educated" bourgeoisie to perform this role. He was proposing that former capitalists, under Communist Party supervision, build socialism. He then divided the working class into two groups: those who were "conscious," meaning those who were willing to learn from capitalists, and those who were not. Workers' control gave way to workers' discipline. Lenin was now proposing state capitalism, a goal that the onset of the Civil War in June 1918 undermined.[6]

The Creation of a State out of Nations and Nationalities

The Bolsheviks, the founders of the Communist Party of the Soviet Union, thought that all peoples progressed from clans and tribes to ethnic groups, then to nationalities, or nations, and finally to socialism. When this final stage was reached, national distinctions would fade away and be replaced by a socialist consciousness. Just as the state would disappear when communism arrived, so would nations (peoples with a defined territory) and nationalities (peoples without a defined territory). Hence the Bolsheviks needed a short-term solution to the nationality problem. Resentment at Russian imperial rule, thought Lenin, could be turned to the advantage of the Bolsheviks. Only about 60 percent of the Russian Empire's population in 1914 was comprised of ethnic Russians. Many parts of the empire had once been sovereign states. There was also a religious dimension. Whereas ethnic Russians were generally members of the Russian Orthodox Church, Ukrainians had their own Orthodox Church as had the Georgians and the Armenians. In Azerbaijan and Central Asia as well as present-day Tatarstan and Bashkortostan, the predominant religion was Islam.[7]

The nationalities question was handed to a rising star in the Bolshevik camp, Joseph Stalin, who was a Georgian. In *Marxism and the National Question* (1913), Stalin, coached by Lenin, sought to offer the prospect of autonomy or even secession to nations within the Russian Empire. A nation was defined as a "historically formed, stable community of people, united by community of language, territory, economic life and psychological make-up."[8]

Before the Communists consolidated their control over Russia, the non-Russian areas of the former Russian Empire pressed for self-government. Finland, Estonia, Ukraine, and the former Polish territories, all under German occupation until 1918, as well as Georgia, Armenia, Azerbaijan, and Turkestan, aspired to self-rule. They envisaged their future within a vast multinational federation or, perhaps, confederation. It was unwise to claim independence, as they were militarily weak and feared invasion by a power such as Germany, hence Lenin's policy of national self-determination appealed to many.[9] The locals wanted control over the land, industry, and natural resources of their territory. There was clearly a tension between the concept of national autonomy and the centralized Bolshevik Party, which claimed a monopoly on political power in the new Soviet state.

In the Decree on Peace, adopted on the morrow of the 1917 Bolshevik Revolution and signaling Russia's withdrawal from World War I, Lenin promised a "just, democratic peace." There would be no "annexations," defined as the "incorporation of a small or weak nation into a large or powerful state without the precisely, clearly and voluntarily expressed consent and wish of that nation."[10] Then he offered Finland and German-occupied Poland independence. He expected a rapid establishment of revolutionary republics, which would immediately join Soviet Russia. Thereafter Lenin expected the whole of Europe to follow suit to create a pan-European socialist state, whose capital would be Berlin.

Joseph Stalin, now People's Commissar for Nationalities, under Lenin's guidance, published the *Declaration of the Rights of the Peoples of Russia* (1917). It abolished all ethnic and national privileges and called for the proclamation of a voluntary union. Although it granted the right of secession to all non-Russian nations, membership in the new Soviet state was expected to be so attractive that the non-Russians would not wish to secede. Only bourgeois nationalists could possibly want to secede, in order to reestablish bourgeois rule, and of course this would not be allowed.

To the consternation of Lenin and Stalin, this declaration had practically no impact.[11] In the Russian borderlands, Russian rule, whether Tsarist or Soviet, was regarded as illegitimate. In 1918 Lenin proclaimed the formation of the Russian Socialist Federal Soviet Republic (RSFSR). The Russian in the title did not signify "ethnic Russians" (*russkaia*) but used the geographical term, *rossiiskaia*, embracing everyone in the RSFSR. Lenin was trying to get across the message that everyone on the territory of the former Russian Empire was welcome to become a citizen of the new RSFSR. Ethnic Russians, though the largest nation, were not to be afforded any privileges.

The 1918 Treaty of Brest-Litovsk ended the war against Germany and Austro-Hungary for Soviet Russia. Lenin was willing to concede almost anything to protect Soviet power. The Bolsheviks were obliged to recognize the independence of Georgia, Finland, and Ukraine but they remained within the German zone of influence. Poland, Latvia, Lithuania, and Estonia fell under more direct German influence. Almost 40 percent of the population of the former Russian Empire, about one-third of the arable land, one-quarter of the railway network, and three-quarters of the iron and coal mines were signed away. Lenin, ever the optimist, regarded this debacle as a temporary setback. Come the socialist revolution in Berlin, this shameful peace treaty would be consigned to the rubbish bin of history.

The treaty prevented the attractiveness of the novel concept of the RSFSR from being put to the test. In the lands occupied by or under the influence of Berlin, local elites were promoted and ties with Moscow broken. The new Ukrainian regime under a German nominee chased out the Bolsheviks. Even worse, by May 1918 three independent states, Georgia, Armenia, and Azerbaijan, had emerged in the Transcaucasian region. The Bolsheviks were even hounded out of Baku, the Azeri capital.[12]

Tsarist Russia's Muslim population had welcomed the fall of the dynasty.

Muslims in Central Asia, although a patchwork of nationalities—Uzbeks, Kyrgyz, Tajiks, and Kazakhs—did not regard themselves as belonging to different nations. They all (except the Tajiks) spoke dialects of Turkish and owed their loyalty to clan and religious leaders. There were no fixed territorial boundaries. In Kazakhstan, Lenin had to fashion a policy that appealed to two disparate groups: the Russian colonists, who regarded themselves as the masters, and the natives. The Kazakhs demanded the return of their ancestral lands. A Kazakh Revolutionary Committee was set up in June 1919 and was parachuted in to establish Soviet power. Violent conflict erupted. During the Kazakh war for independence between 1916 and 1922 about a million perished and another 400,000 fled to China, Mongolia, Afghanistan, Turkey, and Iran.[13]

Moscow came up with an original solution in the rest of Turkestan. There were two irreconcilable revolutions: a proletarian revolution among Russian workers and soldiers, and a nationalist Muslim revolution, led by the educated bourgeoisie, who established an autonomous power base in Kokand. The Turkmen formed a government in the Transcaspian region. The Bolsheviks had little success in promoting revolution outside Tashkent. The Bolshevik Party of Turkestan, composed of Russians, found it impossible to promote national self-determination. It would have swept the Communists off the political map.

In May 1920, Muslims proposed to Lenin that an Autonomous Republic of Turkestan be set up and form part of the RSFSR. He watered down their demands ,but eventually they gained more autonomy than expected. The main reason for this was the distance between Moscow and Tashkent. There was also the fact that the Russian Civil War was ongoing. However, this was only a tactical move by Lenin as he was waiting for the apposite moment to separate and divide the peoples of Turkestan. He did so through the People's Commissariat of Nationalities (*Narkomnats*). It had sections for each nationality and all local demands had to be channeled through it. In 1921 representatives of the Republic of Turkestan were appointed and were to advise Moscow of local problems. They were also to relay Moscow's preferences to the locals. Then federal committees for each policy area were set up. The locals resented Moscow's interference, but the fact that it occurred through Narkomnats, which claimed to represent national interests, sugared the pill. The Bolsheviks turned out to be sophisticated imperialists. In the Transcaucasus, they relied on the Red Army, which retook Azerbaijan in April 1920, Armenia in December 1920, and Georgia in February–March 1921.

The Unitary State and the Soviet Nation

Lenin and Stalin disagreed strongly about the nature of the new state. Stalin favored a unitary state with only one republic, the RSFSR, with all other ethnic regions, such as Ukraine, Belarus, and Central Asia, becoming autonomous republics within the RSFSR. Azerbaijan, Armenia, and Georgia would be grouped together as a Transcaucasian autonomous republic in order to suppress nationalism in each.

Stalin believed that local elites would form, if permitted, their own republics, and make it difficult for Moscow to rule.

Lenin, on the other hand, insisted on a federal state of constitutionally equal republics. This meant that the non-Russian republics, such as Ukraine, Belarus, Uzbekistan, and Turkmenistan, would have the same legal status as the RSFSR within the new Soviet Union. However he agreed with Stalin that Azerbaijan, Armenia, and Georgia should be grouped together in a Transcaucasian Federal Republic, which together would have the legal status of a full republic. The problem of nationalities, such as the Tatars and Bashkirs, within the territory of the RSFSR was solved by making them autonomous republics. They were now clearly subordinate to Moscow, which not only was the capital of the RSFSR but became the capital of the Soviet Union. The conflict between Lenin and Stalin had momentous consequences for nationalities in the new Soviet state. Had Stalin had his way, there would have been no need to establish the USSR, as everyone would have been a citizen of the RSFSR.

Lenin insisted on the formation of the Soviet Union (the only country in the world without a territory in its title) as the only way to overcome the distrust engendered by centuries of Tsarist Russian rule. The republics would run their own economies with Moscow's claiming only the prerogatives of defense and foreign affairs. Lenin thought that local comrades could run their republics better than Russian bureaucrats in Moscow. A policy of promoting local elites was introduced in order to overcome the woeful lack of native cadres, especially in Central Asia. Hence Lenin favored a genuinely federal state. Stalin, in contrast, wanted power concentrated in Moscow, replicating the traditional Great Russian model that Lenin called Great Russian chauvinism. The row came to a head over Georgia. The Georgians strongly objected to joining the Soviet Union as part of the Transcaucasian Federal Republic. They wanted their own republic on a par with the RSFSR.

At this critical point when the Soviet Union was coming into existence, Lenin fell ill. On 9 March 1923, he suffered a massive stroke that ended his political career. He entrusted the defense of a genuinely federal state to Leon Trotsky. However, Trotsky, in turn, fell ill. Hence, at a critical juncture, the country was deprived of the two main actors who would have defended a federal state. The first Soviet constitution, establishing the Union of Soviet Socialist Republics, came into force in January 1924. Had Lenin lived—he died on 21 January 1924—the Soviet Union would have evolved quite differently. Instead, Stalin concentrated power in Moscow and turned the nominally federal state into a unitary state.[14]

In the Soviet Constitution of 1936, drafted under Stalin, replacing the 1924 Constitution, drafted under Lenin, the Soviet Union consisted of eleven republics: the RSFSR, Belarus, Ukraine, Azerbaijan, Armenia, Georgia, Kazakhstan, Kyrgyzstan, Uzbekistan, Tajikistan, and Turkmenistan. Hence the Transcaucasian Federal Republic was dissolved. A cynic remarked that the new federal constitution was primarily for foreign consumption. At a time when German national socialism was on the rise, the Soviet Union paraded in its most democratic clothes. Appearance and reality diverged dramatically. Although the new Soviet Constitution of 1936 cemented Lenin's vision of the new federal Soviet state, the Soviet Union was, de facto, a unitary state. Interestingly enough, the Communist Party made an appearance, near the end of the constitution, and was described as the power in the land. The class electoral system was abolished, and everyone now had the right to vote. The republics were granted the right to secede from the Union, but any attempt to implement this clause would have been classified as "bourgeois nationalism" and punished severely. The Soviet Union was declared a socialist state—the most democratic state in the world.

The federal state required people to identify themselves by nationality. Each republic had its emblems, flags, government, national language (but Russian was recognized as the lingua franca), and even a Communist Party (except the RSFSR). This, of course, promoted local nationalism, but that was not regarded as a threat to Soviet rule. Only bourgeois nationalism and the nationalism of diaspora nationalities (those nationalities that also had a motherland outside the Soviet Union) were perceived as a threat to the integrity of the Soviet state. The Soviet Union was seen as a country of over one hundred nationalities, which were united and harmonious, and progressing toward socialism.[15]

Two years previously, at the Seventeenth Party Congress in 1934, Stalin had proclaimed the victory of socialism. One might have expected nationality to become less significant in official thinking as the country consolidated socialism and moved forward toward communism. However as class was deemphasized, nationality was accorded greater significance in the search for internal enemies of the new order. With socialism victorious, internal opposition could not be based on class—the rich peasants (kulaks) and old bourgeoisie had been vanquished.

At the congress, Stalin warned that the remnants of capitalism were "much more tenacious in the sphere of the national question . . . because they were able to disguise themselves in national costume."[16] Party leaders increasingly identified disloyal groups within the population in national terms. Those who had a motherland outside the Soviet Union, particularly Poles, Germans, and Greeks, became suspect because their national and cultural consciousness was held to be non-Soviet. If forced to choose, their loyalty would rest with a foreign state. A rebellion against collectivization on the Polish-Ukrainian borderlands resulted in many Polish families seeking refuge in Poland. The Politburo response was to order the deportation of thousands of kulak families, first and foremost ethnic Poles. The latter were referred to as counterrevolutionaries and spies. Another group to come under suspicion were ethnic Germans. About half of ethnic Poles and Germans inhabiting the Ukrainian border areas were deported from 1935 to 1936.

During the 1930s, the Soviet authorities reduced the number of ethnically based territorial units by consolidating them into nations. For example, the various Kazakh ethnic groups now formed a nation, it was claimed. This underlined the belief that ethnic groups were coalescing into nations. They would then move on to acquire a socialist consciousness that would gradually obliterate their national identity.

The more perceptive locals realized that Moscow's goal was to elevate Russians to a position of first among equals. The Russian language became more important, as the various nationalities could communicate only in Russian. A reappraisal of Russian history and culture—which resulted in a return to Russian national values—got under way in the mid-1930s. There was a new interest in national identity in the republics. Each nationality was expected to write accounts of its past highlighting friendship and cooperation with the Russian people. Those who had worked closely with the Russians were treated as heroes. The Soviet Union became a fraternal union. The Russians were called the "elder brother" and everyone else the "little brother." The eleven republics were referred to as "sisters." In such a male-dominated country as the Soviet Union, this imagery could not go unnoticed. National self-determination was becoming Russian national self-determination and assimilation.

The constant official harping on ethnic identity and nationality, epitomized by the flags, internal passports recording nationality, quotas for recruitment, and native language instruction, gradually led Soviet citizens to think in these categories. In other words, official policy was producing the opposite of the desired goal. There was little sign that a new, distinctly Soviet nation was coming into being. Nor could it be claimed that socialist consciousness was replacing ethnic and national identity as the country moved toward the socialism enshrined in the new Soviet Constitution of 1936. Inadvertently, the Bolsheviks were reinforcing local nationalism with these mistaken policies.

When Japan invaded China in 1937, Stalin deported all ethnic Koreans from the Soviet Far Eastern border regions to Central Asia. Ethnic Chinese soon followed. The partial deportations of Poles, Latvians, Germans, Estonians, Romanians, Finns, Greeks, and Iranians from border regions came next. During World War II, beginning in 1944 whole nationalities, such as the Chechens, Ingushi, Kabardins, Balkars, and Crimean Tatars were deported. Over the following two years more than fifty nationalities, in whole or in part, were dispatched to the east. The ostensible reason for this policy was the need to eliminate "espionage and sabotage groups" within these nationalities.[17] During the Great Terror of 1936–38, in the hunt for spies and saboteurs, ethnic minorities had accounted for one-fifth of all arrests and one-third of all executions.[18]

Stalin concluded, based on the experience of World War II, that the most loyal citizens of the Soviet Union were ethnic Russians. The onset of the Cold War in 1947 increased concerns about ethnic identity and the loyalty of diaspora nationalities. With the founding of the state of Israel in 1948, Stalin was dismayed to discover that Soviet Jews identified with the new state. Thereafter he singled out Jews as "rootless cosmopolitans" to be dismissed from their posts, arrested, imprisoned, and executed.[19]

The rise of Great Russian nationalism was accompanied by claims that Russians had invented everything worth inventing. In the postwar period ethnic Russians came to dominate more and more top posts in Moscow. All higher education in science and technology was conducted in Russian. The obverse of the promotion of Great Russian nationalism was the resentment felt by other nationalities. They saw themselves as second-class citizens. There was also the simmering distrust of the deported nationalities.

The Economic Foundations for State Building

In October 1917, Lenin would have preferred an economy akin to the present Chinese model. That is, the party managing a capitalist economy with the commanding heights (utilities, defense industries, and the like) in public hands. This model of state capitalism failed because few entrepreneurs were willing to trust the Bolsheviks, and industrial labor aggressively took over industry and services. Lenin then dreamed of jumping over capitalism, which was only just developing in Russia, to communism. This implied the elimination of money and value, among other things. Amazingly, this experiment was attempted amidst a civil war, when Lenin and the Bolsheviks engaged in an astonishing volte-face from state capitalism to its opposite pole: war or military communism.[20]

The first constitution of the RSFSR, promulgated in July 1918 by Lenin, defined the state as a "dictatorship of the urban and rural proletariat and the poorest."[21] All those who employed labor for profit, who were involved in family businesses, or who derived income from investments were deprived of the vote. Members of the Romanov dynasty, former members of the Tsarist secret service, and the clergy were also disfranchised. The RSFSR was a republic of soviets that was to effect the "transition" to socialism. It was unequivocally a class dictatorship. The Communist Party was not mentioned in the document. Clearly Lenin wished to mask the reality of party power.

War communism obliged Lenin to revise his views on the dictatorship of the proletariat and the state. In *The Proletarian Revolution and the Renegade Kautsky* (1918), he robustly defended the Bolsheviks against the barbs of the German social democrat Karl Kautsky, who vehemently criticized the violence of the Bolshevik regime, arguing that Russia lacked the industrial and democratic prerequisites for socialism. In late 1918, Lenin added an addendum to *The State and Revolution.* He now argued that the Russian Civil War was a new, higher phase of the class struggle. During this period the petty bourgeois allies of the working class would gradually dilute their support of the proletariat. The nationalization of land, in February 1918, was presented as bringing to an end the bourgeois revolution in Russia, but it was not possible for the outnumbered working class to defeat the bourgeoisie. The "exploiting classes" possessed certain innate advantages: greater human and material capital, and foreign support. This had even led a part of the proletariat to support them.

The tasks of the dictatorship of the proletariat became destructive: smash the resistance of the bourgeoisie; instill fear among "reactionary" forces; and develop the potential of the secret police and Red Army so as to crush opponents with extreme violence. Those Marxists who denied the utility of violence were "renegades." Those who supported it were "true" Marxists. Law and morality were trampled on in a coercive state bent on protecting the revolution. During the years of war communism (1918–21) the Bolsheviks eliminated all private enterprise, monopolized foreign trade, and forcibly requisitioned food from the countryside. As a result, production imploded.

Ever the realist, Lenin again changed course. In *Left-wing Communism: An Infantile Disorder* (1920), he warned against attempting rapid social change and hinted at political compromise. He recommended emulating West European socialists who worked within trade unions and parliaments to promote Marxism. The Bolsheviks should revert to educational and organizational work—and reject oppression—in promoting the new society.[22] This second astonishing volte-face was possible because the civil war had almost been won. It reveals that war communism, with its unbridled violence, had proved an unmitigated disaster. Hunger stalked the land. The industrial labor force in Petrograd, the bedrock of Bolshevik support, dwindled to one-third of its 1917 numbers. The population of Moscow had halved by 1921. The state rationed bread and essentials but most of these goods were traded on the black market. Leon Trotsky proposed, in late 1919, conscripting workers into labor armies to improve discipline. Extreme violence and tremendous willpower saved the Bolsheviks. One of the keys of success was morale. Trotsky skillfully developed a system of political commissars in the military in order to boost morale and ensure party loyalty. This civil-military model was to be adopted in all Communist states but most successfully in China.

The need to win the civil war led to the centralization of power as scarce resources had to be deployed for optimal effect. In 1921 the weakness of the economy led to the reemergence of the market economy and guidance, rather than management, from the center.

This was the great retreat revealed in the proclamation of the New Economic Policy that ushered in a mixed economy. Capitalism was again acceptable in trade and small-scale industry. Guided capitalism was no longer perceived to be a threat to the Soviet state. However, the Bolsheviks clung to the concept of a political monopoly since a multiparty system might have removed them from power. Stalin's succession set the stage for a second attempt to move to communism. The model adopted by the Bolsheviks was the planned economy. This envisaged the elimination of the market economy.

Under Stalin, private enterprise, permitted during the New Economic Policy, was eliminated, with all enterprises falling under state administration. Likewise, agriculture was collectivized and investment capital was extracted from the rural sector to help fund Stalin's forced-draft industrialization projects focusing on the production of armaments. Depressed living standards in both rural and urban areas were necessary to fund Stalin's many industrialization projects. He administered Soviet economic development through a succession of Five-Year Plans, beginning in 1928, which rapidly developed heavy industry at a time when the capitalistic world foundered during the Great Depression. The standard of living in key metropolitan areas, particularly Moscow, was far higher than in provincial cities, let alone the countryside, where collectivization caused famine (1932–33) and a decline in agricultural output.[23] Total state management of the economy proved unattainable, and elements of the market were again legalized, including collective farm markets where peasants could sell the surplus from their private plots. The shadow economy (outside the plan) developed for industrial goods.

The launch of forced collectivization and rapid industrialization presaged greater centralization of power in Moscow. Mass mobilization was needed to achieve objectives to which the working class and peasantry would never have voluntarily agreed.

Stalin was the patron and his top aides were his clients. They, in turn, became patrons as they recruited subagents to achieve the ever-increasing economic demands of the master. The Soviet Union became a state based on patronage.[24] It was vertically integrated while horizontal integration was blocked. The latter, if it had been allowed to flourish, would have restricted the power of the center. Of course, horizontal links were established, but because they were unofficial, they functioned only in the shadow economy. Widespread corruption was the natural concomitant of this process. Party officials became mired in corruption as they negotiated deals to overcome supply and sales bottlenecks in the imperfectly functioning planned economy.

The party apparatus was weak during the 1930s and even weaker during World War II. However, Stalin found it useful to revive it after 1945. It was shorn of its economic duties in 1946, but quickly regained these functions. At the Nineteenth Party Congress in 1952, economic departments were reinvigorated. Clearly, Stalin wanted to play off government and party functionaries against one another— a standard tactic by the master.[25]

Under Stalin, the Soviet state acquired more and more aspects of the previous imperial Tsarist state. Continuities included the centralization of decision making; the adage that Moscow rules; the power of the bureaucrat and the need to obtain official permission for every initiative; the increasing dominance of ethnic Russians and the Russian language; the rise of nationalism in non-Russian republics; the ruling ideology and the caste of philosophers who articulated and guarded this orthodoxy (akin to the Russian Orthodox Church and its priests); the emergence of a ruling bureaucracy; the development of an elite, which served to protect the power of the leader and his cohorts; the utter lack of accountability of this elite to the people; and the cult of the leader—the tsar in imperial times and the red tsar, Lenin and then Stalin, after the revolution.

Originally, Lenin had seen the party as providing ideological guidance with the Council of People's Commissars (*Sovnarkom*) running the economy. He had no official party position, although he was recognized as primus inter pares in the Politburo, and chose to be chair of Sovnarkom. Stalin built up an alternative power base in the party apparatus and used this effectively to secure the leadership of the country by 1929. During industrialization, all members of the Politburo played key economic roles. The party apparatus was expected to supervise the implementation of government and party directives but, to a large extent, this task was beyond it. It became involved in corruption and colluded with economic managers to claim fulfillment of the planned targets. The result was that many cadres became disillusioned and left the party. They were to pay a heavy price for this during the Great Terror of 1936–38 when they were regarded as disloyal to the regime.

The Great Terror can be viewed as an attempt by Stalin to eliminate clientism and localism. In other words, he was trying to erase the patron-client networks and the tendency of regions to act in their own interests and ignore national needs. He wanted to put principal-agent relationships in their place. This was a vertical division of power with the principal (Stalin) issuing orders to his agents (members of his team), who in turn gave orders to their subagents. It was like a properly functioning military. This was critically important, since the command economy required a flow of instructions from the center to replace market signals. All those who stood in the way of this new model were to be ruthlessly eliminated. The threat of war (against Japan and then Germany) made it urgent to develop the defense industries as fast as possible. The forced development of industry and harsh collectivization secured the Soviet victory over Hitler's Germany. One can argue that without these harsh policies the Soviet Union would have lost the war. This is the measure of Stalin's economic achievement. The stupendous achievement of reuniting the Russian Empire shattered by World War I and then beating Germany in World War II legitimized the Soviet state model, transformed Stalin into a national hero, and made the Soviet economic and political model attractive to emerging nations in the postwar wave of decolonization.

The Influence and Demise of the Soviet Union

The Soviet state evolved into a party-state. This was an original contribution to the Russian government. Lenin and Stalin's model for reconstituting an old state, fallen on hard times in the industrial era, proved extraordinarily influential first in China, where Communists, many trained in the Soviet Union or influenced by Soviet advisers, unified China after forty years of civil war and foreign invasion. After World War II, many Western colonies fighting for independence also followed the Soviet economic and political model because of its great efficacy in wartime. The model explained how to form a party to take political power, how to use the party to create an army to take control over a war-ravaged country, and how to assert control over the economy to marshal the resources to fund both the party and the military. The Leninist-Stalinist model fell short not in wartime, but in peacetime.

Lenin and Stalin failed to create a long-lived empire for several reasons. First, the constitutional equality granted to the many republics of the Soviet Union falsely assumed a disappearance of nations. Lenin perceived clans and groups merging to form nations and then all nations coalescing as socialist consciousness developed.

This would eventually lead to the disappearance of nations. Part of Lenin's problem was that he was a Great Russian nationalist without realizing it. He took it for granted that the Russian language would be the lingua franca of the new Soviet state. He never doubted that he knew what was best for the working class of all nations. By establishing republics that were constitutionally equal he was sowing the seeds of nationalism and separatism.

Second, a new Soviet nation never came into being. Instead, the Great Russian nation took precedence, which it retained until the collapse of communism in 1991. The vertical integration of the political and economic structures, with Moscow presiding at the summit of the hierarchy, precluded the horizontal homogenization among the republics that might have facilitated the creation of a Soviet nation. Instead the Soviet empire became increasingly brittle over time, with deepening fault lines between the republics. Not surprisingly, Russia became the successor state to the Soviet Union in 1992, while the other republics sought independence.

Third, although Stalin's mode of economic development rapidly restored the economy, devastated by World War I and the ensuing Russian Civil War, and produced the vast war materiel vital for defeating Nazi Germany in World War II, the Soviet economic model proved incapable of delivering a high standard of living even for its Great Russian citizens. It turned out that light industry, consumer products, and the civilian economy were critical both for sustained economic development and for military-related industries. These problems did not become clear until long after Stalin's death in 1953, really not until the late Brezhnev era (1964–82). Over time the growing disparity in living standards between the Soviet Union and the West and within the Soviet Union among the republics proved highly destabilizing. It cast doubt on the viability of the model.[26]

Notes

1. Karl Marx and Friedrich Engels, *Werke* (East Berlin: Dietz Verlag, 1962), 7.

2. Jukka Renkama, *Ideology and Challenges of Political Liberalisation in the USSR, 1957–1961* (Helsinki: Suomalaisen Kirjallisuuden Sura, 2006), 58.

3. Vladimir Lenin, *Polnoe sobranie sochinenii,* vol. 33 (Moscow: Izdatel'stvo politicheskoi literatury, 1969), 83.

4. Renkama, *Ideology,* 73.

5. Vladimir Lenin, *Polnoe sobranie sochinenii,* vol. 36 (Moscow: Izdatel'stvo politicheskoi literatury, 1969), 309.

6. Martin McCauley, *The Rise and Fall of the Soviet Union* (Harlow, UK: Longman, 2008); power in the new Soviet state is presented in figure 3.1, 12; the concepts of power, authority, and legitimacy are defined in figure 12.4, 207.

7. Ronald Grigor Suny, *The Revenge of the Past: Nationalism, Revolution and the Collapse of the Soviet Union* (Stanford, CA: Stanford University Press, 1993), 19.

8. Ibid., 31.

9. Richard Pipes, *The Formation of the Soviet Union: Communism and Nationalism, 1917–1923,* 2nd ed. (Cambridge, MA: Harvard University Press, 1964), passim.

10. Martin McCauley, ed. *The Russian Revolution and the Soviet State 1917–1921, Documents* (London: Macmillan, 1975), 142–43.

11. Robert Service, *A History of Modern Russia from Nicholas II to Putin* (London: Penguin Books, 2003), 83.

12. Martin McCauley, *Afghanistan and Central Asia: A Modern History* (Harlow, UK: Longman, 2002), passim.

13. Martha Brill Olcott, *The Kazakhs* (Stanford, CA: Stanford University Press, 1995), passim.

14. Moshe Lewin, *Lenin's Last Struggle* (London: Macmillan, 1975), 87.

15. David L. Hoffmann, *Stalinist Values: The Cultural Norms of Soviet Modernity, 1917–1941* (Ithaca, NY, and London: Cornell University Press, 2003), 172.

16. Ibid., 173.

17. Ibid., 174.

18. Ibid., 175.

19. Jonathan Brent and Vladimir P. Naumov, *Stalin's Last Crime: The Plot against the Jewish Doctors, 1948–1953* (New York: HarperCollins, 2003), passim.

20. Alec Nove, *An Economic History of the USSR* (London: Penguin, 1969), 28; see also Alec Nove, *The Soviet Economic System* (London: Macmillan, 1977), passim.

21. Vladimir Lenin, *Polnoe sobranie sochinenii,* vol. 37 (Moscow: Izdatel'stvo politicheskoi literatury, 1969), 296.

22. Renkama, *Ideology,* 78.

23. Gregory L. Freeze, ed., *Russia: A History* (Oxford: Oxford University Press, 2002), 303.

24. McCauley, *Rise and Fall of the Soviet Union,* figure 11.4, 191.

25. Ibid., 277–95.

26. Yegor Gaidar, *Collapse of an Empire: Lessons for Modern Russia* (Washington, DC: Brookings Institution Press, 2007), 162–200.

6

Mustafa Kemal Atatürk and the Creation of the Turkish Republic

ALEXANDER LYON MACFIE

Abstract: *Alexander Lyon Macfie emphasizes an unexpectedly favorable international and domestic environment (not much recognized at the time), in combination with extraordinary leadership, to explain the success of Atatürk in creating the modern Turkish state. Internationally, the loss of the Christian and Arab parts of the Ottoman Empire during the Balkan and First World Wars left a cohesive Turkish "national" core in Anatolia, while revolution and civil war in Russia put Turkey's principal enemy out of action during the early stages of the struggle. Domestically, the survival of Turkish units of the Ottoman army left an institution capable of imposing order, while the survival of elements of the Committee of Union and Progress, the party that ruled over the Ottoman Empire both before and during World War I, left an organization capable of providing an institutional framework for the development of civil institutions. In addition, mainly Turkish Ottoman scholars had written extensively on the possibility of using Turkish national identity as the basis for a future state. Mustafa Kemal (Atatürk) then astutely used the power afforded by his position as a military officer in Anatolia to unite rival political movements in a Turkish national movement capable of laying the foundations of a new secular (nation) state.*

The achievements of Mustafa Kemal Atatürk (c. 1880–1938), the so-called founder of modern Turkey, must be considered by any standards remarkable. In a few short years, from his dispatch as inspector of the Third Army to Anatolia in May 1919, to his election as president of the first Turkish republic in October 1923, he succeeded, with the help of a small, select band of like-minded colleagues, in forging a Turkish national movement of exceptional strength and unity, capable of challenging the authority of the Sultan and his government in Constantinople (Istanbul), imposing its authority throughout the greater part of Anatolia, confronting the occupation forces of the western Entente powers (Great Britain, France, and Italy), expelling a Greek expeditionary force dispatched by those powers to Izmir in May 1919, and finally concluding at Lausanne in 1923 a treaty of peace with the western Entente powers and their allies, securing the independence and integrity of a newly created Turkish state, the last of the successor states of the Ottoman Empire. Moreover, in

102

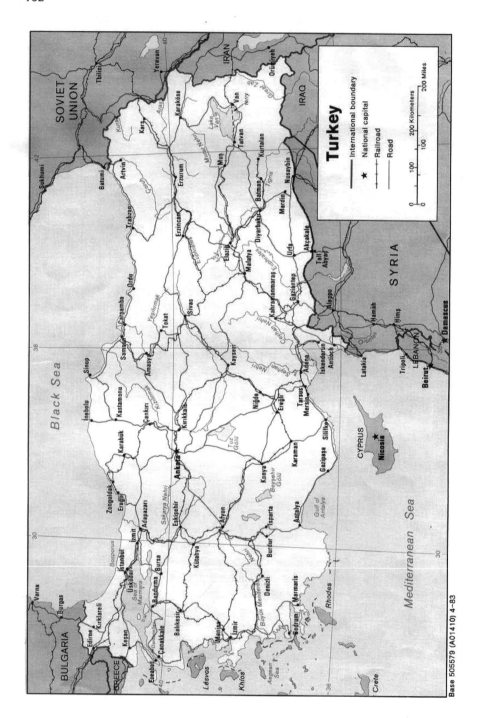

Base 505579 (A01410) 4-83

the remaining years of his life he succeeded in carrying through a series of major reforms, radically transforming the traditional, Islamic structure of Ottoman society and laying the foundations of a modern, westernized, secular nation-state.[1]

When the conditions prevailing in what remained of the Ottoman Empire in the period immediately following the end of the First World War (1914–18) are taken into account, Atatürk's achievements and those of the national movement with which he was associated appear even more impressive. In Constantinople, where a supine government timorously awaited the arrival of the Entente occupation forces, the structure of government, both central and local, had all but broken down, while in Anatolia and eastern Thrace near-anarchy prevailed as more than a quarter of a million deserters, seeking refuge in the hills, raided towns and villages in search of food and the other necessities of life. As a result, among the Turkish-speaking Muslim inhabitants of those areas (some twelve million or so in number, for the most part small peasant farmers, ninety percent illiterate) support for the Ottoman government (widely considered incompetent and corrupt) had all but disappeared, as had the will to further resistance. Indeed, according to one British observer writing at the time, so great was the prevailing despair that had the Allies but acted with dispatch, they might well have imposed virtually unopposed whatever peace terms they wished.[2]

Nor would Atatürk's achievements, and those of the national movement with which he was associated, appear in any way diminished were a comparison to be made with those of other leaders and movements appearing in Europe at the time. Where else among the defeated imperial powers did a movement emerge capable of challenging the armed might of the enemy and obliging him to conclude a satisfactory peace settlement securing the independence and integrity of the nation, and where else did a leader emerge capable of forging such a movement?

In Germany, cowed and humiliated by defeat, the leaders of the recently established Weimar Republic were obliged to accept the harsh terms of the Treaty of Versailles (1919), a fertile source of future conflict. In Russia the recently installed Bolshevik government, desperate for peace, was obliged by the Central Powers, Germany and Austria-Hungary, to accept the terms of the Treaty of Brest-Litovsk (1918), sacrificing extensive territories in western Russia, the Baltic, and the Ukraine, while in Austria-Hungary a settlement loosely based on the principle of nationality was simply imposed, willy-nilly, with little or no consideration for the interests of the former imperial powers.

Only in the Ottoman Empire, it would seem, did a movement arise capable of building a new, stable order on the foundations of the old, and only in the Ottoman Empire did a leader emerge capable of forging such a movement. Small wonder that Lloyd George, the British leader, whose career Atatürk effectively ruined, was wont to refer to Atatürk as the man of the century, and that others have compared him, in the range and quality of his achievements, with such historical figures as Genghis Khan, Tamerlane, and Napoleon, not to mention Alexander the Great, Aristotle, and Lenin.[3]

An Unexpectedly Favorable International and Domestic Environment

It is obvious then that Mustafa Kemal, known from 1934 as Atatürk (meaning father of the Turks), was a remarkable man, and that his achievement in securing, against all the odds, the creation in Anatolia of an independent Turkish Republic, based on the national principle, was impressive. What is less obvious is the extent to which, in the period immediately following the end of the First World War, he benefited from a peculiar concatenation of circumstances favorable to his enterprise.

Yet it is doubtful that Mustafa Kemal and his colleagues would have recognized the circumstances as favorable. These circumstances include:

(1) The defeat of the Ottoman Empire in the Balkan Wars (1912–13), a defeat that led to the expulsion of the Ottomans from the greater part of their remaining territories in Europe (Macedonia, Albania, southern Bulgaria, and western Thrace), territories inhabited mainly by Christians.

(2) The defeat of the Ottoman Empire in the First World War, a defeat that led to the expulsion of the Ottomans from the Arab provinces (today Syria, Lebanon, Iraq, Jordan, Palestine, and Arabia).

(3) The defeat and collapse into revolution and civil war, in the closing months of the First World War, of Russia, a state that in other circumstances might well have hindered, if not actually prevented, a Turkish recovery in Anatolia.

(4) The survival in Anatolia, at the end of the First World War, of substantial Ottoman (Turkish) military forces, for the most part well disciplined and equipped, and capable—despite prolonged Entente (British, French, and Italian) attempts to disarm them—of securing nationalist control of the interior and resisting Greek and Entente attempts to impose their will there.

(5) The parallel survival, in both Anatolia and Istanbul, of branches of the Committee of Union and Progress (CUP), the secret society that organized the Young Turk revolution of 1908 and later, as a political party, ruled over the Ottoman Empire in the period of the Balkan and First World Wars.

(6) The existence in the Ottoman Empire in the previous half century or so of a number of Ottoman/Turkish scholars and intellectuals, many of whom vigorously promoted the idea that the Turkish-speaking peoples of the Ottoman Empire might solve their political problems by adopting a Turkish national identity, an idea that Mustafa Kemal and his colleagues, in the changed circumstances created by the defeat and fragmentation of the Ottoman Empire in the First World War, had no difficulty in adopting.

The defeats inflicted on the Ottoman Empire in the Balkan and First World Wars, which deprived the empire of almost all of its remaining territories in Europe and the Arab provinces, proved immensely damaging. Nevertheless, as a number of commentators pointed out at the time, the loss of the Balkan (mainly Christian) and Arab provinces opened the way to the creation of a mainly Turkish/Muslim nation-state in Constantinople, eastern Thrace, and Anatolia (where the majority of the Turkish-speaking Muslim population of the Ottoman Empire lived). As Mustafa Kemal himself later remarked, the dismembering of the Ottoman Empire, which had occurred during the Balkan and First World Wars, combined with the more or less complete alienation of the Greek and Armenian communities, had made irrelevant the concept of a multinational empire and the associated ideology of Ottomanism, while the expectation that pan-Islamism and pan-Turkism might fill the breach had been largely discredited by the failed policies of the Ottoman leadership during the First World War. Apart from a further fragmentation, therefore, the only possibility remaining was the creation of some kind of nation-state, based on the Turkish-speaking Muslim peoples of Anatolia and eastern Thrace.

The collapse of Russia in the period of the Bolshevik Revolution and its aftermath can be looked on as a decisive factor in the shaping of events in Constantinople and Anatolia in the period of the Turkish war of independence. Had Russia emerged victorious from the First World War, there is little doubt that she would have continued her policy of seeking the opening of the Turkish Straits to Russian warships and their closure to the warships of the Western, non–Black Sea powers. This might have involved a Russian occupation of Constantinople and the Straits—a long-standing Russian objective—promised to the Russians in the so-called Constantinople Agreement of March 1915 and allowed for in the Sykes-Picot Agreement. It might also have involved a Russian occupation of some or all of the eastern provinces of Anatolia (particularly those of Van, Bitlis, Trabzon, and Erzerum), also allowed for in the Sykes-Picot Agreement—acquisitions that would have greatly strengthened Russia's position and influence in the area. At the same time a Russian occupation of some or all of the eastern provinces might well have obliged the Western Entente powers to implement their plans for a partition of the rest of Anatolia, as agreed at Sèvres in August 1920.[4]

The survival of a substantial part of the Ottoman army in Anatolia in the period following the signature of the Armistice of Mudros of 30 October 1918—the armistice that ended Ottoman participation in the First World War—was clearly central to the creation of an independent Turkish state in Anatolia by Mustafa Kemal and his colleagues (in particular Ali Fuat, commander of the Twentieth Army Corps, based in Ankara; Kiazim Karabekir, commander of the Fifteenth Army Corps, based in Erzerum; Hüzeyin Rauf, a naval commander famous for his exploits in the Balkan Wars; and Refet [Bele], commander of the Third Army Corps, based in Sivas). These forces initially numbered some 110,000 men or so, and later, following a period of demobilization and disarmament—never fully enforced by the Entente—perhaps about half of that number. The survival in Anatolia of an Ottoman army, in places well equipped and supplied, and supported by various government agencies (such as *Teşkilati Mahsusa* [Special Organization] and *Karakol* [Guard] and a series of Defense of Rights associations), enabled Mustafa Kemal, appointed in May 1919 inspector of the Ninth Army, later designated the Third Army, and his colleagues to impose their control rapidly on most of the interior in the early stages of the nationalist struggle. Later, expanded and reorganized, it enabled them to defeat the so-called Army of the Caliphate, sent against them by the Sultan in Constantinople, to confront the Entente forces stationed in the area of the Straits and southern Anatolia, and eventually to drive the Greek expeditionary force, based in Izmir, out of western Anatolia.[5]

Teşkilati Mahsusa was a special organization, set up by the CUP sometime before the outbreak of the First World War to strengthen the authority of the government and promote the causes of pan-Islamism and pan-Turkism in the east. *Karakol* was a secret organization, set up by the CUP in 1918 to prepare for resistance following the defeat of the Ottoman Empire in the First World War and to protect CUP officials wanted by the Entente for war crimes, particularly the Armenian massacres committed in the course of the war. Many of the Defense of Rights associations were established, at the instigation of the CUP government in Constantinople, to take advantage of U.S. President Woodrow Wilson's famous Fourteen Points, the peace proposal put forward in January 1918, one clause of which promised the peoples of the Ottoman Empire a peace settlement based on the principle of nationality.[6]

In the fifty years or so preceding the loss of the remaining Balkan and Arab provinces in the Near and Middle East, the Ottoman elite had made the foundation of their multinational empire the twin concepts of Ottomanism—an ideology based on the expectation that the subjects of the Ottoman Sultan would henceforth identify with a new entity known as the Ottoman nation—and pan-Islamism—an ideology based on the idea that Muslims from all parts of the world enjoyed a common identity. Ottoman sultans found pan-Islamism particularly useful as an instrument of foreign policy. Meanwhile, Ottoman scholars and intellectuals (Mustafa Celâleddin Pasha, a Polish exile, who had converted to Islam; Ahmed Vefik Pasha, the grandson of a Greek convert to Islam; Ahmed Midhat Pasha, a leading Ottoman intellectual; Yusuf Akçura, a Tatar educated in Istanbul and Paris; Mehmed Emin, an Ottoman poet; Ziya Gökalp, a half-Kurdish poet and scholar; and many others), much inspired by the work of various European historians and orientalists, had begun increasingly to emphasize the Turkish identity of the Turkish-speaking peoples of the Ottoman Empire. Previously the Turks had looked on themselves simply as Muslims: the word *Turk* was, more often than not, used to denote a backward Anatolian peasant or yokel.

As a result of these and other ideological developments, in the early years of the twentieth century the idea that the Turkish-speaking peoples of the Ottoman Empire might rediscover their lost racial and national identity, and incidentally save the Ottoman Empire from ruin, was widely propagated, in particular in a series of clubs and journals set up in the capital and elsewhere in the period immediately preceding the First World War. These included *Türk Derneği* (Turkish Association) (1908), *Genç Kalemlar* (Young Pens) (1910), *Türk Yurdu* (Turkish Homeland) (1911), and *Türk Ocağı* (Turkish Hearth) (1912).[7]

Competing Intellectual Movements

Ziya Gökalp (1876–1924) was almost certainly the most influential Ottoman intellectual grappling with the problems of religious, cultural, and national identity in the period preceding the Balkan and First World Wars—though in some respects Yusuf Akçura might be considered the most interesting. As Gökalp saw it, the Turkish nation would come into existence as a result of the breakdown of the Islamic *ümmet* (community of Islam), a breakdown caused by the impact of modern (technological) Western civilization. The so-called Westerners, much impressed by recent developments in Europe, wished to adopt all things Western unconditionally; the Islamists wished to revive traditional Islam; and the pan-Turkists wished to revive the ethnic customs of the pre-Islamic Turks. But a nation was neither a collection of individuals united by the common ties of a modern economy, nor a religious community, united by faith. Nor, for that matter, was it a racial or ethnic group united by archaic tribal customs. It was a community united by a common set of national ideals. Western technology could be adopted unreservedly, but the cultural elements of the West should be appropriated only insofar as they promoted a modern national culture. The first aim of any movement concerned with reform should be the promotion of a national culture based neither on the Şeriat (religious law), nor on the pre-Islamic ethnic culture of the Turks, nor on the culture of the Western nations, but on a set of ideals integral to the new Turkish nation.[8]

Yusuf Akçura (1876–c.1935), in an article entitled "Three Policies," published in a small journal, *Türk,* in Cairo in 1904, similarly doubted whether the ideologies of Ottomanism and Islamism, adopted by the Ottoman government, and the policies of pan-Ottomanism and pan-Islamism identified with them, would work. This was because the interests of the three major elements in the Ottoman Empire—the Turks, the non-Turkish Muslims, and the non-Muslims—were simply incompatible. In due course the Ottoman government would have to recognize the national aspirations of the non-Turks and non-Muslims. Hence there was only one thing left for the Turks: recognition of their own national aspirations. They should forget about being Ottomans and be content with being Turks. A Turkish national policy based on the Turkish race would rally the loyalties of the dominant Turkish race within the Ottoman Empire and reinforce it with the support of many millions of Turks in Russia and elsewhere.[9]

As far back as 1822, one Akif Efendi, an Ottoman government official, had written a memorandum laying out the three choices for the Muslim (Turkish) peoples of the Ottoman Empire, then threatened with destruction by Russia and the other European great powers: a defense of the empire, as champions of Islam, regardless of cost; a reduction to slavery, similar to that experienced by the Muslim inhabitants of the Crimea, India, and Kazan; and a withdrawal to Anatolia, from which the Turks had first crossed into Europe. During the century that followed, as one commentator later remarked, the Turks unsuccessfully attempted the first, successfully avoided the second, and finally, under the pressure of events more than of ideas, successfully adopted the third.[10]

It should not be supposed that opposition to the Turkish national movement, organized in Anatolia by Mustafa Kemal and his colleagues, was confined to elements loyal to the Sultan. In western Anatolia, irregular forces, opposed to the Greeks, such as those led by "Çerkes" Ethem, asserted their independence, resisting all attempts on the part of the Grand National Assembly to integrate them into the regular army. In eastern Anatolia, Kurdish tribes of uncertain disposition constantly threatened rebellion. At the 1919 Congress of Sivas, Mustafa Kemal and his colleagues were for a time threatened by Kurdish tribesmen intent on their destruction. In many areas, armed gangs, led by local brigands, taking advantage of the weakness of the new (and old) regime, seized control, raiding towns and villages.[11]

Meanwhile, throughout Anatolia, Islamic societies, left-wing intellectuals, and other groups loyal to what was known at the time as the "Eastern Ideal" were busy promoting ideas of class war and revolution. As a result, in the period of near civil war that followed the dispatch by the sultan of the so-called Army of the Caliphate to Anatolia, socialist ideas spread rapidly. A number of parties and organizations, adopting a left-wing or populist stance, were established, including in the national assembly a People's Group of deputies committed to the propagation of socialist ideas or at least the supposedly socialist precepts of Islam; the so-called Green Army, a secret society established by the People's Group and their supporters to propagate socialist ideas and fight the forces of reaction; and a People's Communist Party of Turkey. Many members of the People's Group of deputies and the Green Army, it was said at the time, remained loyal to Enver Pasha, the exiled CUP leader and Ottoman minister of war during the First World War who, following his flight to the Crimea in October 1918, had made contact with the Soviets and supposedly adopted the socialist cause.[12]

The Leadership of Mustafa Kemal

Mustafa Kemal's response to the threat posed to his position by the People's Group of deputies and their supporters was both devious and cunning. Convinced of the urgent need to secure Soviet support for the national movement's struggle with the imperial powers, and determined to secure the backing of the People's Group and its supporters in the ongoing war against the antinationalist forces, he first reacted sympathetically to requests from a number of leading Communists that they be permitted to organize in Anatolia and he encouraged the formation of the Green Army. But when the Green Army proved more effective than he had expected, infiltrating the irregular forces (in particular those of "Çerkes" Ethem), he quickly changed tack.

First he requested the voluntary dissolution of the Green Army, and then, in a move designed to secure political control of the situation without sacrificing Soviet aid and support, he persuaded a number of the more moderate members of the People's Group, together with some of his own closest supporters (including Ali Fuat, Refet [Bele], and Ismet), to found a new, official Communist Party of Turkey. This party was ostensibly committed to the principles of international socialism, but was really opposed to them, as secret instructions dispatched to the military commanders, ordering them to prevent the spread of such "illegitimate" ideas, made clear.

Having thus effectively isolated the genuine revolutionaries, in particular those with international connections, Mustafa Kemal then moved quickly to suppress them, launching a campaign in the nationalist press accusing them of acting without the consent of the "official" party, arresting and expelling their leaders, and closing down their parties and organizations, including the People's Communist Party of Turkey, founded by leading Communists, following the establishment of the "official" party. Meanwhile vigorous steps were taken to prevent Enver Pasha's return to Anatolia and orders issued for his arrest should he succeed in doing so.[13]

As for the irregular forces and the armed bands, they were variously suppressed by units of the nationalist forces loyal to the movement, compelled to integrate with the regular forces, or otherwise dealt with. Great care was taken throughout not to alienate the Kurdish tribes, who as Muslims were invited by Mustafa Kemal to unite with the Turks in their struggle for independence. So successful, indeed, was Mustafa Kemal in suppressing all forms of opposition to both the national movement and himself that, in the period following the foundation of the republic, he was able effectively to set up something approaching a dictatorship, in which, as president of the republic, commander in chief of the armed forces, and president of the People's Party, he controlled all the important instruments of power.

Mustafa Kemal's many contributions to the success of the national movement include: the defining of its aims at the congresses of Erzurum and Sivas; the sustaining of these throughout the long years of struggle; the uniting of the various resistance movements, irregular forces, and Defense of Rights associations; the convening of a Grand National Assembly in Ankara in April 1920 (following the closure of the Chamber of Deputies in Constantinople); the defeat of the Greek expeditionary force at Sakarya; the later expulsion of that force from Anatolia; the successful negotiation of the Treaty of Lausanne; the abolition of the Sultanate and the Caliphate; and the proclamation of the first Turkish Republic in October 1923.[14] But his greatest contribution was probably the keen understanding he displayed of the realities of the situation prevailing in the Near and Middle East in the period immediately following the end of the First World War—an understanding that contributed significantly to the ultimate success of the national movement. In particular he displayed a keen understanding of what was possible in the circumstances and what was not.

What was possible, as events proved, was the construction in Anatolia of a strong Turkish national movement, capable of asserting its authority in the area. What was almost certainly not possible was a reestablishment of Ottoman control in the Balkan and Arab provinces lost to the Ottoman Empire in the Balkan and First

World Wars, a conquest or reconquest of the various territories in Transcaucasia lost by the Ottomans in the nineteenth century and earlier, and an assertion of absolute Turkish sovereignty over the Turkish Straits (a new Straits regime, accepted by the Turks, was negotiated by the great powers at Lausanne).

The Antecedents to Mustafa Kemal's Reforms

In Europe and America, Mustafa Kemal is perhaps as much known for his implementation in Turkey of a program of secular reform as he is for the extraordinary contribution he made to the creation of a Turkish republic. This is probably because in Europe and America people are impressed by his apparent success in laying the foundations in the republic of a modern, westernized secular state, radically different from the traditional (Islamic, theocratic, eastward-looking) structure of its predecessor.

In fact Mustafa Kemal's reforms were by no means as radical as they have sometimes been made to appear, for it is evident that the roots of the reforms he implemented in Turkey lay deeply embedded in the political, constitutional, intellectual, and cultural history of the Ottoman Empire. Already in the nineteenth century, in the period of the *Tanzimat* (Reform or Reorganization, 1839–76) and the First Constitution (1876), Ottoman statesmen had laid the foundations of a secular system of government and law, including the promulgation of a constitution, the opening of a parliament, and a substantial reform of the legal system, based on the principle of the absolute equality of Ottoman subjects before the law, irrespective of religion. In addition, they had created a state-controlled system of education, later expanded by the governments of the Young Turk period. Writers and intellectuals, including many members of the newly formed Ottoman Scientific Society and Academy of Learning, had experimented with language reform and new versions of the Ottoman script, some involving the use of a Latin alphabet. Later, in the reign of Abdul Hamid II, others had proposed even more radical changes, including the closure of the dervish orders (popular Muslim brotherhoods); the banning of the fez (the traditional Ottoman flat-topped, brimless, red felt hat), and the introduction of equal rights for women. Mustafa Kemal's reform program should, therefore, be seen not as a radical innovation but as the culmination of almost a century of change, remarkable for its thoroughness and consistency. In reality the reform program was, as one commentator puts it, the "child of the Second Constitutional Period (1908–1918), the step-child of the era of Abdul Hamid II (1876–1908) and the grandchild of the era of reform (1826–1878)."[15]

Kemalism

In the early 1930s the followers of Mustafa Kemal, determined to create an ideology comparable to the ideologies of fascism and communism, then popular in Europe, assembled the six basic principles underlying his policies, identified as republicanism, nationalism, populism, statism, secularism, and reformism, in an all-embracing master doctrine known as Kemalism. In 1931 these principles were incorporated into the Turkish constitution—though Mustafa Kemal frequently stressed that they should not be applied in a doctrinaire way, for the essence of his approach was pragmatic, based not on faith but on reason. That the individual principles underlying the ideology of Kemalism were important in shaping events in the period of the war of independence and its aftermath is not in doubt, but it is evident that it cannot, as an ideology, be compared with the dynamic and formative ideologies of Marxism-Leninism and fascism, which in the period of the First World War and its aftermath proved so influential in shaping the course of events. Unlike Marxism-Leninism and fascism, Kemalism was an ideology created after the event. Only in 1929 or thereabouts was the word Kemalism first coined and only in the 1930s did it find an adequate adumbration.

Nevertheless, the influence of Kemalism should not be underestimated, for in the following decades it was to prove a potent force, helping to shape the history of the republic. In the 1940s, 1950s, and 1960s, the Republican People's Party—as the People's Party soon became known—continued to base its policies on the six principles, and, even in the 1970s, when it increasingly adopted class-based policies in line with its new stance as a social democratic party, it continued to assert its allegiance. Likewise, the Democratic Party and its successors (in the 1950s a multiparty system was introduced) were wont to refer to themselves as Kemalist parties, though their tolerance of religious reaction and their promotion of private enterprise frequently made such claims suspect. In the 1970s, however, as Turkish society became increasingly polarized between a fragmented, Marxist left and a reactionary right, and as violence escalated, the influence of Kemalism suffered a sharp decline, becoming only one of many competing political forces in Turkish society—though the army remained throughout loyal to the cause, invariably evoking the spirit of Atatürk in justification of its numerous interventions in the politics of the republic.[15]

How far, it might be reasonably asked, can the creation of the Turkish republic be seen as a model to be followed by those engaged in the business of nation building? Not in my opinion very far, for as I think I have shown, the creation of the republic was the product of a complex set of historical circumstances, peculiar to their time. Nevertheless, it is possible, I think, to identify a number of conditions likely to promote the success of such an enterprise. These might include:

1. The existence, in a clearly defined geographical area, of a more or less homogenous population, united by race, religion, language, culture, and identity—in Turkey this was achieved in part by historical accident (the defeat of the Ottoman Empire in the First World War and the expulsion of the Ottoman Turks from the Balkan and Arab provinces) and in part by the massacre and expulsion of the minority Greek and Armenian populations (the survival in southeastern Anatolia of a substantial Kurdish population has since been the cause of unending difficulty).

2. The existence of a well-educated and well-informed elite, capable of uniting the population and providing leadership—in Turkey the Ottoman military and bureaucratic elite, to which Mustafa Kemal belonged, was accustomed to govern and to lead: they had never been subjected to foreign control.

3. The availability of a well-worked-out ideology, already adopted by significant elements within the elite—in Turkey's case the ideology of Turkish nationalism was already well established in the period preceding the First World War.

4. The absence of any significant opposition—in the Ottoman Empire, in the period of the Balkan and First World Wars, the ideologies of pan-Islamism, pan-Ottomanism, and pan-Turkism, which an opposition movement might have promoted, had been proved largely ineffective.

5. The absence of any significant great power interest in the area, at least to the point that one or more of the great powers might feel compelled to intervene directly to defend its interests—in Turkey great power interest was largely confined to the area of the Straits.

6. A recognition on the part of any leadership of a "national movement" of the limitations of the power they exercise—in Turkey, Mustafa Kemal was at pains in the period of the national struggle and even later not to provoke a direct confrontation with the great powers: with regard to the questions of the Turkish Straits and Mosul (an area now part of Iraq but then claimed by the Turkish nationalists in the National Pact of 28 January 1920), he was prepared to compromise.

Would the existence of these conditions in Anatolia in the period of national struggle that followed the end of the First World War have guaranteed the creation of an independent Turkish (nation) state in Constantinople, eastern Thrace, and Anatolia, without the exceptional leadership of Mustafa Kemal? Many people in Turkey today believe that it would not.

Notes

1. A.L. Macfie, *Atatürk* (London: Longman, 1994), 1–3. This article is based on the contents of four books, all written by the author: *The Eastern Question* (London: Longman, 1989), revised edition, 1996; *The Straits Question, 1909–1936* (Thessaloniki: Institute for Balkan Studies, 1993); and *The End of the Ottoman Empire* (London: Longman, 1998).

2. B. N. Şimşir, *British Documents on Atatürk,* vol. 1 (Ankara: Turk Tarih Kurumu, 1973) no. 22, enclosure.

3. Macfie, *Atatürk,* 3.

4. Macfie, *The Straits Question.*

5. Macfie, *Atatürk,* chapter 3.

6. Erik Jan Zürcher, *The Unionist Factor* (Leiden: E. J. Brill, 1984), chapter 3.

7. Niyazi Berkes, *The Development of Secularism in Turkey* (Montreal: McGill University Press, 1964), chapter 11.

8. Ibid., 345–46.

9. Ibid., 321–22.

10. Bernard Lewis, *The Emergence of Modern Turkey* (Oxford: Oxford University Press, 1961), 319–20.

11. Mahmut Gologlu, *Sivas Kongresi* (Ankara: Başnur Matbaasi, 1969), chapter 3.

12. Macfie, *Atatürk,* chapter 6.

13. G.S. Harris, *The Origins of Communism in Turkey* (Stanford, CA: Stanford University Press, 1967), chapters 1–4.

14. Mustafa Kemal Atatürk, *Nutuk* (Speech) (Ankara: Turk Tarih Kurumu, 1981).

15. R.H. Davison, *Essays on Ottoman and Turkish History* (London: Saqi Books, 1990), 259.

16. Macfie, *Atatürk,* 151–52.

7

Mao Zedong: Utopian Visions and Practical Realities

WARREN SUN

Abstract: *Warren Sun describes Mao Zedong's creation of a New China. Mao jet-tisoned China's ancient Confucian and imperial institutions to follow the Soviet model. This entailed collectivizing agriculture, nationalizing industry, governing through five-year economic plans, and channeling resources from the rural to the urban economy. Mao's risky decision to intervene in the Korean War forced a stalemate against a great-power coalition, winning himself both domestic prestige and international standing, but at the price of total diplomatic isolation from the West. Mao, however, stressed national independence from both the East and the West. The Great Leap Forward reflected his determination to improve on the Soviet model, to Sinify Marxism-Leninism, and to restore China's historical position as a great power, all to be accomplished at breakneck speed. The introduction of the commune system in combination with unrealistic urban and rural production tar-gets disrupted production, caused a lethal nationwide famine, and contributed to the break in relations with the Soviet Union. Nevertheless, Mao believed his basic approach to be correct and made a second attempt to Sinify Marxism-Leninism with the equally disruptive Cultural Revolution. Immediately upon his death his successors abandoned the Cultural Revolution. Nevertheless, they remained equally determined to restore China's international position.*

At the turn of the twentieth century, sixty years after the Opium War (the first of a series of imperialist encroachments), the reformist leader Liang Qichao implicitly described China as "an old country striving to be young."[1] Some fifty years later on the Tiananmen rostrum, Mao Zedong (1893–1976), the charismatic revolutionary leader of the Chinese Communist Party (CCP), proclaimed the birth of the People's Republic of China (PRC), declaring that "the Chinese people have stood up."[2] Against the backdrop of China's descent into domestic disintegration and repeated losses of the previous century to foreign powers, Mao's words encapsulated the enormous sense of liberation felt by the Chinese people as well as the basis for his and the CCP's legitimacy and mandate to rule.

With an unbroken civilization of more than 2,000 years' duration, China was by no means a newly emerged nation, even though PRC historians have regularly referred to Mao's regime as "New China." In fact, at the peak of her prosperity, with less than one-sixth of the world population, premodern China's gross domestic product accounted for more than one-third of the world GDP at the time of Emperor Qianlong's reign (1735–99), when Confucian China was an inspiration to the Enlightenment movement in Europe.[3] But the imperialist advance of Western capitalism and industrialization changed the equation. Imperial China not only was in decline, but soon fell victim to the success of Western civilization. In the face of the Western and later the Japanese challenge, survival and revival through modernization became the principal goal for China as a nation in deep crisis since the mid-nineteenth century. The early years of Mao's China were no exception. From the onset Mao set the goal of creating an industrialized economy and a socialist state. He saw catching up with the industrialized West as a prerequisite for China's survival. In the wake of China's plight in modern times, ideologically committed Chinese Communists embraced Marxism and socialism on both *logos* and *pathos* grounds—meaning both as a rational and a moral choice—as well as out of emotional resentment and rejection of Western capitalist wars, invasions, and exploitation.

The PRC could be considered to be a newborn country because the Communists rejected the Confucian norms and imperial institutions that had long prevailed, so that, in Mao's words, "China was poor and blank"[4] at the time of the Communist takeover. Under Mao, for the first time in the modern era, China became a unified and sovereign entity (minus Taiwan, Hong Kong, and Macao) under the most powerful central government in its entire history. More significantly, Mao embarked on unprecedented social engineering, which, successful or not, profoundly transformed Chinese society. The Chinese tale of national restoration is even more remarkable because China carried such a heavy historical burden when Mao attempted to "destroy the old world and create a new order."[5] Today Communist China still soldiers on, while the first socialist state, the Soviet Union, was created and collapsed within the twentieth century.

Collectivization and Nationalization

Unlike the many dynastic changes in China's long history, the daunting tasks of national restoration facing the Communist leadership entailed much more than restoring national unity, social order, and peace. This was a formidable task in and of itself, given that China had suffered endemic civil warfare from the fall of the Qing dynasty in 1911 until the Communist victory in 1949, a devastating Japanese invasion (1931–45), and inclusion in the world war (1941–45). The ideological commitment to Marxism and Leninism of the CCP went far beyond economic restoration to the intent to build a full-blooded socialist state. This set China on a completely new course.

The CCP was deeply influenced by the Soviet Union, which also came into

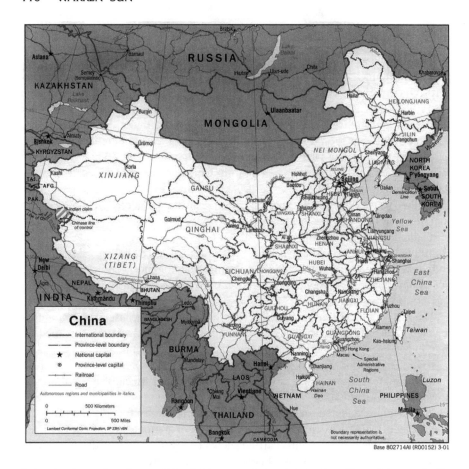

Base 802714AI (R00152) 3-01

being in the wake of a terrible civil war and despite the hostility of the capitalist world. The Soviet experience seemed to offer Chinese revolutionaries the most relevant model for organizing a political party capable of creating a military from scratch, seizing power in a hostile national and international environment, and mobilizing the economy to sustain economic development and political power. The Soviet Union was eager to help revolutionaries abroad in order to overcome its own diplomatic isolation and to vindicate its political and economic model at the expense of the reviled West.

The CCP not only adopted the Soviet system of government, but also emulated the Stalinist economic model of collectivization, centralized planning, high rates of reinvestment, the transfer of resources from agriculture to industry, capital-intensive infrastructural projects, large-scale modern plants, and prioritization of heavy industry over light industry and of military production over consumer goods. Mao also followed the general Soviet sequencing of land reform, nationalization, collectivization, and forced-draft industrialization. Although both Mao and Stalin began with the rural economy, their goals were primarily directed toward the urban economy and specifically industrialization.

In addition to overcoming the severe inflation and urban unemployment of the war-torn economy, one of the remarkable efforts in the early years of the People's Republic was land reform. At the time of the PRC's establishment in October 1949, in the so-called old liberated areas, 120 million rural residents out of a combined rural-urban population of 130 million had undergone land reform. The newly liberated and yet to be controlled areas, where peasants accounted for 280 million out of a total population of 340 million, had not undergone agrarian reform. Land reform had begun in the small Jiangxi Soviet (1929–35), but was later carried out in villages nationwide through a moderation of approaches and the codification of practices under the Land Reform Law of June 1950.[6]

In old China, landlords and rich peasants monopolized up to 80 percent of the cultivable land yet accounted for only 10 percent of the rural population that constituted nearly 90 percent of the entire Chinese population (450 million in 1949). This land ownership system had survived more than 2,000 years. It had entailed the "feudal" exploitation by the gentry and landlords, who served as the economic bedrock for all previous ruling regimes.

Before pushing for cooperativization in 1953, Mao's earlier approaches to this perennial problem ranged from land rent and loan interest reduction to the confiscation and redistribution to landless peasantry of landlord land, equipment, and cattle and to the execution of local bandits and village bullies. Village militia and poor peasant associations were set up to assure order and support. Land reform eliminated rural capitalism as well as the traditional power and influence of the landlords over the peasantry, and thoroughly restructured the social hierarchy at the grassroots level in the countryside. Through such a fundamental and profound transformation, Mao "had in fact rewritten China's socioeconomic history."[7] Never before had the state's political control penetrated so deep into rural society.

Mao was not content with the policy of "land to the tillers" advocated by Sun Yat-sen (1866–1925), the founder of the previous Nationalist regime and icon of modern China in both the PRC and Taiwan. Since China's small-scale, private-enterprise peasant economy was incompatible with socialized industrialization, Mao intended to "get the peasantry organized" and move toward collectivized agriculture.[8] He promoted mutual aid teams from 1949 to 1952 for pooling peasant labor and then established agricultural producers' cooperatives (APCs) in order to transfer land ownership rights to the collective and to pay individual peasants strictly according to their labor. In the meantime, he put in place a new state monopoly for purchasing and marketing grain and other rural products.

Mao assumed that full collectivization could proceed before the mechanization of agriculture. He displayed impatience with his colleagues' gradualist and conservative approach, ridiculing his minister for rural work as "tottering like a woman in bound feet."[9] Vigorous but hasty implementation of cooperativization began in summer 1955 when Mao took personal command over the movement and declared "the high tide of agrarian cooperativization is about to arrive."[10] By the end of 1956, with mass mobilization, 97 percent of Chinese peasant households joined the APCs.[11] Ideological motivations aside, Mao favored cooperatives in the belief that they would significantly increase agricultural production, which was crucial for the overall industrialization effort.

Though born to a peasant family, from as early as 1944, Mao believed China required "new style industry"[12] and industrialization in order to overcome its poverty and backwardness as well as to guarantee its national independence and sovereignty. On the eve of the Communist takeover, he made it the priority of the CCP to "transform China from an agrarian nation to an industrialized state."[13] For Mao, New China meant above all an industrializing China, the first objective in his subsequently formulated program of China's Four Modernizations of industry, agriculture, technology, and defense.

In the early days of the PRC, Mao remarked that a most beautiful picture would be a skyline of the Forbidden City filled with factory chimneys and smoke.[14] Equally indicative of Mao's vision of China as a strong industrial power was a remark made during his twilight years, at the Tenth Party Congress in 1973, when he commented that the surname of the CCP should be "Mr. Gong" (Mr. Worker) because it was the party of proletariat. Presumably this meant that it was not a party of the peasantry, who remained the vast majority of the population.[15]

Land reform and the agrarian revolution served the purpose of freeing rural productive forces and paving the way for industrialization. Agriculture would be a major source of funds for industrial growth, especially for investment in heavy industry. Industry could in turn support the rural sector by mechanizing agriculture, providing chemical fertilizer, and so on.

As soon as Mao had a good grip on agriculture, quite logically his next priority became the transformation of handicrafts and the modern sectors of capitalist industry and commerce. In 1953 Mao put forward the "General Line for the transitional period" aiming to achieve the "three socialist transformations" of handicrafts, industry, and commerce within fifteen years in order to "bury capitalism and all exploitative systems."[16] This broke with the CCP's earlier moderate and conciliatory approach of establishing and upholding the New Democratic order that had allowed private and multiple forms of economic ownership. During the civil war, the CCP had agreed to a moderate approach in order to form a United Front with other small political parties to topple the Nationalist regime of Chiang Kai-shek (1887–1975). Once in power and in a position of strength, the CCP dealt equally ruthlessly with these minor political parties.

Mao modeled his ambitious time frame for complete nationalization on the Soviet experience, which had required three Five-Year Plans. Typical of Mao's impatience and creative experimentation, he pressed for an even more ambitious schedule. Consequently, by 1956, in less than four years and in the wake of the "high tide" of agrarian cooperativization, Mao combined persuasion with coercion to nationalize urban industry and commerce, and collectivize handicrafts.

Mao based his acceleration of the socialist transformation of China on his certitude of socialism's superiority over capitalism and the anticipated great improvements in production. Ideological reasons aside, the dire state of China's existing capitalist industry at the time of the Communist takeover also helps explain Mao's fixation on socialism in order to industrialize. In fixed 1952 currency, China's entire industrial sector in 1949 was valued at slightly over two billion reminbi out of a gross agricultural and industrial product in 1952 of 82.7 billion reminbi.[17] According to Mao, "the capitalist approach could boost production, but it would take much longer and be a painful road."[18]

As a result of the socialist transformation, state and collective ownership dominated the national economy: By 1956 the public sector accounted for 92.9 percent of national income, a complete reversal of the 1952 situation when the private sector had accounted for 78.7 percent. Mao attributed to his reforms the remarkable annual growth rate of 19.6 percent in annual gross industrial output and 4.8 percent in agricultural product for the transitional period of 1953–56.[19] Yet these statistics also reflected the pent-up economic energy after decades of civil war and foreign invasion. For the first time since 1911, China was at relative peace, so that general postwar reconstruction contributed to this rapid economic growth.

Foreign Affairs

National security concerns hampered Mao's development strategy virtually from the start. The PRC came into being in the thick of the Cold War and faced a hostile international environment including sabotage operations by Chiang Kai-shek's forces across the Taiwan Strait. U.S. reluctance to recognize Mao's regime and the growing anticommunist hysteria of McCarthyism left China with little chance to establish normal diplomatic and trade relations with Western countries. Moreover, the new structure of the Chinese economy and intense resentment against multinational corporations precluded normal capitalist transactions and contract arrangements. The United States and most of its European allies continued to recognize Chiang Kai-shek's government as the legitimate government of China and imposed a punishing economic embargo even before Mao decided to intervene in the Korean War. He did so because he believed the security of the industrial heartland in Manchuria to be at stake, but at the cost of any hopes of improved relations with the West. The Communist bloc saved China from complete diplomatic isolation.

Against the reservations of most of his colleagues and at the sacrifice of economic construction, Mao's daring decision to take on a coalition of the world's foremost powers and his ability eventually to force a stalemate in Korea seemed incredible given the relative size of China's industrial base. In 1950 China's annual steel output was 610,000 tons compared to America's 87.82 million.[20] China suffered enormous casualties in the war, 750,000 compared to 142,000 for the United States.[21] Among the dead was Mao's favorite son, whom Mao had sent to the battlefield to lead by example. Unknown to Mao, prior to the Korean War the United States had planned to abandon Taiwan and expected a successful PRC conquest of the island in July 1950, but the Korean War broke out in June, changing the strategic equation and triggering a U.S. reassessment to resume aid to the Nationalists.[22] Thus Mao's intervention in Korea came at the price of an independent Taiwan.

China's entry into the Korean War not only achieved the immediate objective of preserving a friendly North Korea, but also miraculously restored the national economy in the face of enormous adversity. The war mobilization unleashed intense patriotic spirit and a burst of productivity. China's national pride and international prestige grew as did Mao's personal reputation as a military genius and brilliant leader. The war reinforced Mao's prioritization of investment in heavy industry, strengthened his emphasis on the steel industry, and buttressed his faith in the invincibility of the Chinese people. These attitudes had a major bearing on the ensuing Great Leap Forward.

In these formative years, given the hostility of the Western capitalist countries and the inexperience of the Chinese in building socialism, Chinese leaders took the approach of "learning from the Soviet model."[23] The Soviet Union was, after all, the first socialist country with significant achievements and long a source of technical advice and military and financial aid to the CCP. Mao was particularly attentive to the Soviet model in the early years of the People's Republic, when he chose to "lean to one side"[24] in seeking an alliance with the Soviet Union for the sake of China's national interests despite his personal tensions with Joseph Stalin.

However, seeking friends did not mean forsaking oneself, let alone depending on others—as Mao conveyed to the U.S. ambassador to China, Leighton Stuart, when hoping to win over America's support on the eve of forming the Communist government.[25] One of the most striking aspects of Mao's leadership philosophy was the principle of self-reliance or standing on one's own feet[26] in order to ensure independence in both domestic and foreign policy. Thus the line "learning from Russia,"[27] meaning its achievements, quickly turned in late 1955 into "learning lessons from the Soviet Union,"[28] meaning its failures.

In April 1956, Mao's speech on "Ten Great Relationships" made a critical appraisal of the Soviet model and recommended departures for China. Mao demonstrated a growing awareness of the key economic role of agriculture and an intent to overcome the rigidities of the excessive economic centralization, which was undermining his strategy of "mobilizing all positive factors" for economic development. Mao's recommendations included more local- and enterprise-level autonomy as well as more small- and medium-scale industry.[29] By 1958 Mao openly criticized dogmatic copying of Soviet (or any foreign) experience.

Mao's approach to national development emphasized self-reliance and China's unique history and domestic conditions to chart an independent and innovative path to modernity. This was the essence of Mao's lifelong effort to Sinify Marxism. Deng Xiaoping (1904–1997) continued in this vein with the formulation "building socialism with Chinese characteristics."[30] Mao, however, violated this formula in his attempt to take personal command of the economy, an area where he acknowledged from the start he had no particular understanding. He sent China into uncharted waters when he attempted to demolish what he considered to be the superstition that only professors and professionals could run the economy. This was the Great Leap Forward.[31]

The Great Leap Forward

The Great Leap Forward movement of 1958–60 was Mao's great experiment in the search for a distinctly Chinese alternative to the Soviet model for large-scale economic construction. The unfolding Anti-Rightist Campaign, cracking down on intellectual dissent, contributed to the Leap Forward both by creating a supercharged political atmosphere with strong overtones of class struggle and by spreading doubts that China's Western-influenced intellectuals could guide economic development. Mao's approach emphasized mass mobilization and jettisoned the experts.

With the official approval of the "General Line of Building Socialism in a More, Faster, Better, and Economical Fashion," Mao formally launched the Great Leap Forward campaign in May 1958 at the second session of the Eighth Party Congress.[32] On the one hand, this was a logical step forward after Mao fast-tracked and completed the Three Socialist Transformations of handicrafts, industry, and commerce. On the other hand, it had a foreign policy dimension. Mao's trip celebrating the fortieth anniversary of the Russian Revolution followed immediately after the 1957 Soviet launch of Sputnik, the world's first satellite and precursor for nuclear weapons delivery. In Moscow, Mao declared, "The east wind is prevailing over the west wind."[33] When Stalin's successor, Nikita Khrushchev, predicted that the Soviet Union would overtake the United States economically in fifteen years, Mao, out of national pride and with a vision of a modern and strong China, announced that China would surpass Britain, the motherland of the Industrial Revolution, in the same period. From the onset, he presented the Great Leap Forward campaign as a "race against time with Western imperialism."[34] This vision set in motion China's attempt to catch up by leaping forward.

An emphasis on breakneck speed, ambitious plans, willpower, and human labor characterized Mao's unprecedented program to catch up to the advanced industrial powers. The slogans extolled rapid transformation: "Speed is the soul of the general line" of socialist construction,[35] and "one day is the equivalent of twenty years."[36] Overly ambitious plans and targets quickly produced economic dislocation. Other slogans, such as "with enough boldness on the field, the sky is the limit,"[37] reflected a faith in the triumph of willpower and enthusiasm from below. Mao believed that human initiatives and working-class creativity could make up for China's shortage of natural resources, just as its immense but largely unskilled labor pool could compensate for its lack of capital for industrial expansion. Therefore, he emphasized mass mobilization and party leadership over technical expertise. In order to maximize local- and enterprise-level initiatives, he called for radical decentralization at the price of economic coordination. By this time Mao had dismissed Soviet central planning as a "dogmatic" methodology.[38] These elements contributed to a frenzy of unrealistic targets goaded on by Mao.

Minister of Metallurgy Wang Heshou's report entitled "Overtake America in Fifteen Years" confirmed the reliability of ludicrously high steel production targets of 12 million tons for 1959 and 30 million, 70 million, and 1.2 billion tons respectively for the three ensuing Five-Year Plans ending between 1962 and 1972.[39] Such flights from reality in response to pressure from above and below characterized the widespread false production reports during the Great Leap Forward period, which then misled the party leadership. As a result, the Ministry of Metallurgy doubled the 1962 steel target to 60 million tons and, more imminently, to 25 million tons in 1959, an increase of almost fivefold in the two years from the 1957 steel output of 5.35 million tons. Mao then concluded that China could surpass British steel production in two years, not fifteen.[40]

Mao was obsessed with steel. A few years earlier, he had lamented: "China can make tables, chairs, teapots. Chinese peasants can produce grain and make flour. Alas, we're still unable to make a car, an airplane, a tank, and even a tractor."[41] At the official launch of the Great Leap Forward, Mao once again reiterated the primacy of China's steel industry, attributing Stalin's defeat of Adolf Hitler to Soviet possession of 18 million tons of steel. "Chiang Kai-shek was doomed to fail because he was merely able to increase China's steel output by 40,000 tons after twenty years rule of the country."[42]

Unrealistic production targets unbalanced other branches of the economy. The mass movement of "the whole people making steel"[43] undermined both agriculture and the natural environment. Mao's 1958 steel target of 10.7 million tons, double the previous year's output, entailed the mobilization of 90 million people and massive deforestation to man and fuel backyard furnaces. This left inadequate farm labor to harvest the bumper crop of 1958, which resulted in unmet state grain procurement targets. The introduction of people's communes then exacerbated food production problems.

A striking innovation at the height of the Great Leap Forward was the launch of the commune movement that virtually eliminated private property in the countryside and created new forms of communal living on the promise of full communism within a few years. These so-called people's communes served both as local-level government organs and as key economic units, which took control not only over agricultural production but also over local industry, commerce, education, and the militia.[44] They organized peasants into production brigades or teams. When the introduction of mess halls and free meals encouraged consumption not production, the people's communes employed a work-point system to calculate rewards. In practice, rural consumption increased, rural production declined, and urban procurements of rural products increased in order to meet investment targets and to raise funds through the export of agricultural products.

The Great Leap Forward sought not only a technological revolution through the transformation of agriculture and industry, but also a "cultural revolution" through the elimination of illiteracy and the promotion of higher education so that "in fifteen years time everyone can read and understand *Das Capital;* every production team can produce its own Li Bo [the foremost poet of the Tang dynasty], Lu Xun and Nie E [respectively, the well-known twentieth-century writer and musician], and Mei Lanfang [the famous Beijing opera singer]."[45]

These genuine collective efforts of "striving hard for three years to change fundamentally the face of the whole country"[46] went horribly wrong. Production in agriculture and light industry plunged. Excesses of all kinds ran riot and resulted in widespread chaos and waste. The overall economic loss over these three years reached 120 billion yuan and it required five additional years to restore the derailed national economy.[47] The initial slogan of "more, quicker, better, and more economical" produced a catastrophe of less, slower, worse, and wasteful, not to mention the human cost.

During the six years affected by the Great Leap Forward, 1958 to 1963, between 22 and 36 million people, if not more, died from starvation and malnutrition.[48] In contrast to all previous Chinese famines, the Great Leap Forward Famine was largely man-made and national, not regional, in scope. Three years of natural disasters, from 1959 to 1961 then exacerbated the situation. Disaster of unprecedented dimensions engulfed the nation because of economic choices made by Mao, a man who dismissed economics and expertise in general as attributes of the despised bourgeois social hierarchy.

At the root of the debacle lay Mao's utopian conviction that China would soon become a Communist society where problems of scarcity and exploitation would disappear; hence his emphasis on eradicating "the ideology of bourgeois right,"[49] eliminating wages, abolishing the commodity economy, and even doing away with money as a medium of exchange. Mao rejected the notion that smooth and sustainable economic development occurs gradually through a long process of acquiring the necessary expertise from experience and of testing plans empirically. Instead, he mandated utopian visions top-down in keeping with China's long imperial tradition. Idealism and heroism, although widely shared among China's elite and populace at the time, were no substitute for economic rationality in pursuit of national greatness.

In the fall of 1960—after convoluted events including the dismissal of Defense Minister Peng Dehuai who dared criticize the Great Leap Forward—the dire nature of the situation became so apparent that even Mao belatedly opposed the "communist wind."[50] A systematic retreat from the Great Leap began. Mao withdrew to the "second line," leaving the task of cleaning up the mess he had created to Liu Shaoqi (1898–1969), Zhou Enlai (1898–1976), Deng Xiaoping, and others on the "first line." The cleanup included drastic cuts in industrial investment, the shift of resources to agricultural and consumer goods production, a restoration of economic coordination at the expense of decentralization, the reform of the people's communes to vest authority in production teams, the restoration of peasant private plots and free markets, and a return to material incentives.

The Cultural Revolution

Nevertheless Mao's emotional attachment to *his* Great Leap Forward never waned nor did his determination to lead on the "first line." On the contrary, he concluded that his economic revolution required a comprehensive political revolution: "Seize the revolution [meaning combat revisionism and capitalism] in order to boost [socialist] production."[51] The result was the Cultural Revolution.

Like the Great Leap Forward, the notorious Great Proletarian Cultural Revolution, which Mao personally launched to the consternation of his colleagues, was another Herculean attempt at social engineering and economic development that went conspicuously wrong. Mao suspected that the first-line leaders had degenerated, if not into capitalism, then into "revisionism." This, to him, represented a fundamental departure from the Marxist-Socialist path of development. They had allowed the return of practices he reviled such as private and individual household farming, the payment of material incentives in the factories, a two-track educational system divided between occupational and academic subjects, and the depiction of traditional (hence feudal) themes in literature and the arts.[52]

The conservative pace of their economic development program ran up against Mao's habitual impatience. In late 1964, he railed against the slow implementation of his proposed third-line construction to funnel investment funds to China's interior; he called the State Planning Commission under Li Fuchun and the Party's Secretariat under Deng Xiaoping "two independent kingdoms in Beijing."[53] In early 1965, Mao set up the "Small Planning Commission," led by Yu Qiuli and Chen Boda, to replace the State Planning Commission, which in Mao's eye was overly influenced by the ossified Soviet central planning model.

Mao strove not merely to fight corruption, bureaucratization, and the perceived restoration of capitalism in both society and state, but also to uproot the inherent selfishness in every individual's private mind. The Cultural Revolution was about shaping China's future, transforming people into renaissance men, and transforming human nature by banishing selfishness. It was meant to be a "great revolution that touches people in their very souls."[54]

On the eve of the Cultural Revolution, Mao, in his famous "May 7 Instruction," disclosed his version of Plato's republic. He demanded "new and complete men for Communism." Everyone would be "a worker, a farmer, a soldier, a writer, and a fighter against the bourgeoisie, all in one, producing and exchanging goods for his/her own needs."[55] His radical activism at the beginning of the Cultural Revolution, his "sweeping away all demons and monsters"[56] in society, harkened back to his vision at the height of the Great Leap Forward of clearing the way so that "the 600 million Chinese people can all become Yao and Shun," the mythic sage kings of China's antiquity.[57] This surrealistic vision had no place for the division of labor, the specialization of knowledge, or the reliance on expertise pervading modern economies.

Out of his quixotic quest for ideological purity, Mao, the restless revolutionary, embarked on an intense nationwide mass mobilization, especially in urban areas. He incited millions of students, organized into armed Red Guards units, along with factory workers to "bombard the headquarters," to expose the dark side of the authorities, to seize power from the establishment, and, not least, to drag out "capitalist roaders" at every level, while he himself took action to cleanse the upper ranks of the CCP, including most notably the State President Liu Shaoqi and Party General Secretary Deng Xiaoping.[58] He sent countless officials and intellectuals to May 7 Cadre Schools for reeducation and ideological remolding. Yet even the loyal social groups he helped to unleash were soon at each other's throats all in the name of defending Chairman Mao's Thought.

The grand vision proved to be removed from reality, too idealistic, too nostalgic, and too far-fetched altogether. The Cultural Revolution initially inspired millions of young people but grievously damaged the Chinese body politic. Utopia building proved to be detrimental to nation building. Contrary to Mao's initial desire to bring in a new political and social order and national rebirth in the aftermath of toppling the old regime, the Cultural Revolution brought chaos, anarchy, and vicious factionalism. It shattered families, left a generation without formal educations, and entailed the widespread persecution of veteran CCP cadres, government officials, professionals, and scholars. The violent struggle sessions and armed factional fighting caused an enormous loss of life among China's most educated and experienced, and left behind a deeply scarred society with a disillusioned and alienated population, especially youth and intellectuals. Their frustration and anger eventually erupted in the first Tiananmen mass protest, in April 1976, just months before Mao's death. This became known as the Tiananmen Incident; crowds gathered to mourn Zhou Enlai's death and to condemn the Gang of Four, led by Mao's wife, who were attempting to consolidate power as Mao's health failed.

In 1967 and 1968, the Cultural Revolution reached the nadir of "knocking down everything and engaging in extensive civil wars," to use Mao's own description.[59] Nevertheless, by his own reckoning, the Cultural Revolution was "70 percent correct and 30 percent deficient."[60] The death of Minister of Defense Lin Biao (1907–1971) in September 1971 intensified people's doubt over Mao's infallibility. At the beginning of the Cultural Revolution, Lin Biao had become Mao's designated successor, but just as suddenly he fell from grace, dying in a plane crash while fleeing China.[61]

Mao, in order to rescue *his* Cultural Revolution, made concerted efforts to rectify the "30 percent mistakes" first by sanctioning Zhou Enlai in 1972 to combat anarchism and ultraleft practices and then by licensing Deng Xiaoping in 1975 to tackle factionalism and advance the national economy. In 1973 Mao rehabilitated so-called successfully remolded veteran cadres, of whom Deng was the most notable case. By 1974 Mao demanded "stability and unity" in the new order, in particular, solidarity between Deng and the Gang of Four, who were identified with the radicalism of the Cultural Revolution.[62]

Notwithstanding his acknowledgment of some shortcomings, Mao would not brook doubts about the sanctity of the Cultural Revolution. As soon as he sensed that Premier Zhou had overstepped the mark, he launched a Second Cultural Revolution in 1974 that was officially labeled the Campaign to Criticize Lin Biao and Confucius,[63] but actually targeted Zhou Enlai. Likewise, Mao's Anti-Right Deviationist and Anti-Reversal of Verdict Campaign of early 1976 removed Deng Xiaoping for failing to live up to a pledge and precondition for his rehabilitation that he "would never reverse the verdict" on the correctness of the Cultural Revolution.[64]

Not long before his death, Mao made a final and uncharacteristically modest assessment of his eventful career, saying that he "had achieved only two things in life": driving out the Japanese and Chiang Kai-shek (thus establishing the PRC), and launching the Cultural Revolution.[65] Apparently, he wished his people to remember him for these two achievements. These remarks speak volumes about his obsession with the Cultural Revolution as well as his conviction that re-revolutionizing Chinese society was "necessary and timely." He remained adamant even though "not too many [of his colleagues or his people] supported it" as he himself acknowledged on the same occasion.[66]

The Legacy of Mao Zedong

Given Mao's absolute authority, understandably, only after his death could his surviving colleagues, led by his anointed successor, Hua Guofeng (1921–2008), quickly and decisively move away from Cultural Revolution policies. As soon as Mao passed away, Hua staged an unprecedented coup by arresting the Gang of Four, including Mao's widow, Jiang Qing (1914–1991), whom Mao had entrusted to carry on the ideological thrust of the Cultural Revolution. Through Hua and the return of Deng Xiaoping, the new era of reform and openness started to unfold.

In fact, the disruptive Cultural Revolution had not prevented the Chinese economy from making some headway. China was not far from having an "independent, self-reliant and relatively comprehensive modern industrial system of its own"[67]—a mission put forward by Mao in the early 1950s and accomplished around 1980, soon after the CCP shifted its priorities to economic construction under Hua Guofeng and Deng Xiaoping's leadership.

In 2007, fifty years after setting the goal in 1958, China's economy became the world's fourth largest in terms of GDP by surpassing that of Great Britain.[68] Many attribute China's recent economic success to the reforms of Deng Xiaoping, which they portray as a radical departure from the policies of Mao Zedong. This view fails to do justice to Mao's Herculean effort to lay a solid foundation for China's development. Even Deng himself, a major victim of Mao's various political campaigns, duly acknowledged, "What we did . . . were simply undertakings to restore those correct policies made by Comrade Mao Zedong. We are simply doing an accurate and comprehensive learning and practicing of Mao Zedong Thought. . . . In so many respects, what we're up to at present are still those tasks initiated by Mao but not yet completed."[69] Deng's once designated successor, Zhao Ziyang (1919–2005), carried the thought further but with a new twist that tacitly acknowledged Mao's destructive legacy, saying, "if it had not been for the Cultural Revolution during which everything had been driven to extremes, we would not have been able to see things so clearly as we do today."[70]

However flawed Mao's various national development programs, during the twenty-seven years of his rule, China became a major industrializing power, ranked the sixth in the world by the mid-1970s. Industrial output increased thirtyfold and heavy industrial output increased by ninetyfold. Despite the chaos and dislocation of the Great Leap Forward and the Cultural Revolution, and the difficult Cold War international environment, overall industrial growth still advanced at the average annual rate of 11.2 percent. In 1952 industrial production accounted for only 30 percent of GDP, while agriculture accounted for 64 percent. By 1975, one year before Mao's death and the completion of the fourth Five-Year Plan, this ratio had been completely reversed to 72 percent for industry and 28 percent for agriculture. Similarly, the urban workforce also expanded from 3 million in 1952 to 18 million in 1975.[71]

Deng's much-lauded policy of "opening up" to the Western world actually followed Mao's lead. Late in life, in order to bring the Soviet Union to its knees Mao reversed his original course of cutting contacts with the non-Communist world. Initial Soviet help had been welcome, but disagreements over nuclear weapons and increasingly intrusive Soviet interference and unwillingness to treat Mao as the elder statesman of international communism upon Stalin's death in 1953 culminated in the 1960 Sino-Soviet split. In March 1969, Mao orchestrated the battle on Zhenbao Island on the Amur River to highlight China's long-drawn-out border dispute with Russia. This small-scale clash (the main engagement lasted for only seventy-eight minutes),[72] forced an economically unsustainable Soviet militarization of the long Sino-Soviet border. In 1971 Mao played the so-called ping-pong diplomacy that attracted President Richard Nixon's visit in the following year and culminated in the normalization of Sino-American relations in early 1979. Together these events helped overturn the Cold War balance of power at Soviet expense by contributing to the overextension of the Soviet economy that in turn contributed to the implosion of the Soviet Union in 1991. In the meantime, improved relations with the United States proved to be conducive to China's own national development. Mao, not Deng, began the large-scale importation of advanced equipment and technology from capitalist and developed countries with the ground-breaking "4.3 billion USD Import Program" in 1973.[73]

Likewise China's recent initiative to spur the economic development of the interior harkens back to an earlier initiative by Mao. In 1964 against the backdrop of the escalating U.S. involvement in the Vietnam War and increasing Soviet troop deployments along China's northern borders, Mao focused on massive so-called third-front construction in China's hinterland in order to develop the interior and mitigate the development gap between eastern and western China.[74]

Mao may well deserve to be brought to account for his people's misfortune, as suggested in the accusation that he was "the biggest feudal tyrant in Chinese history" (as alleged by Lin Liguo, the son of Mao's once heir apparent, Lin Biao)[75] and the accusation that his twenty-seven years at the helm were "a reign of terror" (as alleged by Li Shenzhi, the renowned Chinese liberal intellectual).[76]

Notwithstanding this, Mao was both a blessing and curse, both an asset and a liability, for the Chinese people who have learned from Mao's mistakes by shaking off various extreme aspects of Maoism. The fact remains that Mao was the founder of the nation and that the People's Republic was created in Mao's character. Mao's powerful legacy through his charisma and status as the nation's father if not the founding emperor of a new dynasty, whether positive or negative, remains relevant to China's ongoing nation building. His actions serve both as a source of inspiration and as hard lessons to be learned. This includes Mao's developmental model prioritizing heavy industry and the inland economy in order to catch up to the leading industrial powers. However, his impatient and over-ambitious nation building was counterproductive, especially when nation building turned into utopia building. That was China's tragedy.

Notes

1. In Liang's original words, "lao guo cong si xinshaonian," Liang Qichao, *Yinbingshi shihua* (Commentary on Poetry from the Ice-Drinker's Studio) (Beijing: Renmin chubanshe, 1982), 32. Liang expanded on the same theme in his 10 February 1900 speech entitled "Shaonian Zhongguo shuo" (On China as a Youthful Country), http://blog.sina.com.cn/s/blog_4a045b7401000aet.html.

2. Li Shenzhi, "Fengyu canghuang wushinian—guoqingye duyu" (Fifty Years of Storms and Disturbances—Soliloquy on National Day Evening), http://www.boxun.com/hero/lisz/22_1.shtml.

3. Yuan Weishi, *Jindai Zhongguo lunheng* (Essays on Modern China) (Hong Kong: Roundtable Enterprise, 2006), 107.

4. Mao's speech on "The Ten Great Relations," 25 April 1956, http://www.marxists.org/chinese/17/marxist.org-chinese-mao-19560425.htm; Pang Xianzhi et al., eds., *Mao Zedong zhuan* (Mao Zedong Biography), vol. 1 (Beijing: Zhongyang wenxian chubanshe, 2003), 811.

5. Mao Zedong, "Address to the Preparatory Meeting of the New Political Consultative Conference" (June 15, 1949), http://www.ahgzw.gov.cn/dangwei/m_wxuan/4_58.htm.

6. Chen Feng, "Dalu jianguo hou tudi gaige he Taiwan tudi gaige zhi bijiao" (A Comparison of the Land Reform in Taiwan and the Mainland after 1949), *Guangxi jiaoyu xue yuan xuebao,* vol. 1 (2001), 123.

7. Dong Zhikai, "Mao Zedong yu xin Zhongguo jingji jianshe" (Mao and the New China's Economic Construction), *Ningbo gangxiao xuekan,* vol. 2 (2004), 45; Frederick Teiwes, "The Establishment and Consolidation of the New Regime, 1949–57" in *The Politics of China,* 2nd ed., ed. Roderick MacFarquar (New York: Cambridge University Press, 1997), 33–36.

8. Mao, "Get Organized!" November 29, 1943, http://www.marxists.org/reference/archive/mao/selected-works/volume-3/index.htm.

9. Pang Xianzhi et al., eds., Mao Zedong Biography, vol. 1, 386.

10. Ibid., 413–15.

11. Frederick Teiwes, "The Establishment and Consolidation of the New Regime," 58; Liu

Guoguang, ed., *Zhongguo shige wunian jihua yanjiu baogao* (Research Report on China's Ten Five-Year Plans) (Beijing: Remin chubanshe, 2006), 83.

12. Guo Haiqing, "Shilun xin Zhongguo Mao Zedong jingji shehui fazhan zhanlue xixiang" (On Mao's Socioeconomic Development Strategies for the New China), *Qiushi*, vol. 10 (2007), 7.

13. Ibid.

14. "Liang Chen fangan" (Liang Sicheng and Chen Zhanxiang's Designs of the City of Beijing), http://baike.baidu.com/view/887942.htm.

15. Gao Wenqian, *Wannian Zhou Enlai* (Zhou Enlai's Later Years) (Hong Kong: Mirrorbooks, 2003), 486.

16. Ma Qibin, *Zhongguo gongchandang zhizheng sishinian* (The Forty Years of the CCP in Power) (Beijing: Zhonggong dangshi chubanshe, 1991), 64.

17. Sha Jiansun, "Guanyu shehui zhuyi gaizhai wenti de zai pingjia" (A Reassessment of the Issue on Socialist Transformations), *Dangdai Zhongguo shi yanjiu*, Beijing, vol. 12 no. 1 (2005), 105; Fang Weizhong, ed., *Zhonghua Remin Gongheguo jingji dashiji* (A Chronological Account of Major Economic Events of the PRC) (Beijing: Zhongguo shehui kexue chubanshe, 1984), 86.

18. Sha Jiansun, Reassessment of the Issue on Socialist Transformations, 105.

19. Ibid., 113–14.

20. Fang Weizhong, ed., Chronological Account of Major Economic Events, 37–38; Dong Zikai, "Chaoxian zhanzheng yu xin Zhongguo jingji" (The Korean War and New China's Economy), *Zhonggong Ningbo shiwei dangxiao xuebao*, vol. 23 no. 5 (2001), 6.

21. Dong Zikai, The Korean War and New China's Economy, 12; Alan Palmer, *The Penguin Dictionary of 20th Century History, 1900–1989* (London: Penguin, 1990), 238.

22. *Foreign Relations of the United States 1950*, vol. 6, *East Asia and the Pacific* (Washington, DC: United States Government Printing Office, 1976), 340; Glenn D. Paige, *The Korean Decision* (New York: Free Press, 1968), 62.

23. Zhang Ruimin, "Mao Zedong dui Sulian zhizheng he jianshe jingyan jiejian de lishi yiyi" (The Historical Significance of Mao Zedong's Learning from the USSR's Experience of Government and Construction), *Zhenzhou daxue xuebao*, vol. 39 no. 2, 2006), 47.

24. Pang Xianzhi et al., eds., Mao Zedong Biography, vol. 1, 56–57.

25. Wang Guoxue, "Dui jianguo chuqi Mao Zedong 'yibiandao' zhanlüe fangzhen de zai tantao" (A Reexamination of Mao's Guiding Strategy of "Leaning to One Side" in the Early Period of the PRC), *Mao Zedong xixiang yanjiu*, Beijing, vol. 22 no. 4 (2005), 58.

26. The original Chinese is "*zili gengsheng.*"

27. The original Chinese is "*yi E wei shi.*"

28. The original Chinese is "*yi Su wei jian.*"

29. Frederick Teiwes, "The Establishment and Consolidation of the New Regime," 68–73.

30. *Deng Xiaoping sixiang nianpu* (A Chronological Account of Deng Xiaoping's Thought) (Beijing, Zhongyan wenxian chubanshe, 1998), 230–31.

31. For a study of this Great Leap Forward campaign, see Frederick Teiwes and Warren Sun, *China's Road to Disaster: Mao, Central Politicians, and Provincial Leaders in the Unfolding of the Great Leap Forward, 1955–1959* (Armonk, NY: M.E. Sharpe, 1999).

32. Pang Xianzhi et al., eds., Mao Zedong Biography, vol. 1, 796, 800, 814, 822.

33. Ibid., 732.

34. Li Wei, "Dayuejin yundong yanjiu de xinjinzhan" (New Studies on the Great Leap Forward), *Beijing Dangshi*, vol. 1 (2006), http://myy.cass.cn/file/2006122926715.html.

35. *The People's Daily*, editorial, 21 June 1958.

36. For the slogan advanced by Chen Boda and various local leaders, see http://www.cdds.chengdu.gov.cn/detail.asp?id=2862; *Guanxi Dangshi*, no.4 (2006), 52.

37. "Ren you duo da dan, di you duo da chan" first appeared in *The People's Daily* on 27 August 1958.

38. Pang Xianzhi et al. eds., Mao Zedong Biography, vol. 1, 790–92, 823.

39. Frederick Teiwes and Warren Sun, *China's Road to Disaster,* 103–4.

40. Luo Pinghan, "Bada er ci huiyi yu Dayuejin de quanmian fadong" (The Second Session of the Eighth Party Congress and the All-Out Launch of the Great Leap Forward), *Wenshi Jinghua,* no. 2 (2004), 26.

41. Hu Wenchao, "Shixi Mao Zedong de Dayuejin qingjie" (On Mao's Great Leap Forward Complex), *Jiangxi langtian xueyuan xuebao* (June 2007), 80.

42. Luo Pinghan, The Second Session of the Eighth Party Congress, 25.

43. Su Donghai et al., eds., *Zhonghua Renmin Gongheguo fengyun shilu* (True Account of the Turbulent History of the PRC) (Shijiazhuang: Hebei renmin chubanshe, 1994), 573.

44. Kenneth Lieberthal, "The Great Leap Forward and the Spirit in the Yan'an Leadership" in *The Politics of China,* ed. Roderick MacFarquar, 95.

45. Luo Pinghan, The Second Session of the Eighth Party Congress, 30.

46. *The People's Daily,* editorial, 3 February 1958.

47. Chen Weihua, "Dayuejin yundong dui Zhongguo xiandaihua de liangcongxing yingxiang" (The Dual Impact of the Great Leap Forward on China's Modernization), *Dangshi yanjiu yu jiaoxue,* no. 1 (1998), 28.

48. The figure of 22 million comes from Li Chengrui, "Dayuejin yinqi de renkou biandong" (The Population Change Caused by the Great Leap Forward), *Zhonggong dangshi yanjiu,* no. 2 (1997), 1–14. The figure of 36 million comes from Yang Jisheng, *Mubei* (Tombstone) (Hong Kong: Cosmos Books, 2008), 7. Jasper Becker in his book *Hungry Ghosts: Mao's Secret Famine* mentions 46 million peasant deaths. http://www.chinaeforum.com/viewtopic.php?f=3&t=1894&start=0&st=0&sk=t&sd=a.

49. Fang Weizhong, ed., Chronological Account of Major Economic Events, 225.

50. http://www.epochtimes.com/b5/8/4/26/n2095633.htm.

51. For the expression, *"zhua geming; chu shengchan,"* see Chen Donglin and Du Pu, eds., *Zhonghua renmin gongheguo shilu* (True Account of the History of the PRC), vol. 3, part 1 (Changchun: Jilin renmin chubanshe, 1994), 188.

52. Harry Harding, "The Chinese State in Crisis, 1966–9" in *The Politics of China,* ed. Roderick MacFarquar, 152–53.

53. Liu Guoguang, ed., Research Report on China's Ten Five-Year Plans, 274.

54. Wang Nianyi, *Dadongluan de niandai* (Age of Great Turmoil) (Zhengzhou: Henan renmin chubanshe, 1988), 2.

55. Liu Guoguang, ed., Research Report on China's Ten Five-Year Plans, 349.

56. *The People's Daily,* 1 June 1966, in *The Chinese Cultural Revolution Database CD-ROM,* ed. Song Yongyi et al. (Hong Kong: USC, CUHK, 2002).

57. *Mao zhuxi shici* (Chairman Mao's Lyrics) (Beijing: Renmin wenxue chubanshe, 1976), 35.

58. Mao Zedong, "Wo de yizhang dazibao" (My Big-Character Poster), 5 August 1966, in *The Chinese Cultural Revolution Database CD-ROM,* ed. Song Yongyi et al. (Hong Kong: USC, CUHK, 2002).

59. Pang Xianzhi et al., eds., Mao Zedong Biography, vol. 2, 1771.

60. Ibid., 1756.

61. Frederick Teiwes and Warren Sun, *Riding the Tiger during the Cultural Revolution—The Tragedy of Lin Biao* (London: Hurst, 1996).

62. Frederick Teiwes and Warren Sun, *The End of the Maoist Era: Chinese Politics during the Twilight of the Cultural Revolution, 1972–1976* (Armonk, NY: M.E. Sharpe, 2007), 187, 367.

63. The original Chinese is *"pi Lin pi Kong."*

64. "Deng Xiaoping's Letter to Mao," 3 August 1972, in *The Chinese Cultural Revolution Database CD-ROM,* ed. Song Yongyi et al. (Hong Kong: USC, CUHK, 2002).

65. Pang Xianzhi et al., eds., Mao Zedong Biography, vol. 2, 1781–82.

66. Ibid.

67. Wu Li, "Zhonghua renmin gongheguo 50 nian jingji fazhan yu zhidu biange fenxi" (An Analysis of the Economic Development and Institutional Changes of the Last 50 Years in the PRC), *Dangdai Zhongguoshi Yanjiu,* no. 5 (1999), 55.

68. In October 2006, officials from the Bureau of Statistics of the PRC reported: "By the end of 2005 China's GDP has reached 2235 billion U.S. dollars, ranked only behind the U.S., Japan, and Germany." http://finance.qq.com/a/20061010/000050.htm.

69. Deng Xiaoping's October 1980 speech. See Li Xiangyong, "Mao Zedong yu xin Zhongguo xiandaihua de qibu" (Mao and the Beginning of New China's Modernization), *Xinan minzu xueyuan xuebao,* no. 8 (1999), 57.

70. Cited in Frederick C. Teiwes, "Restoration and Innovation," *The Australian Journal of Chinese Affairs,* no. 5 (1981), 167.

71. Dong Zhikai, Mao and the New China's Economic Construction, 51; Zheng Hong, "Mao Zedong yu xin Zhongguo de shehui zhuyi gongyehua daolu" (Mao and New China's Road to Socialized Industry), *Liaoning xingzheng xueyuan xuebao,* no. 3 (2004), 128–29; Luo Pinghan, The Second Session of the Eighth Party Congress, 25.

72. "Xiao Quanfu Recollection," unpublished internal material; Li Danhui, "1969 nian Zhong Su bianjie chongtu: yuanqi he jieguo" (On the 1969 Border Clash Between China and the USSR: Its Origin and the Consequence), in *Huishou Wenge* (Looking Back at the Cultural Revolution), ed. Zhang Hua et al. (Beijing: Zhonggong danshi chubanshe, 2000), 903–22.

73. Chen Jinghua, *Guoshi yishu* (A Retrospective Account of National Policies) (Beijing: Zhonggong dangshe chubanshe, 2005), 3–40.

74. Chen Donglin, *Sanxian jianshe* (The Third-front Construction in China's Hinterland) (Beijing: Zhonggong Zhongyang Dangxiao chubanshe, 2003), 408–17.

75. Shu Yun, *Lin Biao shijian wanzheng diaocha* (The Full Investigation into the Lin Biao Incident) (Hong Kong: Mirrorbooks, 2006), 405.

76. Li Shenzhi, Fifty Years of Storms and Disturbances, http://www.boxun.com/hero/lisz/22_2.shtml.

8

Nasser's Egypt: A Quest for National Power and Prosperity

KIRK J. BEATTIE

Abstract: *This case study discusses how Egypt's Gamal 'Abd al-Nasser led a successful coup d'état and, once firmly in power, sought rapid modernization. His efforts to promote a grand Arab nation notwithstanding, he never faced a problem of nation building, because Egyptians already had a strong sense of national identity, in part based on the antiquity of Egyptian civilization. His challenges concerned state building, with priority to creating a strong military, and promoting socioeconomic development. Unflinching pursuit of these objectives had a great, unanticipated impact on Nasser's foreign and economic policies. Initially he followed U.S. recommendations of land reform and institutional models like the Tennessee Valley Authority as pathways to national prosperity. He also followed Western economic advice to concentrate on import substitution industrialization (ISI). These policies, however, did not deliver rapid economic progress. Given Soviet willingness to provide key weapons systems in the face of Western intransigence and support for Israel, Nasser gravitated from state-guided capitalism to an Arab socialist model for economic development. Simultaneously, he raised the banner of Arab nationalism in order to unite Egyptians at home and to elevate Egypt's regional influence. The nationalization of Egyptian enterprises to fund his costly quest for regional influence, combined with the failed ISI strategy, caused economic overextension and stagnation that undermined his dreams to create a stable and prosperous society. Any attempt to evaluate Nasser's nation- and state-building endeavors, which are obviously long-term by nature, must take into account his premature death at age fifty-two.*

What causes some nations to unify and flourish while others languish in discord and poverty? What special mix of political and economic ingredients places certain nations on a path to national peace and prosperity, and others to disarray and destruction? The questions are germane to an analysis of all peoples and nations for all time, but two historical waves have yielded two sets of scholarly examinations of these questions over the past half century. First, the decolonization process of the 1950s and 1960s brought keen interest in the fate of numerous, newly independent countries. Purely scholarly pursuits combined with Cold War–induced strategic interests to foster more sophisticated modes of comparative political enquiry in general, and specific theoretical formulations like modernization theory and its critical offspring, dependency theory. Second, during the 1990s and the first decade of the new millennium, the collapse of Eastern European Communist regimes, the success of the Four Asian Tigers alongside other "failed states," and last but not least, the appearance of "rogue states" and situations growing out of the George W. Bush administration's war on Islamist extremism, all created a second wave of scholarship, much of which is focused on the issue of nation building. Two issues of key concern to the U.S. government, the fates of Afghanistan and Iraq, have brought special poignancy to solving the puzzle of what is commonly referred to as nation building.

Before launching into this chapter's examination of nation building in Egypt, however, it is essential to clarify the meaning of the term itself. As Francis Fukuyama notes, Americans often misuse "the term *nation-building,* reflecting as it does the specifically American experience of constructing a new political order in a land of new settlement without deeply rooted peoples, cultures, and traditions. . . . What Americans refer to as *nation-building* is rather state-building—that is, constructing political institutions, or else promoting economic development."[1] For Fukuyama, *nation building* should refer to the formation of a nation, meaning a people, typically rooted in a particular location, and sharing a common history and culture.

Fukuyama's point is well taken, but in recent years the concept has been given a broader meaning. What *nation building* now connotes in common parlance is not just the construction of political institutions or economic development, but the creation of a political order generating greater prosperity for its citizenry and enjoying widespread legitimacy. My understanding is that the editor's intent with regard to this volume's studies of nation building is for the authors to focus heavily on state-building endeavors, but with an eye to whether those efforts have successfully created and bound a nation and its will to those institutions by significantly improving its standard of living. For this analysis, therefore, I see my task as multifaceted: first and foremost, to study the Nasser regime's efforts at state building, as defined by Fukuyama; second, to explore the regime's success in building an Egyptian or alternative national identity; and third, to establish whether Nasser succeeded in building a state that acquired widespread, performance-based legitimacy in the eyes of that nation. With regard to the first and third dimensions, I will examine the difficulties encountered by Egypt's leaders in these endeavors, offering insight as to why nearly two decades after the real sons of Egypt began to engage in state-building activities to create legitimate, prosperity-generating political institutions, their work remained far from complete. With regard to the second dimension—nation building, narrowly defined—I will analyze how the twists and turns of Egyptian history afforded greater latitude for national identity formation, or "imagining" a national community, than one might surmise.

In brief, the substantive, spatial, and historical scope of this chapter covers nation-

134

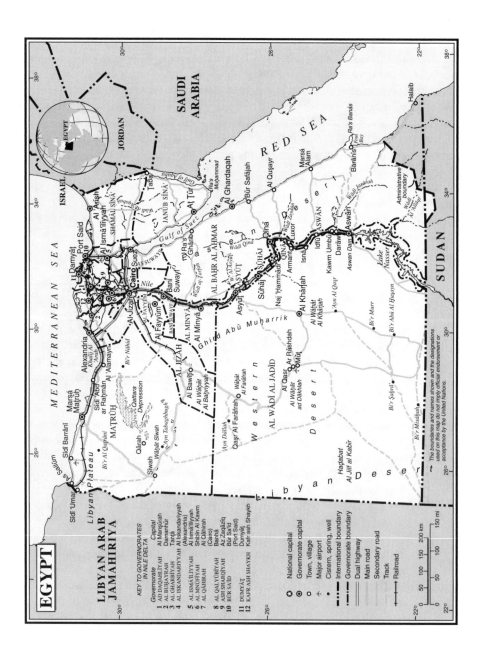

building efforts in Egypt during the Nasser era of 1952–70. Although Gamal 'Abd al-Nasser (1918–1970) did not take control of the presidency until late November 1954—that role having been initially entrusted to a more senior and nationally known officer named Muhammad Nagib—it was Nasser who formed the small group of young military officers, the Free Officers, that carried out the July 1952 overthrow of King Farouk's constitutional monarchy. Once Nasser engineered Nagib's removal from the presidency in 1954, he retained that position until his death in September 1970. As I address the contextual and substantive concerns of nation building mapped out by this book's editor, I will examine the fascinating interplay between Nasser, as he sought to mold state, nation, and economy, and other political actors, ranging from internal regime elements to foreign powers, as they presented varying degrees of cooperation and resistance to his plans.

The Setting

When the Free Officers arrived in power, the regional security environment was rich with challenges. To the far west, in the Maghreb (Morocco, Algeria, and Tunisia), France remained firmly in control of high political matters, and French government officials were wary of the example that Egypt's young, nationalistic officers might set for Arabs chafing under France's imperialist yoke. To the immediate west, in Libya, King Idriss felt threatened by the antimonarchical thrust of the Free Officers' movement, a tension reinforced by Libya's hosting of Wheelus Air Base, a key component in the Anglo-American defense strategy for North Africa. To the south, Sudan remained under British domination.

Even greater challenges to Egyptian national sovereignty were found within Egypt itself and to the east. Egypt remained very much under the British thumb. Over 30,000 British troops were stationed along the Suez Canal, a legacy of the Second World War and British strategic concerns. To the east, another threat to Egyptian and other Arabs' sovereignty arose in the form of the newly created state of Israel. In 1948 Egypt committed forces to quash the Zionist settlers' goal of establishing Israel, but the Zionists' victory cut Egyptian officers' sentiments to the quick. Indeed, this humiliating loss became a major motivational factor behind the formation of the Free Officers group. The realization of genuine national sovereignty through removal of the British military presence in Egypt, or writ large, an end to Western imperialism, along with the creation of a strong military, to prevent a repetition of the 1948 debacle or perhaps reverse it, were enshrined as two of the celebrated Six Principles of the 1952 "revolution." The strategic choices made to accomplish these objectives shaped to a great degree the parameters of decision making in the political and economic domains.

In 1952 Egypt's social and economic situation was, like most of its population, unhealthy. Human capital was weakly developed, with illiteracy afflicting 75 percent of the citizenry. Of all 21.4 million Egyptians, only 1.8 million were enrolled in school. Life expectancy at birth hovered in the low forties due to poor nutrition, inadequate health care, and an irrigation system rife with parasites. The last of these factors was all the more destructive because Egypt remained primarily an agricultural country, with a ten-to-one ratio of employment in agriculture versus industry. Although long benefiting from a rich agricultural base, and despite high hopes for land reclamation and irrigation of desert lands, the agricultural sector was perceived as labor saturated and incapable of providing new jobs for the rapidly growing population. Peasants accounted for the lion's share of the population; nearly all were illiterate, lived in grinding poverty, and subsisted on a diet of bread, watercress, and onions. The distribution of wealth in the agricultural sector was very heavily skewed; in 1952, 6 percent of Egypt's landowners held 65 percent of cultivable land and the royal family alone held over 600,000 acres.[2]

Egypt possessed some interesting mineral deposits, and not insignificant reserves of oil and natural gas, but nothing to rival those of its hydrocarbon-rich neighbors to the east and west. Although Egypt's industrial and service sectors had experienced greater development than those in other countries in the region, wealth remained concentrated in the hands of a very small number of national capitalists and *mutamasriyun* (individuals of Levantine, Jewish, Greek, Italian, and other European backgrounds, often of long residence in Egypt, but most of whom held foreign passports). Indeed, much of the economy's modern sector was dominated by *mutamasriyun,* who typically practiced discriminatory hiring practices. A significant portion of Egypt's infrastructure, including the Suez Canal, was foreign owned, and, true to imperialist form, much of this infrastructure (rail lines and roadbeds) had been constructed to facilitate the passage of raw materials and goods to Egyptian ports for shipment to European metropolises, not neighboring countries.

When a greater degree of national independence was achieved in 1923, new governments promoted a rapid expansion of education. However, emphasis was placed on expanding cheap education at all levels rather than on primary education for the broad peasant masses. Thus, while most peasants remained illiterate and mired in poverty, a newly educated stratum of middle-class aspirants emerged. Unfortunately, many in this latter category were blocked by foreign and *mutamasriyun* control of the modern sector of the economy, factors that reinforced their attachment to nationalist movements of various ideological colorations.

With over 7,000 years of civilization, Egypt has few peers. But beyond the grandeur and prowess of its pharaonic period, the past 2,000 years more often saw Egypt as a province than a power center. Egypt's agricultural richness and geostrategic location attracted Persian, Greek, and Roman conquerors before yielding to longer-lasting rule under the great Arab-Islamic and Ottoman empires. The latter empires, in control for most of the time from the mid-600s until the twentieth century, planted and preserved new Arab and Muslim elements on Egyptian soil. Arab invaders brought the new faith of Islam and implantation of the Arabic language, and the Ottoman Turks helped sustain the predominance of Islam in Egypt.

Egypt remained primarily a mix of eastern Hamitic and Arab peoples, with the former including the ancestors of the Nubian minority. The Ottomans brought a new genetic link to southeastern Europe, but the bulk of Egypt's population remained little changed from an ethnic perspective. Politically, most twentieth-century Egyptians identified themselves with alacrity as Egyptians, not Arabs, whom they associated with the people of the Arab peninsula. Still, cultural ties and considerable shared history left many Egyptians with a strong sense of attachment to and concern for their Arab cousins and coreligionists scattered across the Levant, the Arab peninsula, North Africa, and beyond.

In general, Egyptians of all faiths maintained a high degree of religiosity. With the Arab conquest, Islam became and remained the dominant faith, accounting for roughly 90 percent of the population. Although Christianity had flourished in Egypt from its earliest years, over the centuries it was reduced to a minority faith, with most of its contemporary members belonging to the Coptic Christian branch of eastern Orthodoxy. Significant disagreement existed over the exact percentage of the population that was Coptic. Copts claimed that they represented some 15 percent, whereas government sources proffered a statistic roughly half that figure. At mid-twentieth century, Egypt was also home to a small, yet dynamic, Jewish community.

Nasser's Rise to Power and the Goals of the "Revolution"

Despite Egypt's relative ethno-religious homogeneity when Nasser took power, there was little in the way of widespread consensus over core political values. From the late 1910s onward, four rival political ideological camps emerged in the Egyptian polity, each attracting a significant share of Egypt's citizens. In rough order of membership size and political significance, these camps included liberal democrats, Islamists, national socialists (proto-fascists), and Marxists. The major parties associated with each of these currents were, respectively, the Wafd, the Muslim Brothers, the Young Egypt and Watani parties, and a mishmash of Marxist organizations, among which perhaps the most influential was HADETU (*al-Haraka al-Dimuqratiyya li'l-Tahrir al-Watani* or Democratic Movement for National Liberation). Beyond their common anti-imperialist and largely antimonarchical positions, the depth of distrust and lack of value consensus among these camps produced an inability for political actors in civil society to unite and overthrow the stagnant political economy of the monarchy. There was simply too little agreement on, and too much fear of, what might come next.

It took Nasser's political perspicacity to visualize and piece together in microcosm, among younger members of the military officer corps, what the major civilian political actors could not realize on the grand civil societal stage. Playing upon bonds of personal friendship and strong nationalist sentiments, galvanized by powerful socialization experiences like the humiliating military defeat in 1948, Nasser convinced his colleagues to overcome differences based in social class and commitments to rival ideological groups and mold a small, yet effective, group—the Free Officers. Then, through secret, bilateral communications, Nasser turned his considerable political skills to persuading domestic (Wafdist, Muslim Brother, Marxist) and foreign (American) political actors that his group's intentions were nonthreatening. Consequently, none of these forces reacted in a hostile manner to the Free Officers' July 1952 coup.

Once in power, Nasser could not get civilian political leaders to bury their ideological differences for the sake of national development. Angered by their constant bickering, Nasser assumed greater political power to realize the primary developmental objectives of his "revolution." By January 1953, all political parties were formally banned and their leaders imprisoned or otherwise sidelined; only the Muslim Brotherhood (MB) organization was left standing. The last broad-based civilian challenge to Nasser's power consolidation came in March 1954, but failed when the MB leadership withdrew its followers from the fight.

The MB, however, was not about to fold. It had grown to an organization capable of mobilizing as many as two million members, and its leaders had many reasons to believe that Nasser's 1952 coup was made for them. In the late 1940s, Nasser swore a secret oath of fealty to the MB, as had other key coup conspirators. After coming to power, however, most Free Officers, Nasser included, acquired as much disdain for the MB as they had for their civilian rivals. Inability to harness the MB to the new regime on regime terms brought a showdown in November 1954. With secular civilian political actors either refusing or unable to rally to the Brotherhood's side, the regime imprisoned thousands of Brothers and frightened many others into exile. In the mid-1960s, Nasser faced one more scare from the MB, albeit on a significantly smaller scale, but by and large, the events of 1954 sealed the Brothers' fate for the balance of the Nasser era. Consequently, Nasser was able to steer the Egyptian polity down a fairly secular path, and in this sense fulfilled the hopes and expectations of modernization theorists and Western diplomats of that time.

One might quickly add that Nasser and most of his close colleagues saw themselves as devout Muslims with a modern outlook on life. Thus, the Brotherhood's demise should in no way be construed as an attack on Muslim values from the regime's perspective. Most regime leaders continued to refer to Islamic values in their political and personal lives. Still, one should note that Nasser's choice of a relatively secular path—certainly a more secular path than would have been taken by the MB—kept most individuals in the significant Coptic Christian minority somewhat more receptive to his regime.

Nearly all of the Free Officers were Muslims. Non-Muslims experienced discrimination in government employment during Nasser's regime. The greatest discrimination was experienced by members of Egypt's tiny but dynamic Jewish community, with most of that tension growing out of Arab-Israeli warfare. Government agencies tended to exacerbate, rather than diminish, that tension, ultimately resulting in a massive exodus by Egyptian and non-Egyptian Jews after the 1956 Suez War.

Nasser's objective was the creation of a modernized, economically diverse country enjoying a far more equitable distribution of its wealth, a goal shared by nearly all Egyptians. Only the tiny elite of large landowners and monopoly capitalists stood to lose as a result of the economic reforms Nasser originally envisioned. Most Egyptians had grown sick of foreign political and economic influence, and of socioeconomic stagnation. So the catalyst for change was inspired by internal forces and enjoyed broad civilian support, with specific external actors, like the U.S. government, hopeful that these reforms would reduce the likelihood of Egypt's experiencing a Communist revolution.

The specific goals of the new regime were spelled out in the "Six Principles of the Revolution." These included: (1) an end to imperialism; (2) an end to feudalism; (3) an end to monopoly capitalists' influence; (4) a strengthening of national defense; (5) greater social justice; and (6) a return to parliamentary rule. Translated, these goals signified the regime's ardent desire for termination of British control and the realization of genuine national independence. Construction of a strong military was deemed essential to deter major powers from future interventions, respond to the defeat of 1948, and promote Egypt to regional-power status. Other principles were inspired by a will to extinguish the political and economic power of the king, the large landowning elements, and a small group of super-capitalists. The principles also signaled the regime's hope to promote economic development; to lift the broad peasant masses out of their lives of poverty, poor hygiene, and illiteracy; and to create increasingly interesting job opportunities in the economy's industrial and service sectors.

As events played out, the pursuit of national security not only constituted one of the regime's highest priorities, but also had important, unanticipated implications for many other developmental objectives. It therefore merits primary consideration.

Nasser and his closest colleagues were first and foremost military men. Due to Egypt's low level of industrial and technological development, rapid construction of a strong military necessitated importing large quantities of sophisticated, potentially costly weapons. Because the high-end arms market was an oligopoly, purchases from leading suppliers were fraught with international political ramifications. To make a complicated story short, the major Western producers of weapons (the United States, Great Britain, and France) refused to sell Egypt the type and quantity of weapons deemed necessary. This derived from their agreement to curb arms sales to the Middle East under the 1950 Tripartite Declaration. Failing to obtain weapons in the West and then learning in early 1955 that the French were violating the Tripartite commitment by selling weapons to Israel, the Egyptians decided to shop elsewhere. By September 1955, a deal was struck for a "Czech" (read, Soviet) arms sale to Egypt, an unpalatable move for Western Cold Warriors. In fact, this deal, reinforced by other Egyptian foreign policy changes viewed unfavorably by Western governments, set in motion a long chain of tit-for-tat exchanges culminating in the cancellation of U.S. and British aid to Egypt; Egypt's nationalization of the Suez Canal; and the attack on Egypt by Great Britain, France, and Israel in the Suez War of 1956. The fallout from that war, in turn, had a very heavy impact on Egypt's economic strategic options.

State-Sponsored Economic Development and the
Arab Nationalist Dream

How Nasser's desired socioeconomic changes were to be accomplished was an enormous question mark. Nasser initially held no clear-cut ideological orientation, even laughing when one political journalist asked whether he had one. Nasser's attitude, as I learned through interviews with several of his closest aides, was to proceed by trial and error.[3] Whatever economic policies or strategy produced the desired results would be kept; whatever failed would be quickly jettisoned.

All told, Nasser's regime took Egypt through several phases of economic experimentation. From 1952 to 1956, "Egypt promoted public sector growth but . . . did so either to help the private sector or to undertake projects the private sector could not finance or manage,"[4] such as the Aswan Dam, rural electrification, and the Helwan iron and steel complex. From 1956 to 1960, Egypt experienced "state-guided capitalism,"[5] 1960–63 saw the transition to socialism; and 1963–64 brought a measure of socialist deepening. Finally, in 1968, in the aftermath of the disastrous 1967 Arab-Israeli War (the so-called Six Day War), the country entered into its final phase under Nasser, one involving a small degree of international economic liberalization.

Although these shifts in economic orientation reflected rough economic sailing, often prompted by foreign crises, none of the phases was lacking in method. Indeed, on balance, it is not unfair to regard Egypt and Nasser as repeat, unintended victims of early economic planning models designed by the Western world's leading economists. Western experts of the 1940s and 1950s used the term *modernization* to encompass not only technological change but also social and political change. Many Western experts on Asia believed that poor countries required the state to promote modernization, as had been done so successfully by Japan during the nineteenth-century Meiji reforms. Such experts assumed that countries fresh from decolonization lacked the strong civil societies and institutions, particularly in education and commerce, necessary to promote economic growth. The Sinologist and public figure John King Fairbank believed that such New Deal organizations as the Tennessee Valley Authority could serve as models for government action to fill gaps unmet by the private sector. These ideas reflected the prevailing assumption that "states built nations."[6]

Precisely such thinking was at the forefront of strategic planning regarding Egypt. In many ways Nasser and his closest associates anticipated the 1959 arguments of Seymour Martin Lipset with regard to the social requisites of liberal democracy.[7] They saw Egypt as lacking crucial requisites, such as a large, stable middle class and a literate public, and felt it essential to use the state to create these conditions. But this was no mere coincidence; many of Nasser's key economic advisers had "imbibed" Western development models by studying in the United States, and adopted the Tennessee Valley Authority as a model for rapid economic development in Egypt.

In the regime's early years, there was an obvious willingness to allow capitalists the opportunity to produce positive gains for the entire country. Over time, however, the perceived failings of domestic capitalists combined with a specific unfolding of foreign events to encourage Nasser to adopt an increasingly state-interventionist economic strategy. Although this generated genuine concern in the United States that Nasser's Egypt was "going socialist," ironically the initial inspiration for state-led development projects came from the United States and other Western countries.

One of the regime's first aggressive policies was its 1952 land reform, a policy promoted by the U.S. government in Egypt and numerous other countries at the time. As conceived, the policy was far from anticapitalist. Land reform, it was hoped, would reduce the power of large landowners, create middle-class property holders, decrease the prospects of a peasant-based revolution, and promote economic diversification by pushing large landowners to invest in industry. In practice, large landowners, stung by land reform and wary of the regime leaders' long-run intentions, failed to respond to the regime's repeated pleas for cooperation. While these developments were playing out, Nasser seized upon the 1956 Suez Crisis and war as an opportunity to Egyptianize the economy through the extensive nationalization of foreign assets in addition to the canal itself, leading overnight to the creation of a large public sector. With this new public sector in place and domestic capitalists failing to meet the regime's expectations (and in the eyes of many, incapable, due to their small numbers), Nasser pushed more forcefully for a heavier state role, engendering a transition to a fuller-throated commitment to socialism by the early 1960s.

Egyptian leaders increased their commitment to another Western-inspired economic development strategy, the highly touted strategy of Import Substitution Industrialization (ISI); put simply, the idea that a national economy would reap multiple benefits from the domestic production of goods imported in large quantities. ISI was an important part of Egypt's First Five-Year Plan (1961–65). In addition, the regime invested heavily in human capital. Although the conceptualization and fuller appreciation of human capital was just emerging in the late 1950s, the Nasser regime, motivated by the earlier promises of other nationalist parties, made a concerted effort to improve national literacy, public health, and the overall quality of life. Unfortunately, a closely related concern, family planning, was not given comparable attention until the mid-1960s.

Nasser clearly transgressed the logic of Western planners by embarking on a fuller commitment to socialism in the early 1960s, and by accepting economic advice and assistance from Eastern European Communist states. Reflecting that commitment were policies such as guaranteed full employment to all high school and university graduates, state appropriation of medium- and smaller-size businesses, and state control of prices for housing and a broad range of commodities.

Movement down the socialist path was accompanied by efforts to construct a new, Arab nationalist identity. All prima facie evidence would suggest that few nations on the planet have been better endowed with the requisite elements for the creation of a strong sense of national identity than the ancient people of Egypt. Significantly, Nasser opted to think outside the Egyptian nationalist box and became one of the preeminent Arab nationalist figures of all times.

Nasser initially embraced Arab nationalism in the context of efforts to achieve genuine Egyptian independence and fears of Western imperialism. This "was a policy choice rooted in the utility of Arab solidarity for the achievement and maintenance of Egyptian independence."[8] But in many respects, the Arab nationalist dream took on a life all its own. Individual Arab nation-states turning into provinces within a grand Arab nation-state, spreading across all of North Africa, including the Sudan, and encompassing the Arab nations of the Levant and the Arab peninsula constituted a powerful image. One need not tax the imagination to appreciate the potential political and economic power accruing to a single country in control of 60 percent of the world's proven oil reserves.

Nasser's use of new forms of communication rapidly promoted this vision. The creation of the Voice of the Arabs radio program (*sawt al-'arab*) and a powerful broadcast tower transmitted to a much broader Arab public Nasser's Arab nationalist message, enhanced by his own charismatic oratory. A Western scholar described how he was once listening to a broadcast of a Nasser speech on his balcony in Beirut, only to realize that he need not use his own radio to hear the speech given the great number of others tuned in on their own radios in his neighborhood.[9] This provides ample testimony to what a powerful mechanism the *sawt al-'arab* broadcasts constituted. In this case, the radio broadcasts fulfilled the same crucial function as the spread of print literature had in earlier formations of new national identities elsewhere.[10] But what were the benefits of Nasser's Arab nationalist bid? What is one to make of Nasser's overall nation-building efforts?

One may begin by repeating that Nasser, in contrast to so many other developing nations' leaders, did not face the oftentimes insurmountable challenges posed by the issues of national integration and identity formation. Egypt was no Yugoslavia, Nigeria, Sudan, or Iraq, and its relatively high degree of ethno-religious homogeneity and strong Egyptian identity offered a propitious starting point for any nation-building effort—so propitious, in fact, that he could feel comfortable in going beyond that starting point to promote an Arab nationalist identity. What did confront Nasser were the no less daunting tasks of state building and economic development.

As regarded the creation of a legitimate political order, an initial obstacle was the existence of four rival ideological camps, each with sizeable proponents. Cooperation across these camps was virtually impossible. Yet by playing upon the widespread sentiments of a citizenry that had grown weary of the bickering among rival civilian actors, and exploiting his own enormous charisma, Nasser moved Egypt toward a relatively stable authoritarian political order with a fairly strong secular orientation. Over time, most diehard ideological opponents were imprisoned, exiled, or recruited to regime service. Some, but no great number, were killed.

Most ironically, although many of Nasser's policies eventually earned his regime great antagonism from U.S. policy makers, his initial attitude toward state building and economic development might have made him a veritable poster child for mainstream American diplomats and scholars. On the political front, Egypt was seen as lacking the necessary requisites for a liberal democratic political order. Therefore, it was best for a benign authoritarian ruler to oversee a major socioeconomic transformation to create those conditions. Once that mission was accomplished, that leader would, it was hoped, take his bow and exit the political stage. On the economic front, diversification, and utilization of policies like land reform (Egypt would experience three) and import substitution industrialization (ISI), were the recommendations of the day. Cutting-edge economic policy makers in American and other Western universities touted the virtues, even necessities, of state planning and state-led projects akin to the Tennessee Valley Authority. These ideas were gobbled up by many of Egypt's best and brightest minds, and carried home for implementation by 'Abd al-Nasser's economic advisers.

Dreams Dashed: A Crushing Military Defeat and Economic Stagnation

Middle East realities, however, created major sticking points, especially concerning national independence and national security. What turned Nasser from a "Western" poster child into a scapegoat owed greatly to fallout from his insistence on ensuring Egypt a strong system of defense and on promoting his foreign policy making. With young officers controlling the reins of political power—officers who had suffered a humiliating military defeat and perceived a continuing, regional threat from Israel—his priorities were understandable. Through his dogged pursuit of genuine national independence and the construction of a strong military, Nasser brought Egypt to a critical juncture by 1956. The political victory registered by Nasser by the end of the Suez War sent his popularity through the roof, not only in Egypt, but throughout the region and most of the Third World. He had successfully nationalized the Suez Canal, and U.S. and Soviet pressure forced Britain and France to relinquish control of the strategic waterway. As a new, major figure in the struggle against Western imperialism, Nasser's stock rose precipitously in the Soviet Union and other Communist countries. This yielded significant economic and military benefits from the East, and also positioned him to play off the East against the West for the extraction of strategic rent. But an enormous price would be paid for his opposition to conservative Arab regimes, his advocacy of Arab nationalism and eventually Arab socialism, his enmity toward Israel, and his antagonism of major Western powers.

To begin, the 1956 effort to Egyptianize the economy compelled a significant number of highly talented entrepreneurs and professionals to exit Egypt. This included many foreigners and *mutamasriyun* Egyptians who dominated modern sector positions. Extensive nationalization of foreign companies was accompanied by discrimination against expatriates, "foreign" minorities, Levantine types, Greeks, Jews holding foreign passports, and Egyptian Jews whose love for Egypt was immense. As a group, many of these individuals were playing a developmental role comparable to that later played by ethno-religious minorities in Southeast Asia. Thus, the loss of this human capital was inestimable—a serious setback to hopes for rapid economic development.

Second, what were the fruits of imagining an Arab nation? If Arab nationalism initially struck many as more mirage than manifest destiny, Egypt's and Syria's founding of the United Arab Republic (UAR) in 1958 raised the prospects for an actual payoff. This effort, which collapsed in 1961, was followed by unity discussions involving Egypt, Syria, and Iraq in 1963 that also proved stillborn. Nonetheless, both efforts demonstrated the possibility of utilizing a common Arab identity to create a grand Arab nation, thus perpetuating the dream in many Arab minds. Nasser, himself, may have become even more convinced of the usefulness of the idea over time.

But other consequences of Nasser's pursuit of Arab nationalist objectives merit examination. Although greatly reluctant to sign on to Syrian pleas for unity in 1958, and chastened by the UAR experience in practice, Nasser was convinced through the UAR's demise that Arab capitalists, conservative regional actors (Saudi Arabia, Jordan), and international capitalist interests in general were actively involved in choking off Arab unity undertakings. This belief, in turn, fueled his desire to clip the wings of additional strata of Egyptian capitalists in 1961, introduce the June 1962 National Charter embracing "an Arab application of scientific socialism," and open registration in early 1963 for a new regime party, the Arab Socialist Union (ASU). It also prompted military intervention in North Yemen's civil war from 1962 to 1967 on behalf of the radical republican regime. Ultimately, upward of 70,000 Egyptian troops struggled against pro-royalist guerrilla forces in a draining, futile effort.

The farther Nasser advanced down a pro-socialist, anti-monarchical, anti-Zionist, anti-Western imperialist strategic path, the more he invited a regional and international backlash. Regime elites took careful note of U.S. support for the removal of pro-socialist or pro-Communist Third World regimes: Patrice Lumumba's assassination in the Democratic Republic of the Congo in 1961; the intervention in Vietnam in 1963; and the overthrow of Brazil's Goulart regime in 1964, Ghana's Kwame Nkrumah in 1966, and Indonesia's Sukarno in 1966. Egypt's leaders became convinced that their regime was on an American hit list. They suspected Saudi and CIA figures were involved in reactivating domestic opponents (the Muslim Brothers and Wafdists) and abetting the 1965 Brotherhood conspiracy. With the U.S. government cutoff in food assistance in 1966, Egyptian leaders believed that U.S. President Lyndon Johnson had declared a "silent war" on Egypt, and they knew that the Saudis were heavily backing their adversaries in North Yemen. From their perspective, U.S. support for Israel in its crushing defeat of Egypt in June 1967, including occupation of Egypt's Sinai Peninsula, was the consummate act in this series of events.

In the end, the Nasser regime does not appear to have benefited very greatly from its effort to bolster Arab nationalist sentiments. There is no gainsaying that Nasser's charisma and popularity extended well beyond Egypt's borders and touched the hearts and minds of countless Arab cousins, but efforts to destabilize Arab monarchies were successfully resisted in many countries and induced costly reprisals. True, the spirit of Arab solidarity led conservative, oil-rich Arab nations to come to Egypt's financial assistance in the aftermath of the disastrous 1967 war, but this aid was contingent on Egypt's promise to end its promotion of radical Arab positions and withdraw its forces from North Yemen. Had Nasser lived to a ripe old age, his dream of creating a grand Arab nation might have gained traction, but this is highly conjectural. During Nasser's lifetime, the tangible costs of his Arab nationalist bid appear to have outweighed its benefits. Unlike Atatürk, Nasser failed to appreciate what lay beyond his grasp. He saw the opportunities not the constraints. The obligations of Arab nationalism helped carry Nasser into the 1967 war, and that war—so costly in blood and treasure—shook Egypt to its core. It caused Egyptians to question their alliance with the Soviet Union and search for alternative development strategies, triggering the rebirth of the Islamist movement.

Meanwhile, due to the absence of family planning and other factors, Egypt's population grew from 21 million to 33 million from 1952 to 1970, a 57 percent increase. This growth rate nearly overwhelmed government efforts to improve national literacy and public health. Improvements were made; for example, life expectancy at birth increased from 42.4 to 49.7 years from 1955 to 1970,[11] and illiteracy decreased by nearly 5 percent from 1952 to 1970. However, GDP per capita rose from $147 in 1960 to just $218 in 1970;[12] and enormous inequities remained along social class and regional (urban vs. rural) lines. The state heavily subsidized many basic goods, but in a manner that it could not afford.

The structure of education caused difficulties in combating illiteracy, with excessive emphasis and expenditure on higher education and subsequent employment. From 1961 to 1964, the regime introduced free university education to all secondary school graduates and, inspired by an Eastern socialist logic, guaranteed employment to all secondary school and university graduates. In a decade, university graduates doubled without any accompanying increase in job possibilities and created twice the percentage of university students as in Great Britain.[13] Moreover, higher education remained skewed in favor of the arts, law, and commerce (70 percent), rather than the more needed science, medical, and engineering disciplines (30 percent).[14]

A more educated public is a more politically demanding one, and the question became "What is to be done with these graduates?" In practice and again in keeping with its socialist orientation, the regime placated graduates with bureaucratic and state-owned-enterprise jobs, creating a large pool of redundant labor, a bloated bureaucracy, and low productivity and low job satisfaction among the country's most educated citizens. The only good news for Nasser was that, unlike his successors, he never really faced the hair-pulling consequences of this enormous misallocation of human resources. He witnessed very little labor unrest. The biggest anti-regime protests were caused by the 1967 war, not economic considerations, and were led by students infuriated by the leniency shown to Egypt's wartime military commanders. Most students remained largely supportive of Nasser.

On the economic scene, ISI proved as problematic in Egypt as it did elsewhere because the cost of the requisite technology and capital goods imports outpaced the strategy's putative benefits at reducing imports. Although Egypt registered a fairly impressive 6 percent growth rate for much of 1956–63, the economy fizzled in the mid-1960s in large part because ISI, through the creation of a severe foreign exchange shortage, had run its course.[15] Also, by casting their lot with Eastern European nations and alienating many Western capitalists, Egyptian leaders reduced to almost nil foreign direct investment from the far more prosperous West, and lost potentially large tourist revenues from far more affluent Westerners. Following the 1967 war, improved relations with conservative, oil-rich Arab nations encouraged Nasser to open up Egypt's economy to attract greater foreign investment, but on balance, rebuilding the military while simultaneously fighting the 1968–70 War of Attrition with Israel weighed heavily on the country's resources and made significant economic advances impossible.

The Trials and Tribulations of State Building

Finally, what was the result of Nasser's state-building efforts? Did he create institutions enjoying widespread legitimacy? One of the greatest inherent difficulties faced by any authoritarian regime is its lack of mechanisms to determine what degree of support it retains from its citizenry. Genuine elections are not held and public opinion polls are unreliable because many people are wary of expressing dissenting views. Absent demonstrable measures of one's own popularity or legitimacy, paranoia often ensues, fostering a proliferation of costly intelligence apparatuses designed to protect the regime from its enemies. In Egypt, such conditions emerged and prevented Nasser from fully appreciating and exploiting his own popularity. This may have impaired his efforts to take even bolder domestic policy initiatives for fear of a military coup or strong civilian opposition.

During most of the 1950s, the regime lacked effective, internal watchdog institutions. Regime elites were allowed to enjoy the spoils of power, perhaps in part to retain their loyalty. Although Nasser personally led a Spartan existence, this was not true of many others, including his erstwhile best friend, 'Abd al-Hakim 'Amer, and many who served (or "served" themselves) under him. There was great corruption in the military, which was 'Amer's preserve, and beyond, as the military provided public sector sinecures for retired officers, family members, and friends. The concomitant decline in military preparedness also helped set the stage for the June 1967 debacle.

Once a greater commitment to socialism was made and socialist watchdog institutions were erected in the Arab Socialist Union, intra-regime discord developed.

This friction, most of which escaped the public eye, helps explain many regime shortcomings during the 1960s. In essence, Nasser had to fight many battles with his peers. I became aware of the depth of this discord when I interviewed former military Chief of Staff Muhammad Fawzi. The aging general literally reduced himself to tears recounting how difficult 'Amer's cronies had made his life. So although Nasser successfully used his charisma to build the party institutions of the ASU, he failed to use them to maximum effect against major regime-based opponents of his socialist transformation. While the entire world saw Nasser as the lion of Egypt, many regime insiders considered 'Amer to be the most powerful man in the country.

If Nasser failed to exploit fully the ASU to remove corrupt and obstructionist regime elements, he also refrained from using that organization's full potential to mobilize broad social support for economic development purposes. In nearly all industrially advanced countries, whether in the West or the East, the jump to a higher material standard of living depended on impressive capital accumulation and investment. Typically, this resulted from squeezing the citizenry to pay the development bill. In Egypt, Nasser oversaw the construction of a regime capable of such change. The ASU recruited and trained enough cadres, and created enough believers in Nasser and his regime, to make the general public endure a period of sacrifice and austerity for the sake of future generations, as evidenced by the many advocates of belt-tightening in the mid-to-late 1960s. In short, he had laid the foundation for a legitimate political order.

Yet Nasser eschewed the more difficult path. He chose not to utilize fully the ASU's potential and not to make the broad public pay the price for development.[16] In the 1950s, he extracted resources from existing repositories of accumulated wealth, both domestic and foreign. In the early to mid-1960s, he moved against domestic capitalists. In both cases, he crossed his fingers that state bureaucrats could manage these assets more effectively than their capitalist creators, and simultaneously, he sought to maximize the extraction of strategic rent from both the West and the East. When U.S. aid was no longer forthcoming to pay the development bill in the mid-1960s, when push came to shove, he backed away from taking the required steps for economic development through a genuine "socialist deepening."

By 1965–66, Nasser had subdued his greatest civilian opponents, the Muslim Brothers and pro-capitalist liberal democrats (Wafdists). Most Marxists—the Egyptian Communist Party unilaterally dissolved itself—were working for the regime. Nasser's popularity was enormous. He could have exploited it to democratize politics, along either socialist or liberal democratic lines, and squeezed the Egyptian public to pay for an economic takeoff. He failed to do so. Again, part of the problem may have resided in his fear of 'Amer, the military, and numerous intelligence services. Once the 'Amer threat was snuffed out in the aftermath of the 1967 war debacle and 'Amer's mysterious suicide, Nasser focused on the need to rebuild Egypt's shattered military. But rapid reconstruction of the military brought an unprecedented dependence upon the Soviet Union, fostering fears that the Soviets might exploit their enhanced influence by backing more pro-Soviet elements within the Egyptian regime. These factors may help explain why Nasser—who was staunchly antiCommunist on the home front—forsook austerity and a socialist deepening at this critical juncture.

Alternatively, Nasser might have chosen to open up the system, leading the ASU into competition in a multiparty format with genuine elections. If so, it seems highly probable that Nasser would have won strong electoral support for his policies. Unfortunately for Nasser, he refrained from measuring his popularity in genuine elections. Instead, presidential plebiscites were held in which his astonishing victories—for example, 99.999 percent in 1965—remained completely unconvincing.

In the end, Nasser's personal health became his biggest problem. He did not take power with any term limit in mind. Coming from a family whose members were long-lived, he hoped to enjoy a comparable fate. He believed, despite his debilitating diabetes, that he could oversee major transformations in Egypt's political economic situation, including a possible return to civilian rule, in his own lifetime. (For comparison, Fidel Castro, though slightly younger, was Nasser's contemporary.) Nasser, it turns out, miscalculated his own life expectancy by several decades, dying at the age of fifty-two. This is significant in that the shifts of his rule leave room for speculation across a fairly broad array of possibilities as to where he would have taken Egypt had he lived as long as Castro. Committed socialist? Highly likely. But liberal democrat or single-party authoritarian? Who really knows?

Ultimately, all assessments of Nasser's strategies versus results are clouded by his physical inability to see them through. The millions who grieved his death showed how tremendously popular he remained with Egypt's broad masses, such that one wonders what might have happened if he had lived long enough to oversee the "victory" of the 1973 war. But in the end, having disparaged the ASU himself, Nasser died without leaving any stable, fully legitimate political order in place, thereby facilitating his successor's ability to lead Egypt in a very different direction just years after his passing.

Notes

1. Francis Fukuyama, ed., *Nation-Building* (Baltimore: Johns Hopkins University Press, 2005), 3.

2. P.J. Vatikiotis, *The History of Modern Egypt,* 4th ed. (Baltimore: Johns Hopkins University Press, 1991), 335.

3. Kirk J. Beattie, *Egypt During the Nasser Years* (Boulder, CO: Westview Press, 1994). Many of the observations in this chapter are drawn from this book, which relied heavily on over 200 formal interviews with Nasser regime elites, key opposition members, and other well-informed observers.

4. Alan Richards and John Waterbury, *A Political Economy of the Middle East,* 3rd ed. (Boulder, CO: Westview Press, 2008), 188.

5. Patrick O'Brien, *The Revolution in Egypt's Economic System* (London: Oxford University Press, 1966).

6. David Ekbladh, "From Consensus to Crisis: The Postwar Career of Nation-Building in U.S. Foreign Relations," in Fukuyama, ed., *Nation-Building,* 21.

7. Seymour Martin Lipset, "Some Social Requisites of Democracy: Economic Development and Political Legitimacy," *American Political Science Review* 53, 69–105.

8. James Jankowski, "'Nasserism' and Egyptian State Policy," in James Jankowski and Israel Gershoni, eds., *Rethinking Nationalism in the Arab Middle East* (New York: Columbia University Press, 1997), 161–62.

9. Michael Hudson, Professor of Government, Georgetown University, Washington, DC.

10. Benedict Anderson, *Imagined Communities: Reflections on the Origins and Spread of Nationalism,* 2nd ed. (London: Verso, 1991).

11. United Nations Common Database. See http://globalis.gvu.unu.edu/indicator_detail.cfm?country=EG&indicatorid=18.

12. The World Bank. See http://earthtrends.wri.org/text/economics-business/variable-638.html.

13. Vatikiotis, *History of Modern Egypt,* 477.

14. Ibid.

15. John Waterbury, *The Egypt of Nasser and Sadat* (Princeton, NJ: Princeton University Press, 1983), 90.

16. These views are shared by John Waterbury. See ibid., 307–36.

Part III

Creating New States:
Divergent Pairs

9

Underdevelopment in Haiti

PHILIPPE R. GIRARD

Abstract: *This case study describes Haiti's transition from the richest colony in the New World in the eighteenth century to one of the poorest countries in the twentieth century. Large plantations were subdivided into subsistence plots in the early nineteenth century, and subsequent environmental degradation through deforestation and erosion destroyed formerly productive lands. Haiti's precipitous economic decline, however, took place after the colonial powers—Spain, France, and the United States—had left, most notoriously under the three-decade-long rule of the Duvalier family. The Duvaliers feared and persecuted the educated elites who might contest their rule, causing an exodus of educated Haitians. The Duvaliers' hopes for economic development based on tourism, labor-intensive exports, and foreign aid could not keep up with population growth. Their overthrow, however, brought political instability that undermined hopes for prosperity. Despite a stable international security environment, a rich endowment in natural resources, and proximity to the U.S. market, Haiti has been unable to move beyond a tradition of strongman rule and highly flawed political leadership.*

Haiti stands out among its Caribbean peers as the first country in the region to obtain its independence, following the only successful slave revolt in the history of the world. Since most of Haiti's white planters were killed or exiled shortly after independence, its population is noticeably darker-skinned than those of its neighbors, the Dominican Republic in particular. The dual French and African culture it inherited from its colonial past also distinguishes it from the largely Iberian world of Latin America. The dominant Créole (Kreyol) language originated as a mixture of African languages and the slave owners' French, while Vaudou (Vodun) is a syncretic religion combining Catholic saints with spirits worshiped in Dahomey (Benin) and the Congo. Both Créole and Vaudou are uniquely Haitian cultural artifacts, yet they have been denounced by outsiders (and, until recently, elite Haitians as well) as uncivilized and barbaric.

Haiti is also uniquely poor. The World Bank estimates that Haitians have a gross national income (GNI) of $480 per capita and a life expectancy at birth of fifty-nine years.[1] UN statistics differ slightly, setting the per capita Haitian gross domestic product (GDP) at $390, but these numbers all put Haiti well below the

154

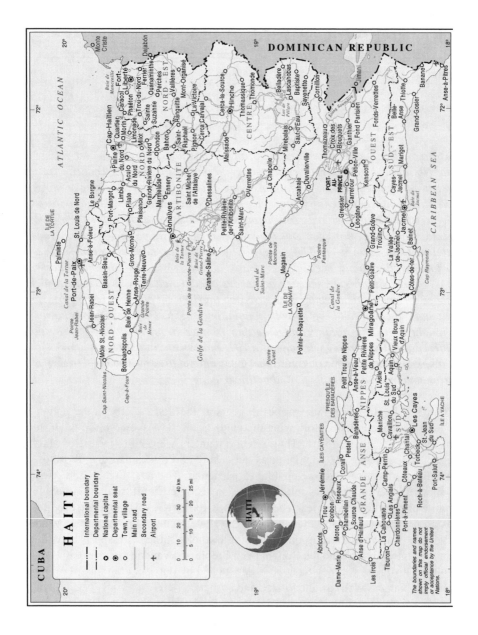

HAITI

International boundary
Departmental boundary
National capital
Departmental seat
Town, village
Main road
Secondary road
Airport

0 10 20 30 40 km
0 5 10 15 20 25 mi

CUBA

DOMINICAN REPUBLIC

ATLANTIC OCEAN

CARIBBEAN SEA

Monte Cristi
Dajabón
Fort-Liberté
Caracol
Ferrier
Ouanaminthe
Perches
Vallières
Mont-Organisé
Fort-Quartier
Morin
Phaëton
Sainte-Suzanne
Cap-Haïtien
Trou-du-Nord
Limonade
Milot
Bahon
Acula
Plaine du Nord
Grande-Rivière du Nord
Dondon
Ranquitte
Saint-Raphaël
Pignon
La Victoire
Cerca Carvajal
Limbé
Plaisance
Pilate
Port-Margot
Le Borgne
Marmelade
Saint Michel de l'Attalaye
Bassin-Bleu
Gros-Morne
Terre-Neuve
Ennery
Dessalines
La Chapelle
Verrettes
Maïssade
Cerca-la-Source
Thomassique
Thomonde
Hinche
Belladère
Lascahobas
Baptiste
Savanette
Cornillo
Jimaní
St. Louis de Nord
Anse-à-Foleur
Jean-Rabel
Môle St.-Nicolas
Anse-Rouge
Anse-à-Foleur
Gonaïves
Petite-Rivière de l'Artibonite
Saint-Marc
Arcahaie
Duvalierville
Thomazeau
Croix des Bouquets
Ganthier
Fond Parisien
Fonds-Verrettes
Pétion-Ville
Grand-Goâve
Léogâne
Carrefour
Bainet
Jacmel
Côtes-de-fer
Belle-Anse
Thiotte
Grand-Gosier
Banane
Anse-à-Pitres
Miragoâne
Petit-Goâve
Vieux Bourg d'Aquin
Aquin
St. Louis du Sud
Les Cayes
Cavaillon
Torbeck
Chantal
St. Jean du Sud
Maniche
Baradères
Anse-à-Veau
Petite Rivière de Nippes
Petit Trou de Nippes
L'Asile
Camp-Perrin
Côteaux
Roche-à-Bateau
Port-Salut
Les Anglais
Chardonnières
La Cahouane
Tiburon
Anse-d'Hainault
Les Irois
Dame-Marie
Moron
Chambellan
Source Chaude
Corail
Pestel
Roseaux
Bonbon
Jérémie
Trou Bonbon
Abricots
Chalon
Coteaux

PORT-AU-PRINCE
Gressier
Kenscoff

NORD-OUEST
NORD
NORD-EST
ARTIBONITE
CENTRE
OUEST
SUD-EST
SUD
NIPPES
GRANDE-ANSE

Île de la Tortue
Île de la Gonâve
Île à Vache

Golfe de la Gonâve
Canal de Saint-Marc
Canal de la Gonâve

PRESQU'ÎLE DES BARADÈRES
PRESQU'ÎLE DU SUD
ILES CAYEMITES

Dominican Republic ($3,088 and seventy years, respectively) and the Caribbean average ($4,985 and sixty-seven years). Forty-six percent of Haitians do not have access to the minimum dietary requirements.[2] The Haitian minimum wage doubled from thirty-six to seventy gourdes in 2003, but the new standard only amounted to two dollars a day. Taking inflation into account, the International Monetary Fund concluded that the 2006 minimum wage represented a mere 17.9 percent of its 1981 counterpart.[3] Even this paltry sum was an unattainable dream to many Haitians given the country's chronic unemployment rate and poor enforcement of labor laws.

Strangely, Haiti, the poorest country in the Western Hemisphere, was the New World's most prosperous colony in the late eighteenth century, when the city of Cap Français was known as the "Paris of the Antilles" and "rich as a Créole" was a common expression.[4] What led to this stunning reversal in Haiti's economic fortunes has been the subject of much historiographical inquiry. In the nineteenth century, Western writers were prompt to point to the black race's inferiority as the main reason for Haiti's decline after French rule ended.[5] This school of thought is largely discredited nowadays, though some scholars still emphasize specifically Haitian traits (cultural, not racial) that impede economic development.[6] The dominant paradigm today, particularly in Haitian and liberal academic circles, points to Haiti's economic and political dependency on its more powerful neighbors. It emphasizes the legacy of colonialism and neo-imperialism, first Spanish, then French, and now American.[7] A third school of thought, embraced by Western conservatives and, to a large extent, this essay, focuses on more recent developments. While acknowledging the brutality of the colonial experience, it concludes that contemporary internal factors—racial tensions, political instability, and poor governance in particular—are the primary reasons for Haiti's current poverty.[8]

Haiti's Environment and Colonial Legacy

A dearth of natural resources is no impediment to economic development (as Japan and Singapore have shown), while an embarrassment of geological riches can coincide with abject poverty (as in the Congo-Zaïre). Haiti's environment, while challenging in some respects, offers a few significant opportunities. Haiti occupies the western third, or 10,641 square miles, of the island of Hispaniola in the northern Caribbean (the Dominican Republic occupies the rest). Though large by Caribbean standards, Haiti's land mass is only partially usable due to its mountainous topography. Sheltered from the moist trade winds, Haiti also tends to be more susceptible to drought than the Dominican Republic, particularly in the arid Northwest. Like all Caribbean islands, Haiti is occasionally plagued by hurricanes, earthquakes, and tropical diseases.

Among Haiti's assets are some bauxite, marble, gold, and copper deposits and, until modern times, its rich soil and tropical woods. Haiti also occupies a strategic location along the Windward Passage, is home to one of the best natural harbors in the region (Môle Saint-Nicolas), and is located close to rich potential markets in North America. Its balmy climate and long, picturesque coastline make it as good a candidate for mass tourism as any other Caribbean island.

Environmental degradation is a leading factor in Haiti's economic decline.[9] Haiti's once-luxuriant forest cover first receded in the eighteenth century, when the French cleared the plains to make way for plantations.[10] As Haiti's population grew from 300,000 at independence to its current 9 million, its largely agrarian workforce gradually occupied all the arable land.[11] By the 1940s, a land shortage forced Haitians to clear ever more marginal lands on steep hillsides, leading to significant soil erosion and economic problems depicted in Jacques Roumain's novel, *Master of the Dew* (1944). The process worsened in the 1970s as growing poverty incited peasants to cut the remaining trees and sell them as charcoal. Today, only 3.8 percent of Haiti's land area is forested, compared with 28.4 percent in the Dominican Republic.[12] This natural disaster is largely manmade. When faced with deforestation in the 1970s, Dominican dictator Joaquín Balaguer embraced proactive land-use policies, which averted the environmental catastrophe that befell his neighbor.

Haiti's colonial experience began in December 1492, when Christopher Columbus reached the northern coast of an island he called Española (Hispaniola) during his first voyage to the New World. Though Spaniards found very little gold, Haitian nationalists point to the subsequent Spanish colonization, which lasted until 1697, as the first incident in a long history of foreign exploitation of Haiti's riches that led directly to today's economic predicament.[13] More significantly, war, hard work, famine, and disease led to the virtual annihilation of the indigenous Tainos within fifty years of Columbus's arrival, a process vividly described in Bartolome de las Casas' *Short Account of the Destruction of the Indies* (1552).

French colonial rule—which began in 1697 (when France and Spain divided Hispaniola into what became Haiti and the Dominican Republic) and ended with the Haitian slave revolt of 1791 to 1804—was marked by unprecedented economic prosperity, but also widespread labor abuse. France imported over one million African slaves to Saint-Domingue, as the colony was called.[14] At the colony's height in the late 1780s, it was a world leader in the production of sugar (80,000 tons) and coffee (40,000 tons). It had 7,000 plantations, including 800 heavily capitalized and profitable sugar plantations. The value of French assets (including slaves) amounted to 1.5 to 3 billion livres, depending on estimates.[15] The colony's trade employed 15,000 sailors and over 1,000 U.S. and French ships.[16] In the 1790s, the colony became the second-largest U.S. trading partner after England.[17] France, which suffered from a 70-million livres deficit in its balance of trade in European markets, ran an 80-million livres surplus overall thanks to re-exports of colonial produce.[18] Profits from the plantation system, however, were unevenly distributed. The emancipated "people of color" (*gens de couleur*) owned plantations and slaves of their own, particularly in the coffee industry, but the bulk of the profits went to French merchants and planters, while 90 percent of the colonial population consisted of slaves.

The plantation system withered after independence. Most cities and plantations were destroyed during the long, brutal war of independence, along with half of the island's population. Haiti's first independent leader, Jean-Jacques Dessalines, faced an economic quandary as he debated whether he should break apart the large colonial estates and distribute the land to the former slaves—a policy that would please his subjects but dramatically reduce the sugar exports that had made Saint-Domingue so prosperous in colonial times—or preserve the plantation system—an option that would allow continued exports but also require forced labor. Dessalines embraced the latter system, as did his successor, Henri Christophe, but such policies were eventually abandoned due to popular opposition.[19]

By the 1820s, most plantations had been divided or abandoned, and Haitian agriculture was characterized by small subsistence farming supplemented by limited coffee exports; the pattern has continued to the present time, except for a short-lived attempt to re-create large estates during the first U.S. occupation of Haiti, in the 1920s.[20] Subsistence farming yielded a modest, but sufficient, income as long as land was plentiful; but productivity was low and conditional on a supply of additional land to accommodate larger generations. When the supply of available land ran out in the middle of the twentieth century, overpopulation, deforestation, and hunger ensued. Other legacies of the slavery era were a pattern of black-mulatto rivalries, lack of qualified labor, and adversarial relations with neighboring slave powers.

Those who view foreign exploitation as the source of Haiti's current economic ills point out that imperialism continued to affect Haiti even after independence. In 1825 France imposed a 150-million-franc indemnity in exchange for diplomatic recognition; the indemnity was never fully paid, but it contributed to the nation's budgetary instability in the nineteenth century. Other practitioners of gunboat diplomacy, such as Germany, used various diplomatic disputes as an excuse to exact further payments later in the century. The United States, citing security concerns and political instability, invaded and occupied Haiti from 1915 to 1934, and repeatedly meddled in Haitian politics thereafter. In 1937 Dominican dictator Rafael Trujillo expelled most of the Haitian migrant workers living in the Dominican Republic and ordered as many as 25,000 of them killed. Exploitation of Haitian cane-cutters in the Dominican Republic, itself a reflection of the two countries' tense relations, has endured until the present time.[21]

Some of Haiti's troubles, however, were self-inflicted. From the end of Faustin Soulouque's reign in 1859 to the U.S. invasion in 1915, Haitian politics grew increasingly unstable, leading to constant upheaval, destruction of property, budget deficits, and, ultimately, U.S. invasion. Widespread graft resulted in a skewed allocation of resources. Infrastructure and education were neglected, except under Fabre-Nicolas Geffrard (1858–67) and Lysius Salomon (1879–88), while corruption, payments on foreign debts, and the army absorbed a disproportionate share of the national treasury.

Haiti's history offers fascinating insights into its citizens' worldview, society, and politics. Blaming all of Haiti's problems on the legacy of foreign imperialism, however, fails to take into account the fact that the Haitian economy began the most precipitous segment of its long-term decline only in the 1960s, by which time Spanish, French, and U.S. colonial rule had been over for 260, 160, and 30 years, respectively. Accordingly, one cannot fully understand Haitian underdevelopment without a thorough analysis of the failed development strategies of Haiti's more recent rulers.

Consolidation of Power Under Papa Doc

In 1960, three years after François Duvalier (a.k.a. "Papa Doc") took over as president, Haiti was no longer the nexus of world trade it had been in the 1780s, but it was by no means impoverished either. At $800, its GDP per capita was almost identical to that of the Dominican Republic. Over the next forty years, Haiti's GDP was cut in half, to $430, while that of the Dominican Republic tripled, to $2,500.[22] Haiti and the Dominican Republic's 1960 per capita GDPs were equivalent to those of North and South Korea, two countries that were also destined to follow markedly different economic paths.

To speak of a development strategy during Papa Doc's rule (1957–71) is somewhat anachronistic, since economic development ranked low in his priorities. Faced with a succession of coup attempts and an insatiable thirst for power, Papa Doc focused almost exclusively on political survival at the expense of everything else, the welfare of his constituents included. His rule was marked by a level of political oppression that was unusual even by Haiti's standards as real or suspected rivals, along with their most distant relatives, were arrested, tortured, and executed.[23]

Papa Doc's stated aim was to institute a black revolution. With some historical justification, he lamented that Haiti had thrown off French colonial rule only to look up to its culture, religion, and race as superior. The pattern was particularly noticeable among the urban mulatto elite, including President Jean-Pierre Boyer (1818–43), which was predominantly French speaking, French educated, Catholic, Francophile, and eager to lighten its skin through careful marriage strategies.[24] Only with the U.S. occupation of the 1920s did a black nationalist cultural movement, known as *noirisme,* appear in reaction to the racism of occupation troops and the humiliation of foreign rule. Jean Price-Mars, a leading figure of the *noiriste* school, asserted that Haiti's African heritage was an integral part of the country's national identity and that the Créole language, black race, and Vaudou religion should be celebrated, not scorned.[25] Papa Doc, himself an eager ethnologist and practitioner of Vaudou, publicly celebrated the nation's revolutionary heroes (Dessalines in particular), changed the national flag from blue and red to black and red in his honor, and stridently denounced foreign imperialism (even as he allied himself with the United States and signed a concordat with the Catholic Church).

Despite Papa Doc's lack of interest in economic matters, his policies had notable economic consequences. Embezzlement, always a problem in Haitian politics, grew as he aggressively sought funds to finance his massive internal security apparatus, including the Haitian Army and the dreaded Tontons Macoutes, the personal secret police of the Duvalier family. (The name Tontons Macoutes derives from the Haitian Créole fairytale figure, a Christmas-eve kidnapper of bad children, who then never return.) Meanwhile, Papa Doc neglected to maintain the country's infrastructure and even banned a promising literacy organization for fear that it was infiltrated by left-wing opponents. The illiteracy rate stood above 60 percent at the end of the Duvalierist era. Wanton political violence, which did not spare even well-connected officials and foreigners (the son of the military attaché in the U.S. embassy was kidnapped), scared away foreign investors and brought an end to the uptick in tourism experienced during the mellower years of President Paul Magloire (1950–56).

Educated elites, who were the most politically rebellious and least receptive to the regime's black nationalist agenda, bore the brunt of Papa Doc's rule of terror. The period thus saw a notable rise in the emigration rate of Haitian nationals, a brain drain that has yet to reverse. Haiti had been a leading destination for U.S. freedmen in the nineteenth century. As land grew scarce in the twentieth century, it provided migrant workers to Cuba and the Dominican Republic. The Duvalier era witnessed a new phenomenon as the country's wealthiest citizens fled to New York, Montréal, and Paris.

Economic Development and Foreign Aid Under Bébé Doc

With Papa Doc's death in 1971, the presidency passed to his son, Jean-Claude Duvalier (a.k.a. "Bébé Doc"). A mere eighteen years of age when he took over, plump, harmless-looking, and more interested in fast cars than politics, Bébé Doc was expected to bring about a softening of the murderous Duvalierist regime. Such expectations went unmet. Bébé Doc publicly expressed his commitment to human rights to placate foreign critics, but he kept his father's torture chambers and Macoute militia largely intact.

The Haitian economy revived during the first decade of Bébé Doc's rule as a less visible political repression brought back foreign tourists. The country's natural beauty and vibrant folk art proved particularly attractive to Canadian, French, and African-American tourists, and, less appealingly, sex tourists. The latter grew scarcer after awareness of an epidemic of acquired immunodeficiency syndrome (AIDS) spread in the early 1980s. Haitians resent being targeted as an at-risk population similar to homosexuals or heroin addicts, but scientists have now concluded that rumors on the prevalence of AIDS in Haiti were no urban myth; AIDS indeed transited from Central Africa to the United States via Haiti circa 1969.[26] AIDS infection rates now approach those found in the most affected regions of sub-Saharan Africa.[27] In Haiti as elsewhere, AIDS has proved to be not only a human tragedy, but also a significant drag on the economy, as it primarily affects young adults and its treatment involves lengthy, costly tri-therapies.

The second pillar of the Haitian economy under Bébé Doc was the export industry. Haitian businessmen capitalized on the country's abundant, low-paid, unskilled labor and proximity to the massive U.S. market to become noted exporters of textiles, garments, handicrafts, and various labor-intensive manufactured products such as baseballs. Unfortunately, the number of jobs in the export sector (80,000 at its peak) failed to match natural population growth and the rural exodus from drought-ridden provinces. By the early 1980s, the exile of upper-class political activists was thus dwarfed by the large-scale emigration of lower-class Haitians motivated by economic, rather than political, reasons. Haitian boat people, even though they were generally prevented from immigrating legally to other countries, eventually formed communities in the United States, France, the Dominican Republic, Canada, and the Bahamas that now top 2 million people compared with Haiti's home population of over 8.5 million.

The third and final pillar of Bébé Doc's development model was foreign aid, even though he would have resented being portrayed as an international beggar given the Duvalierist regime's denunciation of foreign imperialism. The United States, France, and international financial institutions—moved by the plight of the impoverished Haitian peasantry, but also eager to support a stable ally in the Cold War—dramatically increased the trickle of foreign aid that had been made available to Bébé Doc's *papa*. By the late 1970s, a full 70 percent of the national budget stemmed from foreign aid, but the reliance on foreign donors had some unforeseen economic and political consequences. It became difficult for Haitian rice farmers to compete with U.S. agricultural surpluses donated at minimal or no cost. The textile industry also faced unfair competition from used clothes donated by the United States, nicknamed *kenedis* after the U.S. president. A significant portion of the national treasury (and hence of the foreign aid that financed it) was siphoned off by Bébé Doc and his associates.

Reliance on foreign donations also made Haiti dependent on donors whose political agendas, however well intentioned, did not always match Haiti's. In the early 1980s, fears that a swine fever epidemic might spread from Haiti to North America led the United States to call for the slaughter of Haiti's pigs. Bébé Doc complied with the request to placate a crucial ally and donor, but it proved ruinous to the Haitian peasants who used pigs as a literal "piggy bank" whose resale value represented the bulk of their savings. By the 1990s, foreign donors were setting lengthy lists of prerequisites before disbursing cash. The increasingly stringent rules were intended to prevent the continued embezzlement of foreign aid; but they also gave aid managers virtual proconsul status over crucial domestic policy decisions. Foreign donors, for example, insisted that state companies be privatized; the reform was probably in Haiti's best interest, but it showed how much national sovereignty had been surrendered in exchange for the biblical bowl of lentils.[28] By 2006, UN representative Juan Gabriel Valdés openly considered turning Haiti into an international protectorate.[29] Foreign aid, which originated in part as an attempt to correct the wrongs inherited from colonial exploitation, had in the end re-created the very colonialist mentality it was supposed to redress.

Post–Duvalier Era Political Instability and Jean-Bertrand Aristide

Despite initial successes, Bébé Doc's development model was largely considered a failure by the mid-1980s. The growth from the export industries and tourism had failed to keep up with population growth, while the foreign aid windfall had been squandered on First Lady Michèle Bennett's fur collection. Popular frustration with corruption, repression, and the Duvalierist black revolution led to demonstrations and Bébé Doc's exile in 1986. Various neo-Duvalierist regimes followed in rapid succession before democratic elections—Haiti's first—were finally organized in December 1990.

The winner, Jean-Bertrand Aristide, seemed destined to offer a radical shift with Haiti's past. Born to a family of black peasants, Aristide tapped into the same hunger for racial pride and social change that Papa Doc had once exploited. But Aristide loudly and courageously denounced the neo-Duvalierist regimes for their human rights violations. An ordained priest, he also invoked liberation theology and advocated the redistribution of the national wealth. His rhetoric struck a chord with Haiti's poor, whose political importance grew as they migrated, by the hundreds of thousands, from the overcrowded countryside to Port-au-Prince slums.

Upon his inauguration as president in February 1991, Aristide announced that social justice and economic development would be his priorities in office. He spoke of achieving "poverty with dignity" and of giving every Haitian a chance to eat one full meal a day.[30] To achieve these goals, he embraced some liberal policies, such as raising the minimum wage. He also intensified the free trade policy initiated in the 1980s to lessen the cost of living of ordinary Haitians. This had the less appealing consequence of exposing Haitian farmers and industrialists to crippling foreign competition. In the name of better government, he fired thousands of excess public servants. Combined with the increase in foreign aid rewarding Haiti's democratic transition, lower expenditures allowed Aristide to balance the national budget.

Aristide's progressive measures, which married a capitalist framework with a social conscience, might well have helped improve Haiti's economic fortunes in the long term. Haiti's competitive political environment, however, overthrew Aristide before his policies had a chance to show positive results. The conservative elements of the Catholic Church, Haitian army, and bourgeoisie, already aghast by the election of a leftist priest of the slums, became alarmed when Aristide allowed (or, some suspected, incited) his more radical supporters to burn to death former Macoute sympathizers in a form of summary justice.[31] In September 1991, a military junta led by Lieutenant General Raoul Cédras overthrew Aristide, allegedly with the acquiescence of the U.S. ambassador.[32]

No Haitian president had ever returned from exile, but Aristide was adamant that, as the first democratically elected president in Haitian history, he should be allowed to finish his five-year term. His reasoning was sound in principle, but his quest for political survival forced him to embrace policies detrimental to Haiti's economic well-being and national sovereignty. Aristide, who had heretofore been known for his anti-Americanism, settled in Washington, D.C., hired lobbyists with Haitian government funds, and cultivated the friendship of the Congressional Black Caucus and the Haitian-American community, whom he used to pressure the Clinton administration.

Aristide first employed his lobbying apparatus to support economic sanctions that eventually placed most of the Haitian economy under an international embargo. The tourist industry, which had already declined in the politically unstable 1980s, disappeared. Foreign aid packages were cancelled. The export sector was crippled; exports of goods and services, which represented 25 percent of the Haitian GDP in 1980s, only amounted to 14 percent in 2006.[33] The boatfuls of emigrants leaving Haiti were a reliable indicator of the severity of the political and economic crisis.

When Cédras reneged on a 1993 agreement to solve the crisis, Aristide found himself with only one remaining option: to advocate a U.S.-led invasion of his own country. Motivated by democratic idealism and the political consequences of the Haitian refugee crisis, the Clinton administration eventually concurred and, on 19 September 1994, the second U.S. occupation of Haiti began. Virtually no fighting was necessary as Cédras fled the country and the Haitian population celebrated the return of their elected president.

Aristide remained a dominant force throughout the next decade as he served out the remainder of his term (1994–96), undermined the policies of his successor, René Préval (1996–2001), then began a second term as president (2001–04). Having returned through the intercession of a U.S.-led multinational force, Aristide initially toned down his criticism of foreign imperialism and advocated class reconciliation. He also benefited from a steep increase in foreign aid as donors pledged an impressive $3.4 billion for 1994–97.[34] Not all the money was eventually disbursed, but it was accompanied by an even larger flow of private funds emanating from the Haitian community in exile. Annual workers' remittances reached $1 billion in 2006, or 20 percent of the country's GDP.[35] Haiti's growing role as a transit point for cocaine probably brought in some money as well, but reliable statistics on the drug trade are by nature hard to come by.[36]

The massive transfusion of foreign cash should have marked a dramatic shift in Haitian economic history; instead, real growth rates, after a sharp dive from 1991 to 1993 and a partial recovery in 1994 and 1995, remained flat or declining thereafter. As a result of his overthrow and exile, Aristide seemed more interested in jockeying for political supremacy than in the economic well-being of his constituents. A particularly heartbreaking case was that of the homeless children of Port-au-Prince, who occasionally ended as victims of modern-day child slavery.[37] Admired for welcoming orphans into his shelter in the 1980s, Aristide now diverted the shelter's budget to fund his propaganda apparatus and eventually sent the children back to the streets in 1999.[38]

In his efforts to woo the highly nationalist Haitian electorate, Aristide increasingly resorted to denunciations of foreign demands for the privatization of state companies and for investigations into political murders allegedly carried out by his associates. After he returned to the presidency in 2001, he stepped up his anti-imperialist rhetoric in preparation for the bicentennial of the Haitian Revolution. In 2003 he demanded that France repay the indemnity it had obtained from Haiti in 1825; with compounded interest, Aristide's request totaled a precise $21,685,155,571.48. He announced that the massive payment, amounting to four times Haiti's annual GDP, would finance new schools, roads, and electrical power plants, and generally set Haiti on a new economic footing.[39] More immediately, the claim sought to redirect his supporters' anger at the lack of economic progress. France immediately and predictably announced that it would never pay. The Haitian population, which had so fervently supported Aristide during his first mandate, remained largely passive when a coalition of former army officers overthrew him for a second time in 2004, allegedly with the backing of France and the United States.[40]

Haiti's Chances

Haiti's unique historical trajectory makes this nation intriguing; but the more singular aspects of its national experience occasionally represent a significant drag on its economic possibilities. Foremost among them is the cult of presidentialism, which harks back to the military regimes inherited from the war of independence. Starting with Dessalines, top-down strongman rule has been the overarching ambition of every political hopeful; checks and balances, coalition building, and the rights of the opposition are anathema to those who see politics as a zero-sum game. Even Aristide, whose rise to the presidency in the 1980s was facilitated by a multiplicity of grassroots organizations, chose to embrace a ruinous embargo rather than abandon his presidential aspirations from 1991 to 1994, and then to precipitate a clash with Préval and the fellow members of his Lavalas Party that paralyzed the country in 1999 and 2000.

The exclusivist approach to presidential power leaves much potential for abuse. Repression and corruption have been the norm ever since Dessalines told his subordinates to "pluck the hen as long as it does not protest too loudly."[41] In 2004, just as Haiti was celebrating the bicentennial of its independence, it reached the top spot in Transparency International's annual survey of the world's most corrupt countries.[42] Conversely, in the absence of a proper venue where ideologies can compete peacefully, aspiring politicians have regularly employed force as the only instrument of political change, leading to a devastating pattern of political instability.

Another potent legacy of the revolutionary era is the explosive nature of Haiti's racial and international discourse. Haitians' well-founded pride in their ancestors' achievements makes them an easy prey for populist orators who tap the popular yearning for patriotism and racial pride, even as they court foreign support and marry (as Bébé Doc and Aristide did) light-skinned upper-class women. Basing an international development strategy on foreign aid even as one bases one's domestic political career on jingoistic diatribes is a difficult balancing act. In Aristide's case, both foreign monies and domestic support collapsed in 2004, sending him into exile for the second time. Misguided nationalist fervor is also responsible for a variety of counterproductive legal provisions, such as the rule that bans expatriates from voting in Haitian elections even as workers' remittances represent a fifth of the Haitian economy.

On a more positive note, the fact that Haiti's downward economic spiral can be traced back to inadequate political leadership also means that a changing political culture can turn Haiti around. Aside from a dispute with the United States over the uninhabited islet of Navassa, Haiti faces no threat to its territorial integrity; the sole risk is that disaffected former officers of its army, which was disbanded in 1995, might decide to invade their own country, as they did in 2004.[43] No underlying factor prevents Haiti from becoming a tourist destination as popular as neighboring Cuba, Jamaica, or the Dominican Republic; tourists merely need some reassurance that political convulsions will not erupt during their vacation. Haiti's large population and close proximity to North American markets make it a prime candidate for an export-based economy; one needs only to lower the staggering non-wage costs of doing business in Haiti (such as poor security and an unreliable electricity supply).[44] The racist comments of nineteenth-century historians notwithstanding, there is nothing wrong with the genetic profile of the Haitian people; but the most enterprising and educated Haitians must be given a chance to practice their trade in Haiti instead of being pushed into emigrating. Only then will Haiti's remarkable potential be fully realized.

Notes

1. http://devdata.worldbank.org/external/CPProfile.asp?PTYPE=CP&CCODE=HTI.

2. United Nations, *Statistical Yearbook for Latin America and the Caribbean 2006* (March 2007), available at http://websie.eclac.cl/anuario_estadistico/anuario_2006/eng/index.asp.

3. International Monetary Fund, *IMF Country Report no. 07/292* (August 2007), 66, available at http://www.imf.org/external/pubs/ft/scr/2007/cr07292.pdf.

4. Pamphile de Lacroix, *La révolution de Haïti* (1819; reprint, Paris: Karthala, 1995), 7, Moreau de Saint-Méry, *Description de la partie française de l'isle Saint-Domingue,* vol. 1 (1795; reprint, Paris: Larose, 1958), 111.

5. Spenser St. John, *Hayti or the Black Republic* (1884; reprint, London: Frank Cass, 1971); Charles Mackenzie, *Notes on Haiti Made during a Residence in that Republic,* vol. 1 (1830; reprint, London: Frank Cass, 1971).

6. Jacques Barros, *Haïti de 1804 à nos jours,* 2 vols. (Paris: L'Harmattan, 1984); Lawrence E. Harrison, *Underdevelopment Is a State of Mind: The Latin American Case* (Cambridge, MA: Harvard University Press, 1985).

7. Immanuel Wallerstein, *World-Systems Analysis: An Introduction* (Durham, NC: Duke University Press, 2004); Noam Chomsky et al., *Getting Haiti Right This Time: The U.S. and the Coup* (Monroe, ME: Common Courage Press, 2004); Paul Farmer, *The Uses of Haiti* (Monroe, ME: Common Courage Press, 1994), Pat Chin et al., eds., *Haiti: A Slave Revolution: 200 Years after 1804* (New York: International Action Center, 2004); J. Christopher

Kovats-Bernat, *Sleeping Rough in Port-au-Prince: An Ethnography of Street Children and Violence in Haiti* (Gainesville, FL: University of Florida Press, 2006).

8. David Nicholls, *From Dessalines to Duvalier: Race, Colour, and National Independence in Haiti* (Cambridge: Cambridge University Press, 1979); Robert D. Heinl, Nancy G. Heinl, and Michael Heinl, *Written in Blood: The Story of the Haitian People, 1492–1995* (New York: University Press of America, 1996); Philippe Girard, *Paradise Lost: Haiti's Tumultuous Journey from Pearl of the Caribbean to Third World Hot Spot* (New York: Palgrave MacMillan, 2005); Laura Jaramillo and Cemile Sancak, "Growth in the Dominican Republic and Haiti: Why Has the Grass Been Greener on One Side of Hispaniola?" *IMF Working Paper WP/07/63* (March 2007), 23, available at http://www.imf.org/external/pubs/ft/wp/2007/wp0763.pdf.

9. Jared Diamond, *Collapse: How Societies Choose to Fail or Succeed* (New York: Viking, 2004), 329–57.

10. Roger Norman Buckley, ed., *The Haitian Journal of Lieutenant Howard, York Hussars, 1796–98* (Knoxville: University of Tennessee Press, 1985), 46.

11. Gérard Barthélémy, *Créoles-bossales: Conflit en Haïti* (Petit Bourg, Guadeloupe: Ibis Rouge, 2000), 41.

12. http://devdata.worldbank.org/external/CPProfile.asp?PTYPE=CP&CCODE=HTI; United Nations, *Statistical Yearbook for Latin America and the Caribbean 2006* (March 2007), available at http://websie.eclac.cl/anuario_estadistico/anuario_2006/eng/index.asp.

13. Jean-Bertrand Aristide and Christophe Wargny, *Jean-Bertrand Aristide: An Autobiography* (New York: Orbis Books, 1993), 143.

14. David P. Geggus, "The French Slave Trade: An Overview," *William and Mary Quarterly* 58, no. 1 (January 2001), 125–26.

15. R. Lepelletier de Saint-Rémy, *Saint-Domingue: Etude et solution nouvelle de la question haïtienne* (Paris: Arthus Bertrand, 1846), 60–75.

16. Paul Butel, "Succès et déclin du commerce colonial français de la Révolution à la Restauration," *Revue économique* 40, no. 6 (November 1989), 1079–82.

17. Ludwell Lee Montague, *Haiti and the United States* (Durham, NC: Duke University Press, 1940), 32, 47; Tim Matthewson, *A Pro-Slavery Foreign Policy: Haitian-American Relations during the Early Republic* (Westport, CT: Praeger, 2003), 83.

18. Alain Plessis, "La Révolution et les banques en France: de la Caisse d'Escompte à la Banque de France," *Revue Economique* 40, no. 6 (November 1989), 1006.

19. Robert K. Lacerte, "The evolution of land and labor in the Haitian revolution, 1791–1820," *Americas* 34, no. 4 (April 1978), 456–58.

20. Spenser St. John, *Hayti or the Black Republic*, 18; Gérard Barthélémy, *Créoles-bossales*, 26, 84–85.

21. Michelle Wucker, *Why the Cocks Fight: Dominicans, Haitians, and the Struggle for Hispaniola* (New York: Hill and Wang, 1999), 95–137; Maurice Lemoine, *Bitter Sugar: Slaves Today in the Caribbean* (1981; reprint, London: Banner Press, 1985), 53–55.

22. Jaramillo and Sancak, "Growth in the Dominican Republic and Haiti," 4.

23. The following overview of the Duvaliers' presidencies is drawn from Elizabeth Abbott, *Haiti: The Duvaliers and Their Legacy* (1988; reprint, New York: Simon & Schuster, 1991) and Bernard Diederich and Al Burt, *Papa Doc: Haiti and Its Dictator* (1969; reprint, Maplewood, NJ: Waterfront Press, 1991).

24. Mackenzie, *Notes on Haiti*, 35, 107; Fortuna Guéry, *Témoignages* (Port-au-Prince: Henri Deschamps, 1950), 15, 72, 74, 77.

25. Michael Largey, *Vodou Nation: Haitian Art Music and Cultural Nationalism* (Chicago: University of Chicago Press, 2006), 2–4, 6, 10.

26. Michael Worobey et al., "The Emergence of HIV/AIDS in the Americas and Beyond," *Proceedings of the National Academy of Sciences* 104, no. 47 (November 2007), 18566–70.

27. Human Development Sector Management Unit, Latin America and the Caribbean Region, *HIV/AIDS in the Caribbean: Issues and Options: A Background Report, Report no. 20491-LAC* (Washington, DC: World Bank, June 2000), 11.

28. International Development Association, *Haiti: Economic Policy Framework Paper for FY 1996–97 to 1998–99, For Official Use Only* (30 September 1996), 27–38, Microenterprise Collection, USAID Library, Port-au-Prince.

29. Jean-Michel Caroit, "Le bilan de la mission de l'ONU suspendu aux élections haïtiennes," *Le Monde* (7 February 2006).

30. Jean-Bertrand Aristide and Laura Flynn, *Eyes of the Heart: Seeking a Path for the Poor in the Age of Globalization* (Monroe, ME: Common Courage Press, 2000), 79.

31. "Aristide Address 27 Sep After Visit to UN," *Foreign Broadcast Information Service Daily Report* (7 October 1991), 17–19.

32. The following overview of Aristide's exile and 1994 return is based on Philippe Girard, *Clinton in Haiti: The 1994 U.S. Invasion of Haiti* (New York: Palgrave, 2004).

33. International Monetary Fund, *IMF Country Report no. 07/292* (August 2007), 8.

34. World Bank, *Haiti: External Financing* (December 1997), 1, Microenterprise Collection, USAID Library (Port-au-Prince).

35. http://devdata.worldbank.org/external/CPProfile.asp?PTYPE=CP&CCODE=HTI; International Monetary Fund, *IMF Country Report no. 07/292* (August 2007), 6 .

36. Bureau for International Narcotics and Law, *2007 International Narcotics Control Strategy Report* (Washington, DC: U.S. Dept. of State, March 2007), available at http://www.state.gov/p/inl/rls/nrcrpt/2007/v011/html/80857.htm.

37. Jean-Robert Cadet, *Restavec: From Haitian Slave-Child to Middle-Class American; An Autobiography* (1998; reprint, Austin: University of Texas Press, 2002), 4–5.

38. Kovats-Bernat, *Sleeping Rough in Port-au-Prince,* 144–75.

39. "1803–2003: restitution et réparation," *Haïti Progrès* 21, no. 4 (9 April 2003), 1.

40. Randall Robinson, *An Unbroken Agony: Haiti, From Revolution to the Kidnapping of a President* (New York: Basic Civitas, 2007), 153.

41. Thomas Madiou, *Histoire d'Haïti,* vol. 3 (1847; reprint, Port-au-Prince: Fardin, 1981), 161.

42. Transparency International, *Annual Report 2004: The Coalition Against Corruption* (Berlin: Transparency International, 2004), 10, available at http://www.transparency.org/publications/publications/annual_reports/annual_report_2004.

43. Roy F. Nichols, "Navassa: A Forgotten Acquisition," *American Historical Review* 38, no. 3 (April 1933), 505–10.

44. Haiti ranked second to last, before Venezuela, in a 2007 World Bank survey on the ease of doing business in the Western Hemisphere. International Monetary Fund, *IMF Country Report no. 07/292* (August 2007), 16.

10

The Incomplete State: The Dominican Republic, 1844–1961

Frank Moya Pons

Abstract: *This case study examines the importance of war and national security issues for nation building. The Dominicans fought a succession of wars against Haiti and Spain, and fought among themselves over the role of the United States. These wars defined Dominican national identity in terms of who they were not: They were not citizens of Haiti, Spain, or the United States. The chapter also details the limits of Dominican state building. Internal factions favoring a strong legislature versus others favoring a strong executive neutralized each other and inhibited state building in a succession of short-lived governments. In the mid-nineteenth century, the agricultural elite coalesced into a political party that encouraged the development of the plantation economy through foreign investment, immigration, and railway construction. Growing financial and political instability, however, triggered an eight-year U.S. military occupation. The U.S. intervention transformed the Dominican Republic by creating a competent police force, constructing a national highway system, and investing in public health and education. Shortly after the U.S. departure, the army chief of staff, Rafael Trujillo, became dictator for life. He funded numerous public works, public health, and infrastructure projects. At his assassination, he left a legacy of economic development but little improvement on the incomplete state institutions inherited from the United States, so that political successions remain highly destabilizing.*

With very few exceptions, the birth of each modern nation has been preceded or followed by war. Security issues have been, therefore, some of the most important concerns that the rulers of the new nations have had to contend with from independence onward.[1] The Dominican Republic is no exception to this norm. Born out of a political rift within the Haitian political elite, which had forcefully annexed into the Republic of Haiti the eastern part of the island of Santo Domingo in 1822, the Dominican Republic proclaimed its independence in February 1844, and less than a month later its people faced two Haitian armies deployed to revert its separation.[2]

The declaration of Dominican independence briefly united the Haitian elite, but after their armies were quickly defeated in Azua and Santiago in March 1844,

167

168

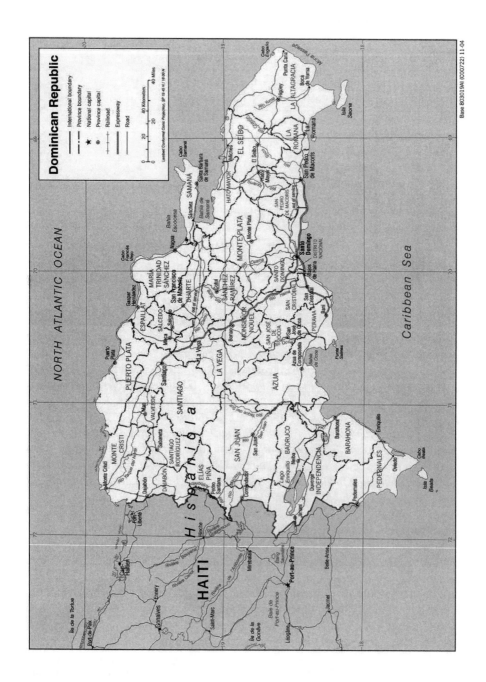

the Haitians could not resolve their own internal disagreements and a series of short-lived governments ensued. This gave Dominicans enough time to organize into a sovereign state. The Haitian army invaded again in 1845, 1849, 1855, and 1856, but each time Dominicans repelled the invasions. Like the Haitians, the Dominicans also fought among themselves and the citizenry split between liberals and conservatives.[3]

Conservative-Liberal Infighting and the Restoration of Spanish Rule

Immediately after independence, the Dominican elite divided into two irreconcilable, regionally based factions. Liberals coalesced in the rich agricultural lands of El Cibao in the middle of the country and in its commercial center in the city of Santiago, while the conservatives dominated the south as well as the government in Santo Domingo. In other words, the Dominican Republic split between a commercial elite in control of money and a political elite in control of military forces.

Conservative domination during the first nine years of the republic produced a hostile reaction from liberals, who demanded the reform of the constitution of 1844, the country's first constitution, in order to remove the legal basis for dictatorship.[4] In February 1853, the liberals finally forced the government to summon a constitutional assembly, which drafted and ratified a liberal constitution, which deprived the executive branch of its authoritarian powers. Less than a year passed before the conservatives denounced the liberal constitution to impose a new one in 1854, which then replaced the Congress with a Consultative Senate of only seven members, thus eliminating most of the democratic gains of the 1844 and 1853 constitutions.

The conservatives installed a corrupt dictatorship, which ruined the economy and provoked a major rebellion in 1857 in agricultural El Cibao, the backbone of the Dominican economy. It produced tobacco, the country's main cash crop and export product. It was the most densely populated region and its population was the most highly educated. Some of its leaders had been educated abroad, particularly in the United States, and resented the conservative abridgement of civil liberties.

As the 1857 rebellion developed into a political revolution, those from El Cibao decided to get rid, once and for all, of the political domination of Santo Domingo. They summoned a constitutional assembly to draft a new liberal constitution with checks and balances similar to those contained in the U.S. Constitution. The vigorous constitutional debates centered on the merits of a federal or a centralist model for the Dominican state. In the end the centralist model prevailed because of the small size of both the country and the population, and the difficulties of internal communication. Since the city of Santo Domingo was the cradle of authoritarianism, the leaders from El Cibao moved the capital to the main commercial center, Santiago.[5]

Conservatives, however, resisted the transfer of the capital to a semirural, although commercial, city in the interior. A counterrevolution in Santo Domingo replaced the Cibao liberal constitution (1858) with the despotic constitution of 1854 and restored Santo Domingo as the capital. Liberal leaders fled the country and a new dictatorship ensued.

The conservative revolution brought inflation, the devaluation of the currency, and economic devastation. Fears grew that Haiti and the United States, respectively, would take advantage of Dominican internal weakness to invade the country and to exploit Dominican resources. Therefore, conservatives sought Spanish protection through a formal treaty. Conservatives believed that separation from Spain in 1821 had left their country vulnerable to Haitian domination.[6] At the time, Spain still ruled Cuba and Puerto Rico, and some Spanish politicians dreamed of restoring the Spanish empire in Latin America. They would start with Santo Domingo. What began as a proposal for a political protectorate soon evolved into a full-fledged initiative for annexation. Santo Domingo would revert to being a province of Spain on a par with Cuba and Puerto Rico.

The idea of annexation captivated many politicians in Washington, Madrid, and Havana. The United States had just annexed Texas and was poised to annex Cuba.[7] Nevertheless, the U.S. government did not support the reversion of Santo Domingo to a Spanish colony because this violated the Monroe Doctrine, which proclaimed Latin America off-limits to the colonial powers of Europe.[8] In March 1861, with the signature of the treaty of annexation, the Dominican Republic dissolved after seventeen years of existence.

Nation Building During the Second War for Independence

The Spanish proved unable to suppress the insurgency that broke out upon their restoration of imperial rule. They soon lost control of most of the country, particularly the northern region and El Cibao. Many Dominicans disapproved of the annexation. The local population approximated 200,000 persons with a median age of fifteen years. This meant that the last two generations born after Spain's colonial domination had ended in 1821, comprised the bulk of the population. Popular political loyalties lay neither with Spain nor with Haiti. Dominicans had endured Haitian military rule for twenty-two years and resented the repeated attempts to subdue them by force. Dominican conservatives failed to understand that a new Dominican nation had emerged out of twenty-two years of Haitian domination and seventeen years of political independence. These thirty-nine years of independence from Spain were sufficient to accentuate the cultural and political differences between a former colony and the mother country.

These differences came to the fore when the first Spanish troops and bureaucrats arrived in Santo Domingo. Since most of these newcomers came from Cuba and Puerto Rico, where black slavery still existed and harsh military rule kept most segments of society racially segregated, the Spanish were dumbfounded that many members of the Dominican elite were colored people. Spanish military officers found unthinkable the plans to integrate into the Spanish army the high-ranking but colored officers of the Dominican army. The Spanish considered the sense of discipline and national pride of these Dominican officers to be entirely at odds with the Spanish military code. Tensions soon surfaced at all levels within the government and precluded the effective suppression of political dissent and opposition.

Rebellion and repression soon followed in succession. In May 1861, the first uprising erupted in the town of Moca, in the heart of El Cibao. In February 1862, another conspiracy was discovered in Santiago. One year later, in February 1863, a much larger conspiracy was crushed in Santiago. Those leaders who were not incarcerated fled to Haiti, where they reorganized. A large-scale uprising began in August 1863 and became known as the War of Restoration. Leaders from El Cibao set up a revolutionary government in Santiago and declared this city the legitimate capital of the republic. Not surprisingly, they restored the 1858 liberal constitution and imposed it, while formally declaring war on Spain.

The war proved to be bloody and financially ruinous for Spain. It lasted two years, ending in July 1865 with Spanish abandonment of Santo Domingo. It cost Spain more than 10,000 casualties and $33 million and contributed to the fall of the liberal government in Madrid that had negotiated the annexation treaty.[9] Moreover, the war stimulated the pro-independence sentiments in both Cuba and Puerto Rico, where similar rebellions broke out in 1868. The Puerto Rican rebellion was quickly put down, but the Cuban rebellion evolved into a large-scale, decade-long war for independence.[10]

Because the Dominican people were poorly armed and clothed, they fought the War of Restoration as a guerrilla war. There was no other way to defeat the better-disciplined and better-equipped conventional Spanish army. Climate, geography, and motivation all favored the Dominicans. Race also played an important role; Dominicans feared enslavement, given that most colored people in Cuba and Puerto Rico were slaves. Racial propaganda spread by the guerrillas and reinforced by the racial prejudices of Spanish soldiers consolidated the opposition to Spanish rule.[11]

The War of Restoration convinced Dominicans and, particularly, the national elite that besides not being Haitian they were not Spanish either. For a people composed mainly of illiterate peasants, their victory over Spain, a major military power in the region, created a deep sense of national pride and shared achievement.

Continuing Difficulties with State Building and the Third War for Independence

The war devastated the country. Even before the Spanish troops evacuated, the old infighting between liberals and conservatives resumed, now complicated by the promotion of hundreds of revolutionaries to the ranks of colonel and general during the war. This introduced a strong military interest group. Even before the war ended, many of the guerrilla groups began fighting to fill the political vacuum left by the Spanish. These new military leaders were known as "caudillos," which referred to the charismatic and often populist military political leaders common in many Latin American countries in this period.

In the Dominican Republic, short-lived governments alternated in power as the new and old caudillos marched on Santo Domingo with their guerrillas to overthrow the latest government. More democratically oriented, the liberals were also more politically divided and could not present a common front against the conservatives, who gradually reunited around former president Buenaventura Báez. After a brief administration, overthrown in 1866, Báez returned to power in 1868 and maneuvered to reimpose the 1854 autocratic constitution, defeating the fragmented leadership from El Cibao. He then installed a bloody dictatorship, which sent hundreds of Dominicans to jail and exile, while killing several hundred of his opponents. A six-year civil war soon erupted. The liberals fought hard, but Báez remained in power. He used his unlimited powers to obtain foreign loans to finance his government.

Báez hoped the United States would annex the Dominican Republic in return for a massive payoff; he saw this as a way to remain in power indefinitely. U.S. President Ulysses Grant supported annexation. The Dominican Congress, which had been reduced to the seven-member Consultative Senate under the reinstated 1854 constitution, approved a draft annexation treaty.[12] The U.S. Senate, however, defeated the treaty by just one vote in 1870, saving the Dominican Republic from becoming a new state of the union before Oregon, Washington, Hawaii, California, and Utah, and just after the Dominican people had fought a second war of independence rejecting annexation to Spain.[13]

The Six Year War (1868–74) against Báez constituted the third war of independence fought by the Dominican people and another step in the process of nation building. It was fought by a wide coalition of politicians, intellectuals, old-school military, and revolutionary guerrillas who simply did not want to return to colonial domination and lose their sovereignty. Dominican intellectual Pedro Henríquez Ureña once said that this war crystallized Dominican national consciousness because Dominicans discovered that in addition to not being Haitians or Spaniards, they also realized that they were not, nor could they be, U.S. citizens.[14] Only after this succession of three successful wars for independence did the Dominican political elite agree in 1881 on a national anthem and on the selection of the founding fathers of the country.

Báez was overthrown in 1873. What followed can only be described as caudillo politics, or a continuation of the series of "revolutions" and short-lived governments that sprang out of the Restoration War. Between 1865 and 1879 the Dominican Republic went through fourteen different governments and twenty-one major military uprisings.[15] Liberals and conservatives fought each other with relentless obstinacy. Caudillos, local and regional, vied for national prominence, continuously failing, and leaving behind a trail of debts that bankrupted the national treasury. When a conservative government took control, it imposed a version of the autocratic 1854 constitution. When a liberal government came to power, it reinstituted the 1858 constitution in its 1866 variant.

Economic Development Under the Blue Party

Gradually the different regional and particular interests of the leaders of El Cibao coalesced into a coalition called the Blue Party, which opposed the southern interests represented by Báez's political clientele, now named the Red Party. The Blue Party represented the tobacco cultivators and merchants from the central part of the country, whereas the Red Party responded to the cattle ranching and forestry interests of the south.

Eventually the Blue Party won out. In 1879 it set up a series of governments, which, as before, were legitimized by indirect elections, but now changed according to agreed-upon two-year terms, giving many a turn at the presidency in the hopes of reducing internal instability. The system worked for nearly a decade. In 1886 the chief of the army and minister of interior, who had already been president between 1882 and 1884, broke the party rule of no reelection to seek the presidency again. This divided the party. Elections were rigged, fraud was widespread, and civil war erupted again. This was a short but violent conflict, which left almost 600 dead, mainly in El Cibao. Ulises Heureaux, the army chief, defeated his opponents and established a dictatorship, which lasted until his assassination in July 1899.

Under the Heureaux and the Blue Party's administrations, the Dominican Republic underwent a first wave of economic modernization. Because the liberals believed foreign investment necessary to develop the country's natural resources, they offered tax incentives and free land to those willing to invest in sugar, coffee, and cacao plantations.[16] Much of the country was virtually uninhabited territory; with an area of more than 48,000 square kilometers, it was populated by just 300,000 people. Most land belonged to the state or was cultivated communally under a land tenure inherited from the colonial period. Land was cheaper in the Dominican Republic than in any other part of the West Indies, as were oxen and human labor. At a time when world sugar demand was quickly growing, the fertile flatlands of the island's southeast were a natural frontier on which to set up a modern sugar industry composed of large central factories.

In addition to incentives laws and negligible taxation, the promotion of immigration also encouraged the development of the sugar plantations. The Blue Party administrations promoted immigration of people from the West Indies, the Spanish—particularly from Cataluña and the Canary Islands—Sephardic Jews from Aruba and Curacao, Chinese from Cuba, and Syrians, Lebanese, and Palestinians from the Ottoman Empire. By the late nineteenth century, the incipient urban centers of the Dominican Republic were becoming a melting pot of races and nationalities. Some towns, like Puerto Plata and San Pedro, had many West

Indians, while other towns, like Santiago and La Vega, as well as Puerto Plata, had many Cubans. In Santo Domingo, the capital, most of the immigrants were of Spanish origin.

This industrialization by invitation produced a "sugar revolution" that changed forever the pastoral economy of the southeast and moved the country's economic center from Santiago and Puerto Plata, in the north, to Santo Domingo in the south. This change undercut the regional base of the Blue Party, forcing some power sharing with Báez's Red Party. Coffee, cacao, and banana plantations also multiplied in the interior of the country, along with the expansion of the sugar plantations in the southeastern plains.

To facilitate the transportation of the new products, both the government and private corporations built railroads.[17] The Heureaux administration borrowed heavily to finance the railway construction linking most of the Cibao towns with the two main harbors of Sánchez and Puerto Plata. Heureaux also borrowed to finance the government deficit, as taxes were insufficient to cover public expenditure. When foreign credit dried up, Heureaux and his associates resorted to printing money, with predictable inflationary results. He then demanded loans from sugar corporations and other reluctant plantation owners. The government financial situation was in shambles when Heureaux was assassinated in late July 1899.[18]

The U.S. Occupation and State Building

For the next seventeen years the Dominican Republic followed a dual track: On the one hand, the plantation economy continued to expand at a rapid pace. Foreign capital poured in. U.S. investments dominated the sugar industry, while a combination of Dominican, American, and European money developed new cacao, coffee, and banana plantations.[19] Good rain precipitation, large expanses of well-irrigated and fertile flatlands, low population pressures, low taxes, and generous legal incentives designed to attract foreign investors together produced an economic revolution in the Dominican Republic.

On the other hand, the Dominican state underwent a very serious and sustained financial crisis, which culminated in the personal intervention of U.S. President Theodore Roosevelt and the imposition of a political and financial protectorate on the Dominican Republic.[20] Security concerns about the future Panama Canal influenced Roosevelt's decision to send troops to Santo Domingo in 1905 and appoint a financial adviser to determine the real external debt of the Dominican Republic. In 1907 the United States took over the administration of Dominican customs, in the manner that Britain had long administered Chinese customs. The 1907 Dominican-American Convention transformed the Dominican Republic into a political and financial protectorate of the United States. Dominican nationalists fiercely attacked the convention, yet it produced several years of political stability and economic growth. President Ramon Cáceres was the main political beneficiary. His regime invested the customs revenues in public works and, more importantly, used the funds to appease the caudillos by recruiting them into his political entourage or into the government bureaucracy.

After President Cáceres was assassinated in November 1911, one of the most unstable and violent periods in Dominican political history ensued. In the following six years, seven governments succeeded each other in a chain of uprisings and coups d'état equivalent to an unfinished and resilient civil war.[21] No ideology or political doctrine sustained these parties and their caudillos. Their programs and manifestos revolved around the personal interests of their leaders and very few, if any, expressed or reflected a vision of national development or modernization.

While the country was regressing politically, it was progressing economically. This was the period when large, new plantations were developing extensive tracts of fertile land in most regions, except the most arid areas in the northwest and southwest. Thus, the Dominican Republic functioned in a two-tiered world: One was a traditional society run by caudillo descendants of Spanish immigrants, while the other was the world of the plantations, normally foreign owned, which functioned as true enclaves with their own borders, their own security forces, their own stores, their own railroad lines, and even their own currencies.[22]

Despite continuous U.S. diplomatic pressure and threats of U.S. military intervention, the caudillos continued their infighting and rejected U.S. demands for military and financial reforms. The caudillos did not understand that changes in the international political environment were influencing U.S. decisions regarding the whole Caribbean area, most notably the opening of the Panama Canal in 1912 and the outbreak of World War I in 1914. In 1914 the U.S. Marine Corps was sent to Nicaragua to impose order and protect the American-owned banana plantations in Central America. That same year, U.S. troops also disembarked briefly in Veracruz, Mexico. The following year, U.S. troops deployed to Haiti to put down a guerrilla uprising and contain German banking interests during World War I. Haiti remained under American military control until 1934.[23] With continuing political chaos in the Dominican Republic, in May 1916, U.S. President Woodrow Wilson ordered the U.S. Marine Corps and the Department of the Navy to take over the Dominican government. Thus began a military occupation, which lasted until 1924 and transformed the state, as well as Dominican society and culture.[24]

Two of the first acts of the American military rulers were the universal disarmament of the population and the creation of a national constabulary to impose public order. This immediately reduced the numbers of caudillos and their followers despite a five-year peasant resistance in some regions. Initially the United States organized the constabulary as a national police force that soon became a national guard with police duties.

In 1917 the military government began the construction of three highways to link Santo Domingo with the rest of the country. By 1922 the basic network extended to the northwestern, southeastern, and southwestern limits of the country, effectively centralizing the political and military administration of the republic. As the number of trucks and automobiles grew, the Cibao railroads gradually became obsolete.

Trucks moved cargo more quickly, cheaply, and efficiently than did railroads. The military government also invested heavily in education and public health, making primary education mandatory. The health campaigns to combat malaria, syphilis and other venereal diseases, and the intestinal parasites affecting most of the Dominican population also ushered in new hygiene and public health practices.[25]

The changes introduced by the American military government transformed not only the state but also the economy as sugar plantations expanded their domination throughout most of the southeastern and southwestern flatlands. Several new, gigantic sugar mills were built during the occupation, while numerous American companies obtained enormous land grants to exploit the country's virgin forests and mines.[26]

Transition to Independence

As soon as the First World War ended, civil resistance to the occupation coalesced around a political movement called the Dominican Patriotic Union (*Unión Patriótica Dominicana*) headed by a coalition of political leaders of the traditional political parties. Differing from their Haitian counterparts under U.S. occupation, the most prominent Dominican politicians declined to participate within the military government and always demanded the restoration of independence. After a long series of demonstrations inside and outside the country, and following negotiations in Washington, the newly elected U.S. president, Warren Harding, agreed to terminate U.S. military rule in 1924 once new democratic elections were held to select a national government.[27]

When the U.S. occupation ended, there had been at least four generations born since the declaration of independence from Haiti. Despite their failure at building a stable democracy, Dominicans considered themselves a mature nation. They had a national anthem, a flag, a coat of arms, and a patriotic pantheon of war heroes, who had fought for independence against the Haitians, the Spaniards, and the Americans. The nationalist campaign against the U.S. military occupation had reinforced this sentiment. Many saw the elections for a new government as an opportunity to create a functional democracy. In July 1924, upon the withdrawal of U.S. troops, Dominicans began speaking of the birth of "the third Republic."

Dominicans elected the old caudillo Horacio Vásquez as president. He ruled over a pacified country with a booming economy and a national professional army without regional caudillos, and his four-year term was a model of democracy and political tolerance as well as economic modernization. New roads were built, new schools and hospitals constructed, new private buildings in the main cities were erected, and the press was free to criticize the government. But ominous signs appeared in 1927.

Just as some journalists and writers were promoting the chief of the army, Rafael Trujillo, as a possible future president, Vásquez repeated an old political pattern by amending the constitution, in 1928, to extend his presidential tenure for two more years. He used the dubious argument that he had been elected while the 1908 constitution (which provided for a six-year presidential term) was in effect. His opponents rejected this maneuver, arguing, quite reasonably, that he had been sworn in under the newly written 1924 constitution, which clearly set a four-year term limit. The disagreement precipitated a serious political crisis, but Congress approved the extension of his mandate for two more years, until August 1930. As Vásquez clung to power, his adversaries began conspiring to overthrow him. They sided with Trujillo, who finally overthrew Vásquez in late February 1930. After a series of political maneuvers, terrorist tactics, and political repression, Trujillo assumed the presidency on 16 August 1930. Between Vásquez's resignation and Trujillo's election on 16 May, the army violently forced all other candidates to quit the race. Trujillo was the sole candidate and, naturally, "won" the elections.[28] The Vásquez regime, despite its shortcomings, was the longest lasting democratic experiment in a country that had been swinging between democracy and dictatorship for more than eighty years.

Rafael Trujillo (1930–61)

Trujillo's thirty-one year authoritarian rule further transformed the Dominican state and the Dominican nation. Many studies portray the Trujillo regime as a totalitarian dictatorship fashioned in the style of the regimes of Adolf Hitler, Benito Mussolini, Francisco Franco, Juan Perón, Getúlio Vargas, and other twentieth-century dictators. Like these dictators, Trujillo built his regime with the support of the peasantry and the lower middle classes, whose economic advancement he championed. With about half of the population initially against him, Trujillo strove to become accepted by all social classes by answering to long-felt social needs.[29] He rapidly reconstructed the capital after the devastating hurricane of 1930 and manipulated the symbolism of a nation to be constructed from the ruins left by a cyclone. He called this nation the New Fatherland, and gave himself the title "Father of the New Fatherland," among many others.[30]

In order to consolidate his power, he gave sinecures to local and regional caudillos loyal to the regime, but crushed and killed the last remaining caudillos from the old days who were still plotting with the traditional politicians to overthrow the government. In 1931 he founded the Dominican Party (*Partido Dominicano*) and obliged every male above the age of sixteen to join. By 1934 Trujillo's rule was monolithic and he had himself unanimously reelected as president for a second term.[31]

Not only did Trujillo eradicate the caudillos, but he also dealt equally decisively with Haiti. A treaty negotiated in 1929 set the boundary, but much to the widespread resentment of Dominicans, since 1874 Haitians had occupied at least 20 percent of Dominican territory. The two countries negotiated a protocol to the treaty in 1936. In 1937 Trujillo forcefully expelled all Haitians living in the country, except those working in foreign-owned sugar plantations.[32] In the process, Dominican soldiers and paramilitary forces killed several thousand Haitians. Nevertheless, even today many Dominicans believe that the expulsion of the Haitians was necessary for the complete integration of the nation.

Much has been written on both sides of the island regarding this event and Trujillo's subsequent campaign for the "Dominicanization of the borderlands" used to unify the Dominican people around the threat of Haitian occupation. As in the nineteenth century, Trujillo used a foreign national security threat to unify the country in the face of endemic internal instability. As the Pacific War broke out in 1941, he saturated the country with anti-Haitian propaganda.[33] Dominican agriculturalists colonized the frontiers. New administrative units were created, and a series of forts and fortresses were built to maintain a strict military control of the frontier.[34]

During Trujillo's thirty-one-year rule, he funded numerous public works projects and extended to more than 5,000 kilometers the road network begun by the U.S. military government. He consistently funded public health programs, particularly those aimed at parasitic ailments, malaria, and tuberculosis. He prioritized irrigation projects and agricultural development programs. Food production rose rapidly. Rice, banana, coffee, cacao, and sugar production sustained both high levels of exports and population growth. The economy grew steadily from 1939 to 1960 on par with the population, which grew from 1.2 million in 1935 to 3 million in 1960, but the per capita standard of living grew only slightly. Rapid urbanization accompanied this demographic revolution. In 1920, 84 percent of the Dominican population lived in the countryside, whereas in 1960 the proportion of the rural population had decreased to 40 percent.[35]

Trujillo and his propagandists claimed that a new nation or a "new fatherland" had been created. They proclaimed the end of the age of instability and attributed all economic and social progress to the order and discipline imposed by Generalissimo Trujillo, the "Benefactor of the Fatherland." One of his favorite titles was "Restorer of the Country's Financial Independence." His propagandists continuously emphasized that he was the father of national independence because he had restored national control over the customs offices in 1941 and had paid off the foreign debt in 1947, thus ending the U.S. protectorate imposed by the Dominican-American Convention of 1907.[36]

While Trujillo's accomplishment in the areas of economic development and internal stability were significant, nation building had occurred prior to his tenure in office as a result of the Dominican Republic's three wars for independence against Haiti, Spain, and the United States, which together created a negative national identity defined in terms of what Dominicans were not, rather than a positive identity of what they were. State building, however, accelerated primarily during the U.S. occupation, which produced far stronger national military than civil institutions. Trujillo then used these more effective state institutions to finish off the traditional caudillos and modernize the economy. Modernization occurred before, during, and after the U.S. occupation.

In May 1961, Trujillo was assassinated by a group of his friends and collaborators. His regime then quickly crumbled. Ever since, Dominicans have been struggling to establish a functional democracy in a country that has historically alternated between instability and dictatorship. The primary obstacle has not been nation building or economic development, but rather state building.

After a series of fraudulent presidential elections from 1966 to 1994 and several constitutional overhauls, the Dominican state still cannot provide the most basic services: Neither electric nor postal service is dependable. The public health system remains in disarray. The educational system ranks among the bottom of Latin American systems. The national police force is openly corrupt and unable to control violence, while the prison system routinely degrades those incarcerated. Politics and money overwhelm the justice system. The government is the first to violate the laws passed by Congress. Public works projects are seldom allocated on the basis of open bids. The army and the Catholic Church retain enormous political influence. The tax system remains among the most regressive in Latin America; customs taxes are selectively levied; and foreign companies operate mining, tourist, and sugar enclaves virtually independently of the state.

For these reasons, the 2005 index of failed states compiled by *Foreign Policy* listed the Dominican Republic together with Haiti and North Korea among the top twenty contenders for this unenviable title.[37] This statement was an evident exaggeration, as the Dominican Republic did not make the 2008 list, which stops at sixty countries.[38] Thus, Dominican state building remains incomplete, although much progress has been made compared to the days of caudillo-led civil wars and also compared to neighboring Haiti.

Notes

1. Anthony D. Smith, "War and Ethnicity," *Ethnic and Racial Studies,* 4 no. 4 (1981), 375–97.
2. Frank Moya Pons, *La Dominación Haitiana, 1822–1844* (Santiago: Universidad Católica Madre y Maestra, 1973); Frank Moya Pons, *The Dominican Republic: A National History* (Princeton, NJ: Markus Wiener, 1998), 153–83.
3. Emilio Rodríguez Demorizi, *Guerra dominico-haitiana* (Ciudad Trujillo: Academia Militar Batalla de las Carreras, 1957), 73–137.
4. Frank Moya Pons, "Acerca de las luchas constitucionales dominicanas en el siglo XIX," *Eme-Eme Estudios Dominicanos,* 5 no. 30 (June 1977), 3–15.
5. José Gabriel García, *Compendio de la historia de Santo Domingo,* vol. 2 (Santo Domingo: Sociedad Dominicana de Bibliófilos, 1979), 221–82.
6. Emilio Rodríguez Demorizi, *Antecedentes de la Anexión a España* (Ciudad Trujillo: Editora Montalvo, 1955), and *Relaciones dominico-españolas* (Ciudad Trujillo: Editora Montalvo, 1955).
7. Philip Foner, *A History of Cuba and Its Relations with the United States* (New York: International Publishers, 1962), and Robert E. May, *The Southern Dream of a Caribbean Empire, 1854–1861* (Baton Rouge: Louisiana State University Press, 2003).
8. Sumner Welles, *The Naboth's Vineyard,* vol. 1 (New York: Payson and Clarke, 1928), 239–40; Charles Hauch, *La República Dominicana y sus relaciones exteriores, 1844–1882* (Santo Domingo: Sociedad Dominicana de Bibliófilos, 1996), 129–31; Luis Fernández

Martínez, "Caudillos, Annexation, and the Rivalry between Empires in the Dominican Republic, 1844–1874," *Diplomatic History,* 17 no. 4 (Fall 1973), 571–97.

9. Hauch, *La República Dominicana,* 151; Charles C. Hauch, "Attitudes of Foreign Governments towards the Spanish Occupation of the Dominican Republic," *Hispanic American Historical Review,* 27 no. 2 (May 1947), 247–68.

10. Frank Moya Pons, *History of the Caribbean* (Princeton, NJ: Markus Wiener, 2007), 243–52.

11. Frank Moya Pons, *The Dominican Republic,* 196–226, 255–63.

12. B.F. Wade, A.D. White, and S.G. Rowe, *Report of the Commission of Inquiry to Santo Domingo* (Washington, DC: Government Printing Office, 1871).

13. Frank Moya Pons, *The Dominican Republic,* 477–79; Hauch, *La República Dominicana,* 233–50.

14. Pedro Henríquez Ureña, "Cartas a Federico García Godoy, desde México, para la Cuna de América, 5 de mayo de 1909," *Obra dominicana* (Santo Domingo: Sociedad Dominicana de Bibliófilos, 1988), 538–41.

15. Frank Moya Pons, *Manual de Historia Dominicana* (Santo Domingo: Caribbean Publishers, 2008), 371–412.

16. José Del Castillo, "The Formation of the Dominican Sugar Industry," in *Between Slavery and Free Labor,* eds. Manuel Moreno Fraginals, Frank Moya Pons, and Stanley S. Engerman (Baltimore: Johns Hopkins University Press, 1985), 215–34.

17. Harry Hoetink, *The Dominican People 1850–1900* (Baltimore: Johns Hopkins University Press, 1985), 52–56.

18. Mukien A. Sang, *Ulises Heureaux* (Santo Domingo: Instituto Tecnológico de Santo Domingo, 1987); Jaime de Jesús Domínguez, *La dictadura de Heureaux* (Santo Domingo: Instituto Tecnológico de Santo Domingo, 1987), 169–215.

19. César Ayala, *American Sugar Kingdom* (Chapel Hill: University of North Carolina Press, 1999); Moya Pons, *History of the Caribbean,* 372–74.

20. Sumner Welles, *The Naboth's Vineyard,* vol. 2 (New York: Payson and Clarke, 1928), 49–99.

21. Luis Felipe Mejía, *De Lilís a Trujillo* (Caracas: Editorial Elite, 1944), 52–79.

22. Frank Moya Pons, "Modernization and Change in the Dominican Republic," in *Dominican Cultures,* ed. Bernardo Vega (Princeton, NJ: Markus Wiener, 2007), 209–21.

23. Antonio de la Rosa, *Las finanzas de Santo Domingo y el control americano* (Santo Domingo: Editora de Santo Domingo, 1969), 209–50.

24. Bruce J. Calder, *The Impact of Intervention: The Dominican Republic during the U.S. Occupation of 1916–1924* (Austin: University of Texas Press, 1983).

25. Marlin D. Clausner, *Rural Santo Domingo: Settled, Unsettled, Resettled* (Philadelphia: Temple University Press, 1973), 174–81.

26. Melvin Knight, *The Americans in Santo Domingo* (New York: Vanguard Press, 1928), 97–107; Mejía, *De Lilís a Trujillo,* 147–55.

27. Kenneth J. Grieb, "Warren Harding and the Dominican Republic U.S. Withdrawal, 1921–1923," *Journal of Inter-American Studies,* 11 (July 1969), 425–40.

28. Víctor Medina Benet, *Los Responsables* (Santo Domingo: The Author, 1976), 351–466; Mejía, *De Lilís a Trujillo,* 230–50; Bernardo Vega, *Trujillo y las fuerzas armadas norteamericanas* (Santo Domingo: Editora Cultural Dominicana, 1992), 49–68.

29. Richard Lee Turits, *The Foundations of Despotism* (Stanford, CA: Stanford University Press, 2003); Orlando Inoa, *Estado y campesinos al inicio de la Era de Trujillo* (Santo Domingo: Librería La Trinitaria, 1994).

30. Frank Moya Pons, *El ciclón de San Zenón y la "nueva patria" dominicana* (Santo Domingo: Academia Dominicana de la Historia, 2007).

31. Jesús de Galíndez, *La Era de Trujillo* (Santiago de Chile: Editora del Pacífico, 1956), 9–62.

32. Bernardo Vega, *Trujillo y Haití, 1930–1937* (Santo Domingo: Fundación Cultural Dominicana, 1988); Bernardo Vega, *Trujillo y Haití, 1937–1938* (Santo Domingo: Fundación Cultural Dominicana, 1995); José Israel Cuello, *Documentos del conflicto dominico-haitiano de 1937* (Santo Domingo: Editora Taller, 1985).

33. Andrés L. Mateo, *Mito y Cultura en la Era de Trujillo* (Santo Domingo: Editora Manatí, 1993); Emilio Rodríguez Demorizi, *Bibliografía de Trujillo* (Ciudad Trujillo: Editora Montalvo, 1955).

34. John P. Augelli, "Agricultural colonization of the Dominican Republic," *Economic Geography,* 38 no. 1 (January 1962), 15–27.

35. Frank Moya Pons, *Breve Historia Contemporánea de la Republica Dominicana* (Mexico City: Fondo de Cultura Económica, 1999), 89–139; Frank Moya Pons, "Los motores del cambio económico y social," *El siglo XX dominicano* (Santo Domingo: Codetel, 1999), 15–132.

36. Ramón Marrero Aristy, *La República Dominicana,* vol. 3 (Ciudad Trujillo: Editora del Caribe, 1958), 9–111; Gilberto Sánchez Lustrino, *Trujillo, el constructor de una nacionalidad* (Ciudad Trujillo: Editora Montalvo, 1938), 173–253; Joaquín Balaguer, *Dominican Reality* (Mexico: The Author, 1949).

37. "The Failed States Index Rankings," July/August 2005, http://www.foreignpolicy.com/story/cms.php?story_id=3100&print=1. For the reaction of the president of the republic, see "Leonel dice que República Dominicana no es Estado fallido," *El Caribe* (Santo Domingo), 14 July 2005, 3.

38. "Failed States Ranking," 2008, http://www.foreigpolicy.com/images/fs2008/failed_states_ranking.jpg.

11

Jordan: Among Three Nationalisms

PHILIP ROBINS

Abstract: *This case study describes Jordan's remarkable success in transforming the weakest Arab state into a nation. A strong sense of Jordanian nationalism has developed despite the competing claims of Arab nationalism and Palestinian nationalism. During the colonial period, Britain subsidized state building in what became Jordan, put the Hashemites on the throne, and helped form an effective police force that remained loyal to the postindependence government. The Hashemites have survived despite being surrounded by unstable, interventionist, and more powerful neighbors. They have done so through astute leadership, the cultivation of a Jordanian national identity, and the reliance on at least one powerful ally. They have used this ally to counterbalance their neighbors and to provide infusions of economic aid to help compensate for a very poor resource endowment. Thus, they have survived by transforming Jordan into a rentier state dependent on strategic rents from the outside. The Hashemites provide a lesson on what astute leadership can achieve in a very unpromising national security and economic environment.*

As little as ninety years ago the idea of Jordan was undreamt of.[1] Even during the frenetic period of state building in the Middle East between 1918 and 1923, the existence of Jordan was improbable. What we now know as the territory of the country seemed destined either to be absorbed into the mandate of Palestine, or to have bits of it incorporated into other entities: Maan south to the Red Sea into the Hijaz, itself soon to be conquered and absorbed into Saudi Arabia; the north, as befitting part of the southern area of *bilad al-sham* (the lands under the sway of Damascus), into whatever state was controlled from Damascus. Even its name seemed unpromising. After all, at the time, the country was known by what it was not: "Transjordan," the land across, and hence beyond, the River Jordan.

The early 1920s was not the only time when Jordan's existence seemed fanciful. In the mid- to late 1950s and then again in 1963, after it had been recognized as an independent, sovereign state, Jordan came under fearful pressure from the forces of Arab nationalism. Jordan's existence was further challenged between 1968 and 1971 by the Palestinian national movement, narrower in conception than Arabism but more explicit in terms of objectives. This dynamic culminated in the victory of the Jordanian state in the civil war of 1970 and 1971, defeating the Palestinian

Nationalists.[2] Against all expectations, Jordan faced down two of the most potent national political movements of the twentieth century in the region—Arab and Palestinian nationalism—relying on its own nationalism. Jordanian nationalism is the bundle of perceived vested interests, underpinned by tribal values, that regards its prospects as being best served within a political entity based on a Transjordan distinct from the geopolitical space of Palestine. It is only a tad hyperbolic to describe Jordanian nationalism as having won, at least so far, the struggle of the three nationalisms: Arab nationalism, Palestinian nationalism, and Jordanian nationalism.

How to explain the incongruity? This chapter will argue that there was always more raw material for Jordanian nationalism than met the eye as the writ of the Ottoman Empire expired in the area just after World War I. By the same token, though conceptually powerful, the organizational and acquisitive aspects of Arab nationalism were haphazard and exaggerated. The emergence of these two competing bundles of ideas and vested interests will form the second part of this chapter, after a consideration of the prospects for the transformation of the newly created Transjordanian entity into a full-fledged state. Palestinian nationalism, though also potent, was immature, and alienated potential allies at a time when the core of the Jordanian state was growing in strength. The late emergence of Palestinian nationalism and its relationship with its Jordanian counterpart will form the third main section. It was only when Israeli rightist revisionism flirted with the idea of a displaced Palestinian nationalism in the "Jordan is Palestine" thesis of the 1980s that it really presented a dangerous threat to Jordan's existence.

Although as a result of these processes the Jordanian state-nation has proven to be surprisingly durable, even pugnacious, a word of warning is in order. Jordan's long-term survival cannot be guaranteed in a turbulent region where new challenges like the uncertain future of Iraq and Islamist terrorism emphasize the small size and capacity of Jordan relative to its neighbors. In short, Jordan, like all states and all nationalisms, remains a work in progress.

State Building and Nationalism

During the period 1918–23, Transjordan sat patiently in the waiting room of history. Initially Britain, the occupying power, was slow to act on its eventual fate; this was partly a reflection of its relative unimportance and partly a product of the working assumption that it would eventually be fully absorbed into the mandate of Palestine. Jordan only emerged as a separate entity in the early to mid-1920s because of other factors all emphasizing its potential utility as a buffer entity. There was the British need to contain Wahhabi expansionism in the emerging Saudi Arabia. There was the British desire to resist the territorial avarice of the French, whose growing southerly ambitions would have ruptured Britain's land contiguity between Palestine and Iraq. There was the corrosive nature of the politics of Palestine and a growing impetus to ensure that its fractious politics did not spread. In response to these considerations, the British authorities, through the League of

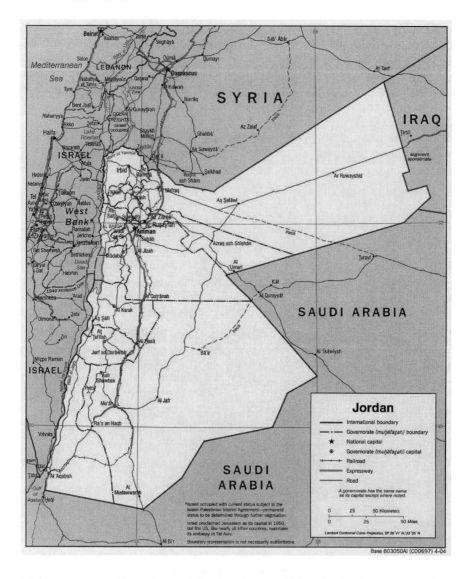

Base 803050AI (C00697) 4-04

Nations, successfully engineered the detachment of Transjordan from the mandate for Palestine in 1924.

Once the reality of a Jordanian entity had been established, the unpromising nature of its potential had to be confronted. Jordan had no city capable of acting as a power center to drive the process of state consolidation. Indicative of its rural nature was the capital of the emerging entity, Amman, a small town that had until relatively recently been abandoned as a human settlement. Rather, Jordan's defining characteristic was its twin mainstays of a hard, marginal ecology, with pastoral semi-nomadism, and upland, rain-fed agriculture. Bedouin tribes pursuing the former roamed widely, in reflection of the unreliability of water resources and seasonal grazing, and of the perpetual intertribal raiding that was in part the product of such a harsh environment. Even agriculture had a partially nomadic element to it, in the form of seasonal labor migration, especially as the rains in Jordan often failed. As a result, the population of Transjordan was, at around 225,000 in 1922,[3] low for the region, and apparently not climbing.

The pioneering state builders in Jordan were the small number of British administrators and officers posted to serve in the mandate. The leading lights among them, such as Frederick Peake, Henry Cox, Alec Kirkbride, and John "Glubb Pasha,"[4] became famous in their own time. If there was one thing that Britain, as a long-standing, global colonial power, was good at, it was state building. Thus the British authorities on the ground set about negating some of the natural disadvantages mentioned above. Consequently, an army and police force were established; the finances of the emirate were taken in hand; thorny issues of border demarcation, in the north with the French and the south with the Saudis, were addressed; the civilian institutions of a state, such as ministries and public sector agencies, were created.

The sine qua non for all of this practical activity at the political center was Britain's willingness to pay a financial subsidy to the emerging state. The marginal economy meant that taxation, where feasible, was insufficient for such an ambitious political project. Moreover, Jordan itself had no raw materials to speak of. The main exception to this day has been mineral fertilizer such as phosphates, which were not at the time commercially exploited. Britain stepped in with a regular budgetary subsidy that lasted for almost three and a half decades, whereupon others took up the fiscal slack. It seems that over time just about any state of note has been a strategic subsidizer of the Jordanian state, including Britain, the United States through the Eisenhower Doctrine at the end of the 1950s, the Arab oil producers in the 1970s and 1980s, the European Union and Japan in the 1990s, and the United States again, especially in 2003, the year of the invasion of Iraq.

This dependence on foreign aid established from the outset Jordan's status as a rentier state, that is to say a state whose domestic, productive activity has never satisfied its indulgent consumption ambitions, both private and public, thereby leaving it crucially dependent on the payment of strategic rents from outside.[5] It really is no exaggeration therefore to say that there would have been no Jordanian state without British diplomacy, the British exchequer, and British colonial administrators.

The Transjordanian Nationalist Narrative for Nationhood

In the Transjordan of the early 1920s, most identities were local ones. Kinship groups were organized into different levels, with the lower levels such as the extended family and clan enjoying the highest level of solidarity, while the larger groupings such as tribe and tribal confederations commanded intermittent solidarity depending on the wider political domain. Nevertheless, at this time, tribal solidarity was still potent, with even the big, seminomadic tribal confederations like the Huwaitat and the Bani Sakhr active entities. The relatively high level of family and clan loyalty to the tribal confederations suggests that there was no competing focus for individual loyalty, such as the state, and that anarchy generally prevailed.

Tribal law regulated the affairs of most people, both in the marginal steppe and in the more sedentary countryside. The focus of the settled peasantry, the majority of the population, was on the village and the locale, especially in the north,[6] where cereal and livestock farming was just about viable. Broader identities, notably religious, though notionally transnational, were expressed in local terms, with the authority of the neighborhood imam and priest dominant. Those with wider horizons, the small traders who had come to Transjordan from Damascus, Nablus, or Hebron on the back of the cereals boom at the turn of the century or to supply the Ottoman army during the war, and the modest Caucasian communities settled by the Ottoman authorities, hardly diluted this reality. It was these local identities that would over time aggregate into a feeling of affinity with the Transjordanian core of the state.

It was in opposition to an external "other" that the first stirrings of Transjordanian nationalism occurred. This is hardly a surprising statement. Nationalism in many cases appears as the counterforce to colonialism in the dialectic of state building in the developing world. What makes the Jordanian case more unusual was that the external "other" was not the British, but a neighboring Arab administrative cadre.[7] As the British authorities set about state building, they became acutely aware of the absence of the bureaucratic raw material for such a task. Notably, the Jordan of the day lacked a rudimentary school system, there being virtually no one with the necessary training to provide the administrative functions of a state. To assist them in this process, the British were obliged to look outside the boundaries of the emirate and imported a cadre of administrators, mostly Arabs from Palestine, defined as the land west of the River Jordan to the Mediterranean Sea. Perceived as untrustworthy urban effendis ("city slickers"), resented for their privileged relationship with the British authorities, and disliked for taking over the administration of the fledgling state, members of the Transjordanian elite distrusted these bureaucratic immigrants. The Sons of the Country Movement had been born.

As nationalist movements go, the Sons of the Country was in many ways a modest affair. It emerged in 1927, but was moribund within five years. It was patchy in its support in Transjordan, being most closely identified with the central-south of the country, notably the small town of Karak and its tribal hinterland.[8] It failed to transcend parochial divisions, even in Karak itself, where the movement was closely associated with the Tarawnah clan and hence cold-shouldered by their perennial rivals, the Majali. The leaders used the movement to leverage political benefits from the British, who provided the benefits to co-opt the leadership, and as a result the movement rapidly declined. Over time, the mandate's newly established schools generated a supply of indigenously trained employees, whom the British pragmatically favored over a renewed recruitment of functionaries from the adjacent outside. But for a couple of years at least it was a movement of spirit. Arguably its real importance was in the way in which it has been invoked in contemporary times by Transjordanian nationalists who seek to establish that their own political identity has a longer pedigree than the controversial period of the late 1960s and early 1970s.

If the Sons of the Country were at the noisy, flag-waving end of territorial nationalism, of more importance were the developments that took place between 1928 and 1946, when Transjordan morphed into the Hashemite Kingdom of Jordan. This was a vital period in terms of the incorporation of the traditional social periphery into the emerging state. There were two aspects to the process. First, the formal and institutional: a small executive council (run by British "advisers") and a modest legislative council were created, as part of the political development with which the mandatory powers had been charged by the League of Nations. Local notables largely alternated between fighting tooth and nail to be included in such institutions and, when on the outside, in a show of contrived radicalism, decrying the foreign control that underpinned them.

Second, and more important, was the role played by the legendary British officer Glubb Pasha,[9] in incorporating the male offspring of Jordan's tribal leaders into the newly formed Desert Patrol of the Arab Legion, the emerging national army.[10] Rather than using coercion to force the loyalty of the tribes, as had initially been the British strategy, from the late 1920s, Glubb allowed the Bedouin to police their own areas, though under his overall direction. Stricken by a prolonged period of drought, the sheikhs were happy to take the state handouts that accompanied the strategy, together with the wages paid to their sons. The fusion of the embryonic state and the culturally distinct social periphery into a mutually, materially complementary relationship steadily deepened. By the time of independence, the Jordan-building project was chugging along nicely, in contrast to Britain's frustrated disappointments in its other mandates, Iraq and Palestine.

The Arab Nationalist Narrative for Nationhood

The transformation of Arab nationalism into an ideology opposed to state consolidation in Jordan in preference for a larger Arab state subsuming Jordan was a wound self-inflicted by the Hashemites. The exploitation of Arab nationalism did not begin with Egypt's Nasser, or even the French-trained intellectuals of Damascus, who would provide the intellectual firepower for Baathism. That all came later. The Hashemite dynasty, which had hoped to inherit the Ottoman provinces in the Mashreq (or Arab east) in their entirety, became the most energetic proponent of pan-Arabism. The post–First World War political settlement installing Hashemite princes incongruously in the mandates of Iraq and Transjordan simply added to their sense of restless irredentism. For the patrician Hashemites, the *noblesse oblige* of ruling over the Arab masses wherever they were to be found was their self-appointed vocation.

Emir Abdullah, the prince nominally responsible for the oversight of domestic politics in Transjordan, was particularly sullen at the prospect of ruling an under-populated and dusty backwater of such little apparent value. Through virtually his whole life he strove to do better. He sought to settle the emerging problems between Arabs and Jews in Palestine by offering to rule them both.[11] His politicking in Damascus for a throne worthy of his person, often ironically against the counter-ambitions of his cousins in Baghdad, was as ceaseless as it was fruitless. It was again ironic that after so much effort Abdullah should have been assassinated in Jerusalem, just months after his kingdom doubled in size, with the 1950 union of the West Bank with the East Bank, the former the Arab rump of a by now divided Palestine.

King Hussein inherited the Hashemite mission from his grandfather,[12] but in times that were far less auspicious. The advent of Nasser meant that Arabism had been transformed from a tool of conservative dynasticism into a radical and un-controllable force for social upheaval. Moreover, under Nasser, Arab nationalism became synonymous with the deployment of state power in the region. Once he had discovered the mobilizing qualities of Arabism, transmitted through the new media of the day, the radio, Nasser could speak directly to the Arab "street" in Jordan and beyond. The message that he preached was one of freeing the Arab nation, through three goals: ending the residual presence of European colonialism; subverting the state system that the imperialists had bequeathed the region; and, more particularly, bringing justice for the Palestinians through territorial liberation. Jordan and its leadership was uncomfortably exposed on all three issues.

Yet for all of Nasser's charisma and the attractiveness of his message, the orga-nizational support to precipitate regime change and the absorption of Jordan into a pan-Arab state was chaotic and erratic. Chances came and were missed. Weeks of political volatility culminated in violent demonstrations against Jordan's join-ing the Baghdad Pact in December 1955. The Baghdad Pact was the British-led Middle East alliance, ostensibly directed at the containment of communism and Soviet expansionism. In reality the threat perception of the alliance tended to con-flate Nasserite nationalism with leftist radicalism, hence the deep divisions that consequently opened up in the region. King Hussein was tempted by membership, partly because Iraq was the Arab world's only pact member, and more especially as material inducements in the form of war planes were on offer. He gave way in the end under pressure from sustained street opposition. Once the specific goal of keeping Jordan out of the pact had been realized, the pan-Arab cause allowed the demonstrations to fizzle out.

Parliamentary elections through the 1950s either returned outspoken deputies or were crudely subverted. An Arab nationalist government under Prime Minister Sulaiman Nabulsi was toppled in April 1957. A motley handful of military plots were preempted.[13] While the towns of Jordan were in ferment, the political center of gravity remained with the conservative countryside, where state and tribalism had fused. Repeatedly, the throne was able to rally the heirs to Glubb's tribal levies, now bolstered by anti-leftist and antinationalist Islamists, against all manner of challenges.

In July 1958, the regime came closest to grief, in the aftermath of the successful anti-Hashemite putsch in Baghdad. America, Israel, and the old colonial power played their part in shoring up the monarchy in Jordan, including the deployment of British troops during the height of the threat. A counterrevolution from the palace followed, with a raft of illiberal measures that lasted for three decades, from the banning of political parties to the sacking of radicals from public sector jobs. A national security state began to emerge, with an extensive intelligence apparatus at its center.[14]

Though previously at odds, in the 1950s and 1960s the Hashemite and Transjordanian causes worked largely in harness, committed de facto to consolidation in one country. The loss of the West Bank in the 1967 Arab-Israeli War, while catastrophic for a Hashemite like King Hussein, brought the territory and demography of Jordan more closely in line with the original spatial conception of the state. Through tenacity tinged with more than a dash of ruthlessness and good fortune, King Hussein had survived, together with his kingdom. While Arab nationalism had proved to be a more potent idea than Jordanian nationalism, the capacity of the Jordanian state, underpinned by an increasing sense of East Bank identity, in the end and against the odds proved to be more durable than Nasserism.

The Palestinian Nationalist Narrative for Nationhood

If by the time of political independence in 1946 the notion of a collective sense of Jordanianness had been quietly gaining in traction, this smooth, quiet, and incremental process was disrupted rudely and indefinitely by the 1948–49 first Arab-Israeli war. The conflict resulted in the displacement of large numbers of Palestinian Arabs from their homes. The largest numbers to be dispossessed fetched up either in Jordan proper, or in the West Bank, which would shortly be incorporated into an expanded kingdom. The 1967 Six-Day War led to a further mass Palestinian refugee flow into the East Bank. Though numbers are inevitably vague, a reflection of their politicization, it has become the practice to parrot that sixty percent of the population of post-1967 Jordan is of Palestinian origin. Virtually overnight, Transjordanians had gone from being the bedrock of an emerging nation-state into being an embattled minority in a contested entity.

The Palestinianization of much of the Jordanian political community quickly led to the loss of political innocence associated with the pre-1946 period. While Jordanians were not unsympathetic to the plight of the Palestinians, conflicting interests quickly began to rub up against each other, embracing a range of socio-economic groups. The relief aid dished out to Palestinian refugees in Jordan by the relevant UN agency, the UN Relief and Works Agency for Palestine Refugees in the Near East, helped to force down wage levels, thereby often pitching East Bank laborers and their families well below the poverty line. Jordanian and Palestinian merchants tussled for the limited number of import permits allocated by the state. The Jordanian security forces struggled to cope with the retaliatory strikes by the Israeli military, perversely in response to the guerrilla raids launched by the disparate Palestinian *fedayeen* groups, many of them not even from the kingdom. (*Fedayeen* means "freedom fighter" or "self-sacrificer" in Arabic, and the term refers to various militant Arab groups.) Palestinians, who settled disproportionately in the towns, were at the forefront of the unruly demonstrations that frequently punctuated the 1950s and early 1960s. For two decades after independence, both Jordanian and Palestinian identity began to crystallize in opposition to one another.

This process came to a head over a four-year period in the aftermath of the 1967 war. Its outcome was not exactly inevitable; the Jordanian army and Palestinian fighters joined forces to repulse a major Israeli push into the Jordan Valley at Karameh in 1968. But both sides learned different lessons from the June war. For King Hussein, the war had shown that the Israelis could not be defeated on the battlefield; conflict would result only in more suffering, dislocation, and loss of territory. For the Palestinians, 1967 had shown that the Arab states could not be relied upon to liberate occupied land; only through their own efforts, including the demonstration of resolve through the deployment of force, could the Palestinians succeed. With radical, leftist ideas the currency of the day, the Palestinian political critique was increasingly focused on Jordan. Only through regime change in Amman might the guerrillas acquire a quiescent base from which to prosecute their military strategy.

For Jordanians, the logic of the state came increasingly to prevail. The Palestinian fighters and their constellation of political groupings were resented and feared because they had come to operate like a state within a state. The *fedayeen* effectively presented society with a parallel police force, a parallel tax-raising power, and a parallel defense and foreign policy. Hence, by definition the guerrillas presented an increasingly existential threat to the Jordanian state. If this was the objective reality of state building, the more subjective aspects of proto-nationalism reflected this too. Organized Jordanian and Palestinian institutions had their own flags, their own insignia, their own discourse, and their own cultural signifiers. The struggle was not just about which organizations held sway in the country, but which values and identities too.

That is not, of course, to suggest that there was a crude ethnic cleavage between the two sides. A small number of urban East Bankers joined the *fedayeen,* either out of ideological conviction or political miscalculation. A much larger collection of Palestinians, increasingly terrorized by young thugs with guns from their own community, acting often without restraint, came to resent and fear the *fedayeen.* The prosperous and the owners of fixed capital among the Palestinians were particularly vulnerable. Thus, when the decisive military showdown took place in September 1970, many Palestinians, craving order, spurned the guerrillas. By the end of 1971, the gun-toting fighters had been killed, disarmed, or expelled from the kingdom.

Regional oil-induced prosperity did much to soften Jordanian-Palestinian tensions in the 1970s and early 1980s. Jordanians increasingly came to fill the leading positions in the bureaucracy, as they had long done in the military, and dominated cabinet government, while Palestinians made money in the private sector or by working in the Gulf. The prevalent political line in Amman on the relationship was that Palestinians enjoyed the rights of citizenship. They would not be made to choose between membership in a Jordanian state and a Palestinian state until, that is, a Palestinian state had come into existence. While small numbers of Palestinian nationalist activists identified openly with the Palestine Liberation Organization (PLO), the vast majority of Palestinians accepted this offer of constructive ambivalence, though warily so. Participation in national institutions, notably elections, was usually low, especially in the refugee camps, but this limited engagement went some way toward reassuring Transjordanians that Palestinians would not try to mobilize their numbers in order to take over the country by stealth, having failed to do so before by force of arms.

Jordanians of all origins were, however, shaken during this time by claims from the Israeli right that the Palestinian people deserved and indeed already had their own state, on the east side of the river. This "Jordan is Palestine" argument rose with the political arrival of the Israeli right in government and was particularly associated with the figure of Ariel Sharon. This slogan coincided with the steady leak of Palestinians from the West Bank into the East Bank, mostly in search of work. Fears of the continuation of war by demographic means were a recurring Transjordanian nightmare. This strategy was largely undermined in the eyes of mainstream rightist leaders, like Yitzhak Shamir and Sharon, following the denouement to the Iraqi invasion of Kuwait in 1991. Though King Hussein was initially ambivalent in the crisis, his decision to deny access to his territory for Iraqi army units brought home the worth of Jordan as a buffer state, even to otherwise hawkish Israeli leaders. Since 1991 the Israeli leadership has shown a marked preference to make peace with a Hashemite-led Jordan, rather than to subvert it.

Though tolerably respectful on the surface, relations between Jordanians and Palestinians have nevertheless remained cool. The harsh recession of the late 1980s reversed the prosperity of a decade and more before. The diplomacy of the 1990s delivered peace with Israel for Jordan but not for the Palestinians. Though Yasser Arafat's unilateral engagement with Israel inadvertently gave King Hussein the political cover to conclude a formal peace treaty in October 1994, every bout of unrest and repression in the West Bank and Gaza since has strained Jordanian-Palestinian relations. In the 2000s it has become increasingly the practice publicly to discuss the interethnic tensions in the East Bank, though to no real avail. With King Abdullah II more of a king for the Jordanians (and hence less of a Hashemite than his father was), Palestinian resentments have grown in the kingdom. Attempts to emphasize modern citizenship over traditional, tribal values as the basis of state identity have resonated little.

Evaluating Nation Building

Jordan emerged in the early 1920s as the runt of the Arab state litter; its creation unexpected, its survival improbable. This perception of a precarious survival is arguably the product of relative state weakness. The West Bank apart, Jordan is surrounded by bigger, stronger, richer, and larger entities. Its dependence on an external strategic rent has appeared to compromise its sovereignty, the very substance of an independent existence. Moreover, the unwilling presence in its midst since 1948 of a very significant proportion of the Palestinians, perhaps even a majority, has reinforced the view of Jordan as an entity lacking in popular legitimacy.

Yet Jordan's track record is more robust than such a view would suggest. To explain the reality, one must look at the pre-1946 period, when the foundation stones of a modern Jordan in premodern guise were laid. Through a combination of the leadership of a handful of British figures and the responses of the social periphery, a solid, conservative, rurally based, tribal set of values and interests, which one may identify as the raw material for Jordanian nationalism, were fused with the new state. Though the capacity of the state remained modest when judged by regional standards, its tenacity in the protection of its collective interests at home was increasingly evident, especially in the mid- to late 1950s, and the late 1960s and early 1970s. Although the twin challenges of Arab nationalism and Palestinian nationalism were less robust than they seemed at the time, this should not diminish the achievement of Jordan's survival.

What can be learned more generally about nationalism and nation building in the twentieth century from the Jordanian case? Clearly this: No matter how unpromising the conditions might appear to be (high levels of illiteracy, entrenched premodern social formations, profound question marks over state viability, critical intervention of a colonial power, and the like), there is always the potential for nation building, and indeed such nation building can actually emerge rather rapidly, certainly well within a period of two generations. In the Jordanian case, this required certain internal and external realities. The former combined an embedded sense of common cultural values and a perceived set of shared vested interests. The external domain provided both an international context that ensured such a project could be nurtured rather than undermined and a perceived strategic value that delivered rents and, when needed, "hard" security. The unpromising nature of the context for the emergence of Jordanian nationalism has been a poor indicator of the vigor of that nationalism once manifest.

Notes

1. For the only narrative history of Jordan, from inception to the new century, see Philip Robins, *A History of Jordan* (Cambridge: Cambridge University Press, 2004).

2. Paul Lalor, "Black September 1970: The Palestinian Resistance Movement in Jordan, 1967–1971," University of Oxford, D.Phil. diss., 1992.

3. This figure, which was generated by the fledgling administration, excludes the area south of Maan, which was, until 1925, governed by the Kingdom of the Hijaz. See Peter Gubser, *Politics and Change in Al Kerak, Jordan* (London: Oxford University Press, 1973), 91.

4. For a sample of their published works and hence their attitudes about the Arab World see: F.G. Peake, *A History of Jordan and Its Tribes* (Coral Gables, FL: University of Miami Press, 1958); Alec Seath Kirkbride, *A Crackle of Thorns* (London: John Murray, 1956); John Bagot Glubb, *The Story of the Arab Legion* (London: Hodder & Stoughton, 1948).

5. For an insightful discussion of how Jordan's search for budget security has affected its foreign policy see Laurie A. Brand, *Jordan's Inter-Arab Relations: The Political Economy of Alliance-Making* (New York: Columbia University Press, 1994).

6. For the definitive studies of north Jordan's villages, especially during the pre- and early state periods see Richard Antoun, *Arab Village: A Social Structural Study of a Transjordanian Peasant Community* (Bloomington: Indiana University Press, 1972), and *Low Key Politics: A Case of Local Level Leadership and Change in the Middle East* (New York: State University of New York Press, 1979).

7. For the discussion of the importance of external elites in the growing consolidation of the mandate of Transjordan see Philip Robins, *The Consolidation of Hashemite Rule in Jordan* (Unpublished thesis, University of Exeter, 1988).

8. For the classic study of the town and its environs, see Peter Gubser, *Politics and Change*.

9. For standard biographies of the life of Glubb Pasha see: James Lunt, *Glubb Pasha* (London: Collins, 1994); Trevor Royle, *Glubb Pasha* (London: Little, Brown, 1992).

10. For the definitive early work on the Jordanian military see P.J. Vatikiotis, *Politics and the Military in Jordan: A Study of the Arab Legion, 1921–1957* (London: Frank Cass, 1967).

11. For a sustained analysis of the subject of Abdullah and Palestine see Joseph Nevo, *King Abdallah and Palestine: A Territorial Ambition* (Basingstoke: MacMillan Press, 1996).

12. For the more useful biographies of King Hussein see: James Lunt, *Hussein of Jordan* (London: MacMillan, 1989); Avi Shlaim, *Lion of Jordan* (London: Allen Lane, 2007).

13. For a detailed discussion of threats to the regime during the 1950s see Robert B. Satloff, *From Abdullah to Hussein* (Oxford: Oxford University Press, 1994).

14. For a study focused primarily on the emergence of the national security establishment and its role see Lawrence Tal, *Politics, the Military, and National Security in Jordan, 1955–1967* (Basingstoke: MacMillan, 2002).

12

Nation-State Building in Israel

GREGORY MAHLER

Abstract: *This case study discusses the realization of the nineteenth-century Zionist dream to create a Jewish state via mass immigration from Europe to the lands of ancient Israel. Extensive lobbying in Britain, the colonial power in control of the Mandate of Palestine, and extensive political preparation for Israel's initial political institutions preceded independence. Israel retained the legal system and many of the administrative institutions from the mandate and later gradually reformed them. From the beginning it had universal adult suffrage. As a result its institutions enjoyed widespread legitimacy among the Jewish population. The Arab population of the region, however, attacked Israel within hours of its independence in 1948. During the eight-month war that followed, Palestinian land ownership dropped from 87.5 to 22.6 percent and has remained a divisive issue ever since. Israel has faced a major war every decade since independence. Despite high defense expenditures, it has a thriving economy and a far higher general standard of living than any other country in the region. Substantial economic aid from Jews internationally, the United States, and Germany has contributed to Israeli prosperity.*

Israel became an independent state after almost a century of efforts by Zionist activists working for the creation of a Jewish state. Their dream became reality after the horrors of the Holocaust with the vote by the United Nations for statehood for Israel in 1948. The founders of the State of Israel created a Western parliamentary-style system of government based on the Westminster model, a strong welfare state, and a highly competent military. In the final decade of the twentieth century, Israel had among the highest gross domestic product (GDP) growth rates in the West, averaging almost six percent between 1990 and 1996, with a per capita GDP in 2002 of $16,950, placing it twenty-first of 200 nations in the World Bank database.[1]

The Creation of a Jewish State

From the end of the Roman period (ca. 600 C.E.) to the Crusades (beginning in 1095), Arabs dominated the lands that are today Israel, Jordan, and Syria, while very small—and politically and economically insignificant—Jewish populations resided there.[2] After the Crusades, the area again fell under the rule of Islamic states. During the fourteenth and fifteenth centuries, many Jews returned to what was known as simply "Palestine,"[3] which a number of Turkish dynasties controlled from approximately 1517 until 1917.[4]

Prior to the nineteenth century the overwhelming majority of the world's Jews had no contact at all with Palestine. The concept of Zionism emerged during the nineteenth century as the rationale for the creation of a Jewish state.[5] Zionism as a national movement had two distinct yet interrelated goals, as articulated by the Zionist leader Theodor Herzl, in his book *Der Judenstaat* in 1896. First, it sought to return Jews to the land for a resurgence of agricultural activities and for a revival of Jewish national life—socially, culturally, economically, and politically. Second, it sought to acquire a publicly recognized, legally secure home for the Jews, free from European-style persecution.[6] By the mid-1860s, an active Jewish community in Palestine had developed.[7] Between 1881 and 1914, events in Europe acceler-ated Jewish migration when a series of anti-Jewish decrees in Russia caused an estimated 2,600,000 Jews to leave Russia and its surrounding territories.[8] In 1898 the Second Zionist Congress passed a resolution sanctioning efforts to obtain a legal charter for Jewish settlement in Palestine.

As the Zionist movement grew, more Jews migrated to Palestine, expanding Jewish communities there and developing new ones. The term *Yishuv* refers to the Jewish communities in Palestine, primarily a direct result of immigration.[9] The immigration came in discernible waves—called *aliyot* (singular: *aliyah,* literally "going up")—starting in the last decades of the nineteenth century in response to growing anti-Semitism in Europe.[10] The five waves are dated from 1882 to 1903, 1905 to 1918, 1919 to 1923, 1925 to 1929, and 1933 to 1936. Immigrants of the first four waves came primarily from Russia and Eastern Europe, while the fifth wave came primarily from Nazi Germany and areas under German control in the 1930s. Over time the Arab population of Palestine became increasingly unhappy with the growth of the Jewish population and with immigration there, generally.

During World War I, the secret Anglo-French Sykes-Picot Agreement of 1916 indicated an intention to put most of what today are Syria and Lebanon under French influence, most of what today are Jordan and Iraq under British influence, and parts of current-day Israel under a "joint allied condominium" for religious and political reasons.[11] By 1917 Britain unilaterally abandoned the condominium, declaring its intention to exercise influence over all of Palestine for strategic con-siderations given the proximity to the Suez Canal.[12] In 1917, with the outcome of World War I still in doubt, America not yet a belligerent, the Russian monarchy overthrown, and the Eastern Front collapsing, the British hoped that the support of Jews throughout the world would aid their war efforts. The British government, accordingly, issued the Balfour Declaration declaring its support for the creation of a Jewish homeland in Palestine.[13]

Although Britain assumed de facto control over Palestine with the Ottoman Empire's defeat in 1918, not until April 1920 did the Supreme Council of the

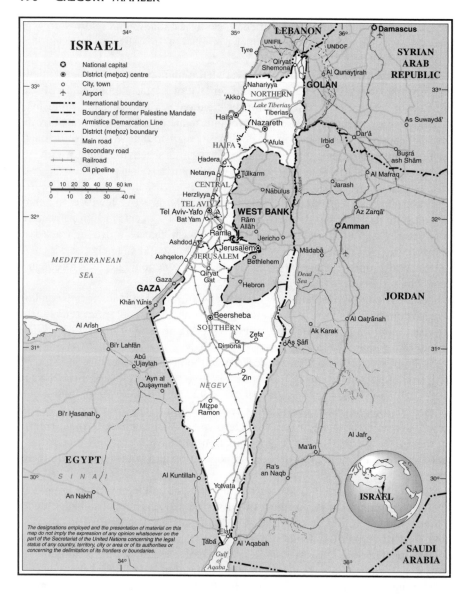

Paris Peace Conference award Britain a legal—de jure—mandate, or control over Palestine.[14] From 1920 to 1922, tensions increased in Palestine between the Arab and Jewish populations, with both sides resenting the British presence. Upon receiving mandatory power, Britain proceeded to partition "Palestine" in 1922 into two territories divided by the Jordan River, one called "Palestine," to the west, and the other called "Transjordan," to the east. Jews were prohibited from settling in the latter. Significantly, the mandate for Palestine formally recognized both Zionist claims and the Zionist movement itself,[15] but its vague wording became the basis of much disagreement.

During the 1920s and 1930s, periods of intense violence plagued relations between the Jewish and Arab communities.[16] In 1937 a British Royal Commission, known as the Peel Commission after its chairman, William Robert Wellesley Peel, Earl of Peel, acknowledged the irreconcilable goals of Arab nationalism and Zionism when it declared that in evaluating the claims of the Zionists and the native non-Jewish population, it found a conflict of "right with right" in Palestine. When, in deference to Arab sentiments, the British tried to limit Jewish immigration in 1939, a struggle erupted between Britain and some of the indigenous Zionist organizations, whom the British considered "terrorist"; the battle lasted until independence.[17]

The Holocaust took the lives of ninety percent of all Jews in those parts of Europe occupied by the Germans, and close to one-third of world Jewry.[18] It also gave increased intensity to Jewish demands for statehood. Two essential lessons came out of the Holocaust for Jews, lessons that are still considered to be important in Israel today. These are, first, that nothing is ever "too horrible to happen"; and second, that Jews must never again depend upon others for their very survival.[19]

After the war, Britain opposed any kind of partition of the Mandate of Palestine, and the Arab states opposed anything other than a single Arab state in Palestine. Both Arabs and Jews had legitimate and incompatible claims. In the end the British decided that they simply could not give all parties involved what they demanded, and returned the mandate to the United Nations. In November of 1947, the United Nations voted thirty-three to thirteen, with Britain abstaining, to create separate Jewish and Arab states in Palestine. Jews in the *Yishuv* as well as Zionists outside of Palestine generally supported the resolution.[20] The United States and the Soviet Union immediately recognized Israel.[21]

The Security Environment

Since independence Israel has operated in a foreign policy setting characterized by hostility and anxiety.[22] This legacy of warfare is significant for its duration, intensity, and policy implications. Within hours of the declaration of Israeli independence on 14 May 1948, Egypt, Syria, Jordan, Lebanon, Saudi Arabia, and Iraq attacked Israel. As a consequence of the eight-month War of Independence, Israel gained almost 2,500 square miles of territory that under the original UN partition plan would have gone to Arab states, primarily on the West Bank and the Gaza Strip.[23] Several different armistices were subsequently signed: with Egypt (February 1949); Lebanon (March 1949); Transjordan (April 1949); and Syria (July 1949).[24]

During the 1948 fighting, hundreds of thousands of Palestinian Arabs fled from the lands occupied by the new State of Israel.[25] In 1882 the non-Jewish residents of Palestine constituted almost ninety-five percent of the population, but by 1948 their proportion had fallen to less than twenty percent as a result of substantial emigration during the period leading up to and during the War of Independence.[26] After the war, hundreds of thousands of Jewish immigrants from communities across the Middle East and Africa, as well as from Europe, streamed into Israel.

Currents of Palestinian nationalism predated the State of Israel,[27] and existed under Ottoman and British rule. Prior to partition, "Palestinians owned about 87.5 percent of the total area of Palestine . . . while Jews owned 6.6 percent of the total lands," with the British holding the balance.[28] By the end of the war, Israel controlled 77.4 percent of the land, and there were 726,000 Palestinian refugees located outside of the armistice lines (Israel's borders) and approximately 32,000 refugees inside the armistice lines.[29] The Palestinians refer to the Israeli War of Independence as *al-Naqba* (the Catastrophe), and argue that the UN partition created a Jewish state with just over fifty-six percent of the land of Palestine at a time when Jews owned less than seven percent and made up about one-third of the population.[30]

The Israelis have fought one major conflict per decade since independence. During the 1956 Suez Crisis, Israel, with France and Britain, took back the Suez Canal recently nationalized by Egypt. Historians disagree about the exact role of the British and the French in leading/inviting Israel into the conflict against Egypt. The French agenda heavily influenced Israel's involvement in the war, which both France and Britain encouraged Israel to join.[31] The United States and the Soviet Union, however, intervened to restore the *status quo ante bellum*. U.S. President Dwight Eisenhower decried the Israeli invasion of the Sinai and promised to ensure that Egypt fulfilled its pledge to keep international waterways open in the future as a part of an agreement with Israel.

In the Six-Day War of 1967, Israel launched a preemptive attack against Egypt and Syria, which were massing troops on their borders with Israel and threatening to attack. When Egypt ordered the UN peacekeeping forces out of the Sinai, where they had maintained a demilitarized zone, moved its own forces toward the Israeli border, and closed the Straits of Tiran to Israeli shipping (cutting Israeli access to the Red Sea), Israel felt that it had to act. A few days later, yielding to strong pressures from Egypt and Syria, Jordan entered the fighting. When Israel sought American support to reopen the Straits of Tiran based upon President Eisenhower's 1957 promise, President Lyndon Johnson—at this time involved in an increasingly unpopular war in Vietnam—responded that the United States was "not the policeman of the world," so Israel would have to take care of its own problems.[32] During the fighting, Israel took the West Bank and Gaza Strip, and also occupied the Sinai Peninsula and the Golan Heights.

In the 1973 Yom Kippur War, Israel repelled an attack by Egypt and Syria. Although Israel was strongly tempted to undertake another preemptive strike against Egypt and Syria as a result of intelligence that an attack by those countries was imminent, it did not do so, at least partially because of promised U.S. support if an attack came. In the event, Israel suffered extraordinarily heavy losses, but managed to hold and then repel the invading armies on both fronts.[33]

In the First Lebanon War (1982–86), Israel intervened in the Lebanese Civil War, claiming as its goal the elimination of Palestine Liberation Organization (PLO) bases on its borders. The PLO bases had been relocated from Jordanian territory to the southern border of Lebanon following fighting between Jordanian and Palestinian forces in September of 1970 (known as "Black September"). Israel found the harassment of its northern border from Lebanese territories by the non-Lebanese PLO to be unacceptable and did not withdraw from Lebanon until 2000.

During the First Intifada or "uprising" (1987–93), the Palestinian population of the occupied territories used political violence within Israel's borders to put a different kind of political pressure on Israel. They resumed the campaign in the Second Intifada (2000–present).[34] During the Second Lebanon War (2006), Israel invaded Lebanon over the kidnapping by Hamas and Hezbollah of Israeli soldiers, but eventually withdrew without securing their release. As a result of this succession of conflicts, Israelis look at virtually all foreign policy issues from a national security perspective.

While Israel and Egypt have been "at peace" since the 1979 Camp David Accords, and Israel and Jordan have been "at peace" since the 1994 Israel-Jordan Peace Treaty, the "peace" has not been sufficiently secure for Israelis to feel that they no longer need to be concerned about their borders. Israel remains technically at war with all of its other neighbors, including Lebanon, Syria, Iraq, and Saudi Arabia, among others. Although the last full-scale Middle East war was in 1973, Israeli defense forces were mobilized from 1982 until 2000 in Lebanon, have continued to be on alert along Israel's borders, and in recent years have remained very active in a struggle against terrorism in the West Bank and in Israel proper. The summer of 2006 saw geographically limited but major warfare in northern Israel and across the Lebanese border that reminded all Israelis of their vulnerability. This was especially true when Hezbollah forces launched missiles from southern Lebanon, hitting Haifa. Because Israel is small and because some of her larger and more populous neighbors remain hostile, the concept of defensible borders is very important to Israelis.

The Legal System

When the State of Israel was created in 1948, the Provisional Council of State announced that all laws from the mandate period would remain in effect until revised. Likewise, it consolidated and transformed into thirteen ministries the former departments that had long been run under Jewish Agency administration. This was the origin of Israel's ministries of defense, education, and health, as well as others. The army and the judiciary were known from the beginning for their high levels of professionalism and immunity from party politics.[35]

The Provisional Council had broad public support, but it was understood that the council was an interim government. The legislature—the Knesset—that became its successor institution was elected according to a proportional system using party lists. Individuals voted for political parties, not candidates, and parties received a proportion of seats in the Knesset that corresponded to the proportion of votes they received. A party receiving twenty percent of the votes would receive twenty percent of the seats in the Knesset. New laws gave all citizens over eighteen the right to vote in the elections for the 120-member Knesset.

Israel's legal system rested on five sources: Ottoman law, mandatory law, British common law, law of the Knesset, and religious law. Initially the laws of the British mandate remained in force and Ottoman traditions concerning land ownership were followed. Over the years, however, the Knesset gradually replaced these bodies of law with its own legislation.[36] Israel followed Anglo-American traditions, emphasizing the protection of civil rights, and British common law. Laws concerning personal status—regulating marriage, divorce, burial, inheritance, and so on—followed the religious traditions of each community, meaning that Israel's Jewish population fell under the jurisdiction of orthodox rabbinical courts.[37]

At the time of independence, serious disagreements erupted over the nature of the future constitution, with religious conservatives arguing for basing the new constitution on the Torah, a position rejected by secularists. The political solution that resulted was to put aside indefinitely plans for a constitution until a consensus could develop, and the *status quo agreement* was born.[38]

Instead of a single written document, eleven Fundamental Laws make up Israel's constitution today."[39] Fundamental Laws are endowed with a "special" position when compared to regular legislation, but since they are decisions of a majority of the members of Knesset they can, in principle, be modified or done away with by a simple majority as well. The eleven Fundamental Laws that have been passed by the Knesset are: (1) The Knesset (1958); (2) Israel Lands (1960); (3) The President of the State (1964); (4) The Government (1968); (5) The State Economy (1975); (6) The Army (1976); (7) Jerusalem: Capital of Israel (1980); (8) The Judiciary (1984); (9) The State Comptroller (1988); (10) Human Dignity and Liberty (1992); and (11) Freedom of Occupation (1994).[40]

In addition to the Fundamental Laws, over the years the Knesset has passed a number of other pieces of legislation that have a quasi-constitutional status in terms of their legal importance and contribution to the country's political culture. These include the Law and Administration Ordinance (1948), establishing a body of Ottoman and British law as Israeli law; the Law of Return (1950), laying out the fundamental principles of the right of Jews to immigrate to Israel and the responsibility of the state to help them in this effort; the Equal Rights for Women Law (1951), giving women equal political and legal rights in the state; the Nationality Law (1952), regulating the naturalization of non-Jews; the Judges' Law (1953), setting up a framework for the appointment of judges; and the Courts Law (1969), establishing several different court systems for different classes of litigation.

The Political Institutions

Israel based the political structure of the Knesset on the British or Westminster model of parliamentary government, which has four defining features:[41] First, the chief executive position is not held by the same person who serves as the head of state. In Israel, there are two executives, the president and the prime minister, not one as in the case of the president of the United States. The Israeli president acts on the advice of the prime minister and Knesset and has very little discretionary power on his or her own (although all Israeli presidents have thus far been men). Second, under the Westminster model, executive powers of government are exercised by the chief executive and his or her cabinet. In Israel, the "real" powers of the government are exercised by the prime minister and the cabinet, while the president serves a primarily symbolic role. Third, the chief executive and the cabinet are all members of the legislature. This has been true for the Israeli prime minister and most of the cabinet except for a brief hiatus between 1996 and 2001,[42] and differs from the relationship found in a presidential system in which there are specific prohibitions against membership in both branches of government. Fourth, the chief executive and the cabinet are responsible to, and can be removed by, the legislature, a right the Knesset can exercise at any time.

The Knesset is constitutionally Israel's supreme political authority.[43] The people elect the Knesset, and the Knesset elects the leader of the executive branch, the prime minister. There is no executive veto of the Knesset's actions, and the courts have hesitated to limit legislative actions by declaring them unconstitutional. There has not been widespread (American-style) judicial review, although this has become increasingly frequent in the last decade or so.[44] The Knesset cannot be dissolved by the head of state (the president); new elections cannot be called by either the head of state or the chief executive, as in other parliamentary systems. Only the Knesset can cut short its four-year term-of-office mandate from the voters, dissolve itself, and call for early elections. The prime minister stays in office only as long as he or she can command a legislative majority. In the Israeli case, this entails the construction and maintenance of coalition governments.

As with other parliamentary political systems, the cabinet, not the legislature, is the day-to-day focus of public attention and is the "engine" that drives the machinery of government. Because of strong party discipline, the role of the individual Knesset member is limited in the legislative process; the political party constitutes the key link between society and the polity.

Political parties explain much of the political turbulence in Israel. The Israeli political system has been referred to as a "party-state."[45] Political parties played an important role in Israel's achieving statehood. It has even been said that the State of Israel "was actually brought into existence by political parties, which were organized and developed entities . . . years before the coming of statehood."[46] Indeed, contemporary Israeli political parties are a direct link to the past in that virtually all have roots in some pre-state political form.[47]

The Israeli political party system could be classified as "overdeveloped." Thirty-one parties ran candidates in the Fifteenth Knesset elections in 1999, and fifteen of these parties won seats[48] by taking at least 1.5 percent of the votes;[49] twenty-seven parties ran in the Knesset elections in 2003, and thirteen parties won seats.[50] In the elections for the Seventeenth Knesset in 2006, fourteen parties were elected to serve.[51] Many of these lists represented temporary coalitions of many separate party organizations.

Regardless of the instability of *coalitions,* Israeli government *institutions* have been relatively stable. From the time of independence, even when Israel's emerging political system was weakly institutionalized, Israelis of all parties have followed the rules of Israel's legal and political institutions. This distinguishes Israel from many new states, which often have large bodies of laws and stated political rules that are honored primarily in the breach.

The Economic Environment

Israel's economy since the time of its creation has resembled other centralized economies, with strong social welfare dimensions.[52] Even before independence, the state played a major role in providing for the well-being of its citizens. This was true in a variety of policy areas, including medical care, housing, employment, education, and the provision of food and transportation. The Israeli economy has, since its inception, been "planned,"[53] although since the 1980s there has been significant deregulation of markets.[54]

Over the years Israel's economy has dealt with four major challenges: guaranteeing national security, absorbing immigration, establishing a modern infrastructure, and providing a high level of public services.[55] During the 1970s and 1980s, Israel spent nearly twenty-five percent of its GDP on defense. This made it extremely difficult to devote substantial resources to domestic items. During the 1990s a wave of almost one million immigrants—primarily from the former Soviet Union—put a huge burden on the economy to relocate and support them. Today Israel spends approximately ten percent of the GDP on defense. The modern infrastructure includes everything from roads and railroads to airports, telecommunications, port facilities, and the national aqueduct. These are major items in the national budget, and, with population growth, the demands on the infrastructure have correspondingly increased. Finally, Israel has a tradition of providing significant social services, but it has been difficult to continue to provide the supports that the growing population expects.

These strains on the economy, especially since the 1973 Yom Kippur War, have caused a retrenchment of government social spending. Given that military and defense expenditures are largely immune from reductions, to control the budget deficit the government has capped or cut its spending in a wide range of social programs. Those with the least financial means, the poor and the unemployed, have borne the brunt of this budget cutting. The cuts, however, have not become a major political issue for the party in power, the Likud, which has a natural constituency among the poorer Sephardic Jews, who came to Israel mainly from countries in the Middle East and North Africa..

Israel's economy grew rapidly between 1948 and 1973, averaging ten percent per year.[56] This was a consequence of factors not found in many other nations, including a rapid expansion of the labor force as a result of immigration and an artificially high rate of investment, substantially provided by Jews living abroad who funneled their contributions to the economy through such organizations as United Jewish Appeal, Hadassah, and other Zionist organizations. There have been three significant foreign sources of Israeli government funding over the years: the world's Jewish population living outside of Israel, and the governments of the United States and the German Republic. These sources have provided both grant funds—not requiring repayments—and loan funds.[57]

After 1973, Israel's economy slowed considerably, with a growth rate of 5.0 percent in 1978–79, 3.2 percent in 1980–81, 1.2 percent in 1982–83, and 1.8 percent in 1983–84.[58] Through the 1980s, the major difficulty was the vast and continuing budgetary increases in the areas of defense and security.[59] These, combined with worldwide inflation and an overwhelming increase in the price of oil, put severe strains on Israeli economic development. In the summer of 1985, the government implemented a radical emergency stabilization program to combat a very serious inflationary cycle. Inflation fell from 445 percent in 1984 to 185 percent in 1985 to 21 percent in 1989.[60] Another difficulty was economic policy making in the occupied territories and, specifically, the appropriate role for the Israeli government there.[61] According to many, the Israeli contribution to West Bank development since the Six-Day War in 1967 has been much more active and constructive than that of Jordan prior to the Israeli occupation.[62]

Generally speaking, Israel's gross domestic product is composed of three parts: (1) general governmental services and private nonprofit institutions, (2) dwelling ownership, and (3) the business sector. The governmental services and nonprofit institutions make up approximately twenty percent of the GDP, dwelling ownership accounts for about ten percent, and the business sector accounts for almost seventy percent.[63] Almost one-quarter of Israel's labor force is employed in industry, which accounts for nearly twenty percent of the GDP.[64] In recent years those working on *kibbutzim* (or collective farms), long thought of simply in agricultural terms in the national economy, began to develop significant industrial output, with individual *kibbutzim* selecting specific products for local production. This production made up five percent of Israel's total industrial output.[65] Complementing this, the *kibbutzim* have developed new techniques in irrigation and hydroponics and new breeding programs for both plants and animals to produce high quality farm exports in a region of the world not traditionally known for its agriculture.

Israel has been able to negotiate free-trade arrangements with the European Community (1975) and with the United States (1985), so its goods can enter both marketplaces without the additional burden of import duties. The United States and the European Community account for over sixty percent of Israel's exports; the United States purchased thirty-two percent and the European Union purchased thirty percent of Israel's exports.[66]

The country's major international financial concern has traditionally been its trade deficit.[67] Israel has a very significant gap between its high level of imports on the one hand and its relatively lower level of exports on the other. Every recent Israeli government has tried to cut the exports-to-imports gap. High defense spending makes it difficult to maintain a trade equilibrium when the nation's major exports include oranges and carnations and a major source of foreign revenue is tourism (which itself has been severely affected by violence and political terrorism in recent years). One report suggested that "it has not been possible for Israel to attain anything even resembling 'economic independence'" since obtaining independence.[68]

Israelis have created a prosperous state despite a very difficult security and economic environment. The key word in understanding the creation and development of the State of Israel has been *diversity,* diversity in terms of culture, social and economic factors, immigration, and many other institutional factors, too. The culture of Israel since prior to independence in 1948 has emphasized pragmatism and survival, and this culture has brought Israel to its present situation.

Why has Israel managed to succeed in the developmental process in ways that many of its neighbors have not? First, the constant existential threat of war has forced groups and individuals who otherwise might have strongly opposed each other to cooperate and work together. Second, the Israeli population has traditionally been highly educated and shared a belief in the importance of the rule of law. This meant that Israel had ample political and economic talent to staff its political, economic, legal, educational, and other institutions, and that Israelis have shared a belief that these institutions should operate according to rules. Thus, despite the numerous political parties and shifting party coalitions, the Israeli political system remains very stable. Governments come and go on the basis of law. Third, even prior to independence Israel received substantial assistance from external Jewish communities, and later from the United States, Germany, and multinational organizations. Finally, Israel's remarkable population growth has contributed at times to remarkable economic growth. This population increase, of course, has cut both ways. Although at times it has entailed a highly unusual influx of well-educated people bringing substantial resources with them, at other times it has entailed large numbers of needy immigrants requiring expensive social support services.

Notes

1. Government of Israel, Ministry of Foreign Affairs, *Facts about Israel, 2006,* "Economy," at www.mfa.gov.il/MFA/Facts+About+Israel/Economy/ECONOMY.htm, accessed 5 May 2008.

2. Haim Z'ew Hirschberg, "Crusader Period, 1099–1291," in Israel Pocket Library, *History until 1880* (Jerusalem: Keter Books, 1973), 185–200.

3. "Mamluk Period (1291–1516)," in Israel Pocket Library, *History until 1880,* 206.

4. Avigdor Levy, ed., *Jews, Turks, Ottomans* (Syracuse, NY: Syracuse University Press, 2002); Haim Z'ew Hirschberg, "Ottoman Period (1517–1917)," in Israel Pocket Library, *History until 1880,* 212–50.

5. Mordechai Chertoff, ed., *Zionism* (New York: Herzl Press, 1975); Israel Cohen, *A Short History of Zionism* (London: F. Muller, 1951).

6. Norman Levin, *The Zionist Movement in Palestine and World Politics, 1880–1918* (Lexington, MA: D.C. Heath, 1974).

7. Dan Horowitz and Moshe Lissak, *Origins of the Israeli Polity* (Chicago: University of Chicago Press, 1978).

8. Jacob Katz, "Forerunners," in Chertoff, ed., *Zionism,* 21.

9. Moshe Burstein, *Self Government of the Jews in Palestine Since 1900* (New Haven, CT: Hyperion Press, 1934); Lawrence Davidson, "Zionism, Socialism and United States Support for the Jewish Colonization of Palestine in the 1920s," *Arab Studies Quarterly* 18, no. 3 (1996), 1–17.

10. Asher Arian, *Politics in Israel* (Chatham, NJ: Chatham House, 1985), 13–19.

11. Howard Sachar, *A History of Israel* (New York: Alfred A. Knopf, 1981).

12. Ibid, 96.

13. J.M.N. Jeffries, "The Balfour Declaration," in Ian Lustick, *Arab-Israeli Relations* (New York: Garland, 1994).

14. John McTague, "The British Military Administration in Palestine, 1917–1920," *Journal of Palestine Studies* 7, no. 3 (1978), 55–76; D. Edward Knox, *The Making of a New Eastern Question* (Washington, DC: Catholic University Press, 1981).

15. Don Peretz, *The Government and Politics of Israel* (Boulder, CO: Westview Press, 1979), 32–33.

16. Mark Tessler, *A History of the Israeli-Palestinian Conflict* (Bloomington: Indiana University Press, 1994), 241–42.

17. Menachem Begin, *The Revolt* (New York: Nash, 1977); Michael Cohen, *The Rise of Israel* (New York: Garland, 1987).

18. Peretz, *Government and Politics,* 45.

19. Gregory Mahler, *Politics and Government in Israel* (Lanham, MD: Rowman and Littlefield, 2004), 34.

20. Phyllis Bennis, "The United Nations and Palestine: Partition and Its Aftermath," *Arab Studies Quarterly* 19, no. 3 (1997), 47–76.

21. John Snetsinger, *Truman, the Jewish Vote, and the Creation of Israel* (Palo Alto, CA: Stanford University Press, 1974).

22. Efraim Karsh, *Israel: The First Hundred Years* (Portland, OR: Frank Cass, 1999).

23. Dan Kurzman, *Genesis 1948* (New York: World, 1970); Joseph Heller, *The Birth of Israel, 1945–1949* (Gainesville: University Press of Florida, 2000).

24. Muassasat al-Dirasat al-Filastiniyah, *The Arab-Israeli Armistice Agreements* (Beirut: Institute for Palestine Studies, 1967); David Ben-Gurion, *Israel: A Personal History* (New York: Funk and Wagnalls, 1971), 94–330.

25. Tom Segev, *1949: The First Israelis* (New York: Free Press, 1986); Benny Morris, *The Birth of the Palestine Refugee Problem, 1947–1949* (New York: Cambridge University Press, 1987).

26. Michael Wolffsohn, *Israel: Polity, Society and Economy 1882–1986* (Atlantic Highlands, NJ: Humanities Press International, 1987), 121.

27. Tessler, *A History of the Israeli-Palestinian Conflict,* 69–126; Ann Lesch, "The Origins of Palestine Arab Nationalism," in *Nationalism in a Non-National State,* eds. William Haddad and William Ochsenwald (Columbus: Ohio State University Press, 1977).

28. Palestinian Academic Society for the Study of International Affairs (PASSIA), *Diary, 2000* (Jerusalem: PASSIA, 2000), 254.

29. PASSIA, *Datebook, 1996* (Jerusalem: PASSIA, 1996), 190.

30. Ibid.; As'ad Ganim, *The Palestinian-Arab Minority in Israel, 1948–2000* (Albany: State University of New York Press, 2001); Avraham Sela and Moshe Ma'oz, *The PLO and Israel* (New York: St. Martin's Press, 1997).

31. David Tal, "Israel's Road to the 1956 War," *International Journal of Middle East Studies* 28 (1996): 59–81; Motti Golani, *Israel in Search of a War* (Jerusalem: Steimatzky's Agency, 1966); Mordechai Bar-On, *The Gates of Gaza* (New York: St. Martin's Press, 1995).

32. Mahler, *Politics and Government in Israel,* 255.

33. Avraham Adnan, *On the Banks of the Suez* (San Rafael, CA: Presidio Press, 1980); Peter Allen, *The Yom Kippur War* (Newark, NJ: Scribner, 1982).

34. Mahler, *Politics and Government in Israel,* 258–68.

35. Sachar, *A History of Israel,* 369–70.

36. Mahler, *Politics and Government in Israel,* 230–31.

37. Sachar, *A History of Israel,* 360–62, 386–88.

38. Mahler, *Politics and Government in Israel,* 119–21.

39. Wolffsohn, *Israel,* 6.

40. Ibid.

41. Gregory Mahler, *Comparative Politics: An Institutional and Cross-National Approach* (Upper Saddle River, NJ: Prentice Hall, 2003), 187.

42. With the exception of the prime minister, cabinet members do not have to be members of the Knesset, and many Knesset members resign from the Knesset after being named to the cabinet to allow party colleagues to inherit their seats in the legislature.

43. Benjamin Akzin, "Israel's Knesset," *Ariel* 15 (1966), 5–11.

44. Eliahu Likhovski, "The Courts and the Legislative Supremacy of the Knesset," *Israel Law Review* 3, no. 3 (1968), 345–67.

45. Emanuel Gutmann, "Israel," *Journal of Politics* 25 (1963), 703.

46. Scott Johnston, "Politics of the Right in Israel," *Social Science* 40 (1965), 104.

47. Benjamin Akzin, "The Role of Parties in Israeli Democracy," *Journal of Politics* 17 (1955), 507–45.

48. http://www.knesset.gov.il/main/eng/engframe.htm > 1999 Knesset Elections > Lists Running in the '99 Knesset Elections. The list of parties winning Knesset seats can be found at http://www.knesset.gov.il/main/eng/engframe.htm > 1999 Knesset Elections > 1999 Elections Results.

49. Central Bureau of Statistics, *Statistical Abstract of Israel* (Jerusalem: 2001), Table 10.2, "Valid Votes in the Elections to the Knesset, by Main List," 10–19.

50. Ministry of Foreign Affairs web page, http://www.mfa.gov.il/mfa/go.asp?MFAH0n130 > The Knesset > Elections in Israel January 2003.

51. http://www.knesset.gov.il/mk/eng/MKIndex_Current_eng.asp?view=1, last consulted May 18, 2008.

52. Benjamin Akzin and Y. Dror, *Israel: High Pressure Planning* (Syracuse, NY: Syracuse University Press, 1966).

53. Raphaella Bilski, *Can Planning Replace Politics?* (Boston: Martinus Nijhoff, 1980).

54. Avi Ben-Basat, *The Israeli Economy, 1985–1998* (Cambridge, MA: M.I.T. Press, 2002); Johnathan Nitzan, *The Global Political Economy of Israel* (London: Pluto Press, 2001).

55. Israel Ministry of Foreign Affairs, "Economy," *Facts about Israel,* online edition 2006, http://www.mfa.gov.il/MFA/Facts%20About%20Israel/Economy/ECONOMY-%20 Challenges%20and%20Achievements.

56. David Horowitz, *The Enigma of Economic Growth* (New York: Praeger, 1972).

57. Mahler, *Politics and Government in Israel,* 105.

58. Edi Karni, "The Israeli Economy, 1973–1976," *Economic Development and Cultural Change* 28, no. 1 (1979), 63–76; Wolffsohn, *Israel,* 223.

59. Eliyahu Kanovsky, *The Economic Impact of the Six Day War* (New York: Praeger, 1970); Marion Mushkat, "The Socio-Economic Malaise of Developing Countries as a Function of Military Expenditures: The Case of Egypt and Israel" *Co-existence* 15, no. 2 (1978), 135–45.

60. *Facts about Israel, online* http://www.mfa.gov.il/mfa/go.asp?MFAH00m70, "Inflation and the Public Sector."

61. Antoine Mansour, "Monetary Dualism: The Case of the West Bank under Occupation," *Journal of Palestine Studies* 11, no. 3 (1982), 103–16.

62. Arie Bregman, *The Economy of the Administered Areas, 1968–1973* (Jerusalem: Bank of Israel, 1975).

63. *Facts about Israel* (1985), 64.

64. *Statistical Abstract of Israel, 2007,* found at http://www1.cbs.gov.il/shnaton58/st14_03.pdf. Table 14.3 is titled "Net Domestic Product and National Income By Industry."

65. *Facts about Israel* (1985), 65.

66. Government of Israel, Ministry of Foreign Affairs, "Economy (2006 Edition) Introduction," found at http://www.mfa.gov.il/MFA/Facts%20About%20Israel/Economy/ECONOMY

67. Haim Levy and Azriel Levy, *The Management of Foreign Exchange Reserves with Balance-of-Payments and External Debt Considerations* (Jerusalem: Maurice Falk Institute for Economic Research in Israel, 1998).

68. Wolffsohn, *Israel,* 255.

13

State Building and Economic Failure in North Korea

Charles K. Armstrong

Abstract: *This case study describes North Korea's descent from being the most industrialized part of the Korean Peninsula to being one of the world's poorest countries, with a fraction of the per capita GNP of South Korea. The North Korean government inherited a strong sense of nation and established strong state institutions, but failed to create prosperity over the long run. It rapidly rebuilt the war-damaged Japanese colonial infrastructure and outpaced South Korea economically until it fully nationalized industry and commerce. It never left a war footing, but approached economic development like a military campaign. In a quest for economic self-sufficiency, it implemented a succession of multi-year plans and collectivized agriculture, but then allowed agriculture and light industry to languish to focus on heavy industry. The Kim family increasingly ruled through a narrow group of family connections and long-time supporters, executing or imprisoning any political opposition. The devastating famine of the 1990s led to a reemergence of private commerce in daily necessities and increasing seepage of information from the outside as Koreans crossed the Chinese border in search of work. The regime has floundered for a solution, but resists political liberalization, having seen its consequences in the former Soviet Union, which collapsed.*

At the end of colonial rule in 1945, Korea was the most industrialized former colony in the Japanese empire, with the bulk of industry concentrated in the northern part of the peninsula.[1] During the Korean War (1950–53), North Korea lost half its industrial output, one-quarter of its agricultural output, and millions of its citizens through death and migration.[2] Postwar reconstruction was an enormous task for both Koreas, but for the first two postwar decades, North Korea appeared to be much more economically successful than the South, which was resource poor, mired in corruption, and overwhelmingly dependent on American aid.[3]

Nation building in North Korea is a complicated area of inquiry. Strictly speaking North Korea is not a nation, but half a nation. Both Seoul and Pyongyang acknowledge only one nation on the Korean Peninsula and consider the other state to be illegitimate. In reality, the two Koreas have developed autonomously since

1945, on the basis of two very different political and economic systems. But the artificial separation of a long-unified nation into two halves, with almost no contact between them for several decades, has greatly affected the economic, political, social, and cultural development of both North and South Korea.

Another problem in studying North Korean nation building is that North Korea was "built" not once, but twice: first under Soviet occupation between the liberation from Japanese colonial rule in August 1945 and the establishment of the Democratic People's Republic of Korea (DPRK) in September 1948, and then rebuilt with Soviet, Chinese, and East European assistance after the Korean War. After the famine at the turn of the twenty-first century, North Korea may be embarking on a third "nation-building" project, with substantial economic aid from China, South Korea, and other countries.

The Creation of a Regime

Between 1945 and 1948, Soviet forces occupied the northern Korean Peninsula and the Red Army left a powerful imprint on the politics, economic system, culture, and worldview of the DPRK.[4] Under Soviet guidance, Korean Communists instituted a highly centralized, top-down system of political control, economic development, and social mobilization even before the regime was officially established in 1948. Kim Il Sung, a young native of the Pyongyang region, who had engaged in anti-Japanese guerrilla activities in Manchuria in the 1930s and early 1940s, and then joined an international detachment of the Soviet army in Siberia, became North Korea's leader in early 1946.

Under Kim and the Soviets, the first major step in North Korea's socioeconomic transformation was land reform, involving the redistribution of farmland to poor and tenant farmers in the spring of 1946. Agricultural output was severely hampered by the separation from the grain-producing areas in the South, as well as by shortages of fertilizer, farm tools, and oxen.[5] This caused a serious food shortage for the first eighteen months after liberation.[6] Throughout the pre–Korean War years and beyond, food was rationed according to type of work, with particular favoritism toward the military.[7] North Korea, like other socialist systems, has always been a "shortage economy."[8]

Although it remained predominantly agricultural in the late 1940s, even then its leaders made heavy industry the centerpiece of their economic plans,[9] much as South Korea's president Park Chung Hee did in the early 1970s. Under the Japanese, Korea's economic development in the 1930s and early 1940s had been concentrated in the mountainous northern part of the peninsula, which had substantial mineral resources and hydroelectric power potential. This gave North Korea a distinct advantage over the South in post-1945 industrialization, and enabled the DPRK to follow a heavy industry-oriented, Stalinist model of development.[10] In August 1946, the emerging North Korean government nationalized the major industries, the last in its series of major social reforms. Overwhelming Japanese control of colonial industry made the transition to state ownership relatively easy.[11]

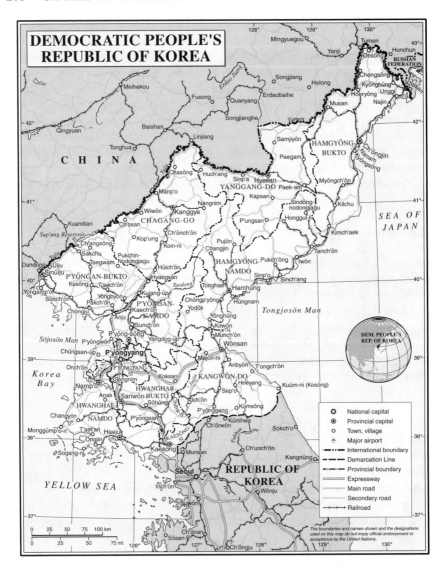

The first of two one-year economic plans was adopted in February 1947. It called for a 92 percent growth in industrial production over the previous year, concentrating on construction, steel, coal, chemicals, power, and transportation, especially railroads.[12] North Korea's state economic planning followed both the Soviet model and also the state capitalism of the Japanese colonial administration.[13] The main architects of the 1947 plan had been trained in Japan, and several hundred Japanese technical experts were retained as advisers in state-run industries.[14]

As in the early years of the Soviet Union and the Peoples' Republic of China, economic development was pursued with the tactics and terminology of war, including "campaigns," "mobilization," and "assault movements." Born out of war, these countries have approached economic development as a violent struggle.[15] The Cold War, which left North and South Korea on a war footing for more than fifty years, reinforced this approach. The line between the army and the civilian reconstruction workforce was often blurry: Korean People's Army draftees were sometimes retained in factory work rather than sent into the army, and active troops were utilized in civilian reconstruction projects.[16]

Postwar Political Consolidation

The Korean War, although devastating economically, at the political level strengthened the position of Kim Il Sung, since many of his political opponents, especially Christians, fled during the war, while the war provided a pretext to purge those who remained. The war intensified North Korea's emphasis on mass mobilization, anti-Americanism, self-reliance, and the "cult" of Kim Il Sung.[17] By 1956 the Korean Workers' Party (KWP) claimed that its membership had increased in the preceding four years from 725,762 to 1,164,945 members or 12 percent of the population, making it proportionately the largest Marxist-Leninist party in the world.[18]

Kim Il Sung used the war to eliminate his rivals, especially his most important rival, Vice-premier and Foreign Minister Pak Hon-yong. Pak had been one of the few Korean Communists to remain in Korea throughout the colonial period and emerge with his life and political integrity intact. Pak commanded enormous respect among Korean Communists, especially those from South Korea, who like himself had moved to the North. After the war, a dozen of Pak's allies in the political leadership were purged, put on trial as spies for the United States, and executed.[19] Pak himself was brought to trial in December 1955 with an incredible list of crimes including collusion with American soldiers, businessmen, and missionaries going back to 1919, and given the death sentence after a one-day show trial.

The biggest postwar leadership challenge to Kim came in 1956, shortly after the Soviet Union's "de-Stalinization" campaign.[20] While Kim was away on a trip to Soviet-bloc states, a conspiracy, led by a group of pro-Chinese and pro-Soviet members of the KWP ruling circles, attempted to eliminate him and his growing cult of personality by introducing a collective leadership. This dispute not only was a matter of political leadership, but also grew out of bitter disagreements concerning economic policy and the relative prioritization of consumer versus military goods. In a widespread purge lasting until the spring of 1958, Kim removed from positions of authority virtually all real or potential threats to his rule. Those who were lucky fled to exile in China or the Soviet Union, others were executed or sentenced to forced labor.[21] From then on, individuals with close personal ties with Kim Il Sung, either through their shared Manchurian guerrilla experience or later through family connections, remained the core of the DPRK leadership.[22]

Despite these power struggles at the top, the postwar social environment in North

Korea was remarkably stable, with few signs of political discontent and opposition, or indeed of crime and violence.[23] Postwar purges and extensive networks of surveillance and control, justified by the ever-present fear of South Korean agents, in combination with intense ideological indoctrination, furthered the penetration of the state into society and the denial of any legitimate forms of criticism against the government. The war also created a new class of suspect persons, those whose relatives had fled to South Korea during the Korean War; they and their descendents lay permanently outside the "core" class of reliable regime supporters.

Postwar Reconstruction

In 1953 Kim outlined the reconstruction program, which continued to emphasize heavy industry. Although he expressed a desire for "simultaneously developing light industry and agriculture," the production of consumer goods and the improvement of everyday life remained secondary to the creation of a powerful industrial state. A long-simmering disagreement erupted over the continued rationing of consumer goods after the war. The KWP leadership debated fiercely about the prioritization of industrialization over the production of consumer goods and the general standard of living. Ultimately the Central Committee decided to retain the rationing system but to reduce the price of certain consumer items and increase wages.[24] In December 1953, the DPRK also cancelled all pre–Korean War debts owed by the peasantry.[25] In the first two years of postwar reconstruction, some 80 percent of industrial investment, or nearly 40 percent of total investment, went into heavy industry, a proportion quite similar to that of China at the time or East European countries a few years earlier.[26] North Korea's emphasis on heavy industry derived not only from the Soviet model, but also from the existence of a prewar Japanese-built industrial infrastructure. Although much of this infrastructure had been heavily damaged or destroyed, rebuilding was a simpler task than building from scratch, as the plans and technical knowledge already existed.

Economic planning advanced through three stages, beginning with an initial period of preparation lasting six months to one year, a Three-Year Plan to bring the economy up to prewar levels, and a Five-Year Plan for industrialization.[27] The North Korean leadership was keen on redirecting industry from the distortions of colonial development. The Japanese had built major factories on the coasts, convenient for export to Japan, but far from the sources of raw materials and poorly suited for Korea's domestic needs. Therefore existing plants should not merely be reconstructed, but new factories and infrastructure should be built in order to make Korea self-sufficient.[28] Industrial development emphasized power generation, raw material extraction, and the production of machine tools, automobiles, and chemicals.[29]

Targets for the first Three-Year Plan (1954–56) were officially reached well before the end of three years, in August 1956; quotas for the first Five-Year Plan, launched in December 1956, were met in 1960, one year ahead of schedule. Given

Table 13.1

North Korean Industrial Growth, 1949–1963

	1949–56	1956–59	1960–63
Official index (%)	9.0	45.2	15.1
Recalculated index (%)	6.6	36.0	7.8

Source: Joseph S. Chung, *The North Korean Economy: Structure and Development* (Stanford: Hoover Institution Press, 1974), 76.

the probable exaggerations in official DPRK estimates, one attempt to recalculate industrial growth produced the pattern above.

The estimate of 36 percent growth in the period of the First Five-Year Plan gives a DPRK growth record matched by few economies in the world. With these impressive growth rates, Kim Il Sung pursued economic autarky, what he called national self-reliance or *juche*, North Korea's leading ideological concept since the late 1950s.

Despite the aspiration for self-sufficiency, in reality, postwar rehabilitation was overwhelmingly dependent on aid from abroad, primarily the Soviet Union but also the labor and assistance of Chinese People's Volunteer troops, who remained in North Korea until October 1958. In 1955 Moscow agreed to transfer technology to North Korea virtually for free. Between 1956 and 1958 alone, the USSR gave North Korea grants and credits of 300 million rubles, and by 1959 total Soviet aid may have reached $690 million.[30] According to contemporary Soviet sources, by the end of the Five-Year Plan in 1960, Soviet aid accounted for 40 percent of North Korean electricity generation, 53 percent of coke production, 51 percent of cast iron, 22 percent of steel, 45 percent of reinforced concrete blocks, and 65 percent of cotton fabric.[31] Thousands of North Koreans received technical training and university educations in the Eastern bloc.

Despite (or perhaps because of) this dependence, in the late 1950s, the DPRK leadership was bitterly divided over North Korea's economic relations with the Eastern bloc. Between 1956 and 1958, Kim Il Sung and his group opposed integration into an international division of labor led by the USSR, in which North Korea would exchange its primary products for manufactured goods from the European socialist countries. Kim's opponents argued against excessive self-reliance, and called for more trade with the Soviet bloc and more emphasis on light industry and consumer goods. In the end, Kim's line of collectivization, nationalism, self-reliance, and heavy-industry-first development won the day.[32] The thrust of the postwar rehabilitation plan remained toward autarky rather than incorporation into a Soviet-centered international division of labor. North Korea never joined the Soviet-directed Council on Mutual Economic Assistance (CMEA), for instance, and even scheduled its economic plans so as not to coincide with those of the other socialist countries.

Table 13.2

Foreign Assistance to North Korea, 1953–1960

TOTAL	879.3 million rubles
USSR	292.5
Others	586.8
China	258.4
East Germany	122.7
Poland	81.9
Czechoslovakia	61.0
Romania	22.0
Hungary	21.0
Bulgaria	18.7
Albania	0.6
Mongolia	0.4
North Vietnam	0.1

Source: SSSR i Koreia (Moscow: USSR Academy of Sciences, 1988), 256.

The economic growth in the first decade after the war was nothing short of astonishing, a record not matched again. The advantages of the North Korean variant of the socialist command economy in the beginning stages of development included opportunities for extensive growth, a high degree of popular mobilization, a preexisting industrial base upon which to build, and an educated and organized workforce. They put the DPRK well ahead of South Korea in economic growth until at least the mid-1960s.[33]

Postwar Social Mobilization

In North Korea, unlike in parts of Eastern Europe, economic mobilization did not lead to worker unrest. Economic reconstruction was geared toward postwar rehabilitation, a widely supported goal. Economic development became a means of "consolidating the democratic base" and strengthening Korean socialism. The government desired "socialist transformation," meaning state direction of the economy and the movement of people into collective forms of association. The collectivization of agriculture and the appropriation of all remaining private industry by the state had been accomplished by 1958, completing the socialist transformation. But as in other socialist countries, beginning with the Soviet Union, nationalization and collectivization had a negative impact on economic growth. These were among the key factors that led to North Korea's economic slowdown in the mid-1960s.

Collectivization had been enshrined as a goal in the 1948 constitution and promulgated as state policy shortly before the war but, as in China and Soviet Russia, was not put into widespread practice until after victory in their respective civil wars. The land-to-the-tiller reform of 1946 had increased the number of private landowners, so that by 1953, 95 percent of agricultural land in North Korea was privately owned.[34] The government quickly set about reversing this process, bringing the entire rural population into farming cooperatives by August 1958, with 13,309 cooperatives each averaging 79 households with 321 acres of land. In October these cooperatives were amalgamated into 3,843 larger units, averaging 275 households and 1,094 acres. Administrative districts were redrawn so that the village, the lowest-level administrative unit, was identical with the cooperative farm.[35] Cooperatives corresponded roughly with the "natural" village of traditional Korea, unlike the large Soviet state farms.[36]

Private ownership in industry also came to an end in 1958. Industry had been biased toward large state-run enterprises since the nationalization decree of 1946 and the First-Year Plan of 1947, but private business had contributed significantly in a number of economic sectors as late as 1957, especially in such small-scale enterprises as food processing and metal-working.[37] In 1958 "complete socialization" of all industries was declared, and all enterprises became either industrial cooperative or, more often, state-owned operations.[38]

If socialism meant state and collective ownership of the means of production, the DPRK had indeed accomplished the socialist revolution by the end of the 1950s, as the party media claimed. North Korea's socialist revolution had been almost too easy. Already when the regime was founded in 1948, more than 90 percent of industrial concerns were state-owned, most of the factories simply having been expropriated from their absent Japanese owners.[39] Nationalization was more thorough in the DPRK than in any of the People's Democracies of Eastern Europe; almost nothing of the private economy remained by the beginning of the 1960s. North Korea developed what Karl Marx might have called "barracks socialism," meaning society as a militarized factory under the leadership of a single supreme leader.

By the middle of the 1950s, North Korea had an impressive industrial economy by Third World standards and a consumer economy able to supply its people with basic necessities. At that point, it could have focused its resources on improving the livelihood of its people, and shifted from a militaristic to a more diversified form of economic development. But, because of the instability in the Communist bloc, the growing Cold War tensions, and perhaps the difficulty of the guerrillas, who ran the DPRK, in seeing economic development as anything *but* war, the regime made a conscious choice to put its resources into a military buildup. Then, just as North Korea was shifting fully into a state-owned, militarized economy in the early 1960s, Soviet-bloc and Chinese aid dropped substantially.

As a result of all these factors—nationalization and collectivization, a drop in foreign aid, and a shift in emphasis from the civilian economy to the military—the North Korean economy began to stagnate and, after a few years, living conditions began a decline that lasted decades. Apparently DPRK planners did not seriously take into account the loss of foreign assistance when they formulated the first Seven-Year Economic Plan (1961–67). As a result, the plan could not be fulfilled and had to be extended three years, making it a de facto ten-year plan (1961–70).

Thereafter, North Korea would never fulfill its economic plans on time and ceased publishing concrete statistics on economic output. The socialist economic show-case of the 1950s sputtered out in the 1960s, just as South Korea's modernization program was beginning to take off.

Toward a Post-Mobilization Regime

Unlike all other Marxist-Leninist states, with the possible exceptions of Enver Hoxha's Albania and Pol Pot's short-lived Democratic Kampuchea, until the famine of the 1990s, the DPRK never moved beyond a mobilization economy to a more consumer-oriented one. The DPRK maintained an extraordinary degree of control over its citizens' movements and activities, and relied primarily on nonmaterial incentives and disincentives to mobilize North Koreans for collective action. From the 1970s on, the North took great pains to shield its citizens from any knowledge of the South Korean economic takeoff and the rapidly widening gap in the standards of living between the two Koreas.[40]

Clearly, a regime that based its legitimacy in part on economic improve-ment and modernity could not sustain such a situation indefinitely. Beginning in the early 1990s there were signs of liberalization and the emergence of lo-cal markets in the North Korean economy, what one American observer called "reform by stealth."[41] At the same time, the acute food shortages of the mid- to late 1990s caused a return to reliance on popular mobilization.[42] During the 1996–99 famine, the public distribution system for delivery of food and other necessities was drastically reduced and, in some areas of the country, collapsed altogether. North Korea probably sustained negative rates of economic growth for the entire decade of the 1990s. Estimates for the famine death toll range from the DPRK figures of 200,000 deaths, to an intermediate number favored by Western academics from 600,000 to one million persons, to a high of three million.[43]

The famine years reduced everyday life to a struggle for survival even for much of the elite. Although conditions improved with the arrival of foreign aid, much of the population remains near the edge of subsistence. The "Arduous March," as the DPRK government called these years, severely weakened the state's ability to provide for its citizens. After the economic breakdown of the mid-1990s, the contours of a "mixed" public-private economy began slowly to emerge. The mar-ket reappeared, at first clandestinely in remote areas and then openly throughout the country.

In January 2001, the Korean Workers' Party newspaper announced a policy of "New Thinking." "New Thinking" entailed the scrapping of outmoded habits and mentalities, technological reconstruction, ideological and economic flexibility, in-dustrial restructuring, and information technology.[44] After decades of self-imposed isolation, North Korea again sent government officials and students abroad to study technical subjects, economics, and business in countries as diverse as China, Malaysia, Australia, and the United States.[45]

The 2002 New Year's joint editorial in the three main official DPRK newspapers celebrated the "successes" of these changes and made a renewed call for "radical change" in the economy.[46] In March 2002, the Supreme People's Assembly, North Korea's highest legislative body, approved a budget emphasizing technical innovation and modernization, and the DPRK began to institute some of the most far-reaching economic changes since 1948.[47] The food distribution system was modified, the price of rice was raised to near-market levels, wages were increased as much as thirtyfold, the official exchange rate for the North Korean won was drastically reduced, and taxation was reintroduced.[48]

This major departure from earlier economic practices moved North Korea away from a central-planning model to a mixed socialist-market economy. Although the reforms stalled as tensions with Japan and the United States rose in the fall of 2002, they were not withdrawn. In March 2006, the DPRK held a conference on national labor planning, the first in ten years, which announced the need to "strengthen [the] economic mentality" in the country and to "create in our own way the most scientific, logical and utilitarian economic management method."[49] Following closely on a visit by Kim Jong Il to China's special economic zones, the conference underscored the North Korean government's attempt to effect and control economic reform.

There is, of course, great danger in this shift, as the regime is well aware. Market-oriented economic reforms encourage self-interest and consumerism. They weaken the dependence of the people on the state and, therefore, the state's control over the people. The DPRK leadership points (with good reason) to such weakening as the source of the downfall of communism in Europe and the rise of revisionism in China. There is as yet little sign of an independent or even quasi-independent civil society emerging. North Korea remains a society of national mobilization, in which civil society is pervaded and dominated by the state.

The social effects of the economic catastrophe of the 1990s and the subsequent economic reforms have been substantial, but the political effects have yet to be felt. Against the government's heretofore strict control of movement within and beyond the country, famine forced large numbers of North Koreans to travel in search of food, including illegal travel to China. Those caught crossing the border or forcibly repatriated from China have been severely punished, many incarcerated in North Korea's notorious prison camps.[50] But the state's ability to restrict internal migration has been weakened, probably permanently. Most North Koreans now obtain the bulk of their necessities from the market (or produce it themselves) rather than from the state. The old social contract, between the paternalistic state and the dependent citizen, has collapsed.[51]

For ordinary North Koreans, the effects of the 2002 economic reforms have been mixed at best. Inflation has been high and sustained. Those with access to foreign exchange and farmers, who can produce their own food, have been able to cope reasonably well with these economic changes and even to profit from them. Others have seen their standard of living decline, as food prices exceed the rise in wages.[52] As in China's early reforms under Deng Xiaoping, the primary initial beneficiaries have been the peasantry. New forms of division between the haves and have-nots have grown. While government control of the mass media is still officially absolute, broadcasts from China and even South Korea are reaching North Korean citizens, and returned migrants from China spread news of their experiences through their networks of friends and family members. The growing presence of aid workers, tourists, and business people from Western countries, China, and South Korea is a visible reminder of the world beyond North Korea. North Korea is no longer the hermetically sealed country it was a decade ago.

Few if any nations in the modern world have shifted from success to failure as dramatically and decisively as has North Korea. Founded as a Stalinist state, the DPRK followed a Stalinist development model. It also absorbed such Maoist influences as an emphasis on self-reliance and "mass line" social mobilization. All this was built on the foundation of Japanese colonial militarism and filtered through a powerful Korean nationalism. The DPRK has known only two supreme leaders since its founding, Kim Il Sung and his son Kim Jong Il. They have merged their highly centralized, personalized leadership with mass mobilization and an emphasis on ideology over material incentives.

In its early period North Korean nation building was highly effective, in the sense of creating political institutions, organizing society, and establishing the basis for economic growth and industrialization, all in a relatively short space of time. Needless to say, North Korea was also highly oppressive, authoritarian, and even brutal. But in its own idiosyncratic way, the system worked.

North Korea's nation building environment is both unique and paradoxical. The DPRK represents the most extreme example of sustained state-led autarkic development in the twentieth century, yet this development was made possible only through substantial foreign aid, particularly in the immediate post–Korean War period (1953–60). North Korea has not been actively engaged in combat since July 1953, yet its society has remained on a war footing for almost the entire existence of the regime. One of the poorest countries in the world, North Korea boasts one of the world's largest armies and recently demonstrated its possession of nuclear weapons. Tied by military alliances to the Soviet Union from 1961 until the end of the Cold War and to China to this day, North Korea has tended to view its regional environment as extremely hostile and to have little trust even in its allies; at various times it has been estranged from both China and Russia, and at present only its relations with China can remotely be described as friendly. In short, North Korea is a highly militarized, deeply suspicious, and largely isolated regime, with profound economic weaknesses, which nevertheless have not substantially altered the overwhelming power and control of the state over its citizens.

North Korea's economic infrastructure was relatively advanced four decades ago, but has steadily deteriorated and is now in critical need of upgrading and repair in every sector. The North has substantial mineral resources and hydroelectric power potential, but little arable land and a short growing season. "Rational" economic management would focus on exporting manufactured goods and importing food,[53] but in North Korea economic rationality has always been subordinate to political imperatives and above all to the aspiration of self-reliance. Unlike many other Third World countries, however, North Korea has a highly educated, ethnically homogenous, and disciplined population. Its potential for economic development is substantial, but remains inhibited by domestic political choices and the international environment.

Although economic growth was North Korea's primary goal in the early years, growth slowed sometime in the 1960s and the system has become increasingly unworkable. Like the erstwhile centralized economies of Eastern Europe, North Korea showed great gains in the early stages of industrialization, but was unable to compete with a capitalism that had developed beyond the stage of mass production to "post-Fordist" or "disorganized" forms of production.[54] In particular, such economies have failed markedly to satisfy popular demand for consumer goods. The socialist "economic miracle" of the late 1950s became the economic catastrophe of the 1990s, when hundreds of thousands, if not millions, of North Koreans died of starvation.

Since the famine, North Korea's primary goal has been survival as a regime and as a society. Although, like other Leninist regimes, North Korea is officially led by the Korean Workers' Party, since the 1990s, the regime has placed greater emphasis on military leadership under the slogan of "Military-First Politics." North Korean propaganda has increasingly emphasized building a "strong and prosperous great state," a slogan reminiscent of Meiji Japan's (1868–1912) slogan of "Rich Nation, Strong Army," suggesting perhaps a new nation-building project in the works.[55]

Whether recent reforms can establish a sustainable economic recovery and create a "strong and prosperous great state," as the regime would wish, remains to be seen. So far the political system appears to be intact and the reform program of the early twenty-first century may constitute a third phase of nation building. On the other hand, if exposure to these new external forces ultimately undermines the regime itself in the manner of Eastern Europe in the 1980s, North Korea may be in the early stages of "un-building" the nation. Nation un-building, meaning disintegration or collapse, which is much less studied than nation building, would then become a useful tool of analysis for understanding North Korea's future.[56] It is too soon to tell. Inasmuch as the founders of the DPRK had intended to create powerful, penetrative, and long-lasting independent state, they certainly succeeded. But North Korea's nation builders also wanted to create a steadily growing, affluent industrialized economy. In this, they clearly failed.

Notes

1. Andrew J. Grajdanzev, *Modern Korea* (New York: John Day, 1944).

2. *Postwar Reconstruction and Development of the National Economy of DPRK* (Pyongyang: Foreign Languages Publishing House, 1957), 8.

3. Central Intelligence Agency, *Korea: The Economic Race Between the North and the South* (Washington, DC: Government Printing Office, 1978).

4. Andrei Lankov, *From Stalin to Kim Il Sung* (New Brunswick, NJ: Rutgers University Press, 2002); Charles K. Armstrong, *The North Korean Revolution, 1945–1950* (Ithaca, NY: Cornell University Press, 2003).

5. United States National Archives and Records Administration, United States Army, Far East Command, G-2 Weekly Summary no. 31 (17 April 1946), 6.

6. National Archives and Records Administration, Record Group (RG) 242, shipping advice (SA) 2005, item 8/59, Haeju People's Court, "Local Situation and Activities," 10 April 1946; *Saegil Sinmun*, 21 March 1946.

7. RG 242, SA 2005 7/57, Supply Section, Pyongyang City People's Committee, "Distribution of Rations," January 1949.

8. Janos Kornai, *The Socialist System: The Political Economy of Communism* (Princeton, NJ: Princeton University Press, 1992), 228–301.

9. RG 242, SA 2007 9/61, Kim Ch'an, *Sangsa taech'a taejop'yo soron* (Outline of Industrial Balance Sheets) (Pyongyang: Munmyông sanôpsa, 1947), 5.

10. Bruce Cumings, *The Origins of the Korean War,* vol. 2 (Princeton, NJ: Princeton University Press, 1990), 337.

11. United States Army, Far East Command, RG 319, *Intelligence Summary North Korea* no. 37 (15 June 1947), 9.

12. Kim Il Sung, "On the 1947 Plan for the Development of the National Economy," *Works,* vol. 3 (Pyongyang: Foreign Languages Publishing House, 1980), 79, 82.

13. United States Armed Forces in Korea, Assistant Chief of Staff, G-2, RG 332, box 57, "North Korea Today," 20.

14. United States Army, Far East Command, Allied Translator and Interpreter Section (ATIS), box 4, item 25, Planning Bureau, North Korean Provisional People's Committee, "Plan of Economic Development to Be Achieved by the North Korea People," 1947, 5.

15. Andrew Walder, *Communist Neo-Traditionalism* (Berkeley: University of California Press, 1986), 8; Stephen Kotkin, *Magnetic Mountain: Stalinism as a Civilization* (Berkeley: University of California Press, 1995).

16. Soviet Embassy in DPRK Report, 30 June 1954, Foreign Policy Archives of the Russian Federation (AVPRF), Fond 0102, Opis 10, Papka 52, Delo 8.

17. Kang Chong-gu, "The Korean War and the Construction of Socialism in North Korea," *Hanguk kwa kukje chongch'i* (Korea and International Politics) 6, no. 2 (Autumn 1990), 95–137.

18. Kim Il Sung, *On the Building of the Worker's Party of Korea,* vol. 2 (Pyongyang: Foreign Languages Publishing House, 1978), 233–34.

19. Dae-Sook Suh, *Kim Il Sung, the North Korean Leader* (New York: Columbia University Press, 1988), 130–34; Koon Woo Nam, *The North Korean Communist Leadership, 1945–1965* (Tuscaloosa: University of Alabama Press, 1974), 92–95.

20. Andrei Lankov, *Crisis in North Korea* (Honolulu: University of Hawaii Press, 2005).

21. Lim Un, *The Founding of a Dynasty in North Korea* (Tokyo: Jiyu-sha, 1982), chapter 6. "Lim Un" is a pseudonym for Ho Chin, a North Korean exile residing in the former Soviet Union.

22. Nam, *North Korean Communist Leadership,* 116.

23. Glenn D. Paige and Dong Jun Lee, "The Post-war Politics of North Korea," in *North Korea Today,* ed. Robert A. Scalapino (New York: Praeger, 1963), 19.

24. Soviet Embassy in DPRK Report, 28 May 1954, AVPRF, Fond 0102, Opis 9, Papka 44, Delo 9.

25. Ibid., 13 January 1954.

26. Masai Okonogi, "North Korean Communism: In Search of Its Prototype," in *Korean Studies: New Pacific Currents,* ed. Dae-Sook Suh (Honolulu: University of Hawaii Press, 1994), 185–86.

27. Kim Il Sung, "Everything for the Postwar Rehabilitation and Development of the National Economy," *Works,* vol. 8, 15.

28. Kim, "Postwar Rehabilitation," 11.

29. Ibid., 11–14.

30. Erik Van Ree, "The Limits of *Juche:* North Korea's Dependence on Soviet Industrial Aid, 1953–76," *Journal of Communist Studies* 5, no. 1 (March 1989), 68.

31. Karoly Fendler, "Economic Assistance and Loans from Socialist Countries to North Korea in the Postwar Years 1953–1963," *Asien* no. 42 (January 1992), 42.

32. Ellen Brun and Jacques Hersh, *Socialist Korea* (New York: Monthly Review Press, 1976), 165; Soviet Embassy in DPRK Report, 30 March 1956, AVPRF, Fond 0102, Opis 12, Papka 68, Delo 5.

33. Central Intelligence Agency, *Korea.*

34. Joseph Sang-hoon Chung, *The North Korean Economy: Structure and Development* (Stanford, CA: Hoover Institution Press, 1974), 10.

35. Mun Woong Lee, *Rural North Korea under Communism: A Study of Sociocultural Change,* Rice University Studies, 62, no. 1 (Winter 1976), 27.

36. Chong-Sik Lee, "Land Reform, Collectivisation and the Peasants in North Korea," *China Quarterly* no. 4 (April–June 1963), 76.

37. Chung, *North Korean Economy,* 60.

38. Ibid., 62.

39. Kim, "Economic Reconstruction," 13.

40. Rudolf Bahro, *The Alternative in Eastern Europe,* trans. David Fernbach (London: Verso, 1981), 237–38.

41. Selig S. Harrison, *Korean Endgame* (Princeton, NJ: Princeton University Press, 2002), 25.

42. James Brooke, "North Korea, Facing Food Shortages, Mobilizes Millions From the Cities to Help Rice Farmers," *The New York Times,* 1 June 2005, http://www.nytimes.com/2005/06/01/ international/ asia/ 01korea.html.

43. Stephen Haggard and Marcus Noland, *Famine in North Korea* (New York: Columbia University Press, 2007), 7.

44. *Rodong Sinmun,* 9 January 2002, 1; "Let Us Examine and Solve all Problems from a New Perspective and Position," *Nodong Sinmun,* 9 January 2001.

45. Nam Kwang-sik, "One Year of a 'New Way of Thinking,'" *Vantage Point* 24, no. 2 (February 2002), 10.

46. *Rodong Sinmun,* 1 January 2002, 1; *People's Korea,* 12 January 2002, 2.

47. "SPA Approves New State Budget Featuring Technical Innovation and Modernization of Economy," *People's Korea,* 30 March 2002, 1.

48. "North Korea Undergoing Economic Reform," *Chosun Ilbo* (26 July 2002); "Stitch by Stitch to a Different World," *The Economist,* 27 July 2002, 24–26.

49. Kyungnam University Institute for Far Eastern Studies, North Korea Brief no. 06-4-03-1, 3 April 2006, http://ifes.kyungnam.ac.kr/eng/references/07_nk_brief_view.asp?nkbriefNO=46&page=1.

50. David Hawk, *The Hidden Gulag* (Washington, DC: US Committee for Human Rights in North Korea, 2003), 56–69.

51. Stephen Haggard and Marcus Noland, *Hunger and Human Rights* (Washington, DC: US Committee for Human Rights in North Korea, 2005), 19.

52. Ibid., 21–22.

53. Marcus Noland, *Avoiding the Apocalypse* (Washington, DC: Institute for International Economics, 2000), 262–63.

54. Scott Lash and John Urry, *The End of Organized Capitalism* (Madison: University of Wisconsin Press, 1987).

55. Ilpyong J. Kim, "Kim Jong Il's Military-First Policy," in *North Korea: The Politics of Regime Survival,* Young Whan Kihl and Hong Nack Kim, eds. (Armonk, NY: M.E. Sharpe, 2006), 66–67.

56. Nicholas Eberstadt, *The End of North Korea* (Washington, DC: AEI Press, 1999); Tanisha M. Faizal, *State Death* (Princeton, NJ: Princeton University Press, 2007).

14

From Anticommunist Industrialization to Civic Democracy in South Korea

Kim Hyung-A

Abstract: *This case study charts the transformation into one of the richest democracies in the world of a country devastated by war and in the hands of a dictatorship and a powerful foreign patron, the United States. Early South Korean governments focused on economic development and anticommunism as their survival strategy in a lethal international environment at the front lines of the Cold War. They produced unprecedented economic growth rates and a thriving middle class, which in turn pushed for political democratization, which was realized in 1987. During the twenty years of democracy since 1987, Korean leaders fell to charges of corruption—the old way of doing business—and were prosecuted through the court system—the new way of doing business. In the process, the role of civil society rapidly grew with the rapid expansion of nongovernmental organizations. Despite a decade-long effort to defuse tensions with North Korea, since the election of the conservative president, Lee Myung-bak, in 2008 tensions have escalated.*

The Republic of Korea, hereafter referred to as the ROK or South Korea, is one of the most successful postcolonial countries in the world, achieving a dual revolution of industrialization and democratization within less than four decades since the early 1960s. The speed and scale of South Korea's transformation from a poverty-stricken client state dependent on U.S. aid after the Korean War (1950–53) into one of the most vibrant democracies in Asia with membership in the Organization for Economic Cooperation and Development (OECD) is remarkable. South Korea today is the thirteenth-largest economy in the world, with a GDP of $971.3 billion and per capita income of $20,045 in 2007. This constitutes a 230-fold growth in per capita income from $87 in 1962. Many countries in the region, including China, have emulated South Korea's technocrat-led rapid development.

South Korea's democratization since 1987 has been equally impressive. Korea has become a civic democracy shaped by over 25,000 nongovernmental organizations.[1] According to the 2006 Freedom House survey, South Korea achieved the highest rating for political rights and the second-highest for civil liberty.[2] In terms of freedom of the press, in 2007 it scored higher than Australia, France, Italy, Japan, and the United States.[3]

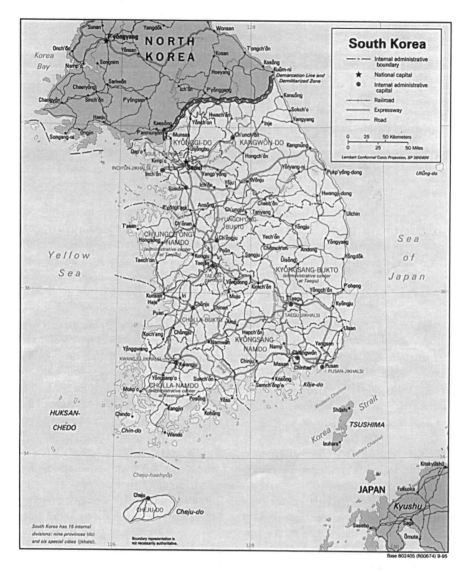

The South Korean population ranks among the most technologically sophisti-cated. There are now over 30 million 3G mobile-phone users, and over 12 million are now broadband subscribers, the highest per capita usage in the world.[4] Perhaps the most striking recent change is the marked improvement in the relations between South and North Korea up to the 2008 presidential elections. In 2005 visitors be-tween the two Koreas exceeded 87,000, which in turn exceeded the total number of visitors since 1945.[5] Commercial trade in the same year between the two countries exceeded one billion U.S. dollars. In 2008, however, newly elected president Lee

Myung-bak declared his conservative "Vision 3000" policy, promising North Korea aid but only on the condition that it abandon its nuclear weapons program.

Two key factors contributed to these stunning achievements. The first was the strong South Korean state in combination with the equally strong and contentious society, each with its own competing vision for economic modernization, democracy, and unification. While the state emphasized anticommunism and industrialization, civil society struggled for democratization against authoritarian governments. Both invoked the language of nationalism and modernization in their distinct agendas.

The second factor was the often controversial role played by the United States, particularly during the early phase of the Cold War. World War II left the Japanese Empire defeated, with Soviet and American troops in occupation of Manchuria and Japan respectively. The United States and the Soviet Union jointly made the decision to divide Korea into northern and southern occupational zones. This division, made soon after the liberation, became the starting point from which South Korea's state building unfolded under the tutelage of the American Military Government in South Korea (USAMGIK), while Kim Il Sung with the support of the Soviet occupation troops swiftly emerged as the leader of North Korea.

The Race to Anticommunist State Building, 1948–61

Founding President Syngman Rhee (1875–1965), like most Koreans, saw Korea in terms of "divided regimes," where state building under each regime opposed the other. Their mutually exclusive visions for a unified Korea locked the North and the South into a race for regime survival.

Unlike the North under Kim Il Sung, however, Rhee's South was extremely unstable and fragile due largely to the sociopolitical conflict between the left and right that erupted in the Autumn Harvest Uprisings of 1946 and the Yŏsu-Sunchŏn Rebellion of 1948, among others, and the escalation of this conflict into the Korean War.[6] The war then worked to cement the political leadership on both sides of the peninsula, with a consolidation of the left in the north and the right in the south.

The USAMGIK relied on the "existing administrative machinery of the Government General"[7] of the Japanese colonial system to control the prominence of leftists in the South. For the same reason, the USAMGIK actively protected Korean conservatives, especially the Korean Democratic Party (*Han'guk Minjudang* or KDP), the "organ of landed wealth and local power," comprised largely of descendants of the landed aristocratic *yangban* families, many of whom had collaborated with the Japanese during the colonial period (1910–45).[8] The KDP was formed in 1945 as a conservative counterweight to moderate nationalist groups, most notably the Committee for the Preparation of Korean Independence (CPKI), later the Korean People's Party. The U.S. occupation force immediately adopted a four-step plan that included: a military build-up to defend at the thirty-eighth parallel, a build-up of the Korean National Police to eliminate Communist sympathizers, the support of conservative political parties, and the suppression of Koreans opposing these measures.[9]

With the founding of the Korean Military Academy (KMA) and the Military English School for potential high-ranking officers, the Korean military grew virtually overnight from a nonexistent force in 1945 to 100,000 men in 1950 and 700,000 by 1955.[10] By the fall of 1946, two classes had graduated from the KMA, including future President Park Chung Hee, whose military coup in May 1961 and rapid industrialization in the 1960s and 1970s would change the face of South Korea.

The U.S. leadership sought to create a containment bulwark in Korea, and Syngman Rhee was their preferred presidential candidate—despite serious reservations—because of his impeccable anti-Communist credentials.[11] Rhee, a descendant of *yangban,* had been imprisoned by the Japanese between 1898 and 1904 and had gone into exile in 1912 in the United States, where he earned degrees from three universities: Washington (B.A.), Harvard (M.A.) and Princeton (Ph.D.).[12] He therefore understood the United States better than any U.S. policy maker understood Korea.

Upon returning to Korea in October 1945, Rhee swiftly aligned with the Korean Democratic Party. In June 1946, while the United States promoted President Franklin D. Roosevelt's idea of a trusteeship in Korea, Rhee publicly declared the formation of a separate government in the South by "kicking out Communist bandits" across the thirty-eighth parallel to the North.[13] For this reason, between 1946 and 1947, the U.S. searched for a more moderate conservative Korean leadership amenable to partition. However, the left and right in Korea, despite having generally antithetical goals, both agreed that Korea must remain undivided.

Contrary to the KDP's expectation that Rhee would support its vested interests, Rhee severely restricted the party's influence in his cabinet by appointing just one KDP member. In the midst of the Korean War, Rhee established his own Liberal Party (*Chayudang*) and in 1953 used martial law to change the constitution, enabling him to run for a third presidential term in 1959. Not surprisingly, he was loathed by many, including in the United States, which attempted to overthrow him in 1953.[14] Despite his turbulent relationship with the United States, Rhee obtained a massive U.S. postwar economic aid package, exceeding $260 million annually, which increased to $383 million in 1957.[15]

Rhee created his own brand of autocracy in the form of a highly flawed "democracy" with the trappings of Western constitutionalism and ostensibly democratic political parties. With this "democratic" autocracy built on U.S. aid, Rhee exploited U.S. Cold War preoccupations to purge the left. In the spring of 1950, 50 to 80 percent of the 58,000 prisoners held in South Korea had been charged under the National Security Law.[16] The execution of Cho Pong-am, the leader of the reformist Progressive Party (*Chinbodang*), in 1959 effectively opened the way for Rhee's one-party system controlled by the conservatives.

Rhee enshrined anticommunism as his national policy (*kuksi*) for the survival of South Korea as a separate and sovereign state, distinct from Stalinist North

Korea. Obsessed with his own style of authoritarian state building, however, Rhee failed to check overt corruption in the civil and military bureaucracies.[17] His demise, following the April 1960 student revolution in opposition to the rigged vice-presidential election, was no surprise for two key reasons. The first was the growing U.S. reluctance to continue to support his leadership. The second was the military unrest, especially among young army colonels who were plotting a military coup. The young colonels had long been frustrated with the stagnation of the military hierarchy, which they saw as the product of both Rhee and U.S. military advisers.[18]

The second republic, established in August 1960 under Prime Minister Chang Myŏn (John Chang in English), lasted only until the military coup of 16 May 1961 led by Major General Park Chung Hee (Pak Chŏng-hŭi, 1917–1979), an enigmatic forty-four-year-old nationalist with a shady past as a colonial soldier under Japan and later as a Communist.[19]

By the time of the coup, South Korea's state-building race against the North had intensified, this time with added purpose: a revolution for the "modernization of the fatherland" (choguk kŭndaehwa), meaning South Korea's rapid industrialization.

State-led Rapid Industrialization, 1961–93

The defining message of the military coup leaders to the Korean people was their "mission" of national reconstruction to save the nation.[20] The military government of Park Chung Hee (1961–79) proved to be very effective, particularly in terms of anti-Communist developmental state building. The Park administration brought the military into government and politics as key administrators and members of political parties, while implanting a hierarchical military culture into the state bureaucracy. It also introduced a planned economy managed through Five-Year Plans, aimed at rapid industrialization. In the process, Park consolidated his authority as a formidable national leader, with a grand vision of transforming South Korea into an industrialized anti-Communist state.

Within the first hundred days of the coup, Park implemented far-reaching administrative reforms of the bureaucracy. He was particularly committed to radical change in South Korea's political and economic structure based on his ideas of "guided capitalism" and "administrative democracy." The former referred to state-planned economic development managed by a technocracy with big business or chaebol as its driving force, and the latter referred to a state-controlled limited democracy designed to serve Korea's "social and political reality, not an unworkable West European democracy."[21] The administrative reforms essentially reflected Park's developmental state building, modeled on the military structure and order.

During the first Five-Year Plan (1962–66), however, Park stumbled through a string of policy failures until mid-1964, when he adopted an export-oriented industrialization strategy, which led to Korea's economic takeoff. During this steep learning curve, Park did not waver from his anti-Communist state-building goals; rather, he adjusted his strategy. He equated South Korea's modernization to "National Restoration" (*minjok chunghŭng*) and "Self-Reliance" (*chaju*), which he later declared as his leadership ideology. Key examples of his anti-Communist state building included his normalization of relations with Japan in 1965, South Korea's participation in the Vietnam War from 1965 to 1971, the launch of the rural New Village and Community Movement (1970–79) to rally national support for his programs, and South Korea's three-stage export-led industrial development with targets of $100 million, $300 million, and $1 billion in 1964, 1967, and 1970 respectively. To achieve these lofty targets, Park hesitated very little in restricting the human rights of the working people (*minjung*), especially after the 1972 declaration of the Yusin (Restoration) Order.

Park shrewdly mobilized the masses to promote Korea's autonomy, particularly from U.S. interference. At the same time, he dovetailed Korea's priorities with U.S. Cold War priorities in East Asia in order to maximize U.S. aid to fund his industrial agenda. By volunteering to dispatch Korean troops to Vietnam, Park ensured that Korea's foreign currency reserves increased to "an all time high of $386 million in 1965."[22] This sudden accumulation of foreign currency reserves was no small matter, given that in September 1963, the month of Park's first presidential election, Korea was on the brink of bankruptcy, with less than $100 million in the Korean National Treasury.[23]

Despite South Korea's dependence on the United States for economic aid and military protection, and U.S. dependence on South Korea to contain communism in Asia, U.S.-Korean relations were rarely without strain. In January 1968, Park became outraged over U.S. inaction after the North Korean assassination attempt on himself, in contrast to its unilateral action over the North Korean seizure of the U.S. spy ship, *Pueblo*. In April the same year, therefore, Park launched a national reserve force of 2.5 million Homeland Guards to create what he called "self-reliant national defense" (*chaju kukbang*) on the grounds that the Korean people must guard their homeland for themselves.[24] In response to the U.S. withdrawal of 20,000 troops from Korea in 1970, he announced a Five-Year Military Modernization Plan (1971–76) in March 1971.[25] Park's all-out campaign for Korean military modernization was a countermeasure to U.S. President Richard Nixon's détente policy highlighted by the normalization of relations with China. The détente policy ultimately drove Park to restructure South Korea into an emergency state system by introducing his Yusin Reform in October 1972, followed by the Yusin Constitution, declared in December 1972.

Park's campaign for Korea's military modernization under the slogan of a "self-reliant military defense" in combination with a "self-reliant economy" turned the entire nation upside down when he, as president with dictatorial power under the Yusin Constitution, imposed centralized control backed by military, bureaucratic, and corporatized social forces, as well as a multi-layered intelligence network. Park used the New Village Community Movement to turn South Korea into one large "training ground" for an anti-Communist homeland force in support of forced-draft heavy and chemical industrialization. Park justified the Yusin Reform and unconstitutional revision of the constitution as necessary to achieve "the Korean people's ardent aspirations for peace, unification and the prosperity of our fatherland."[26] He claimed that the historic Joint Communiqué of 4 July 1972 fostering cooperation between the two Koreas was the result of his own secret initiative for North-South dialogue, but it proved to be little more than a pretext for each side to reinforce Korea's division with its own set of authoritarian powers under its own leadership.

Unlike Kim Il Sung, who rose to supremacy as his people's "Great Leader," Park became the target of the protests of working people (*minjung*), university students, union activists, religious organizations, and liberal intellectual dissidents (*chaeya*), who, from 1977, were the most active nationwide coalition against Yusin rule. Park was resented even by his own protégé, Kim Chae-gyu, the head of the Korea Central Intelligence Agency, who shot him dead on 26 October 1979. Park's assassination threw South Korea into a potential national security crisis, especially following the ensuing military coup of 12 December led by a new autocrat, Major General Chun Doo-whan, the Commander of Korea's National Security Command and chief of the investigation into Park's assassination.

Chun and his military supporters orchestrated a second coup on 17 May 1980 with a declaration of martial law and the purge of 567 leading politicians and high-ranking technocrats, including O Wŏn-chŏl, President Park's senior economic secretary, who had been responsible for the Yulgok military modernization program as well as Park's clandestine nuclear weapons and missile development program. The latter had become the major cause of strain in U.S.-Korean relations. The coup led to a quid pro quo trade-off between Washington and Chun, who offered to dismantle Park's clandestine nuclear program in return for U.S. acquiescence to his seizure of power.[27] By the end of 1982, Chun had dismissed over 800 scientists and closed down the Agency of Defense Development. In doing so, he secured enough U.S. protection so that not only did Korea survive the 1979–80 financial crisis with "U.S.-inspired Japanese financial aid,"[28] but also Chun swiftly consolidated his power base with continued economic growth and a trade surplus of $35 million in 1985, the first trade surplus in modern Korean history.

Korea's trade surplus, however, made no difference to the anti-Chun feelings of the Korean people. Anti-Chun sentiment, fomented by university students over the 1980 Kwangju massacre, in fact, stirred up the radical democratization movement of the 1980s. (There is no exact death toll for the Kwangju Uprising protesting the new military government. Official figures released by the Martial Law Command put the toll at 144 civilians, 22 soldiers, and 4 policemen killed, with 127 civilians, 109 soldiers, and 144 policemen wounded. A Western scholar cites a figure of 4,900 massacred.[29]) *Minjung* activists blamed all political and social ills, including national division, on South Korea's sociopolitical system, and particularly on its "neocolonialist" relationship with the United States. The only cure, they argued, was a revolution against both American imperialism and the military dictatorship.

These demands essentially reflected a generational change from the Korean War generation to the rising younger generation.

The radical 386 generation who were in their 30s (by 2000), attended university in the 1980s, and were born in the 1960s, for example, were the first beneficiaries of Korea's development, but they ironically cared little about either economic growth or American abandonment of South Korea. Unlike their parents' generation, which had been haunted by memories of the Korean War and thus valued anticommunism, economic growth, and the U.S.-Korean alliance, the 386 generation cared more about political freedom and greater equity, and thus radical change in Korean society.

With an outpouring of public protests, the Chun Doo-whan regime (1980–1988) abruptly gave way to Roh Tae-woo (No T'ae-u), Chun's former classmate and a key actor in the 1980 coup, who publicly pledged democratization in his June Declaration on 29 June 1987.[30] Roh won the presidential election in December that year largely because Kim Young-sam and Kim Dae-jung, the leaders of the opposition and also longtime partners in the democracy struggle, failed to agree on a single ticket for the presidency. Although Roh promoted a conciliatory image as a transitional figure in effecting democratization, his rule was the continuation of an illiberal developmental state by other means. He used monetary leverage to achieve what his predecessor Chun Doo-whan had acquired by force.[31] More stunningly, in 1991 Roh made a pact with Kim Young-sam and Kim Chong-p'il, founder of the Korean Central Intelligence Agency and co-planner of the 1961 military coup, to form the Democratic Liberal Party (DLP). Kim Young-sam's rise to the presidency in 1993 was the direct outcome of this elite pact making between "political nemeses and ideological foes."[32]

Civic Democracy Against All Odds

South Korea's democracy, ironically, strengthened amid the elite pact making and structured regionalism exploited principally by the "Three Kims": Kim Young-sam, Kim Dae-jung, and Kim Chong-p'il. Kim Young-sam was the first civilian to be elected president in the thirty-one years following the 1961 military coup. Despite his alliances with military elites and ideological foes, once in power Kim Young-sam swiftly distanced himself by claiming his administration as a "civilian government," and pledged to build a "New Korea." To this end, he purged the *Hanahoe* (One-Mind Club), an elite military clique from North Kyŏngsang, the home region of the three former generals-turned-president: Park Chung Hee, Chun Doo-whan, and Roh Tae-woo.

Kim Young-sam also forged a public consensus, at least initially when he introduced "real name bank account" legislation in 1993, which significantly reduced both electoral and tax fraud. Moreover, he brought Roh Tae-woo and Chun Doo-whan to trial, leading to prison sentences for misappropriation of public funds. Kim Young-sam seems to have sought a genuinely new and more democratic Korea, by promoting civil society to launch his grand plan of "globalization" (*segyehwa*), focused on a "sweeping transformation of society," in 1994. According to Kim, "civic duties" meant to "cultivate a wholesome character and unwavering democratic belief" and to "stop considering narrow self-interests."[33] Riding on Kim's globalization campaign, civic groups and nongovernmental organizations mushroomed from 3,800 in 1996 to 20,000 in 1999 under the leadership of progressive academics and former radical activists of the 386 generation. They became a major political force as public watchdogs and advocates of a "just civil society."[34]

The popularity of Kim's reforms, however, was short lived. His regime became stuck in its inherent limitations, mainly caused by Kim's dependence on supporters from Pusan, the capital city of his home region of South Kyŏngsang. He was thoroughly disgraced in the autumn of 1997 when a series of corporate bankruptcies (Kia Automobiles, Hanbo Steel, and others) rocked Korea with a full-scale currency crisis.[35] At the center of this crisis were the Hanbo conglomerate's financial scandals involving Kim's own son, Kim Hyun-chŏl, with the nickname of "little president." It was generally believed that the cause of the 1997–98 financial crisis was the failure of the previous Roh Tae-woo government, as well as that of Kim Young-sam, "to dismantle the old government-business alliance."[36] Not surprisingly, therefore, political-economic collusion between big business *chaebol* and the conservative elites became the key issue in the presidential election in December 1997. The widespread call for change created the momentum for Kim Dae-jung, South Korea's most famous dissident leader and outsider, to become president in his fourth attempt.

Kim Dae-jung's triumph marked another historic political transition in South Korea when he became the first opposition candidate to be elected president. But the 1997–98 financial crisis involving a $58.3-billion International Monetary Fund (IMF) bailout package overshadowed his triumph. As president-elect, Kim Dae-jung agreed to IMF-imposed neoliberal structural reforms, including reforms in the labor market, banking finance, and corporate governance. Kim's neoliberal policy, contrary to his pledge to promote "democracy and a market economy," brought high unemployment that peaked in 1999 at 6.8 percent with the ratio of temporary workers rising from 40 percent of all wage workers prior to the 1997 crisis to 55.4 percent or 7,840,000 in August 2003.[37]

Yet, Kim's policy, known as DJnomics, created a façade of inclusiveness in the form of the Tripartite Commission on Industrial Relations, which included labor, business, and government and thus created the basis for a neoliberal consensus in South Korean society. Domestic elites such as the leading nongovernmental organizations and many *chaebol* were particularly keen on neoliberal reforms because they thought such reforms would bring "global standards" for efficiency, accountability, and transparency, which in turn would bring not only "economic justice" or "participatory democracy," but also the labor flexibility sought by the *chaebol* together with increased independence from government intervention.[38]

Some analysts credit Kim Dae-jung with bringing the Korean economy out of the abyss of the financial crisis two and a half years ahead of the four-year IMF target.[39] During his presidency, South Korea became noticeably more open and democratic, with an expanded social welfare program and a knowledge-intensive infrastructure wired to the Internet, transforming Korea into one of the most information-technology-sophisticated countries in the world.

These developments, however, had little impact on overall social conditions and outcomes, especially in terms of improving ordinary working people's livelihoods. Some analysts therefore argued that the neoliberal reforms under Kim Dae-jung had hijacked Korea's democracy.[40] The "cash-for-summit scandal," exposed on the eve of Kim Dae-jung's meeting with North Korean leader Kim Jong Il in June 2000, ultimately undermined Kim Dae-jung's reconciliation "Sunshine Policy" toward North Korea. Despite growing support for the Sunshine Policy, especially among progressives and the younger generation, many Korean conservatives were suspicious of Kim Dae-jung's plans to travel to Pyongyang on the eve of the April 2000 general elections.

Although the summit in Pyongyang won Kim Dae-jung the Nobel Peace Prize in 2001, a string of scandals marred his credibility. Ten days before the end of his presidential term, Kim publicly apologized not only for having "bought" the Pyongyang summit by arranging for the Hyundai business group to pay almost $200 million to North Korea, but also for the bribery and corruption charges involving his two sons and his close aides. By then, Kim had become as tragic a figure as his predecessor, Kim Young-sam, leaving a similar legacy of corruption. Thoroughly disappointed with Kim Dae-jung's end, many Koreans, especially the younger generation, demanded an end to the old politics of the Three Kims era. This demand for social change resulted in the presidential election of December 2002, when Roh Moo-hyun, an untested former human rights lawyer, rose to power with the support of the radical leftists and pro–North Korean 386 generation.[41]

Roh Moo-hyun, then the "new face" of the Korean people, actively promoted the strengthening of South Korea's relations with North Korea in keeping with the globalized post–Cold War era. With the same zeal, he opposed U.S. foreign policy, particularly any military option against North Korea's nuclear program. Many regarded Roh's rise to the presidency as the outcome of the citizens' revolution, as the victory of the younger over the older generation, and of progressives over anti-Communist conservatives. Despite his movie-star-like initial popularity, Roh's approval ratings rapidly plummeted. In 2004, to the nation's horror, the National Assembly impeached him on charges of incompetence and illicit fund-raising by his campaign team during his 2002 presidential bid.[42] His popularity hovered around the 30 percent mark, due largely to his controversial Sunshine Policy and his deci-sion to send troops to Iraq, among other things. Nonetheless, many Koreans did not support the opposition-led impeachment, and Roh was subsequently reinstated by the Constitutional Court.

The electorate backlash against the impeachment, therefore, changed Roh's luck overnight and his ruling Open-Uri Party won a landslide victory in the April

2004 general elections. Roh's change of luck was short lived due largely to his controversial "four great reforms" agenda. The ensuing provincial elections in May 2006 virtually wiped out the Open-Uri Party. By then, both Roh and his party were seen as incompetent radical leftists, and the subsequent downfall of the progressives, especially in the 2007 presidential election and April 2008 general elections, surprised very few, even among Roh's own supporters. Two-thirds of the electorate voted for two conservative candidates, Lee Hoe-ch'ang (15 percent) and Lee Myung-bak (48.7 percent or 11,492,349 votes), despite much-publicized allegations that Lee Myung-bak had links to the famous "BBK financial scandal."[43] Lee's landslide victory, together with his party's majority in the National Assembly election on 9 April 2008, reflected the magnitude of ordinary citizens' dissatisfaction with Roh's neoliberal economic policies. His government was seen as having utterly failed to control growing income inequality or escalating real-estate prices fueled by speculation. The gap between the annual incomes of the highest and lowest 20 percent of earners had widened from 4.81-fold to 5.87-fold in the years between the 1997 Asian financial crisis and 2005.[44]

This failure of economic policies does not mean that Roh was a passive leader. To the contrary, he effectively reformed the state bureaucracy in removing the worst aspects of the South Korean state's authoritarian practices, especially in four key agencies: the National Intelligence Agency, the Prosecutor's Office, the police, and the National Tax Service. In the past, these four agencies had been the most effective tools of power readily available to every Korean president, even those with a high reputation for their promotion of democracy. Roh also took a stance independent from that of the United States concerning North Korea.

He defused the North Korean nuclear threat in the historic February Agreement of 2007, showing that a leader of a peripheral, medium-sized state can exert "an outsized impact on the shape of our world."[45] The rapidly growing role of nongovernmental organizations during his tenure, like that of his predecessor, proved central in shaping the character of South Korea's civic democracy. As Ham Chae-bong argues, the "miraculous" character of this democracy has certainly defied almost every norm: "the very events and features which critics point to as signs and symptoms of weakness were . . . turned into opportunities to enact far-reaching reforms."[46] From the perspective of civic participation, Korean democracy appears more robust than anywhere in the region, as demonstrated in the nationwide candlelight vigils initiated largely by high school students in May 2008 against the Lee Myung-bak government's decision to revive the importation of U.S. beef.

Development and Democracy

In 2008 the ROK celebrated the sixtieth anniversary of its foundation, which was originally proclaimed on the third anniversary of the liberation from Japan on 15 August 1945. Despite shaky beginnings, marked by ideological constraints and socioeconomic and institutional instability, South Korea by its sixtieth anniversary had transformed itself into an economically robust and democratic middle power in the region. This remarkable transformation took place in two phases, the first managed by an authoritarian state, which embarked on highly centralized economic development conceived as an ongoing race against North Korea in the difficult years following the Korean War. South Korea's rapid development in effect created a large, vibrant, and highly educated middle class that, by the 1980s, had emerged as a political force demanding democratization. This led to the second phase, begun in 1987 when South Korea began democratizing after the historic June 29 Declaration.

In this process, South Korea's development has benefited from the combination of a strong state and an equally strong and contentious civil society. The state pursued forced-draft industrialization as a means for regime survival, especially during the Cold War, while civil society relentlessly challenged the state to democratize. The fusion of a strong state and a strong society, despite or because of their competing agendas and priorities, created an effective sociopolitical dynamic that, on the one hand, put pressure on the state to bring about better governance and, on the other, enabled fundamental change in South Korean society.

Another significant influence on South Korea's state building, particularly in the early stages, was the world's capitalist system, and especially the United States. The United States, for example, provided massive economic and military aid, spending $12 billion from 1945 to 1965.[47] South Korea's industrialization since the mid-1960s also benefited from U.S. foreign policy, even in the 1970s. When all is said and done, however, no amount of U.S. economic aid or other support could be the core source of South Korea's success, because it was fundamentally the Korean people and their leaders (even dictators) who, against all odds, turned obstacles, national weaknesses, and calamities into opportunities in their unwavering pursuit of national prosperity and democratic development.

Notes

1. The NGO Times, *Directory of Korean NGOs* (1997, 2000, 2003), http://www.ngo-times.net/ (accessed 24 February 2007). The NGO Times (*Simin ŭi sinmun*) was closed in April 2007.

2. http://www.freedomhouse.org/uploads/press_release/fiw07 charts.pdf (accessed 4 April 2007).

3. Cited in *The Canberra Times,* 11 May 2007. Korea ranks 31, Australia and France rank 35, Spain ranks 41, Japan ranks 51, and the United States ranks 53.

4. Peter Lewis, "South Korea Broadband Wonderland," http://www.business.nsw.gov.au/aboutnsw/labour/C12_gross_enrolment_tertiary.htm (accessed 11 December 2007).

5. Key-Young Son, "Entrenching 'Identity Norms' of Tolerance and Engagement," *Review of International Studies,* no. 33 (2007), 507.

6. Kang Man'gil, *Koch'ossŭn Han'guk hyŏndaesa* [A Revised Korean Modern History] (Seoul: Changjakkwa Pipyŏngsa, 1994), 211–13; Bruce Cumings, *Korea's Place in the Sun* (New York: W.W. Norton, 1997), 217–24; Pak Myŏng-lim, *Han'guk 1950: Chŏnjaeng gwa p'yŏnghwa* (The Korean War, 1950: A Reflection on War and Peace) (Seoul: Nanam, 2004), 349–91.

7. Gregg Blazinsky, *Nation Building in South Korea* (Chapel Hill: The University of North Carolina Press, 2007), 15.

8. Bruce Cummings, *Korea's Place in the Sun,* 215.

9. Ibid., 200.

10. Joungwon A. Kim, *Divided Korea* (Cambridge, MA: Harvard University Press, 1975), 216.

11. Bruce Cumings, ed., *Child of Conflict: The Korean-American Relationship, 1943–1953* (Seattle: University of Washington Press, 1983); Frank Baldwin, *Without Parallel: The American-Korean Relationship Since 1945* (New York: Pantheon Books, 1973).

12. For background on Rhee, see Yi Han-u, *Kŏdaehan saengae: Yi Sŭngman 90-nyŏn* [A Great Life: Syngman Rhee] (Seoul: Chosun ilbosa, 1995); Richard C. Allen, *Korea's Syngman Rhee* (Tokyo: Charles E. Tuttle, 1960).

13. Rhee made this controversial but decisive statement in Chŏngup, a small town in North Chŏlla province, on 3 June 1946. See Kang Man'gil, Revised Korean Modern History, 213.

14. Kim Hyung-A, *Korea's Development under Park Chung Hee: Rapid Industrialization, 1961–1979* (London: Routledge/Curzon, 2004), 27–30.

15. U Chŏng-ŭn, "Pi-hamnisŏng imyŏn ŭi hamlisŏng-ŭl ch'ajasŏ–Yi Sŭngman sidae suib daech'e sanŏphwa ŭi chŏngch'i kyŏngjehak," in *Haebang chŏnhusa ui chaeinsik* [A new understanding in the history of pre- and post-liberation], Pak Chi-hyang and Kim Ch'ŏl eds., vol. 2 (Seoul: Ch'aeksesang, 2006), 488.

16. Gregory Henderson, *Korea* (Cambridge, MA: Harvard University Press, 1978), 162–63.

17. James B. Palais, "Democracy in South Korea, 1948–72," in *Without Parallel,* ed. Baldwin, 322.

18. Kim Hyung-A, *Korea's Development,* 60–62.

19. Ibid., 13–31.

20. Minju Han'guk hyŏngmyŏng ch'ŏngsa p'yŏnch'an wiwŏnhoe [Compilation Committee of a History of Revolution of Democratic Korea], *Minju Han'guk hyŏngmyŏng ch'ŏngsa* [A History of Revolution of Democratic Korea], 1962, 26. No mention of place of publication or publisher.

21. Park Chung Hee, *Our Nation's Path,* 2nd ed. (Seoul: Hollym, 1970), 198.

22. Se-jin Kim, "South Korea's Involvement in Vietnam and Its Economic and Political Impact," *Asian Survey,* 10 (1970), 519.

23. Kim Hyung-A, *Korea's Development,* 90.

24. Taet'ongnyŏng pisŏsil [Presidential Secretariat], *Park Chung Hee Taet'ongnyŏng yŏnsŏl munjip* [President Park Chung Hee's Speeches], che 5-chip (vol. 5) (Seoul: Tonga ch'ulp'ansa, 1965), 141–47.

25. Robert Boettcher and Gordon L. Freedman, *Gifts of Deceit* (New York: Holt, Rinehart and Winston, 1980), 95.

26. Park's public announcement on the Joint Communiqué of 4 July cited in *Korea Times,* 18 October 1972.

27. Kim Hyung-A, "Heavy and Chemical Industrialization, 1973–1979: Korea's Homeland Security Measure," in *Reassessing the Park Chung Hee Era, 1961–1979: Development, Political Thought, Democracy and Cultural Influence,* Kim Hyung-A and Clark Sorensen, eds. (Seattle: University of Washington Press, forthcoming).

28. Tat Yan Kong, *The Politics of Economic Reform in South Korea* (London and New York: Routledge, 2000), 247.

29. Cumings, *Korea's Place in the Sun,* 378.

30. At the time, Chun and his military supporters were under heavy pressure from the international community, especially the United States, to relax authoritarian rule in the lead-up to the 1988 Seoul Olympics. Sung Chul Yang, "An Analysis of South Korea's Political

Process and Party Politics," in *Politics and Policy in the New Korean State,* ed. James Cotton (New York: Longman and St. Martin's Press, 1995), 8.

31. James Cotton and Hyung-A Kim van Leest, "The New Rich and the New Middle Class in South Korea," in *The New Rich in Asia,* David S.G. Goodman and R. Robinson, eds. (London: Routledge, 1995), 185–203.

32. Hahm Chae-bong, "South Korea's Miraculous Democracy," *Journal of Democracy,* 19, no. 3 (2008), 134.

33. Cited in Doh C. Shin, *Mass Politics and Culture in Democratizing Korea* (New York: Cambridge University Press, 1999), 201.

34. *Simin sinmun* (2000), http://www.ngotimes.net/ (accessed 24 February 2007).

35. Donald Kirk, *Korean Crisis* (New York: Palgrave, 2000).

36. Barry K. Gills and Dongsook S. Gills, "Globalization and Strategic Choice in South Korea," in *Korea's Globalization,* ed. Samuel S. Kim (Cambridge: Cambridge University Press, 2000), 45.

37. Cited in Hyun-chin Lim and Jin-ho Jang, "Neo-Liberalism in Post-Crisis South Korea," *Journal of Contemporary Asia* 36, no. 4 (2006), 454.

38. Jim Crotty and Gary Dymski, "Can the Global Neoliberal Regime Survive Victory in Asia?" (1998), 24, available at http://www.peole.umass.edu/crotty/lope_fil.df (accessed 11 November 2006).

39. Young-whan Kihl, *Transforming Korean Politics* (Armonk, NY: M.E. Sharpe, 2005), 158–83.

40. Lim and Jang, 447–48; Yi Ch'an-gŭn et al., *Han'guk kyŏnjae-ga sarajinda* [The Korean Economy Is Fading] (Seoul: 21-segi buks, 2004); Chon Ch'ang-hwan and Kim Chin-ban eds., *Wigi ihu Han'guk Chabon juŭi* [Korean Capitalism since the Crisis] (Seoul: P'ulbit, 2004).

41. Song Ho-gŭn, *Han'guk, Musŭn ili ilrŏnagoinna* [Korea, What Is Happening Now] (Seoul: Samsŏng kyŏngje yŏn'guso, 2003), especially chapter 1, 15–33.

42. Roh was impeached on 12 March 2004.

43. Kim Hyung-A, "Video Throws S. Korea's Presidential Election into Turmoil," *The Canberra Times,* 19 December 2007.

44. Kyŏnghyang sinmun t'ŭkbyŏl ch'ijaet'im [Kyŏnghyang Daily's Special Report-team], *Minjuhwa 20-nyŏn ŭi yŏlmanggwa chŏlmang* [Desires and Despairs of Democratization for Twenty Years] (Seoul: Humanit'as, 2007), 14–15.

45. Howard French, "Shuffled Off to History, Veneration of Ro Moo Hyun Will Follow," *Herald Tribune,* 28 December 2007.

46. Hahm Chae-bong, "South Korea's Miraculous Democracy," 141.

47. Kim Hyung-A, *Korea's Development,* 215.

15

Deconstruction in the Republic of the Congo

MBOW AMPHAS-MAMPOUA

Abstract: *This case study shows that despite a rich endowment of natural re-*
sources, fertile land, and repeated oil booms, the Republic of the Congo has been
unable to forge a national identity out of diverse and hostile tribes. Tribes engage
in politics as a zero-sum game, where those in power exclude the rest, and those
out of power plot to retake it. This political culture has led to endemic instability,
corruption, economic decline, and intense intertribal animosity. For the first three
decades after independence, Congolese followed Soviet and Chinese models for
economic development that entailed the nationalization of industry, the neglect of
agriculture and consumer goods, economic development through five-year plans,
and political rule through a one-party state. This model transformed the country, a
food exporter at independence, into a food importer; failed to maintain the trans-
portation infrastructure left by France; and created a proliferation of money-losing
state enterprises and an unsustainable expansion of the state bureaucracy. The
turn to democracy in the 1990s brought not stability but civil war as the tradition
of zero-sum politics lives on.

The Republic of the Congo is a country of paradoxes: Despite its rich endowment
of natural resources, including oil, and its comparatively well-educated population, most of its citizens remain poor, and, since independence from France, it has
suffered from chronic political instability. Although each succeeding government
administration has made revolution its motto, the Congo's problems—a deteriorating infrastructure, endemic corruption, political violence, declining agriculture, high
indebtedness, and inadequate managerial skills—remain remarkably unchanging.
Despite the generally anti-Western rhetoric of these governments, they remain
highly dependent on Western aid. And finally, after years of authoritarian rule,
democracy brought civil war, not stability.

Until 1992 Congolese leaders followed Marxist political and economic models,
had a one-party state led by a charismatic leader, pursued development through five-
year plans, and nationalized the private sector. Although the Congo did not extend
Marxism to the countryside by collectivizing agriculture, it followed the Marxist
emphasis on industry and failed to invest in either agriculture or the transportation

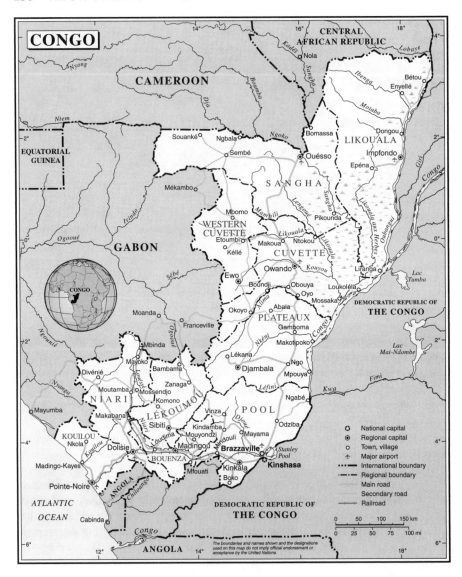

infrastructure to get produce to markets. A food exporter at independence, today the Congo is dependent on food imports. Despite oil booms in the 1970s and 1980s, the economy has stagnated and the colonial-era infrastructure has deteriorated.

The Setting

The Republic of the Congo (hereafter referred to as the Congo) should not be confused with its much larger neighbor, the Democratic Republic of the Congo (Zaire), which was colonized by Belgium. The Congo is roughly the size of New Mexico with an area of 132,047 square miles and a population of four million. Although the population density is low, 85 percent of the Congolese live in the country's two main cities, the capital of Brazzaville and the ocean port of Pointe-Noire, and in the towns along the railway line connecting the two cities, meaning the population is overwhelming concentrated in the coastal south. The Congo River, the world's second-largest river in terms of water flow, after the Amazon, forms the border between the two Congos. Brazzaville serves as a major river port and lies across the river from the capital of the Democratic Republic of the Congo, Kinshasa. The Congo also shares borders with Gabon, Cameroon, and the Central African Republic. The four former colonies comprising French Equatorial Africa (the Congo, Gabon, the Central African Republic, and Chad) plus Cameroon and Equatorial Guinea share the same currency, the CFA franc.

The Congo's abundant natural resources include diamonds, iron, phosphates, potassium, zinc, gold, petroleum, and natural gas. In the early twenty-first century, the Congo was sub-Saharan Africa's fifth-largest oil producer, after Nigeria, Angola, Gabon, and Cameroon. The Congo's natural resources are concentrated in the south, so wealth is also concentrated there. Although the climate is tropical with heavy rainfall, the Congo suffers from neither floods nor droughts. It has a rainy season from April through October and a dry season from November to May. Farmers can reap five cassava harvests per year, four groundnut harvests, and three maize harvests. In 1964 the Congo's principal exports were timber and diamonds, each constituting about 40 percent, while oil made up only 2 percent.[1] By 1982 oil accounted for 80 percent of exports.

In 1960, 47 percent of the population were Bakongo, 20 percent Batéké (Teke), 11 percent Mbochi, 7 percent Mbeti, 5 percent Sangha, and the rest from various smaller ethnic groups.[2] The dominant ethnic group of the south is the Bakongo (also known as the Kongo), who speak Monokutuba and live on the Atlantic coast and particularly in the capital. An important Bakongo subgroup is the Lari, whose members are among the most highly educated Congolese. The Batéké and Mbochi speak Lingala and come from northern Congo. Originally they inhabited the central plateau, but with the rapid urbanization of the Congo, many now inhabit the urban southern coast.

French colonization of the Congo goes back to 1880, when the explorer Savorgnan de Brazza signed a treaty with Makoko, the king of the Batéké people. Brazzaville is named after him. In 1895 France consolidated its West African colonies into a federation known as French West Africa. France ruled the Congo through native political institutions until 1900, when it took direct control in order to exploit the Congo's natural resources as efficiently as possible.[3] In 1910 it created out of its central African colonies a second federation called French Equatorial Africa, which it ruled through a governor-general located in Brazzaville and a reasonably efficient colonial administration.

France created a far better transportation infrastructure than had existed previously. This investment was geared to resource extraction for the benefit of France.

For example, in the 1920s and 1930s, France constructed the Congo-Ocean Railroad from Pointe-Noire to Brazzaville, bypassing the lower Congo River rapids, in order to extract resources not only from the Congo, but also from the neighboring colonies in equatorial Africa. The French built a hydroelectric dam on the Djoue River, the ports of Pointe-Noire and Brazzaville, and the airport for Brazzaville in order to facilitate their import-export business activities.

When France established a customs union encompassing its African colonies, the Congo served as a "staging post for capital in the customs union" by providing essential technical and financial services that were much more developed than those of its neighbors.[4] Key elements of the transportation infrastructure were the shipping lines along the Congo and Ubangi rivers, which extended deep inland, the railway, the road system, and the port of Pointe-Noire. The trade along this transportation net meant half of the credits from the customs union was funneled through the Congo. This wealth allowed for the development of numerous small metalworking shops as well as a number of small- and medium-sized industries producing consumer goods such as cigarettes and beer for markets within the customs union. France encouraged cash crop production. For instance, the French tobacco company Societé Industrielle et Agricole du Tabac Tropical (SIAT) encouraged tobacco production. The Niari valley and the Batéké plateau together produced about 400 tons of tobacco annually.[5] At independence, the Congo provided sugar for the entire customs union.[6] This, however, did not enrich the Congolese, who increasingly resented their political exclusion and the exploitation of their resources for the benefit of outsiders.[7]

Thus colonialism engendered the very local resistance movements that would undermine it.[8] The resistance movement under the Lari leader, André Matsoua (1899–1942), demanded the end of the Code de l'indigenat, France's legal code for the local non-French population that protected French accused of violence against them. The code provided no protections for political rights, the freedom of assembly, or the freedom of speech. It also mandated corvée labor, which the French used to build the Congo's railway line connecting Brazzaville and Pointe-Noire. In the 1920s, the French writer André Gide denounced the Code de l'indigenat in his book Voyage au Congo.

World War II greatly weakened France. In 1946, France established the French Union, composed of itself and its colonies. Costly wars in Vietnam (1946–54) and Algeria (1954–62), however, forced France to withdraw from both colonies, encouraging decolonization movements elsewhere. In 1958 France replaced the French Union with the French Community, which had provisions for the independence of its members via local referenda. As a result, in 1960 France granted independence to all of its African colonies save Algeria.

Independence and the Presidency of Fulbert Youlou (1958–63)

A common desire for independence blurred ethnic divisions. Once France left, however, the "tribalization of the Congo" accelerated, with the key ethnic fault line dividing the north from the south. The deep antagonisms between the Mbochis of the north and the Bakongos of the south constituted a major impediment to creating a unified nation. Ethnicity played an important role in the political ascension of the three crucial Congolese political leaders who emerged before independence: the Mbochi, Jacques Opangault (1907–1978); the Bakongo, Fulbert Youlou (1917–1972); and the Vili, Jean Félix Tchicaya (1931–1988), the father of writer Utam'si Tchicaya.[9]

In the Congo, as in most sub-Saharan African nations, leaders tended to distribute goods to their own ethnic group in return for votes.[10] Therefore, ethnicity and political party membership tended to coincide, meaning that the Congo lacked a political party with a national membership. Each party had a regional following. Upon taking power, each group sought to exclude the others. No group has constituted an absolute majority of the population. At the time of the 1958 referendum to establish a provisional government in preparation for independence, tribalism dominated Congolese politics, with a clear confrontation between North Congolese Mbochis, who formed the membership of the African Socialist Movement (*Mouvement Socialiste Africain* or MSA) founded in 1946, and South Congolese Laris, who formed the membership of the Democratic Union for the Defense of African Interests (*Union Démocratique de Défense des Interêts Africains* or UDDIA) under the leadership of Fulbert Youlou in 1956. Youlou was a former priest and anti-Communist who had served as the mayor of Brazzaville.

Prior to the 28 November 1958 referendum, the Mbochi leader of the MSA, Jacques Opangault, served as the prime minister. Opangault had entered the French administrative service in 1925. The election of Youlou as prime minister in 1958, by twenty-three votes to Opangault's twenty-two, ended the MSA's former monopoly on political power and opened the floodgates for government appointments to Laris. The Laris had been privileged under colonial rule, as France relied on them to provide government and private sector administrators. Youlou transferred MSA civil servants, appointed Bakongo to Mbochi districts, and allowed no opposition portfolios. As a result, the Bakongos in government outnumbered the Mbochis and Youlou created a one-party state. There was a brief civil war in 1959 that avoided the tragedy of genocide because Congolese political leaders were inclined to reconciliation. Although in the Congo the president and the dominant cabinet members tended to come from the same tribe, on 5 June 1961, Youlou appointed his opponent, Opangault, as vice-president. However, the holder of the number two position typically never rose directly to the number one position. Youlou then made the Provisional Republic permanent as the Government of the Republic.

Independence created a shared pride among Congolese. Contrary to popular expectations, however, Youlou was unable to make profound changes. He did not stimulate economic development or improve the general standard of living. The departure of French colonial administrators left a shortage of trained personnel. At independence, there were about five university graduates in all of French Equatorial Africa and virtually no industry in the Congo. The new government continued to rule through French administrative structures, and the French imprint remained strong in educated Congolese, most of whom had studied at French institutions. France also left its linguistic imprint when French became the official language, in 1960, even though it was a first language for virtually no one in the entire population and very few women spoke it fluently. The Youlou administration worked in close collaboration with foreign companies and facilitated the exploitation of Congo's resources by France.[11]

The Congolese perceived foreign investment as benefiting foreigners and local bureaucrats, but not the general population.[12] Unemployment increased, the trade deficit soared, the roads were impassable during the rainy season, and administration consumed three-quarters of the government budget. Youlou had created a "bureaucratic bourgeoisie," who like himself lived extravagantly.[13] Although politically independent, the Congo remained economically dependent on foreign exchange from the foreign buyers of its crops and minerals. Youlou's foreign policy was no more successful than his domestic policy. He backed a secessionist movement in neighboring Zaire. When UN forces crushed the movement in January of 1963, this further eroded Youlou's support at home.[14]

The optimism at independence soon faded. Trade unions became the driving force of the revolution of 1963. Civil servants joined the general strike. Youlou rejected the trade union demands for governmental reforms, the election of a new legislature, and the removal of incompetent and corrupt ministers. When he arrested the two most important trade unions leaders, Gilbert Pongault and Julien Boukambou, demonstrations spread throughout the capital demanding Youlou's resignation. Youlou responded with deadly force. After France turned down Youlou's request for military support—a decision it may have soon regretted—Youlou stepped down rather than risk a civil war.[15]

Socialism Under Alphonse Massamba-Débat (1963–68)

Congolese considered Youlou and his followers to have been a local extension of the French colonial administration, what they referred to as neocolonialists. A Congolese elite had simply replaced France's administrators and now had a cut of the profits, but for all practical purposes the Congo remained a French economic colony. Nineteen sixty-three was the height of the Cold War, when the United States and the Soviet Union aggressively competed to extend their political and economic models to the rest of the world and maintained two vast and hostile alliance systems. It was also the height of the Sino-Soviet split, when the Soviet Union and the People's Republic of China competed for leadership of the Communist bloc. The Congolese were thoroughly disenchanted with the Western model that had brought them colonialism. Many believed the Marxist explanation for the international distribution of wealth that blamed imperialism. Many saw Mao Zedong's China as an appropriate model for the Congo. Whereas the Soviet model emphasized industrial workers, which the Congo conspicuously lacked, the Chinese model promised revolution through the peasantry. Congolese leaders jettisoned capitalism for socialism, and state control became the order of day. The Congo soon cultivated relations with the Soviet Union, China, and Cuba, at the expense of France.

Although the trade unions and not the army played the key role in the overthrow of Youlou, the army played the key role in choosing his successor and excluding trade unionists from the cabinet. The army brought to power President Alphonse Massamba-Débat (1921–1977), a Bakongo. He purged the civil service by eliminating 2,000 of 9,000 posts. In 1964 his young revolutionary supporters founded the National Revolutionary Movement (*Mouvement National de la Révolution* or MNR) as a Marxist-Leninist ruling party and banned all other political parties. Massamba-Débat served as the secretary-general of the MNR and as president of the republic.

The Congo became a single-party state on the rationale that only the homogenizing force of single-party rule could overcome the ethnic divisions fracturing the country. The single-party system attempted to contain tribalism by emphasizing an overarching ideology. Political militancy instead of ethnicity became a route to political appointment. The Central Committee of the MNR soon controlled both the government and the trade union movement, with the pro-China faction in control and other factions purged. Cuban experts arrived to train the Civil Guard and the youth group of the MNR, which operated rather like the Red Guards in China to create a climate of fear. Youth group harassment caused the United States to close its embassy. Although relations with France improved after 1967, a disagreement with Britain over Rhodesia (now Zimbabwe) led to the severance of their relations.

The MNR denounced free enterprise as inefficient and called for state control of foreign trade and the closure of non-state schools. The first Five-Year Plan (1964–68) introduced central planning. The plan made overly optimistic estimates of foreign aid, and plan targets were not met. Nevertheless, from 1964 to 1966 industrialization proceeded rapidly, with the Congo registering the fourth-highest growth rate of French-speaking Africa, and agriculture prospered. The Congo was self-sufficient in cassava, sugar, maize, fruits, and vegetables. The Congolese sugar industry, with a capacity of 100,000 tons, exceeded that of any other French-speaking African country and provided export revenues. This period included the establishment of a cigarette factory in Betou as well as a fish-flour factory, a glassworks, and a cement factory, and the expansion of the oil-palm plants in Owando, Mokouango, and Etoro, each producing 3,000 tons. From 1965 to 1973 the average real GDP grew at 6.8 percent.[16] As a result the unemployment rate declined.

Meanwhile, Massamba-Débat increasingly relied on the Civil Guard to remain in office. His demotion of the charismatic paratrooper Captain Marien Ngouabi (1938–1977) triggered an opposing alliance between his own most radical younger supporters and the left wing of the army. In 1968 he reshuffled the cabinet and combined the offices of president and prime minister in his own person in order to undercut the growing power of radical MNR leaders.

Scientific Socialism Under the Congolese Labor Party

Ngouabi did not take kindly to his demotion. He seized power on 31 July 1968, and for the first time since independence, the Congo was ruled by a military leader. This shift from a civil government at independence to military governments thereafter followed the general trend in Africa that included Algeria, Burundi, the Central African Republic, Dahomey (Benin), Ghana, Mali, Nigeria, Sierra Leone, Togo, Uganda, and Zaire. Ngouabi's succession also marked a transfer of power from the south to the north, as Ngouabi and his two immediate successors were members of the northern Mbochi and Kouyou tribes, whereas Youlou and Massamba-Débat were southerners. Ngouabi claimed that the entire population had joined the revolutionary uprising bringing him to power.[17] In practice, the military officers who effected the coup had been trained at France's foremost military academy, St. Cyr, which stressed the tradition of military nonintervention in politics.[18]

Ngouabi banned the MNR, dissolved the National Assembly, purged the government, and created the National Council of the Revolution to impose his rule. In 1969 he founded the Congolese Labor Party out of the civilian revolutionaries in the National Council of the Revolution, the Civil Guard, and the left wing of the army. Like his predecessor, he banned all other political parties. He justified the one-party state by arguing that only an avant-garde party could mobilize the masses through political indoctrination and defend their interests by deepening the revolution. Ngouabi endorsed a more radical version of Marxism than that followed by Massamba-Débat. Then he turned Marxism on its head, rejecting Karl Marx's formulation "from each according to his ability, to each according to his need" for his own slogan, "He who does not work has no right to a salary."[19] The rhetoric shifted from socialism to scientific socialism and the name of the country changed from the Republic of the Congo to the People's Republic of the Congo. Soviet influence grew with many in the military and the party receiving training in Moscow.

In 1970 the government nationalized industry and transport. The Congo's sugar production fell from 100,000 tons at independence to 7,000 tons, transforming the country into a sugar importer.[20] Palm oil production also declined, with palm oil workers putting in two hours of work per day. High unemployment and the collapse of agriculture brought food shortages. There was a brief oil boom in 1974, followed by a collapse in petroleum production. Oil production declined significantly, and the Holle potash facility closed in 1977 because of flooding.

Many disagreed with this economic strategy. There were coup attempts in 1969 and 1970, and growing student and labor unrest. Ngouabi responded with violent repression. His economic failures became so obvious that in 1975 he purged the Political Bureau of the Congolese Labor Party, created the Special Revolutionary General Staff, and implemented a special three-year economic plan (1975–77). Strikes ensued. He gave the portfolio of defense minister to his protégé, Denis Sassou Nguesso (1943–), a fellow member of the Mbochi tribe, but he did so by bypassing another northerner, Jacques Joachim Yhombi Opango of the Kouyou tribe (1939–), who was connected with the Congolese intelligence services.

On 18 March 1977, Ngouabi, who had taken power in a coup nine years earlier, was assassinated in his palace under murky circumstances.[21] The northern Mbochi and Kouyou tribes retaliated for the assassination by executing Massamba-Débat and assassinating Archbishop of Brazzaville Emile Biayenda, both from the south.[22] Ngouabi's family alleged that Archbishop Biayenda had used magical powers to undermine Ngouabi's invulnerability.[23] On 6 April 1977, another northerner, Yhombi Opango, assumed power over an interim government with the consent of Sassou Nguesso, who, as Ngouabi's defense minister, should have been his successor. Yhombi Opango tried to legitimize the transition by claiming continuity with the Ngouabi administration, but in practice he was not loyal to his predecessor's vision. Many within the military and the Congolese Labor Party favored Sassou Nguesso.[24] The Congolese Labor Party called a Central Committee session approving Sassou Nguesso's succession on 5 February 1979, thus replacing the interim government with his permanent government. Sassou Nguesso remained in power for thirteen years and, after a hiatus of five years, returned to power in 1997.

Upon taking power in 1979, he restored the assassinated president's revolutionary structures shelved by Yhombi Opango. He also tried to claim a restoration of Marxism to garner public support. With the oil boom of 1982, he became known as the "good luck president" and the Congo became sub-Saharan Africa's fourth-largest oil producer. Oil revenues rose from $16 million in 1978 to $250 million in 1982, peaked at $1 billion in 1985, and fell to $800 million in 1986.[25] Rather than use this massive windfall to invest in infrastructure, the bureaucratic elite consumed in luxury homes what was left over from debt repayments. Sassou Nguesso, like his predecessors, failed to increase prosperity. Instead, he created a civil service that devoured state funds faster than they were generated. Agriculture remained in collapse without adequate roads or food storage facilities for farmers to market their produce. Overstaffed state-run enterprises operated at a loss of $80 million in 1983 and consumed 16 percent of the government budget, so that many state-run enterprises had to close.[26]

Economic disaster forced Congolese leaders to temper their ideology with pragmatism. Sassou Nguesso sought improved relations with the West as the Soviet Union, China, and Cuba had failed to provide much aid. In return for financial aid, Sassou Nguesso implemented the structural adjustment program demanded by the World Bank, the International Monetary Fund (IMF), and the United States. The program required the opening of markets to attract foreign investments. The Congo liberalized trade and investment regulations, privatized state-owned enterprises, and emphasized efficiency in the public sector. In 1989 the World Bank provided major loans for road maintenance, education, and urban development. Severe balance-of-payments and budgetary shortfalls, however, increased the debt burden. From 1980 to 1991, enterprises continued to perform poorly, partly because managers received their appointments based on political patronage rather than competence.

Throughout the life of the Congolese Labor Party, the economy continued to deteriorate, due to a combination of budget deficits, a deteriorating infrastructure, and declining agricultural production.

Democracy and Civil War

Mikhail Gorbachev's reforms in the Soviet Union coupled with the fall of the Berlin Wall in 1989 gave impetus to the experimentation with democracy in Africa. In 1991 countries such as Benin, Zaire, Burkina Faso, and Zambia moved toward multiparty political systems. Sassou Nguesso authorized the formation of other political parties and promulgation of the democratic constitution of 1992. Like other one-party-state leaders who encouraged the formation of political parties, such as Mathieu Kerekou in Benin and Kenneth Kaunda in Zambia, Sassou Nguesso lost the ensuing elections. Even though virtually every region produced its own party and only the Congolese Labor Party had a multiethnic and national membership, he still lost, to Pascal Lissouba, a professor of biology and member of the Nzébi tribe. Lissouba, who controlled the South Congo regions of Bouenza, Lekoumou, and Niari, became the country's first democratically elected president.

Lissouba and his party, the Pan-African Union for Social Democracy (*Union Panafricaine pour la Démocratie Sociale* or UPADS) won 36 percent and 61 percent in two rounds of presidential elections, defeating Bernard Kolelas, a member of the Bakongo-Lari tribe and the leader of Congolese Movement for Democracy and Integral Development (*Mouvement Congolais pour le Démocratie et la Développement Intégral* or MCDDI), and Sassou Nguesso's Congolese Labor Party. Victory came in the second round as a result of an UPADS-Congolese Labor Party coalition, but after the election Lissouba failed to share power with his coalition partner. Therefore, the Congolese Labor Party soon formed an alliance with the Union of Democratic Forces (*Union des Forces Démocratiques* or UFD), a Bakongo-Lari political group without a clear ideology, creating a majority in the National Assembly, which Lissouba proceeded to dissolve in 1993. He called for new legislative elections on 2 May 1993.

Although the new, democratically elected government came to power on a wave of optimism and although it immediately launched an economic and social recovery plan, the plan foundered on the familiar external debt problem. To fund the reform package, in 1994 the IMF provided a one-year standby agreement, the World Bank extended economic recovery credit, and the Paris Club agreed to debt reduction. The government negotiated a contract with the French oil company Elf, the main explorer of the Congo's crude oil, requiring Elf to remit 32 percent of oil revenues to the Congolese treasury.[27] But these changes were insufficient to jump-start the stagnant economy.

The multiparty system under Lissouba failed to create political stability. One of the key attributes of effective governance is a monopoly on the use of force.

The central government lost the monopoly. Paradoxically, instead of unifying the country, the multiparty system contributed to its further fragmentation. Lissouba's political rivals, particularly Kolelas and his MCDDI party and Sassou Nguesso and his followers in the Congolese Labor Party, did their utmost to prevent him from succeeding. Lissouba's closest allies focused on personal enrichment, rather than on mobilizing political support. The political parties created their own militias. Soon three militias operated in the Congo. Two represented an ethnic group. The Aubevillois militia represented the Niari, Bouenza, and Lekoumou area under Lissouba and UPADS. The Ninjas militia mainly had support from MCDDI, the political party of the Pool region surrounding the capital. The Cobra militia was associated with Sassou Nguesso and the Congolese Labor Party and was financed by Angola, which was embroiled in its own civil war. The army was divided, and Lissouba lacked the support within the army to disband these militias. Yet the existence of militias undermined the authority of the army.

In 1994 fighting broke out between Kolelas's MCCDI and Lissouba's UPADS militias in the Bakongo quarter of Brazzaville. For the first time in Congolese history, southerners fought each other. In the past, Laris of the south had fought Mbochis of the north. On 30 January 1994, members of parliament from the Pool and Niari areas met and called for peace. In the run-up to the presidential elections of July 1997, none of the three major contenders represented the majority of the electorate, so a democratic solution required a coalition government. But each party intended to exclude the others after victory.

In June 1997, the personal ambitions of Lissouba and Sassou Nguesso brought the country to civil war when Lissouba attacked Sassou Nguesso's heavily guarded home in Brazzaville to disarm the Cobras. Lissouba created a new Constitutional Council and extended his term in office so that he could postpone the presidential elections. Angola intervened on the side of Sassou Nguesso. The ensuing civil war took 10,000 lives and left much of the capital in ruins. In September the militias removed Lissouba from power to reinstate Sassou Nguesso.[28] For the first time in Congolese history, a political leader came to power by winning a war. Many politicians, including Lissouba, sought exile abroad. The United States soon recognized the new government.

Upon retaking power in November 1997, Sassou Nguesso announced a move toward national reconciliation that he failed to follow in practice. He showed little mercy for his political opponents, trying in absentia those who had fled. The Pool region, Kolelas's political base, became a humanitarian disaster. Sassou Nguesso abolished the constitution of 1992 and set presidential elections for 2002, which he subsequently won with 82 percent of the vote after preventing credible political rivals from running. Meanwhile, from 1999 to 2004, oil production fell from 300,000 barrels per day to about 235,000. Since 2006, oil production has increased to about 255,000 barrels and should reach 330,000 barrels per day with the exploitation of the new field at Moho-Bilondo. The IMF, however, has criticized the Sassou Nguesso government for failing to keep adequate records of its oil income and expenditures.[29] Thus, in the past two decades, the Congo has become more polarized than ever.

The Congo, rather than a case of nation building, state building, or economic development, has been a case of "unbuilding," or deconstruction. For all the many problems of colonialism, France left the country with a better infrastructure and more honest administration than the country has had since. When the French departed, they left administrative institutions that might have become the basis for a strong state, but the land they left behind was not a nation, in the sense of a people of a territory unified by a common, overarching identity. Rather, the French left behind competing tribes, whose members engage in politics as a zero-sum game in which the winner takes all and the loser gets nothing. Those who lose and complain face repression. As a result, those who lose gather their forces to fight and win the next round, and those in power grab what they can while they can. Each new administration jettisons the institutions of its predecessor, as indicated by the constantly changing constitutions of the Congo. Political legitimacy comes from revolutionary rhetoric, since the one thing the Congolese do agree on is that the status quo is unacceptable and change is desirable. But there is no agreement on a positive agenda for change, only a negative agenda of destroying what came before and a cat fight over the spoils of the Congo's rich natural resources.

Despite the great good fortune of the oil boom, the Congolese elite have consumed rather than invested this windfall. Investment requires stability, but Congolese political successions are irregular, bitterly contested, and highly destabilizing. The Congo suffers from a failure of leadership at the top and a failure of management in the middle. In this volatile political environment, little economic development has taken place. Many in the countryside live without electricity, roads, hospitals, transportation, or running water. Unemployment remains chronic, while the standard of living continues to fall. Tribalism, political exclusion, and corruption have thrived at the expense of economic development.

Notes

1. The percentages have been calculated from the table provided in Mbow M. Amphas, *Political Transformations of the Congo* (Durham, NC: Pentland Press, 2000), 78.

2. Donald Morrison, *Black Africa: A Comparative Handbook*, 2nd ed. (London: MacMillan, 1983), 13.

3. See Samir Amin and Catherine Coquery-Vidrovitch, *Histoire Économique du Congo 1880–1968* (Paris: Ed. Anthropos, 1969), 25.

4. G. Nguyen and T. Hung, *Agriculture and Rural Development in the People's Republic of the Congo* (Boulder, CO, and London: Westview Press, 1987), 4; Lyn K. Mytelka, "A Genealogy of Francophone West and Equatorial African Regional Organizations," *The Journal of Modern African Studies* 12 no. 2 (1974), 297–320.

5. Janet MacGaffey and Rémy Bazenguissa-Ganga, *Congo-Paris: Transnational Traders on the Margins of the Law* (Bloomington: Indiana University Press, 2000), 40.

6. Hugues Bertrand, *Le Congo: Formation Sociale et Mode de Développement Économique* (Paris: Ed. Maspero, 1975), 86.

7. See Jean Ganiage, *L'expansion coloniale de la France sous la Troisième République (1871–1914),* Collection Bibliothèque Historique (Paris: Ed. Payot, 1968), 45.

8. Rodney Walker, *How Europe Underdeveloped Africa* (London: Bogle-L'Ouverture Publications, 1972), 166.

9. Virginia Thompson and Richard Adloff, *The Emerging States of French Equatorial Africa* (Stanford, CA: Stanford University Press, 1960), 486.

10. Kimuli Kasara, "Tax Me If You Can: Ethnic Geography, Democracy, and the Taxation of Agriculture in Africa," 25 November 2005, paper delivered at "Poverty, Democracy, and Clientelism: The Political Economy of Vote Buying," conference, Stanford University, 28 November–2 December 2005.

11. Rene Gauze, *The Politics of Congo Brazzaville* (Stanford, CA: Stanford University Press, 1973), 175.

12. Pierre-Philippe Rey, *Colonialism et Transition au Capitalisme: Exemple de la "Comilog" du Congo Brazzaville* (Paris: Ed. Maspero, 1971), 518.

13. "Brazzaville: Ten Years of Revolution," *West Africa,* 13 August 1973.

14. Crawford Young, "Zaire: The Anatomy of a Failed State," in *History of Central Africa: The Contemporary Years since 1960,* eds. David Birmingham and Phyllis M. Martin (London: Longman, 1998), 106.

15. Amphas, *Political Transformations,* 27.

16. *Africa South of the Sahara,* 16th ed. (London: Europa Publications, 1980), 387.

17. Marien Ngouabi, "Scientific Socialism in Africa, Congo Problems, Views and Experience," *World Marxist Review,* 18 no. 5 (May 1975), 36.

18. William Tordoff, *Government and Politics in Africa,* 3rd ed. (Bloomington: Indiana University Press, 1997), 181; Theophile Obenga, *La vie de Marien-Ngouabi 1938–1977* (Paris: Présence Africaine, 1977), 46–47.

19. Amphas, *Political Transformations,* 7.

20. "Congo: le marxisme en question: 'or noir' 'or vert,'" *Le Monde,* 2 January 1988.

21. David Lamb, "Congo Finds It Can Exist on Marxism," *Los Angeles Times,* 29 July 1977.

22. Cas De Villiers, *African Problems and Challenges* (Sandton, South Africa: Valliant, 1976), 85.

23. *African Contemporary Report,* 77–8.B.552.

24. Michael Radu and Keith Somerville, *The Congo,* Marxist Regimes series (London: Pinter, 1989), 179.

25. Amphas, *Political Transformations,* 86.

26. *The Economist,* 2 July 1983.

27. Amphas, *Political Transformations,* 104.

28. Ibid., 101–2.

29. John Donnelly, "In Oil-rich Nation, Charges of Skimming: Congolese Officials Said to Reap Profit," *The Boston Globe,* 25 November 2005.

16

The Three Pillars of Power in Gabon: Ethnicity, Family, and France

James F. Barnes

Abstract: *This case study examines the enduring influence of France in its former colony, Gabon. Although Gabon is both politically stable and wealthy, much of its population remains poor and the general life expectancy is low. At independence, the local elite who had cooperated with France during the colonial period took political control, while France retained its economic interests and protected them by overturning a military coup in 1964. The Gabonese used the centralized administrative structures inherited from the colonial period to impose personalistic clan rule. Much of Gabon's middle class works in this government bureaucracy, which controls the economy. The second president of Gabon remained in power from 1969 to 2009 and was, apart from royal families, the world's longest-ruling leader. Although his rule constituted a shift in the ethnic groups controlling the government, he maintained political stability by forging a coalition of carefully balanced ethnic groups, by relying on his own clan to staff his inner circle, and by protecting French interests to retain French support.*

The Gabonese state is an artifact of French colonialism. Following independence in 1960, a conservative Gabonese elite, with the active support and intimate involvement of the French, acquired an autocratic grip on the country's political and economic institutions. A modified symbiotic relationship persists and fundamentally defines the nature of the polity. In the complex narrative of the Republic of Gabon, nation building and democracy are recurrent, perplexing themes. Throughout its postcolonial history, the aspirations of many Gabonese for both independence and self-government remain unfulfilled despite the rhetoric of change in Gabon and the revolutionary, democratic traditions of France.

Gabon shatters Western stereotypes of African nations. It is stable and wealthy. It is also a study in contrasts. Given its plentiful natural resources and relatively small population, it should be able to provide a respectable standard of living to all of its residents with relative ease. The well-being of a substantial number is, however, substandard, whether measured by their health, the distribution of income, or income inequality. For example, life expectancy among men and women is fifty-two and fifty-seven years, respectively, while in France the figures for men and women are seventy-seven and eighty-four years, respectively; the rate of infant mortality at birth is 53.65 deaths per thousand in contrast to 3.41 per thousand in France.[1] The differences are striking. While Gabon's socioeconomic circumstances are similar to those in other African countries, these disparities in health and income are the consequences of several centuries of neglect and indifference. In both urban and rural areas, many Gabonese face a host of serious medical conditions; there is a very high probability of contracting hepatitis A, bacterial diarrhea, typhoid fever, and malaria. Gabon is also plagued by HIV/AIDS and cases of Ebola are still documented in its remote forest areas. Gabonese men and women suffer as well from unusually high rates of sterility, a condition that has been a major topic for Gabonese and French researchers at the Franceville hospital for a number of years.

While credible data about income distribution is difficult to acquire, Gabon enjoys a per capita income four times that of most sub-Saharan African nations, and there appears to have been a sharp decline in extreme poverty. This decline in poverty is, however, offset by substantial income inequality. While approximately 33 percent of the national population reportedly lives in poverty, it appears that just 2 percent of the population controls more than 80 percent of the national wealth.[2] It is apparent that a very large number of Gabonese subsist minimally, in poor health, while a relatively small elite have high incomes and access to health care in Gabon and France that would be the envy of many persons in the developed world.

Clearly the socioeconomic circumstances of a substantial number of Gabonese did not dramatically change in the transition from colonialism to "independence." While many Gabonese have quite obviously improved their standard of living, many others have not been the beneficiaries of Gabon's wealth. What explains such extreme socioeconomic inequality?

The Setting

Although Gabon has an unusually small population, estimated at 1.3 million inhabitants, at least forty distinct ethnic groups live within its borders. Gabon's basic demographic structure is the result of periodic migrations of Bantu peoples from their central African homelands throughout vast areas of sub-Saharan Africa. Four major ethnic groups of Bantu origin—the Fang, Bapounou, Nzébi, and Obamba (each of which is comprised of a number of subgroups)—provide Gabon's extraordinary ethnic and linguistic diversity.

Geographically, Gabon's Fang plurality is the most strategically placed ethnic group. They represent the demographic center of gravity of the Estuary region, including the capital city, Libreville, and are the primary residents of the agriculturally prosperous Woleu N'Tem region, stretching from the coast to the border with Cameroon. The Fang zone—including southern Cameroon, Equatorial Guinea, and Gabon—contains approximately two million Fang.

Rapid urbanization during the twentieth century has forced many of Gabon's

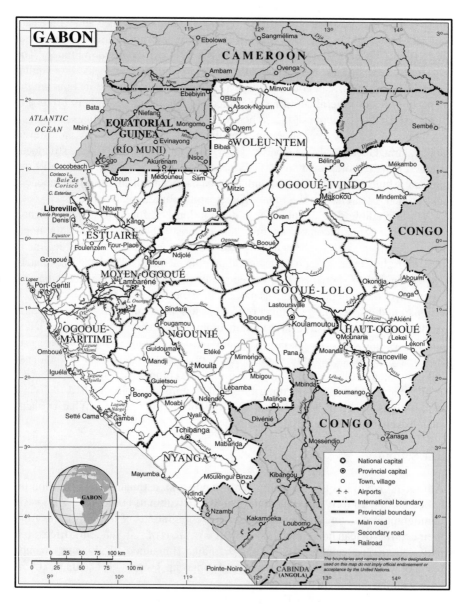

smaller ethnic groups to move from their traditional regions to live in close proximity in and around Gabon's major cities, Libreville, Port Gentil, Lambaréné,
and Franceville, the traditional centers of the French administrative, military, and
economic presence.[3] Thus, a national Gabonese identity has evolved as residents
of various regions have migrated to these "nationalizing zones," where French has
become the common Gabonese language and Catholicism their religion. As in many

parts of the world, these migrations have produced residents who are typically at home in quite complex ethnolinguistic settings.

Gabon is nearly the same size as the American state of Colorado, is roughly divided in half by the equator, and has two substantial deepwater Atlantic ports, Libreville and Port Gentil. Blessed with large stands of timber in one of the world's few remaining rainforests and substantial supplies of petroleum and manganese discovered in the twentieth century, it has been the object of attention of a number of European countries and the United States for virtually all of its existence as an identifiable geopolitical entity.[4]

Gabon's state revenues historically have been based on sales of timber and petroleum. Production of petroleum began in the 1930s, and by the 1960s, petroleum products had replaced timber as Gabon's major export. Although petroleum was discovered initially in the coastal areas, exploration and production have moved almost exclusively to offshore sites in the Gulf of Guinea, prompting occasional tension with Gabon's most immediate neighbors in the region, Equatorial Guinea and the former Portuguese colony São Tomé and Príncipe.

In the early 1960s, manganese and uranium represented important new sources of government revenue. The discovery of manganese led the government to build the Trans-Gabon Railway in the 1970s, to transport it from the remote Belinga region (adjacent to Gabon's borders with Cameroon and the Congo) to the terminus of the railway at Owendo, the port city for Libreville. Gabon's manganese is estimated to be among the world's major reserves and is currently the third leading source of national revenue after petroleum and timber. Supplies of uranium, produced uniquely for the French Atomic Energy Agency, were depleted by the mid-1990s, and the mines were closed in 1999.

Following classic colonial methodology, the French colonial administration monopolized control of Gabon's resources, and strictly monitored contracts with various French and international firms. The pattern of centralized state control established during the colonial era remains the norm. Throughout Gabon's history as a colony and independent nation, the centralized state apparatus has essentially precluded alternative modes of economic development. Gabon, unlike a number of other African states, did not experience a socialist/collectivist period nor, as in the 1970 Biafran secession in Nigeria, have any of Gabon's ethnic groups attempted to seize control of regional sources of timber or petroleum or manganese. The colonial state and its successors, the regimes of Léon Mba (1967–2009) and Albert Bernard Bongo Ondimba (1967–present) and their French partners, have successfully monopolized Gabon's natural resources.[5]

European interest began in the mid-fifteenth century when the Portuguese and, in turn, the British and French, were attracted to Gabon as a deepwater port for their naval and commercial fleets. By the seventeenth century, Gabon was a magnet for British and French commercial interests. Ships from a host of countries visited its coast in search of slaves, gold, and converts to Christianity. It became an important French possession in 1839. American missionaries, representing a consortium of

Congregationalist churches, posed a particularly interesting challenge to French Catholic missionaries in the competition for converts. The decision by French officials, the de facto administrators of the region, to make French the language of religious instruction effectively eliminated an American presence in Gabon until the appearance of Texas oilmen in the petroleum boom years following World War II. The British ultimately ceded power to the French in an important decision to consolidate their interests in Gambia, along the Senegal River. Similarly, Portuguese interests shifted southward to Angola and to Brazil, Portugal's major new possession in South America.

As a result of the agreements reached at the Congress of Berlin (1884–85) by the major European powers on the partition of Africa, France gained control of a substantial part of central and west Africa. France invested in commercial sites and military installations at Abidjan, Bangui, Brazzaville, Dakar, Fort Lamy (Ndjamena), and Libreville. From the late nineteenth century until the outbreak of World War I, Gabon was a classic colonial territory. The war became a crucial turning point in its political evolution, for thousands of Gabonese fought alongside French and allied soldiers in many of the European campaigns and a growing French-educated, Gabonese intelligentsia enthusiastically embraced the ideas of self-government and democracy.

From the end of World War I until the outbreak of World War II, considerable momentum for independence and democratization developed in the colonies. In Gabon, a number of indigenous organizations, despite the opposition of the colonial administration, lobbied initially for liberalization of the colonial system and, eventually, for independence. The idea of democracy and the dream of independence became inextricably linked, leading to a lasting tension between those who used an independent Gabon to further an alternative agenda and those who remained committed to the idea of an independent, democratic Gabon.

The decision of Léon Blum's Popular Front government in 1936 to introduce a degree of self-government in France's African colonies heartened the supporters of change. This entailed the introduction of parliamentary legislative bodies, and Africans, albeit in limited numbers, gained the central instruments of democratic politics: voting, elections, political parties, and regional assemblies. World War II and General Charles de Gaulle then greatly accelerated the pace of change and the ultimate collapse of the French colonial system.

Germany's occupation of France in 1940 and the establishment of the Vichy regime led to de Gaulle's creation of the Free French movement and the establishment of its twin headquarters in London and in Brazzaville, in the French Congo. In 1944, in a fateful speech at Brazzaville to rally black Africa to the Allied cause, de Gaulle promised that an Allied victory with African assistance would bring about liberalization in the colonial system. Although de Gaulle had not envisaged independence, France's loss of Indochina in 1954 and the beginning of an armed movement for independence in Algeria in the same year heralded the end of the colonial system.

Independence

On 17 August 1960, Léon Mba, the prime minister of the colonial assembly, became president of the formally independent Republic of Gabon. In retrospect, at this point Gabon's future course was largely determined. Mba, with the participation of a contingent of the Gabonese elite and major French economic and government interests, ushered in a virtually cooperative system of neocolonialism, meaning a system of power that defined Gabonese interests as the interests of the Gabonese elite and the national interests of France. The accord granting independence was replete with conditions that allowed the French to exercise an extraordinary degree of power over Gabonese affairs so that the country's extensive natural resources remained in the hands of the very same French interests that had exploited them during the colonial era. A symbiotic relationship emerged in which the Gabonese elite supported French interests in return for French support for their interests.

Despite the enthusiasm of many Gabonese for independence, Mba lobbied with the French government for Gabon to remain attached to France as an overseas department (*département d'outre mer*) in the manner of Guadeloupe and Martinique. In addition to his anxiety about Gabon facing the complexities of the world on its own, Mba was an ardent Francophile. The prospect of losing Gabon's intimate association with France appears to have been an issue of great concern for him and for many Gabonese who were proud of their identity as French Africans. President de Gaulle rejected Mba's request for overseas department status, and Gabon embarked uneasily on its eventful journey.[6]

Mba soon revealed his political agenda to the Gabonese. In a series of laws passed by the governing party, the Gabonese Democratic Bloc (*Bloc démocratique gabonais* or BDG), Mba moved decisively toward a one-party state. His major opponents were either imprisoned or sent into exile, and the opposition was reduced to an ineffectual voice in a national legislature dominated by Mba's BDG. Motivated by Mba's efforts to reverse the direction toward democracy, a group of young, French-trained army officers, with the tacit support of key personalities in the opposition, staged a coup d'etat on 17 February 1964. They removed Mba from power and installed a provisional government, largely staffed by members of the opposition.

In 1963, under similar circumstances in the French Congo, France had declined to intervene to save Fulbert Youlou's government, whereupon the new Congolese government proceeded to nationalize French assets. The French took a different course of action a year later in Gabon. Within two days of the coup, they dispatched paratroopers from Brazzaville to restore Mba to power. Along with many of the alleged conspirators, Jean-Hilaire Aubame, Mba's major critic and rival, was imprisoned and, later, exiled to France for his alleged involvement in the coup. There was, as one might suspect, a heated controversy about the French intervention. Some argued that France had intervened at the request of the Mba government, others viewed it as simple French aggression.

Upon Mba's death from cancer in a Paris hospital in 1967, Vice President Albert Bernard Bongo Ondimba,[7] at the age of thirty-one, became the second president of the Gabonese Republic. Again France determined Gabon's fate and accelerated the pace of neocolonial rule. In an important addition to the literature on Franco-African relations, Jacques Foccart, African affairs adviser to French presidents from Charles de Gaulle to Jacques Chirac, revealed that Bongo Ondimba was his choice to serve as Mba's vice president.[8] Foccart recalled that Mba, in his hospital bed in Paris, agreed and the deal was struck. Bongo Ondimba, who had come to Foccart's attention while serving as Mba's chief of staff, aggressively pursued Mba's plan to establish a one-party state. As Mba's successor, Bongo Ondimba faced no serious opposition—Aubame remained in exile.[9]

With the support of his allies in the National Assembly, Bongo Ondimba abolished the BDG, creating a new party, the Gabonese Democratic Party (*Parti démocratique gabonais* or PDG). All Gabonese were urged to join the PDG in a spirit of national reconciliation. Nevertheless, the most important government positions were in the hands of Bongo Ondimba loyalists and, significantly, French nationals routinely filled key civil and military positions until the 1990s, when the substantial French involvement in everyday Gabonese affairs declined. At this time there was an increasing demand from a growing number of educated Gabonese for access to government positions and a corresponding increase in the level of frustration about the extraordinary power of the French in Gabon. This decline in French day-to-day involvement did not, however, fundamentally alter the pattern of relations between the two countries.

Bongo Ondimba's Rule

As many commentators have noted, the momentum toward liberal democratic regimes that began in the post–World War I era was lost and a pattern of centralized oppressive regimes emerged in Africa following independence. This pattern is clearly evident in Gabon in the disposition of political power and economic rewards. In African countries, family and ethnicity are major factors in the world of politics. In Gabon, the truism holds.[10]

Mba's death and Aubame's exile dramatically altered the face of ethnic politics in Gabon. Despite their ethnic kinship, Mba and Aubame came from very different worlds: Mba was a Fang from Libreville and, allegedly, an active member of *Bwiti,* a religious sect, which the French colonial administration had considered sacrilegious and outlawed. Aubame, in contrast, was a Catholic from the more conservative Fang heartland in northern Gabon and was supported by the important Roman Catholic hierarchy. Their absence from the political center stage, applauded by many who were uneasy with the degree of Fang influence, cleared the way for a fundamentally different configuration of power in Gabon.

Bongo Ondimba's accession in 1967 signaled a major shift in the ethnic balance of power away from Fang domination of national politics. He was from the small

Batéké ethnic group in southeastern Gabon centered on the important regional city of Franceville. In his position as heir apparent to Mba, Bongo Ondimba had acquired a reputation as a pragmatist who was willing to establish a dialog with Gabonese of many different ethnic and regional identities. His power base was made up of a number of related ethnic groups in southeastern Gabon, the fabled "Nzébi/Batéké axis."

Bongo Ondimba also persuaded other strategically placed ethnic groups to participate in *le système Bongo*. A prime example was his close alliance with key personalities in the Mpongwé community. One of the oldest and most prestigious ethnic groups in Gabon, the Mpongwé were among the first of the indigenous populations to interact with the European and American arrivals in the coastal regions. They were pushed aside by the massive Fang migration from the north in the nineteenth century, but their alliance with Bongo Ondimba revived their economic and political fortunes. Gabon's petroleum wealth significantly aided Bongo Ondimba's practice of handsomely rewarding those who were willing to play the regime's game. While Bongo Ondimba successfully courted ethnic groups marginalized during the Mba-Aubame era, he did not ignore Gabon's Fang plurality. A basic rule of Gabonese politics is that the prime minister (who is chosen by the president), recently Jean Eyeghé Ndong, is always a prominent member of the Estuary Fang community.

After ethnicity, family is the second pillar of Bongo Ondimba's political alliance. His inner circle is made up of immediate family members, and members of his extended family are strategically placed throughout the extensive civil and military bureaucracy. Two of the many examples are his son, Ali Ben Bongo (Ondimba), formerly his minister of defense, who is now president and his daughter Pascaline Bongo (Ondimba), who was chief of staff. The combination of ethnic and familial relationships is an important component of a system of power that has remained in place for forty years. The family's political longevity and Gabon's stability reflect its ability to fashion a strategically populated ethnic coalition.

French support was the third key factor explaining Bongo Ondimba's political longevity. In 1983, French investigative journalist Pierre Péan described a shadowy body known as *le clan gabonais,* a group of prominent French and Gabonese personalities whose role was to advance French economic and foreign policy interests in the region and to further the political and economic interests of the Gabonese elite. Péan's exposé revealed a history of controversial practices, including allegations of assassination and harassment of anti–Bongo Ondimba exiles in France by the French government.[11]

Despite pronouncements by successive French governments concerning their commitment to change, democratization has not been very high on the list of French priorities. As revealed in a telling assessment by the Economist Intelligence Unit, France's former sub-Saharan colonies have authoritarian regimes (Cameroon, the Central African Republic, Chad, the Congo, Gabon, Niger, and Togo), flawed democracies (Benin and Mali), or a hybrid of the two (Senegal).[12]

It may be in the foreign policy arena that the Franco-Gabonese connection pays the greatest dividends for the French. From the presidency of de Gaulle to that of Sarkozy, the French have successfully maintained an impressive level of influence throughout the African continent. On the military side of the foreign policy equation, the French presence in Africa is clearly strategic. French military contingents are garrisoned in the Central African Republic, Chad, Djibouti, Gabon, Ivory Coast, and Senegal, locations that allow them to support their interests militarily, as they did in Gabon in 1964 and 1993 and Ivory Coast in 2007. In 1993 President François Mitterrand dispatched French marines to restore order after violent protests erupted in several Gabonese cities following Bongo Ondimba's questionable victory in the presidential election. Despite Mitterrand's assertion that he ordered the intervention in order to protect French nationals, the result, regardless of intent, supported a controversial Bongo Ondimba victory.

In 2007 pronouncements by Gabonese President Bongo Ondimba and French President Nicolas Sarkozy are noteworthy examples of a more recent display of Franco-Gabonese harmony. In a visit to the United States in May 2007, Bongo Ondimba publicly supported the George W. Bush administration's decision to invade Iraq. Three months later, in August 2007, shortly after winning the French presidential election, Sarkozy startled the international community and a substantial number of the French by suggesting that France might join the "coalition forces" in Iraq.[13] Sarkozy's comment is particularly interesting in light of his predecessor's well-known opposition to the American-led invasion. Sarkozy also announced shortly after his election that France had decided to annul 20 percent of Gabon's debt to France.[14] One could certainly conclude that this act of generosity was France's acknowledgment of Bongo Ondimba's stature as *le doyen* (the dean) of the French African community and of its continuing commitment to the political and economic stability of one of its most stalwart African allies. There are, nevertheless, indications that France, during the Sarkozy era, may bring about a significant reconceptualization of the French role in Africa. Douglas Yates, who has written on Gabon's political and economic relations with France, suggests that Sarkozy could significantly modify the French presence in Africa in an effort to broaden and diversify the scope of French foreign policy.[15]

One should also note that Bongo Ondimba has, on occasion, played an "American card" to assure good relations with the United States and to keep the French off balance. Whatever his motives, he was certainly correct, at least for the foreseeable future, in assuming that French interest in stability in Gabon would persist and that the regime would likely to get the benefit of the doubt in difficult circumstances. He was also correct in his assumption that policy makers in the United States believe that American national interests benefit from a cordial Gabon-U.S. relationship, a point underscored by increasing U.S. imports of petroleum from Gabon.

At a macroeconomic level, an important Chinese presence in Gabon has complicated the picture. China has assumed a major role in the development of Gabon's manganese, and Chinese construction and manufacturing firms are actively pursuing Gabonese projects. The possibility of increased tension among French, American, and Chinese interests in Gabon is not a farfetched idea. One thing is clear: Africa's involvement in the global economy will erode the established patterns and parameters of colonial and neocolonial economics and politics. A truly postcolonial environment might bring, perhaps realistically for the first time, fulfillment of Gabonese dreams for independence and democracy.

Democratization

In the early 1990s, Bongo Ondimba tried to temper the more autocratic characteristics of the Gabonese system. The end of apartheid in South Africa, the implosion of the Soviet system, and civil unrest in Gabon, including two failed coup attempts, are usually cited as explanations for Bongo Ondimba's announcement that he intended to liberalize the political system. At the time, the government published the only daily newspaper, L'Union, and monopolized radio and television. In a series of important initiatives, the government authorized the formation of opposition parties and the right of political formations to have their own newspapers and independent radio stations.

Bongo Ondimba's decision to tolerate an opposition led to the appearance of a number of new political parties that provided the first opportunity since the immediate postindependence era for opponents of the regime to express alternative views on public policy. A much-heralded National Conference in 1990 that brought together government and opposition organizations ratified Bongo Ondimba's reform initiative. This initiative constituted an implicit invitation to opposition political parties to engage PDG candidates in local and national elections.

In the presidential election of 1993, Bongo Ondimba's most formidable opponent was a Catholic priest, Paul Mba Abessole, the nominal leader for many years of the anti–Bongo Ondimba opposition in France. Returning from a long exile, he was the candidate of the National Assembly of Lumberjacks (Rassemblement National des Bûcherons or RNB). The Lumberjacks represented virtually the same Fang constituency that had supported Jean-Hilaire Aubame. During the campaign, to the dismay and disappointment of many, the government constantly harassed the opposition parties and in an extreme act of repression, Bongo Ondimba's Republican Guard destroyed Mba Abessole's private residence and the Lumberjack's radio station, Radio Liberté.[16] Despite angry voices from Paris, there were no real consequences for the government's actions. This was a striking example of the limits of opposition politics in Gabon and the well-practiced French tendency to turn a blind eye to the excesses of the regime. Nevertheless, Mba Abessole was expected to do well, possibly even defeat Bongo Ondimba. The 1993 election, rather than resulting in the first electoral defeat of the incumbent, was extraordinarily revealing about President Bongo Ondimba, his regime, and the power of "the Gabonese clan."

On election day, before the polls closed and a substantial number of votes were counted, Bongo Ondimba declared himself the victor with 51 percent of the vote, just enough to claim victory and avoid a run-off election. It was disclosed later that Charles Pasqua, the French interior minister and a longtime member of "the clan," dispatched ministry officials, with the approval of his government, to assist Gabonese election officials in falsifying the vote count. Sympathetic observers, including the U.S. State Department, determined that the election was conducted within acceptable parameters despite substantial evidence of fraud.[17]

Anger at the blatant theft of the election, exacerbated by increasing economic tension in the country, led to outbreaks of violence in Gabon's two major cities, Libreville and Port Gentil. A year later, the French initiated a second attempt at rapprochement between Bongo Ondimba and the opposition, the 1994 Paris Accords, which were ignored by the regime. Although "defeated" in the 1993 election, Mba Abessole has served, at the apparent pleasure of the regime, as mayor of Libreville, a Fang stronghold and Gabon's largest city, and is currently the national minister of culture, another stunning example of Bongo Ondimba's success in sustaining an effective ethnic coalition.

In the 1998, 2002, and 2007 presidential elections, Bongo Ondimba easily defeated his opponents. (There were also reports of extensive vote fraud in the 2007 elections.) A notable change in the Gabonese constitution by the governing PDG in 2003 eliminated presidential term limits, in anticipation that Bongo Ondimba would remain in office for some time. Following his unexpected death in 2009, his son, Ali Ben Bongo (Ondimba) was elected president, so the long-awaited post-Bongo Ondimba era would be well into the future.

Civil Society

In the past several decades, the literature of comparative politics has emphasized the significance of civil society in analyses of nation building and democratization. This concept is critically important in understanding the circumstances of the Gabonese state. Civil society provides a mechanism to limit the tendency of centralized governments to extend their power too far into the realm of individual privacy or, in the case of entrepreneurial economic activity, to constrain free market economics with excessive bureaucratic interference and centralization. The concept of civil society highlights the need for independent, intermediate socioeconomic structures to limit and mediate between the state and its citizens, either as individuals or members of a host of societal organizations.

As African states came into existence following their independence from Britain or France, they inherited systems of centralized power that postindependence elites used to further their own agendas.[18] Thereafter, centralized regimes based on European assumptions of bureaucratic rationality gave way to highly personalized systems of authority. When elites rely on the state for self-enrichment, their regimes sacrifice both legitimacy and stability. To remain in power, they must rely on tribal and personal loyalties that do not extend beyond the life of the political leader. By doing so, they prevent the creation of enduring legal systems and governmental institutions.[19]

Although the organizational structures that one would expect to find in a modern state—labor unions and opposition political parties, for example—are, nominally at least, present in Gabon, there is no substantial, independent Gabonese middle class that can effectively check the regime's powers. Many Gabonese who could be considered middle class based on levels of income and education are likely to be employed in Gabon's extensive, many would say bloated, civil service or publicly owned enterprises and are, of necessity, loyal to *le Patron,* Bongo Ondimba. Additionally, the Gabonese government and its economic partners have a virtual monopoly on the nation's wealth, effectively precluding the emergence of countervailing political forces.

In May 2007, the International Monetary Fund (IMF) approved a new $117-million standby loan to support government efforts to expand the nonpetroleum sectors of the economy. The government has a substantial income from petroleum, timber, and manganese. But, because of its overspending, excessive borrowing, and a number of very questionable and expensive national projects, including Air Gabon and the Trans-Gabon Railway, by 2007 Gabon's debt payments amounted to 40 percent of the national budget. Expectations that a number of IMF structural adjustment initiatives since the mid-1980s might catalyze a more privatized, diversified, decentralized, and efficiently managed economy have not materialized. Bongo Ondimba's centralized system appears to be as strong as ever.

Gabon's relatively small population has led to a reliance on foreign workers to supplement the local workforce. Approximately 150,000 non-Gabonese Africans and 10,000 to 12,000 French expatriates currently reside and work in Gabon. One often wonders if the regime might, in fact, prefer an expatriate workforce, despite occasional expressions of concern about an excessive foreign presence. Foreign workers are subject to deportation and pose little threat to the regime. Periodically, the government scapegoats foreign workers for Gabon's most serious crimes, stirring the pot of xenophobia. The practice appears to be successful in diverting popular attention from a host of endemic problems.

Both non-Gabonese African immigrants and French expatriates are relatively passive. Any overt intervention on their part in the political process would prompt some form of retaliation. Gabon's largest cities have a substantial number of French residents, who own and manage an array of services including restaurants, hotels, garages, and pharmacies that cater to the affluent lifestyle of the French expatriate population and a significant number of Gabonese. As Bongo Ondimba has become more comfortable with his power, even French residents are occasionally victims of his periodic recalibration of the degree of French influence in Gabonese affairs.

Gabon is, in the strictest sense, a functioning national entity. It conducts domestic and international business; it has diplomatic representation throughout the world; and its population engages, albeit within carefully circumscribed limits, in the selection of local and national officials. Despite its natural wealth, a skewed income distribution has left nearly half of the population in marginal socioeconomic circumstances. The nexus between politics and economics is key to understanding virtually everything about the Gabonese polity, which rests on three pillars of power: ethnicity, family, and France. Ethnic, family, and extended family connections account for many government appointments and the indigenous makeup of the so-called Gabonese clan. France supports this elite in order to share the wealth from the country's extensive natural resources, while the elite remains in power primarily by relying on ethnic and family ties and French support in potentially destabilizing circumstances.

Speculation about the post–Bongo Ondimba era is a favorite pastime of the Gabonese. Like Bongo Ondimba's mortality, it is also a certainty that global economic issues will directly influence every corner of the African continent. For Gabon, and equatorial Africa in general, vast petroleum reserves in the Gulf of Guinea and the corresponding interest of the world's major consumers of petroleum in the region may soon indicate the contours of the future.

Notes

1. www.cia.gov/library/publications/the-world-factbook/geos/gb.html#Intro.
2. David E. Gardinier, "France and Gabon Since 1993: The Reshaping of a Neo-Colonial Relationship," *Journal of Contemporary African Studies,* 18 no. 2, 225–42.
3. Brian Weinstein, *Gabon: Nation Building on the Ogooué* (Cambridge, MA: The MIT Press, 1966). Chapters 1–4 provide an excellent introduction to the "nationalizing process."
4. James F. Barnes, *Gabon: Beyond the Colonial Legacy* (Boulder, CO: Westview Press, 1992). See chapter 1 for an historical overview of this era.
5. For an excellent analysis of Gabon's dependence on petroleum, see Douglas A. Yates, *The Rentier State in Africa: Oil Rent Dependency and Neocolonialism in the Republic of Gabon* (Trenton, NJ: Africa World Press, 1996).
6. Jacques Foccart, *Foccart parle: Entretiens avec Phillipe Gaillaird* (Paris: Fayard/ Jeune Afrique, 1995), 194.
7. Foccart, *Foccart parle,* 278.
8. Bongo Ondimba was born Albert Bernard Bongo; he has since changed his name twice. After his conversion to Islam, he was known as El Hadj Omar Bongo, and in 2003 he adopted his father's true surname, Ondimba.
9. Aubame returned to Gabon in the early 1990s during a period of reconciliation initiated by Bongo Ondimba. He was given an honorific position in the national judiciary and did not return to electoral politics.
10. For a devastating critique of postindependence African elites, see George B.N. Ayittey, *Africa Betrayed* (New York: Palgrave Macmillan, 1993).
11. Pierre Péan, *Affaires africaines* (Paris: Fayard, 1983), 7–12, 198.
12. www.economist.com/media/pdf/DEMOCRACY_INDEX_2007_v3.pdf. p. 7.
13. *La Lettre du Continent* no. 522 (19 July 2007), www.africaintelligence.com.
14. *La Lettre du Continent* no. 531 (20 December 2007) www.africaintelligence.com.
15. Douglas A. Yates, "The French Connection," *Global Dialogue,* 13 no. 1 (March 2008), 22–23, 50–51.
16. Gardinier, "France and Gabon Since 1993," 229.
17. Ibid., 228.
18. Pieter Labuschagne, "Revisiting Civil Society in Africa," African Studies Association of Australasia and the Pacific, Conference Proceedings, Africa on a Global Stage, www. afsaap.org.au/Conferences/2003/Labuschagne.pdf.
19. Ibid., 8.

17

The Incomplete State and the Alternate State in Papua New Guinea

HANK NELSON

Abstract: *This case study shows the difficulties of forging a national identity and creating effective state institutions in an archipelago state of enormous ethnic and linguistic diversity. Papua New Guinea faces no major international security threats. The former colonial power, Australia, bowed out peacefully, but left behind a population inadequately educated to staff modern state institutions. Although the country has an extensive endowment of natural resources, these have not produced general prosperity. Rather, they have raised the exchange rate, making it more difficult for other sectors of the economy to develop. State services, elementary schooling, the road system, hospitals, and policing do not extend to all parts of the country. Most political parties and political leaders have a very narrow regional following. Although regular and highly contested elections have been held since independence, and despite a free and active press, corruption has increased and violent crime is endemic.*

Lines on the map are one of the most significant and lethal legacies of colonialism. The map inherited by Papua New Guinea has not provided the boundaries to foster an easy growth of a sense of nationhood and the institutions of a state. It is made up of the eastern half of the island of New Guinea and other islands farther to the east. The largest of the Pacific island states, Papua New Guinea has a total land area of 178,213 square miles (461,691 square kilometers) and a population of over 6,000,000. Some of the eastern islands, particularly New Britain, New Ireland, and Bougainville, are significant in terms of both population and area.

Colonial Rule Under a Succession of Powers

The arbitrary border on the west was established early. The Dutch claim to the west of New Guinea was an extension of their possessions in the East Indies, and Dutch sovereignty to the 141st meridian was accepted in 1884 by the British, who laid claim to the southeast, and the Germans, who planted their flag in the northeast. After the Australian colonies federated in 1901, the new Australian nation took over British New Guinea in 1906, and renamed it the Australian Territory of Papua. At

263

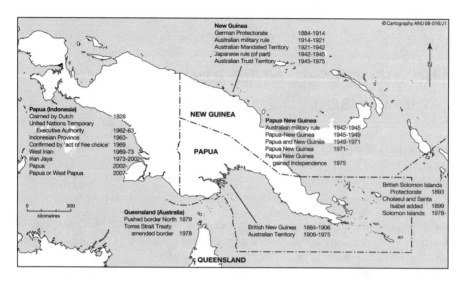

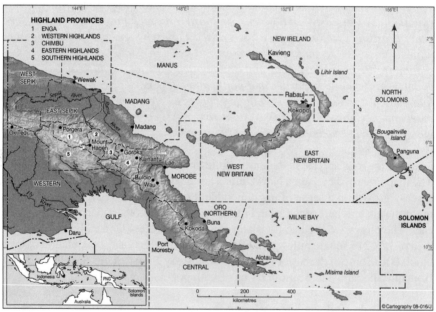

the start of World War I in 1914, Australian troops went north, faced brief opposition, and occupied German New Guinea, which as part of the postwar settlement became an Australian mandate under the League of Nations in 1921. Thereafter, Australia administered all of east New Guinea, but retained separate administrations for Papua and New Guinea. In 1949 the two Australian Territories in the east, combined since 1942, continued under the one administration as the Territory of

Papua and New Guinea—New Guinea was then a Trust Territory of the United Nations. In 1971 the combined territories became Papua New Guinea, the name retained at independence in 1975. Meanwhile, in 1962 Dutch New Guinea passed to the United Nations Temporary Executive Authority and then to Indonesian control in 1963, confirmed by an act of free choice in 1969. Indonesian New Guinea has been successively the province of West Irian, Irian Jaya, and then Papua. In 2007 the province was divided into two, Papua and West Papua.

For a nation that came into being without violence or even a political prisoner, Papua New Guinea has been much concerned with internal and external security. For Australians, the importance of the New Guinea islands was often expressed in two metaphors: they were both island ramparts essential for the defense of Australia and stepping stones ready to be exploited by an enemy eager to grasp Australian lands.

When the Japanese landed at Rabaul on 23 January 1942 and swept aside the small Australian force, Australia's fears were realized. The British, struggling for survival in Europe, could provide no aid, Singapore offered not protection but disaster, and a triumphant enemy was in the New Guinea islands. Pragmatically, Australia shifted its pleas for aid and close military alliance from Britain to America. The Americans and Australians fought the key battles of 1942 in the Coral Sea, at Midway, Guadalcanal, Milne Bay, Kokoda, and Buna, and cemented a long-term shift in alliances in the Pacific; but the war remained in Papua and New Guinea, where over 100,000 Japanese surrendered when the Emperor Hirohito conceded defeat in August 1945.

Previously one of the inhabited areas in the world most lightly tied to the outside, in four years of war, Papua New Guineans had seen over 1,500,000 foreigners pass through their lands, bringing with them the most advanced and destructive engines then known. Papua New Guineans had traveled farther and earned more cash than ever before; they had fought alongside foreigners, and some had excelled and been decorated. At the same time, perhaps a quarter of them had not known that a war was on, and, for those caught up in it, there was no media directed to Papua New Guineans to turn particular events into common experiences. Papua New Guinea emerged from the war with some of its people having a vision of a new and better world. With few exceptions, none of them had a Western education beyond a few grades of primary school. They had no exploitable political or social infrastructure. It was not the generation who experienced the disruption of war, but the next, who founded the first political parties and began talking of a nation.

In the immediate postwar period, Australians thought the critical significance of New Guinea to their defense had been confirmed, but by the late 1960s they had reduced this assessment. For Australia, a continental, rather than a forward, defense seemed appropriate.[1] When the neighboring colonial powers on the west (the Dutch) and the east (the British in the Solomon Islands) withdrew, they went halfway round the globe, but after the Australians ceased being administrators, they shared a border in the Torres Strait and retained a defense interest. That concern with defense was self-interested and practical, with a continuing engagement with the Papua New Guinea Defense Force (PNGDF). As Papua New Guinea declined on international indices measuring corruption and speculation increased about its becoming a failed state, Australia had to consider whether its neighbor could maintain the integrity of its borders and prevent transnational criminals, subversive groups, drug traffickers, and terrorists from finding a haven.[2] By 2003, when the two countries announced their Enhanced Cooperation Program, security was again a motive for Australia's increased engagement with the region.

Security Environment

For an independent Papua New Guinea, security has been dominated by legacies of the map. The long land border in the west—dividing related peoples and cutting through swamps, tropical rain forest, and precipitous mountains—will always be difficult to police. It is more than an international border. Given the number of Indonesians from elsewhere in the archipelago who have settled in west New Guinea, the 141st meridian is now where Southeast Asia meets Australasia and Melanesia, where the lingua franca changes from Bahasa Indonesian to English or New Guinea Pidgin (*Tok Pisin*), and where Islam meets Christianity. A line that is at once a national, regional, and cultural marker and crosses difficult terrain is going to cause problems.

While both sides have generally cooperated, nearly every year there are incidents ranging from minor cases of people avoiding customs or migration regulations, to shots being fired at alleged adherents of the Organisasi Papua Merdeka (OPM)—the persistent guerrilla movement in the western part of the main island—and refugees crossing into Papua New Guinea to escape Indonesian forces harassing OPM and its supporters. The highest number of refugees came in 1984, when over 10,000 crossed; some are still in camps in Papua New Guinea.[3] As the efficiency and resources of the PNGDF have declined or been diverted elsewhere, the country's capacity to monitor the border has diminished. In parliament in 2007, a member for an electorate on the border complained, "Money laundering, sales of illegal firearms, drug trafficking, human smuggling and other illicit activities were becoming common practices and seemed acceptable."[4]

On the east, the colonial border meant that Bougainville, the most northern of the Solomon Islands, was attached to independent Papua New Guinea.[5] Their homeland geographically separate and conscious of their distinctive blackness, Bougainvilleans had already asserted their desire for special consideration from the Australian administration. As Conzinc Rio Tinto developed a major mine at Panguna, prospecting, the acquisition of land, and the arrival of workers from outside the island stimulated separatist sentiment on Bougainville. In 1972, on the eve of self-government, the copper mine at Panguna began production. The Bougainville secession movement increased in strength as independence approached, and in 1975 many Bougainvilleans accepted reluctantly their place in the nation of Papua New

Guinea. The mine was financially significant for the nation (generating just under half of all export earnings) and dispersed funds to local landowners and the North Solomons Province. But disputes over compensation for pollution and arguments about the distribution of landowner payments led to sabotage of the mine, aggressive responses from the police and the PNGDF, the closing and destruction of the mine, intermittent violence, and brutality.

The Bougainville Revolutionary Army could not unify Bougainvilleans—it was guilty of violence against other Bougainvilleans, and some of its policies seemed atavistic to educated Bougainvilleans. The PNGDF performed poorly, and, when the government attempted to introduce mercenaries recruited by Sandline International, the army revolted and expelled the mercenaries. Although there was no coup, the prime minister was forced to stand down and members of the military later faced charges.

After ten years of low-level warfare, the most implacable of the Bougainvilleans were isolated, and in 1997 the majority came together with the government to negotiate a cease-fire. While few had died in battle, many Bougainvilleans had been forced from their homes, nearly all education and health service had ceased, and much infrastructure was destroyed. Under the conditions of the peace agreement of 2001, Bougainville neither remained a province nor seceded. The difficult process of writing and operating a constitution for an island that is both "autonomous" and within the nation of Papua New Guinea continues, and, as the peace settlement includes the right to a referendum, the Bougainville Autonomous Government may be temporary. Where civil wars in other parts of the world with rich resources have often been contests for the control of mineral revenue, on Bougainville the mine was opposed, destroyed, and not reopened—although in future the Panguna mine (or some other mine) may well be exploited.[6]

More people have died elsewhere in resurgent tribal or clan fighting than in the decade of civil war on Bougainville. Even before the Australians left, they found that in parts of the Highlands—meaning the five adjoining Highland provinces of Eastern Highlands, Chimbu (or Simbu), Western Highlands, Enga, and Southern Highlands—traditional warfare, suppressed for a generation, was breaking out and those involved were defying government officers and their armed police.[7] The weapons gradually changed from traditional bows and arrows, clubs, and axes to shotguns and automatic weapons. Just how many weapons are in the hands of rural clans engaged in their own wars is uncertain, but there are alarming newspaper reports of "3000 guns in the Baiyer and Lumusa areas in the Western Highlands";[8] and more reliable claims of up to thirty automatic weapons owned by one clan in Enga Province,[9] and of Highlanders making their own weapons and ammunition.[10] The total numbers being killed is uncertain, but in one prolonged clash in the Eastern Highlands, 500 are said to have died and in Enga the village courts have recorded over 3,000 deaths in ten years.[11]

While sometimes characterized as "ethnic" violence, much of the fighting is between clans and alliances of clans from the same cultural groups. Many of the clan alliances have long histories, and the causes of the disputes (land, murder, revenge, control of women, and theft) recur; but population increases (especially among the young), vehicles and greater mobility, money (and high compensation payments), beer and other drugs, and, of course, guns have transformed traditional warfare. It cannot be controlled by traditional leaders, and hired gunmen from outside the clans immediately involved are not subject to the restraints on local clansmen.

The endemic warfare has disrupted state and economic activities, but it has not threatened the integrity of national borders. The clans have not fought for issues that might engage the sympathies of outsiders, such as protecting rainforests or resisting rapacious foreign mining companies, and the fighting has often gone unreported by the international media. The sum of the clan wars has been as great as a civil war, but not considered as one.

Economic Environment

Papua New Guinea is often seen as a country of potential riches. The contrast is drawn with the small Pacific islands or landlocked sub-Saharan states, which have few possible strategies to escape poverty. With its extraordinary mountains, rainforests, tropical coasts, islands, and diverse cultures, it could have a significant tourist industry, but tourism generates much less income than it does in the smaller state of Fiji. In Papua New Guinea, tourism is restrained by problems of law and order, inadequate material and nonmaterial infrastructure, and malaria.

The first internationally significant mineral find, the alluvial gold dredged from the Bulolo Valley, was not exploited until the 1930s. Mineral production did not recover from the disruption of World War II until the development of several significant gold and copper mines at Panguna, Ok Tedi, Porgera, Misima, and Lihir. Other smaller mines also operate, and new major projects are underway—the most significant being the Ramu nickel-cobalt mine, the largest investment by the Chinese in the Australasia-Southwest Pacific area. Important oil and gas reserves are in or near areas of endemic clan warfare. Securing safe production and passage of oil and gas has been difficult. Ambitious plans to pipe gas to Australia have been delayed, probably abandoned, but there is a chance of Exxon Mobil making a major investment.[12] A decline in oil production, evident in most years since 2000, has been more than offset by increased prices. But inevitably Papua New Guinea remains vulnerable to reverses in world commodity prices for oil, metals, and tropical tree crops.

In 2005 gold, oil, and copper, of almost equal value, made up 75 percent of the country's exports. Agriculture and forestry (log exports) accounted for the rest of the exports, except for a small amount earned by fisheries. Within agriculture, the old industry of copra[13] production has declined, while oil palm has grown and coffee and cocoa have been important cash crops. For reasons of history and proximity, Australia dominates both imports and exports: in 2006 Australia supplied over 50 percent of imports, and Singapore, the second most important source, provided 12.6 percent.[14]

Recent macroeconomic indicators have been favorable, partly as a result of high commodity prices. External debt has decreased, the current account has been in surplus, and the GDP growth estimates for 2007 were over 5 percent. The problem is governance. The state has slight capacity to collect and distribute the benefits of improving national accounts. Firstly, according to Transparency International, over a third of the six billion *kina* government budget is "stolen each year by corrupt politicians and bureaucrats."[15] That may be an exaggeration, but the Transparency International Corruption Perceptions Index for 2007 ranked Papua New Guinea at 130 among 163 listed countries and the press reports alarmingly high totals for misappropriated monies.[16] Secondly, the institutions of government are weak. The state is unable to regulate or provide the infrastructure and security necessary for a growing economy. Thirdly, the advantages that come with the exploitation of minerals and high commodity prices may enable the government to postpone basic reforms; high wages in the mining industry will inflate wages elsewhere; and the currency will be maintained at a high level, making it difficult for other exporters to compete on world markets. In other words, Papua New Guinea will show the symptoms of "Dutch disease," meaning that flourishing natural resource export revenues have raised the exchange rate to the detriment of the development of manufacturing.

A significant characteristic of the Papua New Guinea cash economy is that around 8 percent of the population, dependent on subsistence gardening, is not in it, and about 70 percent has food gardens and a variable income from tree crops (coffee, oil palms, coconuts, betel nuts,[17] and cocoa) and vegetables. As a result, many people are lightly connected to the cash economy. They make enough to meet essential needs and imposts such as school fees, respond to high market prices, and in tough times are able to provide their own food, fuel, and shelter. Except for oil palms, most cash crop production comes from small holders rather than plantations.

Papua New Guinea did not inherit rich social capital at independence, and it has not been able to invest effectively in the health and skills of the population. In 1975 life expectancy was estimated at forty-one, half the children of primary school age were in school, and only one-third of adults were literate. By 2005, life expectancy had increased to fifty-seven, 75 percent of children were in primary school, and over half of all adults were literate. The independent government can therefore point to considerable advances, but Papua New Guinea is still low on international measures of education, health, and income. The United Nations Development Program's Human Development Index (2007/2008) places Papua New Guinea at 145th place out of 177.[18]

Political Environment

The traditional polities and colonial history did little to foster the institutions or consciousness of a nation-state. Much of island and coastal New Guinea was ruled successively by Germany, Australian military and civil administrations, Japan, and again by Australian military and civilian administrations. The longest continuous administration of the northeast has been that of independent Papua New Guinea, beginning in 1975. In the Highlands, home of half the population, the Australian administration only began its exploratory patrols in the 1930s. By the early 1950s, there was still a quarter of the total population completely or partially outside Australian rule. As the Australians left within a generation, many people who had grown to maturity in the traditional society were still active in their communities when the Australians left. At independence, some coastal communities had known a century of colonialism and some had endured what might be called a disruption rather than a period of colonialism.

The ethnic diversity of Papua New Guinea is often illustrated by pointing out that it is a nation of 800 languages. While languages are important markers of ethnicity, they understate the political diversity because the larger language groups are divided. Most traditional leaders held sway over a few hundred people and, through alliances with other leaders, could extend their influence. None had power over an area as large as any of the current eighty-five rural administrative districts. In a few areas, leaders held hereditary positions and were called "chiefs," but most were self-made "big-men." While many of the Melanesian communities have been described as egalitarian and competitive, individuals, families, and clans could often be placed in rank order. It was much more likely that big-men would come from some families rather than others. Even so, big-men had to work constantly to maintain their position against rivals inside and beyond their extended families.

Extensive trade routes across seas and land linked many peoples, but did not result in the formation of political units. The colonial experience gave people a sense of belonging to larger units, such as Sepik, Manus, Milne Bay, or Chimbu, and to Papua as opposed to New Guinea; and some people—such as Bougainvilleans—may be more conscious of their provincial identity than their national. If the people of the five Highland provinces developed a stronger identity and expressed it politically, they could assert influence within the state and perhaps provoke a disruptive reaction from the coast and islands, but as yet no movement has come close to commanding the loyalty of anything like a third or half the nation. Fragmentation has impeded building a nation, but the very extent of the fragmentation has prevented the development of fissures likely to break the nation into two or three incompatible regions.

The Australian administration did not establish a national political institution with a majority of Papua New Guineans—an elected parliament—until 1964, and, at that time, nine years before internal self-government, there were no political parties. The first House of Assembly was a place where individuals made requests, asked questions, and debated, but they did not then aspire to govern. It was not until 1967 that Papua New Guineans formed a political party (Pangu Pati), which operated in the House and aimed for home rule. By 1972, Pangu, in a coalition led by Michael (later "Sir") Somare, had a majority in the House. By then Australia was ready to hand over power. Had a referendum been held then, most Papua New Guineans would probably have voted against ending the colonial ties. Papua New Guinea became self-governing in 1973 and independent in 1975. Generally, nationhood was greeted with enthusiasm by a minority and unease, indifference, or ignorance by many—and outright opposition by those Papuans and Bougainvilleans who did not want to join the new nation.

It was not until the eve of self-government that progressive Papua New Guineans and Australians began to press for the adoption of the most fundamental symbols of a nation: a flag, an anthem, and a name. In the end, the name was a compromise, with the omission of "The Territory of" and the "and" of the old designation of "The Territory of Papua and New Guinea." The institutions of a state were equally late in being possessed by Papua New Guineans. In 1972, of the 3,436 members of the PNGDF, 617 were still Australians; in the police force two-thirds of the commissioned officers were from overseas (mainly Australia). In the public service only one head of a department was a Papua New Guinean and nearly 4,000 overseas officers were serving in the first, second, and third divisions of the public service.[19]

Papua New Guinea came peacefully but suddenly to independence. There was no violence to leave scars, no dominant army, and no heroes of the struggle for independence. There was some emotion to give enthusiasm to those at the center of the new government but not enough to unite a diverse people; and while there was a functioning elected government and public service, and an independent judiciary and media, few Papua New Guineans had the technical skills and experience to make them continue to work efficiently.

Having come into existence with a freely elected government, Papua New Guinea has retained its democracy. Elections to the single-house parliament have been held on time, contested by many parties and individuals, and changed governments. Prime ministers and ministers defeated at one election have won later elections and returned to office. Somare, prime minister at independence, was reelected in 2007 and began his third period in office. The leader of the opposition in 2007, Mekere Morauta, is an ex-prime minister. The institutional monitors of democracy—the media, the ombudsman, the judiciary, and the auditor-general—have retained their independence and sometimes offer frank, even aggressive, criticism of government officers, procedures, and policies.

In spite of obvious evidence of democracy working and being valued by people, there are signs of a system under stress. Corruption has grown in spite of its being exposed in the media and in official inquiries, and despite politicians and civil servants being charged and some jailed. There is much corruption of elections with rolls manipulated, double voting, ballots filled out in batches, votes bought, and in some cases voters intimidated and ballot boxes stolen. But most corruption is organized within electorates, not nationally and there are electorates where there is no or insignificant violation of fair process.[20] The fragmentation of the electorates impedes good governance. In the 2007 general elections, an average of twenty-five candidates stood in each electorate; they represented over thirty parties and included nearly 1,500 independents.

Many candidates can call on family and clan loyalties to secure votes, making party affiliation and policies irrelevant. Even the most successful national politicians, such as Somare, have little influence on any elections outside their home provinces. The result is a government put together postelection from a combination of parties and independents. Rather than being committed to policies, members focus on bringing material benefits to those who elected them, not to an electorate. As many candidates serve just one term, they know that they have a short time in which to secure benefits for themselves and their voters. They need to be in government to have access to resources, not in opposition. In these aggressively competitive elections, no indigenous woman now holds a seat.

This is not a patronage system as found elsewhere: candidates do not owe their election to the support of a national leader. Governments are formed by individuals and groups doing deals. This is a dynamic and competitive system, but it has not generated good policy. There was less violence in the 2007 election than in 2002, but government revenue lost to corruption increased. Attempts to stabilize parties by legislation and changes in the voting system from first-past-the-post to limited preferential have had modest success. In the limited preferential system, voters register their support for three candidates, whom they mark in order of preference. This is an attempt to force candidates to seek votes or "preferences" outside their home areas, and to force voters to consider candidates outside local affiliations. The lower tiers of government, the provincial and local-level governments, hold powers devolved to them from the center, and generally lack funds and competence. So while some of the provincial governments (particularly in the New Guinea Islands) provide a compensating source of government services, most people are dependent on the uncertain capacities of the central government.

The Papua New Guinea state has characteristics alien to the Western experience or expectations. For many people the state does not provide any basic services such as a school, a road, a resident policeman, a medical service within a day's travel, a postal service, a connection to an electric power line or a water main, or a record of births, marriages, and deaths. In some areas warfare has forced the state to withdraw services. For many more the state provides just two or three such services. One of the few times that the state attempts to reach all adult citizens is every five years during a general election, and then voting is not compulsory and the voting rolls are notoriously inaccurate. As a result, people live in what observers from the developed world would think was an incomplete or optional state. If citizens want a state service, they may well have to leave home.[21] And many people are serviced by an alternate state: mining companies build roads, schools, and hospitals as offsets to taxes; Christian churches have long contributed to health and education services; cult movements offer hope and some material services; and foreign government and nongovernment aid donors take over many government functions. With so many "state" services unavailable or coming from another source, many citizens do not have a basic contract with the state—they do not pay taxes in return for services.

Prospects

Papua New Guinea appears to face neither immediate success nor disaster. No external force threatens the nation or even wishes it ill. Within Papua New Guinea no group commands the sympathy of 20 percent or more of the population, a constituency sufficient to sustain a long campaign and fracture the nation. The possible, but remote, exception is a complete breakdown of the government in Port Moresby which then provokes the New Guinea Islands to break away. The other areas of sufficient size—the north coast, the Highlands, and Papua (the south coast)—have geography against them. The Highlands are landlocked and need outlets to the coast, Papua surrounds Port Moresby, and the north coast is ill-defined and currently people from there hold a strong stake in the Port Moresby government.

The PNGDF has defied the government when its self-interest has been involved (and for that reason it is unlikely that its numbers will be reduced to a recommended total of just over 2,000). At the end of 2007, there were rumors of an army plot to arrest the prime minister, but the PNGDF does not possess the tanks, troop carriers, and aircraft to move quickly with intimidating power to critical points. An army coup in Port Moresby would have difficulty imposing its rule in Madang, Goroka, Kokopo, Kavieng, and Alotau. A coup carried out by a combined PNGDF and Royal Papua New Guinea Constabulary would be a greater threat to the democratic state as the police are more numerous (over 5,000) and more dispersed and can call on reserve and auxiliary personnel. But the police and the army have a history of conflict rather than cooperation, and there are divisions within the leadership of both the PNGDF and the police. A force able to carry out a successful coup— such as the combined armed services with the support or sympathy of students or a politician and his followers—currently seems unlikely.

Particular problems of law and order will continue. In lists of the world's most dangerous cities, Port Moresby ranks alongside, and sometimes above, Algiers, Bogota, Lagos, Baghdad, and Johannesburg.[22] Most people who can afford to do so live within razor-wired and patrolled houses or compounds and rarely venture out after dark. Other towns, such as Mt. Hagen and Kainantu, are equally dangerous. Given the protracted traditional fighting in some rural areas, there is an urgent need for the state to assert its monopoly of violence, but little progress has been made in attempts to get guns out of the hands of citizens engaged in crime and warfare. There have already been some unholy associations of politicians and town *raskol* gangs[23] and armed clans, and there is the potential for a part of Port Moresby or another town to decline into a level of chaos that will require a substantial force to reassert control. These are likely to be locally dangerous and destructive, and damaging (but not fatal) to the state.

Political uncertainty also comes with the inevitable change in leaders that will

happen simply because of the age of several of the most prominent of them—
Somare is over seventy, and Julius Chan, Mekere Morauta, Paias Wingti, Bart
Philemon, and Rabbie Namaliu are approaching the end of their political lives. Just
who the new leaders will be is unclear, but it can be assumed they will be different because they will have been educated and grown to political consciousness in
an independent Papua New Guinea, not with memories of Australian institutions,
personnel, and values.

Religion is important in the political and daily life of Papua New Guineans.
The preamble to the constitution refers to the "Christian principles that are ours
now" and to the "guiding hand of God." But the churches in this predominantly
Christian country have been undergoing change. The churches that grew out of
the old Catholic and Protestant missions have been influenced by charismatic and
born-again movements. New fundamentalist groups have formed. Some administrative and technical expertise has been lost, but the churches retain influence and
are increasing their involvement in tertiary education.

The prevalence of HIV/AIDS is close to 2 percent and could reach 10 percent
by 2025.[24] Transmission is by heterosexual sex. If HIV/AIDS cannot be contained,
then it has the potential to reduce the workforce, absorb much of the health and
aid budgets, and dislocate some communities. In rural communities where people
believe that disease is a result of malign sorcery, accusations, counteraccusations,
and severe punishments multiply the impact of an insidious disease.

Australia has provided some fifteen billion dollars in aid to Papua New Guinea
since 1975. While Australia, the major aid donor, has maintained and may increase
its annual aid, its assistance has declined as a percentage of Papua New Guinea's revenue. Through the last thirty years, the manner of delivery and intent of Australian
aid has changed, often following international trends in what is thought to be most
effective. It has shifted from direct aid to the budget to project aid, with emphases
on institutional strengthening, governance, and law and order. Interventions in East
Timor and the Solomon Islands marked an increased Australian engagement in the
region. In 2003 Australia and Papua New Guinea agreed on an Enhanced Cooperation Program, committing Australia to placing civil servants in Papua New Guinea
positions and providing an additional billion dollars over five years.

The context in which Australia provides aid has changed. Where in the past
Australians were by far the most numerous foreigners in Papua New Guinea, they
are now outnumbered by Asians.[25] There are probably more Chinese alone than
Australians, Chinese investment in resource extraction is growing, and China will
increase in importance as a trade partner. At the same time, Japan, the European
Union, the United States, and New Zealand are increasingly seen as alternative
sources of aid, and the health of Papua New Guinea's economy gives its government options.

For Papua New Guineans, the map inherited from the colonial powers made
the development of a sense of nationhood difficult. Their precolonial communities
were among the most fragmented on the globe, and the Australian administration

was benign but late and incomplete in its attempt to create the institutions of a state and a commitment to a nation. Those plagues of the "bottom billion"—civil war, endemic problems of law and order, corruption, and poor governance—have afflicted Papua New Guineans, but their very fragmentation has meant that they must cooperate. No group can come close to dominance, and the history of the peoples of Papua New Guinea has constantly confirmed that families and clans must cultivate alliances.[26] Geography has given Papua New Guinea advantages. It sits at the junction between Australia and Southeast Asia and between Australia and the dominant economies of East Asia, and it has an extensive and diverse land area rich in minerals. It will probably continue to avoid catastrophe while suffering chronic poor governance and occasional crises, but it has a chance to begin to bridge the gap that now separates it from the countries able to offer their citizens literacy, children of average weight, and a life span of over sixty-five years.

Notes

1. H. Nelson, *Fighting for Her Gates and Waterways,* State Society and Governance in Melanesia, Discussion Paper, Canberra, March 2005.

2. Hugh White and Elsina Wainwright, *Strengthening Our Neighbour* (Canberra: Australian Strategic Policy Institute, 2004), 14; Ben Scott, *Re-Imagining PNG* (Sydney: Lowy Institute, 2005), 7.

3. R. May, "East of the Border," in *Between Two Nations,* R. May, ed. (Bathurst, Australia: Robert Brown, 1986), 124.

4. *National* (Papua New Guinea daily newspaper), 8 October 2007.

5. A. Regan and H. Griffin, eds., *Bougainville Before the Conflict* (Canberra: Pandanus Books, 2005).

6. Anthony Regan, "The Bougainville Conflict: Political and Economic Agendas," in *The Political Economy of Armed Conflict,* Karen Ballentine and Jake Sherman, eds. (Boulder, CO: Lynne Rienner, 2003), 133–66.

7. *Report of the Committee Investigating Tribal Fighting in the Highlands* (Port Moresby: Government Printer, 1973), 2–3; Mervyn Meggitt, *Blood Is Their Argument* (Palo Alto, CA: Mayfield, 1977); W. Clifford, L. Morauta, and B. Stuart, *Law and Order in Papua New Guinea,* 2 vols. (Ports Moresby: Papua New Guinea Institute of Applied Social and Economic Research, 1984); Sinclair Dinnen, *Law and Order in a Weak State* (Hindmarsh, Australia: Crawford House, 2001).

8. *Post-Courier* (Papua New Guinea daily newspaper), 9 January 2008.

9. Polly Wiessner et al., "Warfare in Enga Province: From Prehistory to Modern Times," 2007, an excellent unpublished paper.

10. *Post-Courier,* 9 January 2008; Sinclair Dinnen and Edwina Thompson, *Gender and Small Arms Violence in Papua New Guinea,* State Society and Governance in Melanesia, Canberra, Discussion Paper, August 2004.

11. Wiessner, "Warfare in Enga Province," 51.

12. "Cops Deployed to Protect Oilfields," *National,* 22 January 2008; *Sydney Morning Herald,* 30 January 2008.

13. Copra is the dried coconut meat from the coconut palm used to produce coconut oil. Palm oil comes from the oil palms.

14. http://www.dfat.gov.au/geo/fs/png.pdf.

15. Scoop New Zealand News (www.scoop.co.nz), 6 December 2007.

16. *National,* 28 September 2007, and *Post-Courier,* 6 September 2007.

17. Betel nuts, a mildly euphoric stimulant, are chewed throughout much of Asia.

18. http://hdr.undp.org/en/statistics/.

19. *Papua New Guinea Report for 1971–72* (Canberra: Government Printer, 1974), 13, 15, 34, 41.

20. "Papua New Guinea National Election, June–August 2007: Report of the Commonwealth-Pacific Islands Forum Election Assessment Team," http://www.forumsec.org.fj/_resources/article/files/png%20FINAL%20REPORT.pdf.

21. H. Nelson, "Governments, States and Labels," State Society and Governance in Melanesia, Discussion Paper, Canberra, January 2006.

22. *Global Report on Human Settlements 2007,* www.unhabitat.org/downloads/docs/5204_47267_BK percent208.pdf-; "Economist Intelligence Unit," *Guardian,* 22 September 2004.

23. *Raskol,* derived from the English word *rascal,* is a Papua New Guinea Pidgin term for a person, usually a member of a gang, engaged in crime and violence.

24. www.ato.gov.au/budget/2006-07/ministerial/html/ausaid-05.htm.

25. H. Nelson, "The Chinese in Papua New Guinea," State Society and Governance in Melanesia, Discussion Paper, Canberra, March 2007.

26. Paul Collier, *The Bottom Billions* (Oxford: Oxford University Press, 2007).

18

National Identity and Exclusion in Indonesia

ROBERT CRIBB

Abstract: *This case study focuses on a linguistically fractured archipelagic state that is at the center of Southeast Asian civilization. Indonesian national identity developed during the colonial era in reaction to the Dutch. After independence, Indonesian national identity partially excluded those of mixed descent and immigrant heritage, such as the Chinese community. Indonesia's first postindependence leader, Sukarno, tried to deepen this identity through the promulgation of his five precepts: belief in God, nationalism, humanitarianism, social justice, and democracy. Although at independence Indonesia was an exporter of numerous agricultural products and minerals, including oil and gas, Sukarno's expropriation of colonial ownership damaged the country's export potential, and socialistic policies produced starvation in the countryside, a rapid deterioration in the infrastructure, inflation, and a growing Communist movement. The military intervened under General Suharto, who slaughtered the Communists, centralized political power and access to wealth under himself, and transformed the government into a vast club of insider traders. Since the fall of Suharto, political power has become less centralized and Indonesia's tradition of exclusion has focused on non-Muslims.*

Modern Indonesia is a paradox. A century ago the name *Indonesia* itself was hardly known outside ethnographic circles—it was coined in the nineteenth century from Greek *Indos* (India) and *nesioi* (islands) by analogy with Polynesia (many islands) and Melanesia (black island).[1] It consists of about 17,500 islands stretched over a distance greater than that from Dublin to Teheran. Scholars disagree on how many ethnic groups it encompasses, but a rough count based on languages suggests a figure of around 400. No local state ever encompassed anything like its whole territory, and even the Dutch East Indies, Indonesia's immediate predecessor in terms of state succession, only took its final shape in the archipelago in the first decade of the twentieth century. Small wonder that writers on Indonesia often describe it as a thoroughly implausible state and suggest that it may have difficulty enduring.[2]

From a longer historical perspective, however, Indonesia is far from implausible. At its core lies the island of Java, one of the six major centers of civilization and

278

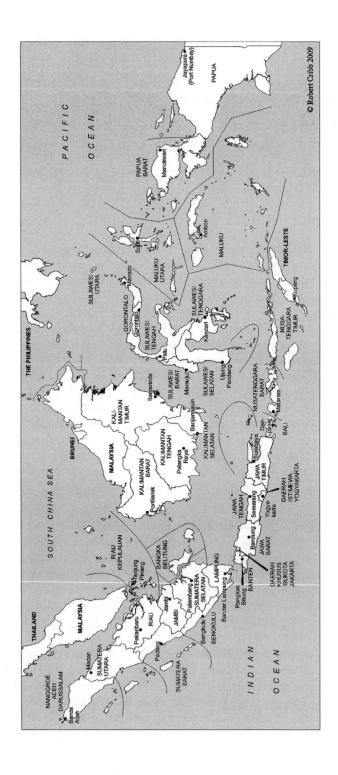

political power that have dominated Southeast Asia for more than 2,000 years. The fertile valleys of the Irrawaddy, the Chao Phraya, the Mekong, and the Red River; the Strait of Melaka; and the island of Java were the heartlands of six sophisticated civilizations—Burmese, Thai, Cambodian, Vietnamese, Malay, and Javanese— whose varied fortunes form the core narratives in the region's long history and for whom the rest of the region was mostly just hinterland. In contrast with the other major states in the region, Indonesia's heritage also draws significantly from a second civilizational center, the Melaka Strait. Until the early sixteenth century, a succession of glittering states in Sumatra or on the Malay Peninsula orchestrated trade between India and China through the strait.[3] The city of Melaka at its height was one of the great cities of the world. But its glitter came to an end in 1511, when it fell to the Portuguese, newly arrived in Asia with cannons and other firearms. From that year until the present, the Melaka Strait region has been divided and thus far weaker than its history and location suggest it should be. The Malay Peninsula, including Singapore, eventually went to the British, Sumatra to the Dutch. But by incorporating Sumatra within their Java-based empire, the Dutch gave what became Indonesia a rich share in Malay culture, expressed most obviously in the national language, Bahasa Indonesia, which is a development of Malay, rather than of Javanese. Together, the Javanese and Malay civilizations have given Indonesia a political and cultural repertoire as deep and versatile as that of any of Asia's medium powers outside the great imperial regions of China and India.

Civilizations, of course, do not exist on ideas alone. The enduring advantage of all the Southeast Asian civilizations was their strong agricultural base. Java, its soil enriched by copious volcanoes, was especially formidable as a producer of rice. As a whole, however, the archipelago has been more or less consistently the source of one or another produce in great demand in other parts of the world. In the very earliest times of trade, the archipelago was a source of gold, of fragrant woods for incense, and of exotic bird pelts. For centuries, the spices of the region—cloves, nutmeg, ginger, and pepper—found markets thousands of kilometers away. In more recent times, Indonesia produced coffee, sugar, tea, tobacco, indigo, copra,[4] cinchona,[5] rubber, and palm oil on a vast scale, and tin, gold, copper, timber, oil, and gas. Dependence on distant markets has sometimes been dangerous—as during the Great Depression when markets shrank, or during the Second World War when hostilities cut the transport route to the usual purchasers of Indonesian produce. But for the most part, the Indonesian archipelago has experienced 2,000 years of integration into global markets, which in turn have generated the capital needed for institution building.

Big-man Rule

Indonesia's politics, however, also display key elements from a still older tradition. Both Malay and Javanese belong to the Austronesian language family. The speakers of Austronesian languages originally inhabited the island of Taiwan, but

5,000 years ago some of them began to migrate to the south.[6] They first occupied the Philippines; then some moved out into the Pacific, and are the ancestors of the Hawaiians, the Maori, and other Polynesians; others moved into what is now the Indonesian archipelago, where they intermarried with what was probably a sparse population of dark-skinned peoples related to today's Melanesians. Some even crossed the Indian Ocean to populate the island of Madagascar. Although we have little direct evidence of the dynamics of this prodigious expansion, there is much to suggest that it had to do with political rivalries. Austronesian societies were dominated by so-called big-men, strong individuals who achieved prominence in their communities by virtue of their personal skills, not their line of descent. Societies based on big-men were volatile. Individual chiefs were always subject to challenge by aspiring successors. The result was a constant tendency to secede. The islands of Indonesia and the Pacific were colonized, it seems, by wave after wave of big-men and aspiring big-men who preferred creating a new society under their own domination to living under the chieftainship of someone else.

This heritage has had two consequences for Indonesia. One is a tradition of restless innovation. The Indonesian sense of tradition is qualified by a deep-seated inclination to abandon the old and construct something new. The archipelago has no ancient cities of the kind found in China, India, the Middle East, or Europe. The glittering centers of early times are sometimes no more than a few stones among the rice fields or the memory of ancient vibrant trade in a sleepy fishing village. Even the location of the capital of Srivijaya, the longest-lasting kingdom on the Melaka Strait, was forgotten until archaeologists managed to pinpoint it in the late twentieth century. In this respect, Indonesia's newness is itself a part of the archipelago's traditions.

The second consequence has been that Indonesian power holders have constantly sought ways to consolidate their fragile power by drawing ideas and institutions from outside. For most of recorded history, Indians and Chinese seldom dared to board boats for the perilous journey to the archipelago across the Bay of Bengal or the South China Sea. Indian (and to a much lesser extent Chinese) political ideas, however, were carried selectively to the islands by local rulers keen to bolster their authority with the trappings and ideologies of great civilizations. Indonesia thus acquired an impressive array of rajas claiming to be incarnations of Hindu gods, building spectacular temples to their divine sponsors, and trying to create a sense of sharp class difference between themselves and their followers. For more than a thousand years, the court civilizations of the archipelago were Indian in appearance and idiom, even if the actual forms were different from those in India itself.[7]

At the same time, however, the opponents of power holders in the archipelago also sought assistance from outside. One of the most important reasons for the spread of Islam in the archipelago from the thirteenth century was that it provided an ideological formulation which devalued the extravagant claims of the quasi-Indian rajas and emphasized instead the authority of individual believers and religious leaders. Islam in effect became the political tool of a merchant class, which came into being in response to the expanding commercial oppor-tunities created by consumption in China, India, the Middle East, and Europe.[8] An enduring feature of Indonesian polities has been the so-called stranger-king, the charismatic outsider who can provide justice because he stands above and beyond the rivalries and antagonisms of the community. Even the spread of Dutch colonial rule from the early seventeenth century took place partly at the initiative of local communities keen to end their internecine feuds by submitting to a disengaged external authority.[9]

The long-term effect of colonialism in the archipelago, however, was stultifying. The Dutch gradually took over the most lucrative commercial opportunities by us-ing first naval power and later a variety of legal techniques.[10] Where they could not exploit commercial opportunities themselves, they favored Chinese, who were, like the Dutch, relatively new arrivals in the region. Coming from a Europe in which class distinction was formalized and entrenched, they constructed a political order that rested on a special relationship with indigenous aristocracies. Half of the ter-ritory that eventually comprised the Dutch East Indies was indirectly ruled—that is, native kings and sultans were left in place as sovereigns but subordinate to the Dutch. Elsewhere, indigenous aristocracies were transformed from the volatile source for pedigreed monarchs to effete agents of colonialism. Their supposedly traditional authority was as much a product of Dutch manufacture as of real tradi-tion. Dutch state building also broke with tradition in funneling wealth out of the Indies. Although debate among historians continues over the extent to which the Netherlands profited from its Indies dominions and the extent to which that profit was at the expense of the Indies, there is no doubt that a significant part of the opu-lence still visible today along the inner-city canals of Amsterdam was the product of a long-term transfer of wealth from the Indonesian archipelago. In the first half of the twentieth century the colonial capital, Batavia, was a spruce and elegant city—Queen City of the East it was called by its boosters—but it was a shallow and modest place in comparison with Amsterdam and other Dutch cities.[11]

National Identity and Exclusion

Dutch colonialism created the geopolitical framework that became Indonesia. The precise shape of this framework was arbitrary. The islands of Borneo, Timor, and New Guinea were partitioned along lines that had little to do with history or culture, and, as we have seen, the momentous division of the Melaka Strait region was preserved.[12] The national aspiration that grew within the framework, however, was no more arbitrary than any other nationalism of the twentieth century. On the one hand, that aspiration rested on a sense of ethnic difference with the Dutch colonialists which subdued the sense of ethnic difference within the archipelago. Javanese, Balinese, and Malays did not lose their sense of specific identity, but they acquired a broader sense of belonging to a new transcendent ethnicity increasingly called "Indonesian," which, they felt, ought to be regarded with the same respect as

Dutch or European ethnicity. At the same time, the shape of national aspiration in the archipelago reflected the older pattern of recruiting outside ideas as a weapon against power holders. One part of this dual character of Indonesian nationalism was expressed eloquently by a young Javanese aristocrat, Suwardi Suryaningrat, in an essay entitled "If I Were a Dutchman," published in 1913, in which he rebuked the Dutch for celebrating their own liberation from Napoleon when they had robbed the people of the Indies of their freedom.[13]

At its noblest, the idea of Indonesia was an assertion of the right of indigenous people in the archipelago to justice and prosperity. It was an assertion of the right to social mobility, which had been the dominant characteristic of the polities of the archipelago since the days of the big-men and which had been closed off by the Dutch, just as it had previously been closed off by rajas. And it was an assertion of the archipelago's right to the proceeds of its own economic wealth. It was a claim for the restoration of the old pattern in which profits from trade went to institution building in the archipelago, not to opulent display and productive infrastructure on the other side of the world. When the constitution of independent Indonesia stated, "The land, the waters and the natural riches contained therein shall be controlled by the State and exploited to the greatest benefit of the people," it was no mere platitude but a central aspiration of the nationalist project.

The other, darker, aspect of Indonesian nationalism, however, lay in its construction as a device for exclusion. Central to the Indonesian national project was the exclusion not only of sunburned Dutch profiteers and adventurers but also the archipelago's large mixed-race Eurasian community, the product of three centuries of intermarriage between Dutch men and local and other Asian women.[14] This community, numbering perhaps half a million at the end of the colonial period, was culturally and psychologically rooted in the Indies, but was marked by the nationalist movement as alien. Thousands were killed in the revolution, which followed the Japanese occupation during the Second World War, and many of the rest ended up in the Netherlands.

Also excluded were residents of Chinese descent. Like the European community, the Chinese were scattered across a spectrum from those who had no other home but the Indies to those for whom the archipelago was no more than a place to make a fortune before retiring to their homeland. All those marked as Chinese, however, were also marked as something less than fully Indonesian, their right to participation in Indonesia always conditional on a special demonstration of loyalty and good citizenship, though the means by which loyalty and good citizenship could be demonstrated was never entirely clear.[15]

The effect of disqualifying Eurasians and Chinese from full, uncomplicated citizenship was to create "Indonesia" as a space within which only the unambiguously indigenous could compete for power and wealth. The provision of the Indonesian constitution that states that "the President shall be a native Indonesian" was no mere casual act of discrimination but went to the heart of the issue of who could share in the justice and prosperity that the Indonesia project offered.

National Principles: Sukarno's Pancasila

Neither the declaration of independence and the creation of the Indonesian Republic in August 1945, nor the final, grudging Dutch transfer of sovereignty in December 1949, after four years of revolutionary war and political negotiations, marked the final resolution of these tensions within the national project. The perception that Indonesia is not just one nation among many but a manifestation of higher human values has been an enduring element in Indonesian perceptions of the meaning of their own society. Whereas Suwardi in 1913 rebuked the Dutch for their hypocrisy, Sukarno, who was the leading nationalist of his generation and soon-to-be first president of Indonesia, established on the eve of the independence declaration a set of national principles that he called the Pancasila (the five precepts): belief in God, nationalism, humanitarianism, social justice, and democracy. These principles, which were incorporated into the preamble of the new constitution, were intended to demonstrate that Indonesia stood for more than just opposition to colonialism (which, after all, the independence declaration was meant to sweep away); that is, it stood for principles that would lead to a just and prosperous society and which might well be an inspiration beyond Indonesia's borders.[16]

Many Indonesians were particularly proud of the precept "belief in God," which, they said, resolved the ancient dispute in Western thinking between secularism and established religion. The Indonesian term *Ketuhanan* translates as something like "God-ness" and was always understood to represent the Allah of Islam, the God of Christianity, and the Yahweh of Judaism (though Jews were an insignificant minority in Indonesia). In this way, Indonesia could be a religious state (very substantial sums were allocated for the support of religion through the Ministry of Religious Affairs) without being committed to any one religion. In this respect, the idea of Indonesia, for all its deep roots in an amalgam of Javanese and Malay civilization, had much in common with the civil nationalism of the United States and its endorsement, enshrined in the Declaration of Independence of "life, liberty, and the pursuit of happiness."

Just as American confidence in the universality of the values expressed in the Declaration of Independence has underpinned an intrusive approach to world politics, Indonesian self-confidence underwrote Sukarno's confrontation with Malaysia in the 1960s. Malaya, which had been devised as the pliant successor state to Britain's small colonial empire in maritime Southeast Asia, stood for much that Indonesia opposed, especially the continued control of the national economy by external interests and the entrenchment of aristocratic power in the form of Malaysia's multiple royal families.[17] Sukarno, however, overestimated the appeal of the Pancasila and the Indonesia project in general beyond the borders of the former Netherlands Indies. His attempt to thwart the creation of Malaysia appeared to the supposed beneficiaries to be no less than bullying. Still more tragic was Indonesia's presumption in 1974–75 that the former Portuguese colony of East Timor would cheerfully integrate in the Indonesian national project. Rather than

gratefully accepting Indonesian citizenship and the alleged benefits of incorporation in what was then one of the world's most dynamic economies, the Timorese
resented Indonesian brutality, and fought so tenaciously (but at huge cost) and
recruited international support so effectively that Indonesia eventually surrendered
the territory in 1999.

Within Indonesia, moreover, the Pancasila itself became a powerful tool for
exclusion. Initially, the key exclusionary talisman was the precept "belief in
God." This precept did double service. First, it stymied the claim by sections of
Indonesia's Islamic community that Indonesia, with a Muslim population nudg-
ing ninety percent, should be an Islamic state or, at the very least, should allow
Islamic law to be applied to its Muslim citizens. This claim was problematic in
the best of times. As in most other Muslim countries, there was a vast range of
belief concerning appropriate religious practice. In Java, in particular, a large
part of the Muslim population, especially in the countryside, followed a religion
that was nominally Islamic but was deeply imbued with mystical and animist
practices absorbed into Islam at the time of conversion. People who revered local saints and spirits, bequeathed property to daughters instead of sons, and saw
no need to fast or to make the pilgrimage to Mekka were pious Muslims by their
own standards, but they had no wish to be subjected to the formalist regulations
of Middle Eastern Islam. For these Muslims, the precept "belief in God" was a
key defense because it seemed to preclude the state from giving any special place
to Islam above other religions.

For the more orthodox, fundamentalist Muslims, by contrast, *Ketuhanan* was
fundamentally disempowering because it marked the Indonesian state as *kafir,* or
infidel, and thus as not deserving the unqualified loyalty of Muslim citizens. Some
Muslims took this insight to its logical conclusion and in the late 1940s launched
a rebel movement, which they called Darul Islam (House of Islam). It aimed to
supplant the Indonesian Republic by force and replace it with an Islamic state. The
consequence was that Islam as a political movement was persistently compromised
within the national polity and orthodox, fundamentalist Muslims were given the
sense of living as a minority in an alien state.

The Pancasila was also deployed against the Left. Marxist analysis had been a
major strand within Indonesian nationalist thinking. The Indonesian Communist
Party emerged after independence as one of the larger forces on the political land-
scape. The presumed atheism at the core of Marxist doctrine, however, compromised
the party in the national project as effectively as did the piety of the fundamentalist
Muslims. Of course real economic and social issues were at stake: How would
land be distributed? What position would women hold in society? What forms of
public morality and political correctness would be applied to Indonesians? The
conflict was raised beyond a policy dispute to one concerning basic understand-
ings of Indonesian-ness.

In all the cases mentioned here, the consequences for the excluded groups
were drastic. Eurasians were killed or expelled. Chinese were subject to a raft

of discriminatory regulations. Chinese education and the public celebration of Chinese festivals, for instance, were banned. Even more seriously, the Chinese as a community became the serial victims of an elaborate protection racket in which even the official armed forces were deeply implicated: security forces stoked and managed the threat of riots and smaller-scale violence against Chinese, especially wealthier Chinese, in order to extract payments for providing protection against that violence. To stave off violence, Chinese have paid vast amounts of money to other sections of Indonesian society, both in the form of direct payoffs to formal and informal security forces and in the form of philanthropic donations intended to buy some degree of respectability. For fundamentalist Muslims, participation in the Darul Islam rebellion led to savage military countermeasures. The internal war, which dragged on from the late 1940s to the early 1960s, was little reported at the time, even within Indonesia, but it was on a much larger scale than the twenty-first century war in Afghanistan and it cost thousands and thousands of lives.[18]

The most dismal fate, however, was that of the Communists. In 1965 right-wing sections of the army, after suppressing a coup, which appears to have been organized by sections of the Communist Party, launched a nationwide pogrom against party members in which an estimated 500,000 people were killed. Of the survivors, more than a million passed through detention camps and, once released, faced systematic discrimination on the grounds of their former political allegiance. Even children born long after 1965 into the families of former Communist Party members faced real, official obstacles to full participation in national civic life.[19]

The nationalist determination to take charge of the resources of the archipelago for the benefit of its people also proved disastrous when it took the form of a nationalization of Dutch interests in 1957.[20] The plantations and other Dutch businesses came into the hands of army managers and gave the military an economic base that enabled it to function largely independently of the budget provided by the civilian government. Three malignant forces, however, were at work in the plantation sector, then the mainstay of the economy. One was the legacy of two decades of underinvestment and destruction, the outcome of the Depression, World War II, and the revolution. Another was the difficulty of reconciling the economic imperatives that kept wages low in the plantation sector with the higher-wage aspirations of the plantation workers. Also decisive was the lack of Indonesians trained in plantation affairs and the consequent assumption of new managers that the sector could simply be milked for income, without attention to reinvestment. In other sectors formerly controlled by the Dutch, Chinese business moved into the vacuum created by the lack of capable Indonesian managers. Confidence, especially on the part of President Sukarno, that Indonesia's natural wealth would inevitably mean prosperity for its people if control were taken out of foreign hands led Indonesia into a ruinous state. By 1965, it had become one of the poorest countries in the world, with starvation stalking the countryside, infrastructure in a state of advanced decay, markets almost empty of goods, and piles of tattered, overinflated rupiah needed for the smallest transaction.[21]

General Suharto and the Insider-Trader Economy

Suharto, however, the general who took over as president in the aftermath of the slaughter of the Communists in 1965, found a far more effective way of marshalling the resources of the archipelago. Rather than preserving those resources dogmatically and exclusively for Indonesians, he presided over a resources boom, based especially on oil, timber, and gold, in which he tapped the outward flow of wealth for the funds needed to restore a decent standard of living to Indonesians and to build the country's infrastructure and human capital. The transformation was remarkable. Economic growth far outpaced the increase in population, and Indonesia climbed rapidly from penury through poverty to the promise of prosperity. By the 1990s, Indonesia seemed firmly established among the so-called Asian Tiger economies.

Suharto's consummate managerial style played a major role in this recovery. On the one hand, he was a fast and intelligent learner. He listened to advice, digested it, and made it his own. He also had the knack of delegation. Across a vast range of policy, he chose capable subordinates, gave them responsibility for a policy field, and left them with the authority to find the best way of achieving the goals. Yet he retained a chief executive's oversight of the whole of government, so that there was no field of government initiative, from industrialization, to environmental protection, to family planning, which was not clearly being steered in a direction set by the president. Central executive power was underpinned by a complex political system in which formally democratic arrangements were so hemmed in with restrictions as to make them almost meaningless. A government party, Golkar, contested elections every five years with two nongovernment parties cobbled together through the forcible amalgamation of parties that had been legal in the 1950s. But campaign periods were short, the parties were not permitted to organize below the level of district capital, and policy differences could not be discussed. The military, whose members were not permitted to vote, had separate institutional representation in parliament, and the parliament as a whole contributed only half the members of the People's Assembly, which elected the president (always by acclamation); the other half was appointed by Suharto himself. Other laws restricted public discussion of politics and punished dissenters.[22]

Suharto's success also rested on a complex exclusionary strategy in the economic sphere. This strategy was based on a parallel, illicit economy. When he died in early 2008, *The Economist* reflected a commonly held judgment when it headed its obituary of him with the description "a crook and a tyrant."[23] It was widely said (though it remained completely unprovable) that Suharto had accumulated a private fortune of $30 billion during his long term in office. But personal greed was never a character of the Suharto presidency; the man lived rather modestly and showed none of the excesses of display that characterized, for instance, President Ferdinand Marcos in the neighboring Philippines. Wealth for him was a means to power rather than luxury.

The French novelist Honoré de Balzac once wrote memorably that "behind every great fortune lies a great crime," but in Suharto's Indonesia even modest fortunes depended on at least small crimes. If not to survive, then at least to maintain the same living standards as one's peers, most members of the new Indonesian elite were forced to engage in one way or another in corrupt activities. Such activities typically included the collection of inflated commissions on government transactions, the use of connections and family relationships in allocating government contracts or posts, the channeling of public resources to private benefit, the privileged flouting of government regulations for personal profit, the collection of payoffs for services that should have been provided in the normal course of employment, down to the common practice of moonlighting to supplement inadequate salaries. The opportunities for such corrupt activity varied enormously and generally increased in tandem with one's social proximity to the presidential palace.

Suharto's political genius and the tragedy for Indonesia lay in the vast number of Indonesians whom he implicated in, and thus compromised by means of, this illegal economy. In effect, he created in Indonesia a vast club of insider traders, people who profited unduly by virtue of their position. Even if individuals were aware that others were making much more out of the system than they were, and even if they would have preferred a clean, well-governed polity, their own involvement in the system was both morally crippling and practically disempowering. How could they seriously criticize Suharto when they themselves were beneficiaries of the system he had created? Those with the courage to step outside the system and criticize its shortcomings—and there were always individuals brave enough to do this—found their access to wealth curtailed at once.

In the 1990s, this system at last showed signs of fraying at the edges. The growing complexity of the Indonesian economy meant that the vast array of corrupt practices was becoming increasingly vexatious for genuine business. Whereas there might have been an argument in the 1970s and 1980s that corruption increased efficiency and worked, albeit in an unorthodox way, to promote capital accumulation, by the 1990s, most observers, from conservative economists to radical critics of the regime, were inclined to see it as counterproductive rent seeking. Rather than recognizing the end of an era and permitting reform of the system, however, Suharto began to restrict its benefits. In particular, he allowed his adult children to build business empires based on a predatory array of monopolies and licenses. A monopoly over clove marketing allocated to the president's youngest son, for instance, generated vast income for him while seriously undermining the income of tens of thousands of small producers, who could no longer get the benefit of market prices. Suharto's former genius in spreading the benefits of corruption across the whole elite was losing its effect.

The Post-Suharto Decentralization

After Suharto fell from office in 1998, therefore, the Indonesian tradition of constructing new institutions and new formats for exclusion kicked in again in unexpected ways. At the national level there was a substantial disempowerment of the president and a corresponding enhancement of the powers of the now freely elected parliament. Although the president remained chief executive, his or her practical authority was seriously constrained by parliamentary oversight. Still more important, there was a substantial devolution of power to the district level. Although this devolution was done in the name of bringing government closer to the people, its practical effect was to increase the power of local positions and to reserve them for local talent by excluding outsiders. Suharto's most baleful legacy was thus to cast serious doubt on whether the Indonesian framework was still capable of delivering its people justice and prosperity.

The process of exclusion has also taken another dimension. Since the 1990s, the Islamic character of Indonesia has become steadily more pronounced. This transformation is publicly visible in a huge growth in the number of mosques being built and in the increasing use of markers of Islamic piety in public behavior—the Islamic greeting, "Assalamualaikum," now opens most public ceremonies and the use of the headscarf by Muslim women has become far more widespread than it once was. Since 1999, in the name of the devolution of power to local authorities, more than forty districts have introduced local regulations that implement some aspect of Islamic law. Except in the special province of Aceh, these regulations are far from systematic. In some districts, they require schoolchildren and government officials to wear Muslim dress (especially the headscarf for women); in others, they restrict gambling and the consumption of alcohol; in still others, they restrict the freedom of women to be outside the home at night or to be in the company of men who are not family members, or they require couples registering a marriage to show that they are able to read the Qur'an. Some districts now collect the *zakat* or Islamic tithe, resulting in a very substantial increase in district government revenue.

These initiatives have led to extensive debate within Islamic circles, but the broader effect has been to make Indonesia's Christian, Hindu, and Buddhist communities increasingly marginal to the national project. At its worst, this phenomenon has led to Muslim-Christian civil war in the Moluccas (the provinces of Maluku and North Maluku) and in central Sulawesi. Thousands have died, tens of thousands of buildings have been destroyed, and hundreds of thousands of people of both religions have been displaced in a process by which the regions have effectively been partitioned into distinct Christian and Muslim cantons.[24]

The prospects for Indonesia, then, are mixed. Over the last century, exclusion has generally been a one-way path. Those removed from the Indonesia project do not come back. Even now, with communism dead as a global ideology and no prospect of a Communist revival in Indonesia, public opinion is vehemently set against any rehabilitation of the Communist Party. On the other hand, the constant, restless search for new institutions to take up the baton in the race for justice and prosperity is likely to continue. The decentralization that has dominated Indonesia's most recent decade is unlikely to be the last word.

Notes

1. Russell Jones, "George Windsor Earl and 'Indonesia,'" *Indonesia Circle* 64 (1994), 279–90.

2. J.D. Legge, "Indonesia's Diversity Revisited," *Indonesia* 49 (1990), 127–31.

3. O.W. Wolters, *The Fall of Srīvijaya in Malay History* (Ithaca, NY: Cornell University Press, 1970), 77–107.

4. Copra is the dried coconut meat used to produce coconut oil.

5. The bark from the cinchona tree is used to produce the antimalarial drug quinine.

6. Peter Bellwood, *Prehistory of the Indo-Malaysian Archipelago,* 2nd ed. (Honolulu: University of Hawaii Press, 1997), 96–127.

7. J.C. van Leur, *Indonesian Trade and Society: Essays in Asian Social and Economic History,* 2nd ed. (The Hague: W. Van Hoeve, 1967), 93–96.

8. Christine Dobbin, *Islamic Revivalism in a Changing Peasant Economy: Central Sumatra, 1784–1847* (London and Malmö: Curzon Press, 1983).

9. David Henley, "Conflict, Justice, and the Stranger-King: Indigenous Roots of Colonial Rule in Indonesia and Elsewhere," *Modern Asian Studies* 38 (2004), 85–144.

10. M.A.P. Meilink-Roelofsz, *Asian Trade and European Influence: The Indonesian Archipelago between 1500 and about 1630* (The Hague: Martinus Nijhoff, 1962), 207–94.

11. Susan Abeyasekere, *Jakarta: A History* (Singapore: Oxford University Press, 1987), 88–130.

12. Robert Cribb, *Historical Atlas of Indonesia* (Honolulu: University of Hawaii, 2000), 115, 121.

13. R.M. Soewardi Soerjaningrat, "Als ik eens Nederlander was, . . . ," in E.F.E. Douwes Dekker, Tjipto Mangoenkoesoemo, and R.M. Soewardi Surjaningrat, eds. *Onze verbanning: publicatie der officieële bescheiden, toegelicht met verslagen en commentaren, betrekking hebbende op de Gouvernements-Besluiten van den 18en Augustus 1913, nos.* 1a en 2a, *Regelende de Toepassing van Artikel 47* R.R. (Schiedam: De Toekomst, 1913).

14. Ulbe Bosma and Remco Raben, *Being "Dutch" in the Indies—A History of Creolisation and Empire, 1500–1920* (Athens: Ohio University Press, 2008), 293–343.

15. Charles A. Coppel, *Indonesian Chinese in Crisis* (Kuala Lumpur: Oxford University Press, 1983), 26, 36–38, 77, 93, 128–29.

16. George McTurnan Kahin, *Nationalism and Revolution in Indonesia* (Ithaca, NY: Cornell University Press, 1952), 22–127.

17. J.A.C. Mackie, *Konfrontasi: The Indonesia-Malaysia Dispute 1963–1966* (Kuala Lumpur: Oxford University Press, 1974), 103–7.

18. C. van Dijk, *Rebellion under the Banner of Islam: The Darul Islam in Indonesia* (The Hague: Martinus Nijhoff, 1981).

19. Robert Cribb, ed., *The Indonesian Killings of 1965–1966: Studies from Java and Bali* (Clayton, Vic.: Monash University Centre of Southeast Asian Studies, Monash Papers on Southeast Asia no. 21, 1990), 42–43.

20. J. Thomas Lindblad, *Bridges to New Business: The Economic Decolonization of Indonesia* (Leiden: KITLV Press, 2008), 177–208.

21. John Bresnan, *Managing Indonesia: The Modern Political Economy* (New York: Columbia University Press, 1993), 51–60.

22. M.C. Ricklefs, *A History of Modern Indonesia since c. 1200,* 4th ed. (Houndmills, UK: Palgrave Macmillan, 2008), 344–62.

23. "The Death of Suharto: Epitaph on a Crook and a Tyrant," *The Economist* (3 January 2008), http://www.economist.com/opinion/displaystory.cfm?story_id=10608377.

24. Gerry van Klinken, *Communal Violence and Democratization in Indonesia: Small Town Wars* (London: Routledge, 2007), 88–106.

Conclusions

S.C.M. PAINE

Choice figures prominently in the movement along three interrelated continua concerning economic development, nation building, and state building. The first continuum is bounded on the extremes by poverty and prosperity; the second ranges from a land fractured into hostile communities on to a unified nation; and the third one progresses from uninstitutionalized personal rule to a state with comprehensive civil and military institutions. Although environmental factors weigh most heavily on the ability to create an overarching nation out of competing communities, choice can trump fate.

The present study takes an inductive approach to analyze these problems: It relies on country experts to explain the course of nation building, state building, and economic development in their country of expertise in order to draw overarching conclusions. The case studies divide into three categories: (1) economic and political development imposed from the outside under colonialism (India under Britain, Algeria under France, the Philippines under Spain and the United States, and Manchuria under Japan); (2) the anticolonial reaction of powerful national leaders (Lenin/Stalin, Atatürk, Mao, and Nasser); and (3) paired case studies of ostensibly similar environments that produced different levels of prosperity (Haiti/ the Dominican Republic, Jordan/Israel, North Korea/South Korea, the Congo [Brazzaville]/Gabon, and Papua New Guinea/Indonesia).

The questions raised in the section of the Introduction titled "The Analytical Framework," divide into two categories: (1) the environmental constraints and opportunities in the areas of national security, economics, and politics, and (2) the choices made by policy makers operating within such an environment. This dichotomy concerns the hand a country is dealt and the way its leaders choose to play that hand. In other words, the questions concern a combination of fate and choice.

The economic success stories of the twentieth century come from some of the most unlikely places if one considers such environmental factors as overpopulation, ecological stress, poor natural resource endowments, and national security threats. Israel, South Korea, Taiwan, and Southeast Asia would seem to be highly unlikely locations for rapid economic development, just as Japan seemed, to Europeans of the late nineteenth century, to be an outlandish spot for the latest rising power.

291

Visible environments, however, do not reveal invisible choices. In national policy, although the road chosen may be visible, the far more numerous roads not taken remain invisible. Still more obscure is the myriad of choices made by citizens concerning the effort and creativity they put into their own work, which aggregate into a gross national product.

Nation Building

Nation building should be conceptualized as a long continuum, with a fractured nation at one extreme and a unified nation at the other. For instance, the American Revolution partitioned the seventeen British North American colonies into the thirteen states in rebellion and a northern loyalist rump that eventually became Canada. The bitterly fought eight-year Revolutionary War transformed an alliance of thirteen autonomous colonies into a federation constituting the United States of America. Yet these states remained divided between free and slave states. Eighty years later, the Civil War, which accounted for more U.S. war dead than all of the country's foreign wars combined, finally eliminated slavery in all of the states. Yet another century elapsed before the passage of the Civil Rights Act and the Voting Rights Act, which belatedly eliminated the legal basis for discrimination against African Americans. The full implementation of the Declaration of Independence's affirmation that "all men are created equal" is still an ongoing process. Thus, nation building in the United States has already taken over two centuries.

Some countries are born more homogeneous than others (Korea for example) and so do not struggle over the issue of nation. Some have a widely shared ancient identity, such as ancient Egyptian civilization for Egypt (albeit in combination with a more recent Arab-Islamic identity), or Han Chinese civilization for China.

Some have tried to homogenize others into empires. France unsuccessfully tried to infuse its colonial subjects with a French identity. Beyond a very small Franco-phone elite deeply influenced by French culture, Haitians, Algerians, Congolese, and Gabonese rejected this identity. Upon independence, these areas rapidly fell into conflict, if not civil war. When France granted independence to Gabon and the Congo, neither had a cohesive national identity. On the contrary, they were fractured by competing and hostile tribes. In the Congo, the northern tribes, under a military leadership, won out and imposed a Soviet-modeled dictatorship on the others. In Gabon, France intervened to prevent this outcome, keeping a pro-French elite in power and preventing the nationalization of French assets. A generation later, when the Congolese government tried to back out of the nonperforming Soviet political and economic model, it turned to democracy, which brought to power an opposition government equally bent on excluding other tribes as the former ruling party had been. Civil war ensued. Vicious conflict is common in poor countries lacking sufficient overlapping identities to blur ethnic divisions.

The Gabonese seem to have benefited from the stability and comparative absence of bloodshed that the continuing French presence afforded. Today the Gabonese have five times the gross national income per capita of the Congolese and approximately that of the Russians or Turks. Yet the distribution of wealth remains highly skewed, so whether or not the general population of Gabon actually has a higher standard of living than that of the Congo remains unclear. For instance, both have average life expectancies at birth of 54 years—extremely low.[1] See the table below, "Statistics for the Case Studies."

Likewise, British India fractured upon independence into a Muslim West Pakistan and East Pakistan on the one hand, and a democratic but divided India containing a large Muslim minority and a Hindu majority divided by caste. Mahatma Gandhi had spearheaded a major pre-independence nation-building effort, which helped mitigate caste divisions and hold together a postindependence Hindu-Muslim, democratic India. In Pakistan, Muhammed Ali Jinnah made no such grassroots effort, but relied on a shared Muslim identity to build a nation.

Spain, however unintentionally, made a greater contribution to nation building in its colonies than did Britain, France, or Japan in theirs. Of the colonial cases examined, Filipinos had the strongest overarching national identity at independence despite their archipelagic geography, normally a serious barrier to national integration. Perhaps this relates to their widely shared Roman Catholicism, a legacy of Spanish colonization, in combination with the long duration of Spanish rule. Those areas most resistant to a Filipino national identity are not Catholic, but Muslim separatist. The Spanish Roman Catholic Church seems to have fostered the process of nation building by imposing a common religious identity, reinforced by the Spanish government's imposition of a common administrative identity. In Latin America, Spain also left behind an enduring and integrating legacy in the Spanish language, but nation building there was a byproduct of genocide, with the obliteration of pre-Columbian civilizations and communities.

The impact of the colonial powers on nation building seems to have been a function of the duration of their control—the longer their rule, the more formative their influence. While Spanish colonial rule endured for three centuries, Britain held India for two, and France controlled many of its colonies for about one century. Perhaps, the longer the colonial administrative divisions endured, the more integrating their impact, but the process was slow. Since most colonial powers were bent on empire, not on the creation of unified foreign nations, it is not surprising that they made only limited and mainly inadvertent contributions to nation building.

Even countries of ancient lineage have struggled to build nations. Java is the center of one of Southeast Asia's six major civilizations. The Javanese have long been connected to many other civilizations by maritime trade routes. However, even though they constitute the dominant ethnic group and their island is the main island of Indonesia, they are but a part of the whole. At times Indonesians have defined themselves by excluding others, notably Eurasians and Chinese in the postcolonial era. At other times, they have forcibly tried to retain those wishing to secede, for example in Aceh, West Papua, and East Timor. Tensions between the small Christian minority and the Muslim majority endure. Periods of extreme

Statistics for the Case Studies

Country	Area[a] Rank	Area Total	Population 2005[b] Rank	Population 2005 Total	Population 1950[c] Rank	Population 1950 Total	GNI per cap 2007[d] US$	GNI per cap PPP	Illiteracy[e] Male	Illiteracy Fem.	Illiteracy ca1950[f] %	Illiteracy ca1950 Year	Life Expectancy at Birth (2008 est)[g]
India	7	3,287,590	2	1,093,563,426	2	369,880,000	950	2,740	31.6	54.6	80.7	1951	69.25
Algeria	11	2,381,740	36	32,560,735	40	8,892,718	3,620	7,640	23.7	43.0	93.8	1948	73.77
Philippines	71	300,000	12	90,435,785	21	21,131,264	1,620	3,730	4.9	5.2	40.0	1948	70.86
Russia	1	17,075,200	8	142,775,578	4	101,936,816	7,560	14,400	0.3	0.6	5–10 est.	1950	65.94
Turkey	37	780,580	17	72,673,810	22	21,121,639	8,020	12,350	6.6	23.5	68.1	1950	73.14
China	4	9,596,960	1	1,306,313,812	1	562,579,779	2,300	5,370	7.9	22.1	50–55 est.	1950	73.18
Egypt	30	1,001,451	15	77,561,884	20	21,197,691	1,580	5,400	33.4	56.2	80.1	1947	71.85
Haiti	147	27,750	88	8,394,520	86	3,097,220	560	1,150	48.0	52.2	89.5	1950	57.56
Dom. Rep.	131	48,730	84	9,088,094	103	2,352,968	3,550	6,340	16.3	16.3	57.1	1950	73.39
Jordan	112	92,300	105	5,759,732	145	561,254	2,850	5,160	5.1	15.7	80–85 est.	1950	78.71
Israel	153	20,770	99	6,742,915	124	1,286,131	21,900	25,930	3.0	7.3	6.3	1948	80.61
No. Korea	99	120,540	49	22,198,568	35	9,471,140	less than $935				60–65 est.	1950	72.20
So. Korea	109	98,480	24	48,005,157	23	20,845,771	19,690	24,750	0.9	3.6	60–65 est.	1950	78.64
PNG	54	462,840	106	5,554,512	119	1,412,466	850	1,870	29.4	43.2	90–95 est.	1950	66.00
Indonesia	16	1,919,440	4	228,895,746	6	82,978,392	1,650	3,580	8.2	18.1	80–85 est.	1950	70.46
Congo	63	342,000	128	3,604,002	137	826,308	1,540	2,750	12.5	25.6	95–99 est.	1950	53.74
Gabon	75	267,667	150	1,395,690	153	415,767	6,670	13,080			95–99 est.	1950	53.52
U.S.	3	9,629,091	3	295,583,436	3	152,271,000	46,040	45,850			2.5	1952	78.14

[a] List of Countries by Land Mass [Ranked by Area] http://www.mongabay.com/igapo/world_statistics_by_area.htm, accessed 12 April 2007. Area in square kilometers. China does not include 1,092 sq. km. for Hong Kong or 25 for Macau. Israel does not include the Occupied Palestinian Territory of 6,220.

[b] U.S. Census Bureau, International Data Base, Country Rankings, 2005. http://www.census.gov/cgi-bin/ipc/idbrank.pl. accessed 14 January 2009.

[c] U.S. Census Bureau, International Data Base, Country Rankings, 1950. http://www.census.gov/cgi-bin/ipc/idbrank.pl. accessed 14 January 2009. The 1950 statistic is for the USSR not just Russia.

[d] GNI=Gross National Income. US$=Atlas methodology. PPP=Purchasing power parity in international dollars. World Bank, "GNI per capita 2007, Atlas method and PPP," World Development Indicators Database, http://siteresources.worldbank.org/DATASTATISTICS/Resources/GNIPC.pdf, accessed 22 December 2008.

[e] Institute for Statistics, Literacy and Non Formal Education Sector, "Estimates and Projections of Adult Illiteracy for Population Aged 15 Years and Above, by Country and by Gender 1970–2015," July 2002, http://www.uis.unesco.org/en/stats/statistics/literacy2000.htm, accessed 25 August 2008. The statistics for illiteracy apply to the year 2000.

[f] UNESCO, "World Illiteracy at Mid-Century" (Paris: UNESCO, 1957), 32–33, 38–42. Statistics for Israel pertain to the Jewish population. For those countries with no census, UNESCO made estimates in 1950.

[g] Central Intelligence Agency, "Life Expectancy at Birth," 2008, *The World Factbook*, https://www.cia.gov/library/publications/the-world-factbook/rankorder/2102rank.html, accessed 15 October 2008.

violence have punctuated the nation-building process in Indonesia, most notably the 1965 massacre of up to 500,000 alleged Communists, many of whom were ethnic Chinese.

Some leaders have tried to construct an overarching ideology to integrate diverse nations. Stalin used Stalinism, Mao used Maoism, Atatürk used Kemalism, Sukarno used his Pancasila, and Nasser used pan-Arab nationalism to create a unifying ideology. Without coercion, however, the Soviet empire fractured. Maoism did not last beyond Mao. The export versions of these two Communist variants have both withered away. The passage of time has diluted the potency of Nasserism, Kemalism, and the Pancasila. During the American Revolution, despite the ethnic diversity of the North American British colonies, the founding generation of the United States created a powerful integrating ideology, which emphasized, not ethnicity, a common history, or a common theory of history as the basis for a nation, but the shared political values embedded in the Declaration of Independence and U.S. Constitution. This ideology survives in both its domestic and export versions.

Democratic institutions in the Philippines and India furthered national integration, but in a severely fractured society, such as the Congo, democracy became the prelude to civil war. Although civil wars tend to retard the unification of diverse communities into a shared nation, regional wars can create powerful accelerants for nation building. A lethal national security threat can create the *force majeure* necessary for diverse communities to compromise, to cooperate, and, in doing so, to blend. Thus, threats of invasion (regional war), unlike civil war, can glue internal communities together, as was the case of Israel's diverse Jewish communities, which faced a common threat of annihilation from neighboring states. Likewise Haitian-Dominican wars reinforced national identities on both sides of the border.

Of the postindependence case studies, Jordan constitutes the only example of successful nation building from scratch. Although Turkey and Israel also built new nations, Atatürk leveraged a preexisting Turkish identity and Israel leveraged an ancient Jewish identity, and both countries have failed to integrate into the nation key minority communities—the Kurds and the Palestinians, respectively.

Jordan had no preexisting Jordanian identity to leverage. The Mandate of Palestine could have been divided in a number of ways or kept whole. The territory that became Jordan is a fabrication of Great Britain, which then imported the Hashemite dynasty to rule it. (The Hashemites hailed most recently from Hejaz, now part of Saudi Arabia.) Yet the Hashemite dynasty transformed into Jordanians the residents of a land bereft of natural resources and lacking even an adequate supply of the most basic resource, water. They did so in defiance of Nasserite Arab nationalism and Palestinian nationalism through astute leadership and the solicitation of foreign financial aid.

Some countries inherit a unified nation; others struggle to create one. The existence of multiple ancient communities within one country is an environmental factor dealt by fate. The direction a country moves along the continuum between a fractured and unified nation, however, reflects choices made by leaders, communities, and individuals. The case studies suggest that those communities not blessed with a preexisting sense of nation can gradually construct one by promoting the development of overlapping communities, for instance, the Congress Party in India. Cross-ethnic religious, regional, linguistic, class, or political party identities can help defuse ethnicity as a cause for conflict.[2] These overlapping identities can become a social glue to bind together disparate communities and contribute to the evolution of an overarching shared identity. This seems to have been the process in the West, where over the centuries feuding communities coalesced into larger communities—nineteenth-century German and Italian history comes to mind.

Attention to the cultivation of such crosscutting loyalties and overlapping group identities may be crucial first steps toward nation building in fractured societies. Public education can contribute to this process of nation building from the bottom up by binding together all children in a shared and integrating educational experience, whose effect will be felt mainly after the students grow up and assume leadership positions themselves.

State Building

The case studies suggest that state building can foster nation building. State building, like nation building, should be conceptualized as a long continuum, with uninstitutionalized personal rule at one extreme, merging into incomplete states, and on to comprehensive state institutions at the other extreme. Uninstitutionalized personal rule characterized the Haitian and the Dominican governments at independence. The endemic personalistic rulers populating Latin American governments during the first century after independences acquired the generic name *caudillo,* Spanish for army chieftain. They were the Latin American equivalent of the Chinese warlord of the pre-Communist era. *Caudillos* produced few enduring institutions but much chaos.

Gradually Haiti and the Dominican Republic acquired a broader set of state institutions: a police force, on-again off-again legislatures, a judicial system, and the like. In the twentieth century, the Dominican government expanded its activities to encompass infrastructure development, public health, public education, and woodland protection. It developed a more complete set of state institutions than did Haiti, which remained stuck longer in the personalistic-dictatorship mode under the Duvaliers. Instability in these two countries comes not from incomplete nation building, but from incomplete state building. There are no secession movements or ethnically distinct communities in either. Rather, instability arises over political succession. Neither country has regular and fairly contested elections. Both remain incomplete states in varying degree.

In Papua New Guinea, state institutions are so incomplete and state services are so sporadic that for some communities the state itself remains optional. Islanders can live their lives entirely outside the purview of the state. This is no recipe for prosperity, but for subsistence living. For other Papua New Guineans, the state remains incomplete, offering some services, not others, so that private organizations such as churches, mining companies, and others fill some of the gaps. Archipelagic geography on the periphery of trade routes, high illiteracy, and the absence of a strong sense of nation make unlikely a rapid change in the situation. Although Papua New Guinea was colonized, most of its population hardly came into contact with each other let alone with the colonizers. Its situation suggests the fate of an uncolonized land lacking an integrative domestic civilization. Although largely spared the violence of colonial wars, interethnic and tribal warfare and high crime rates take a constant toll.

Algeria suffers from incomplete nation and state building. In the tightly controlled elections since independence, political legitimacy has remained tied to the thinning ranks of those who fought for independence from France. The independence generation forms an integrating overlapping community, but as this generation succumbs to mortality, its surviving members provide an ever-shrinking pool of acceptable presidential choices. In such incompletely institutionalized but enduring governments, among the first institutions to develop tend to be the military and intelligence organizations necessary to enforce dictatorial rule. Just three years after independence, the commander of the army leveraged his military and intelligence connections to overthrow the civilian leadership and remain in power until his death thirteen years later.

Overbearing military institutions can stifle the development of civil institutions. Such a situation often produces a contested state because even popular dictators (Nasser) and popular generations from which to pick dictators (Algeria) eventually die off. They take to their graves their personal connections that serve in lieu of institutions. This leaves behind a power vacuum that others compete to fill. Institutions form a "steel frame," as in India, to contain instability precisely because they endure beyond the lifespan of any individual. Succession is the Achilles heel of dictatorships that do not become dynasties.

Great Britain and the United States left a broader colonial institutional legacy than did France. Frenchmen administered French colonies, while Britain and the United States relied much more heavily on a large cadre of local administrators, whom they educated to perform their duties. These local civil servants had a vested interest and expertise in maintaining the administrative structures left by the departing colonial powers. Unlike France, both Britain and the United States deliberately focused on state building in the belief that this promoted administrative efficiency and lowered costs. The United States also did so as preparation for eventual independence.[3] Britain focused on the administrative and police functions of the state, while the United States also emphasized the development of democratic institutions, mass public education, and public health programs. India, Jordan, Israel, the Dominican Republic, and Papua New Guinea all chose to expand upon the institutional legacy left by Britain, the United States, and Australia, respectively, but at best, colonialism left behind an incomplete state (India) and at worst it left armed chaos (the Congo).

The newly independent made critical choices on how much of the colonial institutional infrastructure to retain. India kept much of Britain's colonial administrative structures, the large cadre of Indians manning these organizations, the laws governing them, and the Indian lawyers interpreting the laws. At independence, India chose democratic political institutions. These institutions fostered nation building by creating a shared political experience that became a basis for an overarching sense of nation. But democracy did so in India within a preexisting institutional steel frame.

Likewise, Israelis relied heavily on Britain's colonial institutions, retained British legal traditions, and imported British parliamentary institutions. Israel developed strong state institutions virtually overnight. For nearly a century, Zionists had been preparing for a Jewish homeland. Before independence, the future Israelis drew up electoral laws and procedures for a provisional government. They followed these rules without the turmoil common in Third World political successions. Although Israeli ruling coalitions remain highly volatile, the laws of the land and its civil and military institutions are stable.

The colonial case studies indicate the limits of both domestic coercion and outside interference to force populations to strive in desired directions. Colonial powers can invest enormous sums in state building, but if there is no local buy-in, once the colonial power departs, these institutions disappear overnight—for example, Japanese institutions in Manchuria or French institutions in Algeria. India, Israel, and the Philippines, in contrast, adopted and adapted democratic and other state institutions left by the British and the Americans respectively. Indians, Israelis, and Filipinos made this choice, not the departing colonial power.

As in nation building, an external security threat can facilitate the internal cooperation necessary for state building. Intuitively, a national security threat would seem to create an inhospitable environment for nation or state building. In practice, common fears sometimes create a common cause, which sometimes strengthen a national identity or impel people to cooperate in state building. Israelis and both North and South Koreans had national identities of ancient lineage but polities of recent creation. Yet all three rapidly put together strong state institutions. Perhaps the desperate wars at independence and dire national security environment thereafter made clear to their populations the imperative to create these institutions.

Occasionally, civil war can also promote state building. In the 1990s, a lethal insurgency in Peru precipitated a thorough reexamination of the roots of poverty, which many educated Peruvians presumed to be the source of the insurgency. This research produced the Latin American best seller *The Other Path: The Economic Answer to Terrorism*.[4] It identified the legal system as the culprit for Peru's dilatory economic development. The laws erected barriers to property ownership for the poor and aspiring middle class, while protecting the mercantilistic privileges of the elite. In doing so, the legal system straitjacketed the potentially most vibrant part of the economy, condemning both rich and poor to economic stagnation. The dire nature of the national security threat posed by the Shining Path insurgency spurred the Peruvian government to introduce a program of sweeping legal simplification, but it remains too early to tell whether Peruvians have identified and eliminated the critical barrier to prosperity. Nevertheless, they reduced the insurgency from a serious ideological competitor to mafia status and, as of 2008, had a real GDP growth rate of nine percent.[5] Peruvian success came from internal choices concerning internal problems.

The paired case studies also highlight the importance of choices over environmental determinants. The people of North and South Korea did not differ at independence; neither elite focused on self-enrichment, but rather on competing visions for economic development; and both Koreas benefited from massive foreign aid. The North started out with the larger, richer, and more industrialized piece of territory. Except for the geography, the other factors have reversed since independence. The ideology underpinning the North Korean vision, while highly effective for state building, failed at economic development.

The South Korean model for state building presupposes a strong preexisting national identity. The model includes strong early leaders focused single-mindedly on economic development and a population intent upon securing political freedoms, not just for a minority but for all. South Koreans forced their government to protect these freedoms by organizing themselves into numerous nongovernmental groups. Meanwhile, their government extracted strategic rent from the United States to fund the first two decades of economic development and to provide a security umbrella.

In other words, at numerous levels, ranging from voters at the grassroots, to nongovernmental organizations, to the highest levels of leadership, South Koreans made key choices; the North Korean leadership made other choices including the decision to preserve its monopoly on political and economic power; and these choices had consequences.

Human beings, however shaped by their environments, constantly choose among alternatives in a myriad of big and little decisions. The world is as it is, not just because of the decisions of a few great powers, but more fundamentally because of the decisions made by the far more numerous smaller powers and the citizens of them all. Beyond the ability to take life, even dictatorships cannot totally deprive their subjects of choice. Their citizens choose whether to perform the minimum workload or to strive, and this has enormous implications for economic growth. While the oppressed may not be able to fashion their own plans, they may be able to veto the plans of their oppressors.

Clearly state building is more difficult in some countries than others. What are the main impediments?

The Showstoppers

In the case studies examined, two items precluded state building, while other factors were inhibitors, but not showstoppers. The showstoppers for state building were a missing foundation of prior nation building that led to vicious fighting or an elite engaged in politics as plunder.[6] In countries fragmented into hostile communities— for example, the Congo—either civil war or intense social unrest precluded the stability necessary for either state building or rapid economic development. These internal subcommunities engaged in zero-sum conflicts, where the winner took all and the loser could be starved, jailed, or even executed; at best the losers could expect to be frozen out of promising economic opportunities, which the winning subcommunity monopolized. In short, these were countries without a nation.

Such countries tended to suffer from a rapacious elite for a common reason: If those in power live in constant fear of being overthrown, then they quite rationally focus on maximizing short-term personal benefits so that politics becomes plunder. In Papua New Guinea, many leading politicians tolerated corruption whether in or out of office in anticipation of another turn at raiding the public till.

In other cases, where the infighting and the chaos seemed remarkably similar, the problem concerned not a lack of nation, but a governing elite focused on self-enrichment, resulting in the rape of a country's natural resources rather than the sustained investment necessary to prosper or the sustained commitment necessary to develop lasting institutions. Examples include Haiti, the nineteenth-century Dominican Republic, and the Philippines particularly during the Marcos era.

Some countries had both strong nations and strong states and yet remained poor, for example North Korea. Why? In addition to contested nations, contested states, and politics as plunder, the case studies indicate that the showstoppers for economic development were either the complete nationalization of private enterprise (plus or minus the complete collectivization of agriculture) or a reliance on ideology over empiricism to determine economic policy.

Colonialism inspired a visceral anticolonial reaction. Ironically, the most articulate voices came from ancient empires that had fallen onto hard times after the Industrial Revolution. This economic and technological revolution shifted the international balance of power irrevocably in the favor of the most industrialized states, which initially meant Western Europe. The anticolonial critics of Western imperialism, however, often had a colonial agenda of their own, perhaps to revitalize an ancient empire, in the case of Stalin in Russia or Mao in China, or to promote an expansionist agenda, in the case of Nasser's quest for regional leadership. Atatürk stands apart from this trend because he never tried to reconstitute the Ottoman Empire and because he considered Russia, not the West, to be Turkey's primary national security threat and so never traveled the anti-Western road taken by the others.

Of the anticolonial reaction, Russia produced the most influential ideology of the twentieth century. Lenin and Stalin demonstrated the political efficacy of a vanguard party in control of the military and a state in control of the economy to funnel resources to the military. Their model proved effective at bringing its practitioners to political power. In the wave of decolonization following World War II, first-generation leaders focused first and foremost on seizing power. For this the

Soviet Union offered a highly effective model, but the program never produced affluence in peacetime, but rather long-term economic stagnation, a consequence not generally recognized at the time.

In 1968, fifty years after the Russia Revolution and twenty years before the collapse of the Soviet Union, the distinguished political scientist Samuel Huntington noted that Leninism was an accurate theory for political action but an inaccurate theory of social evolution. It provided the means to take power but not to prosper thereafter.[7] What was a matter of speculation in 1917 became one of accumulated data by 1989, conclusively proving that the model did not deliver prosperity despite the broad natural resource endowment of the Soviet Union, its highly educated population, and its comprehensive state institutions. At that time, the Russian leadership chose to abandon the nonperforming model.

In the meantime, many followed parts of the model, including Nasser, whose nationalization of industry and desires for regional aggrandizement created debilitating complications for Egyptian economic development. China's Mao Zedong and North Korea's Kim Il Sung were among the most literal followers, despite Mao's claims that he had tailored the program to suit a more agricultural economy and Kim's emphasis on self-reliance. Mao's rural tailoring and Kim's self-reliance, like Stalin's collectivization of the Ukraine, produced famine. France prevented Gabon, but not the Congo, from heeding the Siren of Marxism-Leninism and suffering the economic consequences. The showstopper demanded by communism was not nationalization per se but the total elimination of private enterprise. North Korea did relatively well until it ratcheted up state ownership to one hundred percent.

Although the Soviet Union demanded the liberation of the colonies of others, it clung tenaciously to its own. When Soviet resolve weakened, unrest spread throughout Eastern Europe and Central Asia. Lenin and Stalin conspicuously failed at nation building in the empire, leaving a Russian rump state at the collapse of the Soviet Union in 1991. Mao, likewise, clung to China's colonies of Tibet, Xinjiang, and elsewhere, but at the cost of enduring unrest. Although he fostered a strong sense of nationalism among the Han Chinese, this nationalism has not resonated among China's many minority peoples, who, despite their small numbers, occupy two-fifths of Chinese territory. It would seem that beyond a few geriatric dictators, like Fidel and Raul Castro in Cuba, Kim Jong Il in North Korea, and throwbacks like Hugo Chávez of Venezuela, the Soviet model is a fixture of the twentieth century, not the twenty-first.

But ideology itself is far from dead. Other ideologies were also inimical to economic development. This was the second showstopper. In this sense, the Soviet model was not a unique phenomenon. The related ideology of dependency theory also inhibited economic development in Latin America for much of the second half of the twentieth century.[8] Eventually the data piled up, demonstrating that the ideology was not delivering. This took three long generations in Russia. In the more democratic Latin America, it took two generations to push aside dependency theory and to seek government ministers with a graduate education in economics.

Previously, Latin American elites tended to view economic development through the ideological prism of dependency theory, which attributed poverty to expropriative and exploitative activities, particularly of the United States. The success of the so-called Four Asian Tigers (South Korea, Taiwan, Hong Kong, and Singapore) undermined this theory in much of Latin America, because even countries with large U.S. military bases (South Korea) and intimate economic ties with the United States (Taiwan) or under another colonial power (Hong Kong and Singapore) became wealthy. More to the point, by dependency theory, Australia should be as impoverished as any Latin American country, given its long colonial domination by Great Britain, its location on the imperial periphery, and its heavy dependence on raw material exports. Yet Australians have long enjoyed a very high standard of living.[9]

Likewise, radical Islam did not produce prosperity in Iran, which traded authoritarian rule and rapid economic growth under the Shah for authoritarian rule and the stagnation of living standards under the clerics. How long it will take for the proponents of Islamic governance to take a more empirical approach to political and economic development is anyone's guess. The historical record suggests that social change dependent on major shifts in attitudes requires generational change for the older, most ideologically committed, generation to pass from the scene so that their less orthodox children and, particularly, grandchildren, can gradually take over.

Ideological systems share a debilitating flaw: they demand programs consistent with *a priori* assumptions about how the world should work, rather than with empirical evidence on how the world actually functions. Moreover, the most influential ideologies of the twentieth century—communism, dependency theory, and radical Islam—all emphasized the external origins of society's ills. They focused on an external enemy on whom to blame internal problems—the United States, the West, or Israel. This blinded the ideologues to the internal origins of their problems, which, in turn, deflected them from addressing those problems over which they had the most control and which they had the most ability to fix, namely problems of domestic origin. Not surprisingly, prosperity has generally eluded such societies.

Some would argue that the "Washington consensus," meaning U.S. economic development advice doled out from the second half of the twentieth century forward, was also too ideologically driven and not adequately aligned with tangible results. When Nasser followed the recommendations of the leading Western economists of his era, their advice, however ideologically and methodologically correct, failed to produce positive economic results. While Egypt was following flawed Western and Soviet advice in the 1950s and 1960s respectively, the economic model actually working at the time was the postwar version of Japan's Meiji model spreading through East Asia, first to Taiwan and South Korea and a generation later to China. Japan's wartime record, however, made people loath to praise anything about prewar Japan.

Postwar economic growth in Manchuria, Korea, and Taiwan reflected massive Imperial Japanese investments in infrastructure development, mining, heavy industry, and technical education. Japan left behind not only tangible investments but also an intangible reservoir of expertise that the postindependence governments leveraged. These tangible and intangible factors help account for North Korea's early years of substantial economic growth, while North Korea's subsequent full nationalization of private enterprise helps account for its ensuing economic stagnation.

Postwar Japan's highly successful export-led economic model was essential for the economic prosperity of the Four Asian Tigers, but its implementation reflected not Japanese choices but the choices of each of the Four Asian Tigers. Moreover, the model worked when only a small number of countries used it. In the future, the international system, as presently organized—with the United States as the consumer of last resort—may be unable to absorb the quantity of exports necessary for populous countries such as China or India to apply this economic model with equal success to reach parity with the per capita incomes of developed countries.

Turn around the showstoppers for economic development and the prerequisites become: technocratic leaders focused on economic development, meaning that any self-enrichment is a secondary, not a primary goal; and a reliance on technical experts, not political intimates or ideological think-alikes, throughout government institutions, particularly those responsible for matters affecting the economy. These two factors are closely related. The first condition depends on specific individuals in key positions, while the second condition depends on agreement among the elite on the need to rely on technical expertise to guide economic development. Both factors concern people, the choices they make, and the importance of putting those most likely to make good choices in positions of power.

One would think that a leader focused on economic development would naturally seek expert advice and make appointments on the basis of technical expertise. In fact, ideological leaders, such as Kim Il Sung, may aim at economic growth but embrace ideological measures that preclude it. Other leaders may be so preoccupied with retaining power that they funnel state funds not into economic development but into private bank accounts to buy political loyalty.

Like the economic showstoppers, the above prerequisites for growth do not concern immutable environmental constraints but the choices that people make. Of the two showstoppers for state building, one, a missing prior foundation of nation building, is indeed an environmental factor, but the other, an elite engaged in politics as plunder, reflects personal choices more than an immutable fate.

The Inhibitors

The case studies point to a variety of inhibitors to economic development: geography, a capital-intensive resource endowment, concentrated land ownership, gross environmental degradation, high illiteracy, a leadership deficit, and the subordination of domestic policy to a grand foreign policy agenda. These factors have been arranged starting with those that policy makers cannot control at one extreme (the environmental factors), and proceeding to those over which they exercise increasing degrees of control.

Policy makers have least control over geography. The archipelagic geography of Papua New Guinea, Indonesia, and the Philippines constituted a formidable barrier to nation building, state building, and economic development. Scattered islands do not naturally integrate. Indonesia leveraged its centrality to trade routes and Javanese civilization to build a national idea. Roman Catholicism and democratic institutions have integrated the Philippines. Geography, however, remains an unsurmounted barrier to national integration in Papua New Guinea. Yet, the archipelagic geography of Japan did not prevent its transformation into one of the world's most prosperous countries. In other words, even geography does not necessarily dictate fate.

Intuitively a rich natural resource endowment would seem to constitute a major stimulus for economic development. Yet countries reliant on oil production for a significant proportion of their trade revenues do not generally enjoy a high standard of living. Likewise, much of sub-Saharan Africa, despite rich natural resource endowments, remains poor. Perhaps the capital-intensive nature of the extraction of these resources produces an oligopolistic or monopolistic economic environment that allows the few to dominate the many. For a poor country, resource extraction requires large investments that only a government or a multinational corporation can provide. The infusion of external wealth from trade gives those in control of this trade disproportionate power within poor societies.

Natural resource prices reflect the demand and wealth of the importing countries, not the domestic price structure of the exporter. For good or for ill, this disparity in wealth magnifies the impact of such investments in developing countries. If mismanaged, they can potentially retard the development of the other comparatively far less lucrative sectors of the economy, particularly agriculture. Yet agriculture is vital because the poor must eat, and when they no longer produce enough to eat, either they starve or their government must use scarce foreign reserves to import foodstuffs. Moreover, agriculture tends to be the starting point where the poor find work and accumulate the wealth to branch out into other sources of income. If agriculture, handicrafts, and small-scale commerce wither, the poor have few prospects for upward mobility and society loses the benefit of their labor. Inattention to economic opportunities for the poor converts them from a potential source of economic growth to a potential source of social unrest.

Poorly institutionalized governments have great difficulty channeling the wealth from their resource endowments away from the personal bank accounts of those in power and into investments designed to promote development across the rural and urban economy, such as costly infrastructure investments. Russia, Algeria, Papua New Guinea, the Congo, Gabon, Haiti, and Indonesia all suffer from this affliction. There is a temptation to use the windfall not to stimulate growth but to underwrite dictatorships, the role played by Sonatrach, the Algerian oil and natural gas monopoly. This wealth both reduces the pressure to reform and allows otherwise nonperforming dictatorships to linger in power, so that capital-intensive natural resources can become a curse not a blessing for long-term economic development.

In preindustrial or lightly industrialized countries, concentrated land ownership and high farmer-tenancy rates can function similarly. In the preindustrial era, land was the primary source of wealth, so exclusion from land ownership condemned the landless to poverty. The Philippines and much of Latin America have not overcome the inequities of the highly concentrated land tenure pattern established by the Spanish. Concentrated land tenure produced highly skewed income distributions, which produced equally skewed distributions of political power. Although urbanization and industrialization open nonagricultural avenues to wealth, Filipino incomes still reflect the land tenure patterns established under Spain.

Land redistribution would seem to be the solution. Yet in Haiti, Indonesia, and Algeria the elimination of large estates proved economically disastrous. In Haiti and Indonesia, the government redistributed the land, whereas in Algeria, the French loss of the Algerian War entailed the end of French agricultural subsidies and a mass exodus of colonial commercial agriculturists, whose lands were then taken over by others. Whether de jure or de facto, the land redistribution in these three countries resulted in the collapse of agricultural production, which never became the source of wealth that it had been previously. Land reform turns out to be a tricky issue. Simple redistribution does not automatically lead to prosperity. If the necessary economies of scale and the expertise to farm are lost with the expropriation and expulsion of the former plantation operators, land reform can become a fast track to increased rural poverty. In the Dominican Republic, the plantation economy survived and remained a source of wealth for the few and of employment for the many.

South Korea and Taiwan, both high economic performers, underwent significant land redistribution in the 1940s and 1950s. This opened economic opportunities to the formerly landless without destroying the environment in the process. During the colonial period, Japan made enormous efforts in both countries to inculcate good practices in agriculture. Both countries also had strong states, unlike the contested Philippine and Haitian states, which were ill-equipped to enforce government regulations.

At the opposite extreme of environmental riches lies environmental degradation. Although all countries underwent significant environmental degradation during the Industrial Revolution, this did not necessarily undermine economic performance. Some cases of environmental degradation, however, are so severe that they do. This helps account for the economic disparity between Haiti and the Dominican Republic. Virtually no forests remain in Haiti. This preindustrial deforestation caused extensive erosion, which in turn degraded the farmlands the logging was intended to open. In contrast, the Dominican Republic has an extensive park system, which, despite persistent illegal logging, still has kept twenty-eight percent of the country wooded and the surrounding farmland more fertile than Haiti's.[10]

In contrast to these environmental factors, policy makers have a much greater degree of control over literacy rates. Even so it takes at least a generation for schoolchildren to become leaders and for a country to realize the benefits from universal public education. Papua New Guinea, Haiti, India, Egypt, and Algeria all suffer from appallingly high illiteracy rates in the range of one-third to one-half of the population. With the exception of Algeria, they all have extremely low per capita incomes. No society has yet become prosperous with these levels of illiteracy. For Algeria, oil revenue probably helps explain its comparatively high income.

In some countries, an absence of leadership retarded nation and state building as well as economic development. Despite strong democratic institutions, the Philippines has suffered a virtually uninterrupted leadership deficit. Although Corazon Aquino played a key role in the elimination of the Marcos dictatorship, she was unable to address the country's underlying poverty despite high literacy rates among both men and women. Subsequent leaders have fallen over corruption charges. Likewise, the Congo, Gabon, Haiti, the Dominican Republic, and Papua New Guinea have all suffered from a leadership deficit. They have no Atatürk, no Park Chung Hee, no King Hussein, no George Washington. There are degrees of deficiency. For instance, Dominican leaders, however flawed in some areas, made the decision to set aside and to protect parklands, while the government of Haiti did not. This one issue then had enormous economic repercussions.

In other cases the problem was not a deficit of strong leaders, but the choices the leaders made. The strong foundational leaders of the Soviet Union, the People's Republic of China, North Korea, and modern Egypt all focused on promoting their ideological visions abroad. Some attempted to reconstitute old empires, but nationalism had changed the economics of empire, making it a money-losing proposition when subject peoples either failed to put down their arms or resisted in other ways. Even the act of trying to spread a vision to neighbors, as in the case of Nasser, consumed scarce national resources. It turns out that funneling national wealth into foreign policy is a very expensive proposition that does not seem conducive to rapid economic growth. On the other hand, countries that ignore potent national security threats may not survive.[11]

Likewise, domestic policy choices mattered. In the case of the Hashemites, given the cards they were dealt—no resources, poor farmlands, interventionist neighbors, and no preexisting national identity—they did well for their country. In 2008 life expectancy in Jordan was 79 years, putting it in the ranks of developed countries and ahead of all other Muslim Middle Eastern states, in some cases by nearly a decade.[12] At independence, Jordan had an illiteracy rate estimated at 80 to 85 percent.[13] In 2000, when Arab states had the combined illiteracy rate of 28.3 percent for men and a stunning 52.2 percent for women, the Jordanian rates were 5.1 percent and 15.7 percent, respectively. Based on the experience of other countries, the economic effects of this rapid rise in literacy should be felt with a lag of twenty years.[14] Some have argued that poor natural resource endowments actually encourage long-term growth because human beings develop more effective institutions to compensate.[15] In other words, the key to economic growth is not the natural inheritance but the human factor.

The Turkish experience makes a powerful case for leadership. Atatürk avoided the pitfall of imperial overstretch. He perceived and seized opportunities to create a strong state out of the Turkish rump left by the collapse of the Ottoman Empire. Today, his country has a far higher male literacy rate than Egypt or Algeria, earns a per capita gross national income on a par with resource-rich Gabon and Russia, and belongs to the elite Western alliance of NATO.

Leadership also played an essential role in determining the effects of foreign aid. South Korea and Israel invested heavily in infrastructure: power grids, railways, roads, aqueducts, and the like. Both also invested heavily in their children, putting a premium on education, academic performance, and hard work. These investments depended on funds, which in the early and most vulnerable period came from outside aid. South Korea, Israel, Jordan, and Taiwan, another high performer, have all been major recipients of long-term foreign aid. They leveraged their strategic locations to extract money (strategic rent) from the United States, becoming so-called rentier states. South Korea and Taiwan no longer receive generous foreign aid, but Israel and Jordan still do. Although the Philippines for many years was and Egypt remains a major beneficiary of U.S. aid, neither has nearly as much to show for it as do Israel, South Korea, Jordan, or Taiwan. Part of the difference may reflect Egypt's and the Philippines' comparatively larger populations. Yet South Korea surmounted the problem of large population compounded by a devastating war.

The Prospects

The Introduction posed a question: Why do some countries prosper, while others languish?

Countries flounder when fractured into feuding internal communities (meaning they lack a basic foundation of nation building), when their elites engage in politics as plunder, when the public sector eliminates all private enterprise, or when ideological conformity becomes the primary test for policy formation. A country with any one of these four problems will languish. Countries can work their way out of these problems if a domestic leadership emerges that focuses on economic development and that relies on technical expertise over political or ideological conformity to implement reforms. Any of the following factors inhibits prosperity: archipelagic geography, a capital-intensive resource endowment, concentrated land ownership, gross environmental degradation, high illiteracy, an internal leadership deficit, or the subordination of domestic policy to a grand foreign policy agenda. The more of these factors present, the more likely a country will languish.

All of these factors can be overcome by choice. Japan stands out as a country that has faced many of them: it overcame archipelagic geography, concentrated land ownership, high illiteracy, and the subordination of domestic policy to a grand foreign policy agenda. Australia has flourished despite a capital-intensive resource endowment and gross environmental degradation. The brilliant Korean leadership of the second half of the twentieth century emerged after a century of dysfunctional late Yi dynasty rule, a half-century of brutal Japanese colonization, and the catastrophic Korean War.

An examination of the paired case studies in combination with the analytical questions posed in the Introduction indicates that choice can trump fate. The common factors behind the more affluent country in each pair did not primarily concern immutable environmental factors but rather deliberate decisions. The impetus for successful reforms was internal and proactive (Israel and South Korea). Although government planning was important, it alone was not sufficient (North Korea and Communist states in general). Effective economic planning had to be based on technocratic expertise, not ideological consistency (Japan, South Korea, and Israel). Government goals that focused on the military, not civilian economy, and foreign policy over domestic policy, in the long run produced a weak economy incapable of funding military ambitions (Stalinism and Nasserism). Yet a fear for national survival could have a salutary effect by forcing internal interest groups to cooperate (Israel, Jordan, South Korea, North Korea, and the Dominican Republic).

Broad public education was important but not decisive. Latin America has a highly literate population but no area beyond Puerto Rico, a virtual U.S. colony, has broken into the ranks of the developed countries in terms of per capita national income. Likewise, neither natural resources nor foreign aid was decisive. Although foreign aid could substitute for a poor resource endowment (Jordan and Israel), this alone was not sufficient for economic development (the Philippines and Egypt). Moreover, in communities locked into zero-sum conflicts, the aid could serve to entrench a dysfunctional power structure rather than to promote economic development (the Philippines under Marcos). Local leadership was critical and could not be conjured from the outside. Yet, it is difficult to understand why key leaders emerged at a particular time or a particular place.

The obstacles to and prerequisites for prosperity seem to be overwhelmingly domestic in nature. This is both good and bad news. The good news: the problem can be solved and in fact must be solved in-country. Brilliant domestic leadership can overcome daunting combinations of problems, but—now for the bad news— brilliance by definition is a quality in short supply. One of the key attributes of brilliant national leadership is the ability to create an environment in which citizens can develop and use their own talents to the fullest and desire to do so. Such societies become wealthy from the aggregate contributions of the many—the "invisible hand" described by Adam Smith, the father of the field of economics. Communist systems conspicuously failed at this task. Neither regimented nor anarchic societies produce environments conducive to human development.

Irrespective of the caliber of the leadership, there is no quick fix. A strong nation and a strong state are two of the hallmarks of developed countries. Nation and state building can become reinforcing processes, but the dual progression takes generations. This is because human beings acquire a sense of nation over generations.

Nation building becomes tortuously slow for countries caught in an environment of feuding communities. Nevertheless, Europe overcame centuries of warfare between Catholics and Protestants; and Germany and Italy became unified nations.

Likewise, state institutions become strong over many decades. It took nearly a century before the U.S. Congress attempted to levy an income tax. During the American Revolution, the Continental Congress had to beg for revenue because it had no ability to enforce tax levies. The process of state building took time in the developed world. In all probability, this will also be the case for the developing world. Therefore, those attempting to evaluate progress along the three continua of state building, nation building, and economic development require a deep sense of history—of both the developed world and of the country in question. Otherwise, they have no sense of what is feasible within a given timeframe. Overly optimistic timelines lead to the confusion of the incremental steps necessary for progress with a failure to produce rapid success. For instance, to many, the South Korean leadership looked brutal and corrupt from the 1950s through the 1980s, when dictators (often military dictators) were making their many retrospectively wise economic choices.

When Americans were demanding that South Korea move further down the continuum of state building to permit the development of a broader array of democratic institutions, the South Korean leadership chose to focus on advancing further along the continuum of economic development. In Russia, Mikhail Gorbachev chose to focus on state building (political reforms) over economic development, while, in China, Deng Xiaoping chose to make the reverse prioritization.

Gorbachev missed entirely the problem of nation building and lost an empire in the process of making political reforms. Chinese leaders apparently believe that the problem of nation building can be solved by a combination of Han nationalism and coercion of the rest. Although this approach removes the ability of ethnic minorities to rebel, coercion fuels their desire to secede so that incomplete nation building remains a festering problem that periodically erupts into open rebellion. Removal of not just the means but also the will to rebel would require political accommodation (state building) in order to foster nation building. Political reform, however, has stagnated in both China and Russia, as has the Russian economy. Meanwhile, the Chinese economy has taken off.

It is important to recognize that there are three interrelated problems at work—nation building, state building, and economic development. The case studies suggest that a strong state can become a key facilitator for economic development, and that either a weak nation or a weak state is a key "debilitator." There is no linear correlation between a strong sense of nation and economic prosperity: North Korea, Haiti, Egypt, the Dominican Republic, Turkey, and South Korea are listed in order of ascending prosperity, yet all possess a strong sense of nation. Although successful economic development requires an extensive array of strong state institutions, such institutions do not guarantee prosperity. The Communist countries examined had strong states, but none were prosperous.

Nation and state building seem to be prerequisites for economic development because they provide the necessary social stability and institutional framework. Strong nations, by embracing different communities in an overarching nation, avoid civil unrest from a marginalized or persecuted minority and benefit from the contributions of the many not just the privileged few. In anarchic environments, people do whatever they want. No law channels their choices away from destructive directions. Strong state institutions limit people's choices by distinguishing what is legal from what is illegal, and by enforcing prohibitions of the latter. Whether such institutions channel choices in directions conducive to economic growth is yet another issue.

Perhaps nation building and state building conducive to economic development should be conceptualized in terms of their influence on the choices citizens make. While it is important to channel choices in economically constructive directions, it is also important to avoid constraining human creativity, ambition, and drive. It turns out that choices matter—the choices not only of the rich and the powerful, who attempt to dictate, but also those of the poor, who can and do veto the plans of their rulers.

Notes

1. Central Intelligence Agency, "Life Expectancy at Birth," 2008 estimate, *The World Factbook*, https://www.cia.gov/library/publications/the-world-factbook/rankorder/2102rank. html, accessed 14 October 2008.

2. Donald L. Horowitz describes the plight of the minority group in a country split 60–40 between two competing ethnic groups. The minority always loses. Donald L. Horowitz, *Ethnic Groups in Conflict* (Berkeley: University of California Press, 1985), 19, 83–84, 650.

3. Arnold Rivkin, *Nation Building in Africa: Problems and Prospects* (New Brunswick, NJ: Rutgers University Press, 1969), 1–3, 214–15, 222–26. Arnold Rivkin perceived broad differences between British and French colonial methods. He served for nearly fifteen years immediately after World War II in the precursor of the Agency for International Development. Thereafter, he worked for five years at the Center for International Studies at Massachusetts Institute of Technology, followed by six years in the African Department of the World Bank before his untimely death at age forty-nine in 1968 (ibid., vii).

4. Hernando de Soto, *The Other Path: The Economic Answer to Terrorism* (New York: Basic Books, 1989); William J. Baumol et al. also emphasize that constraints on entrepreneurship block economic growth and prosperity. William J. Baumol et al., *Good Capitalism, Bad Capitalism, and the Economics of Growth and Prosperity* (New Haven, CT: Yale University Press, 2007), 131.

5. Central Intelligence Agency, "GDP-Real Growth Rate," 2008, *The World Factbook*, https://www.gia.gov/library/publications/the-world-factbook/rankorder/2103rank.html, accessed 15 October 2008.

6. The phrase "politics of plunder" comes from V.S. Naipaul, the winner of the 2001 Nobel Prize in Literature, and is cited in Lawrence E. Harrison, *Underdevelopment Is a State of Mind: The Latin American Case*, rev. ed. (Lanham, MD: Madison Books, 2000), 117.

7. Samuel P. Huntington, *Political Order in Changing Societies* (New Haven, CT: Yale University Press, 1968), 337–40.

8. François Bourricaud, the French intellectual, labeled dependency theory as an ideology in 1982. Andre Gunter Frank, the most famous proponent of dependency theory, described his

theories in his monograph, *Capitalism and Underdevelopment in Latin America* (New York: Monthly Review Press, 1967). See Harrison, *Underdevelopment Is a State of Mind*, 113.

9. Harrison, *Underdevelopment Is a State of Mind*, xvi, 128–29.

10. Jared Diamond, *Collapse: How Societies Choose to Fail or Succeed* (New York: Viking, 2005), 329–32.

11. Tanisha M. Fazal, *State Death: The Politics and Geography of Conquest, Occupation, and Annexation* (Princeton, NJ: Princeton University Press, 2007).

12. Central Intelligence Agency, "Life Expectancy at Birth," 2008 estimate, *The World Factbook,* https://www.cia.org/library/publications/the-world-factbook/rankorder/2102.rank.html, accessed 15 October 2008.

13. UNESCO, *World Literacy at Mid-Century* (Paris: UNESCO, 1957), 40. UNESCO made this estimate in 1950.

14. Gabriel Tortella and Lars Sandberg, "Education and Economic Development Since the Industrial Revolution: A Summary Report" in *Education and Economic Development since the Industrial Revolution,* ed. Gabriel Tortella (Valencia: Generalitat Valencia, 1990), 5; Boris N. Mironov, "The Effect of Education on Economic Growth: The Russian Variant, 19th–20th Centuries" in ibid., 121; Clara-Eugenia Núñez, "Literacy and Economic Growth in Spain, 1860–1977" in ibid., 133, 135. Núñez argues for a lag of thirty-five years and emphasizes the importance of closing the gap between male and female literacy rates.

15. Daron Acemoglu et al., "Reversal of Fortune: Geography and Institutions in the Making of the Modern World Income Distribution," National Bureau of Research Working Paper 8460, 2001, http://www.nber.org/papers/w8460.

About the Contributors

Kay Adamson is a lecturer in sociology at Glasgow Caledonian University whose research focuses on the different interconnections between Algeria and France concerning French colonial policies in Algeria. She is the author of *Political and Economic Thought and Practice in Nineteenth-century France and the Colonization of Algeria* (Edwin Mellen Press, 2002) and *Algeria: A Study in Competing Ideologies* (Cassell, now Continuum, 1998).

Mbow Amphas-Mampoua, is an associate professor of political science and international relations at the American University in London. He is the author of *Political Transformations of the Congo* (Pentland Press, 2000) and *The United States, Russia, and European Security* (Dorrance Publishing, 2004). He served as a political and economic adviser to the ambassador from the Republic of the Congo at the embassy in Washington, D.C.

Charles Armstrong, associate professor of history at Columbia University, is the author of *The North Korean Revolution, 1945–1950* (Cornell University Press, 2002) and *The Koreas* (Routledge, 2007), and editor of *Korean Society: Civil Society, Democracy and the State* (Routledge, 2nd ed., 2006). He is currently working on a history of North Korean foreign relations since the Korean War.

James F. Barnes is a professor of political science at Appalachian State University. He is the author of *Gabon: Beyond the Colonial Legacy* (Westview Press, 1992) and coeditor of *Culture, Politics, and Ecology in the Gabonese Rainforest* (Edwin Mellen Press, 2003).

Kirk J. Beattie is a professor of political science and international relations at Simmons College. He is the author of *Egypt during the Nasser Years: Ideology, Politics, and Civil Society* (Westview Press, 1994) and *Egypt during the Sadat Years* (Palgrave, 2000). He is currently working on a book about U.S. congressional policy making on the Arab-Israeli conflict.

313

Amy Blitz holds a doctorate from the Massachusetts Institute of Technology. Her book *The Contested State: American Foreign Policy and Regime Change in the Philippines* (Rowman & Littlefield, 2000) is based on Tagalog, Spanish, and English sources. She now focuses on economic growth issues from the private sector.

Robert Cribb is senior fellow at the Research School of Pacific and Asian Studies at the Australian National University. His extensive publications include *Historical Atlas of Indonesia* (Curzon, 2000); *Modern Indonesia: A History since 1945*, co-authored with Colin Brown (Longman, 1995); and *Gangsters and Revolutionaries: The Jakarta People's Militia and the Indonesian Revolution, 1945–1949* (Allen and Unwin, 1991).

Philippe Girard, an associate professor at McNeese University, specializes in Haitian history. He has published *Clinton in Haiti: The 1994 U.S. Invasion of Haiti* (Palgrave, 2004); *Paradise Lost: Haiti's Tumultuous Journey from Pearl of the Caribbean to Third World Hot Spot* (Palgrave, 2005); and is currently working on a book on the Haitian revolution.

Kim Hyung-A is an associate professor of politics and director of the Australia-Korea Leadership Forum at the Research School of Pacific and Asian Studies, Australian National University. She is the author of *Korea's Development under Park Chung Hee: Rapid Industrialization, 1961–79* (RoutledgeCurzon, 2004) and coeditor of *Reassessing the Park Chung Hee Era* (University of Washington Press, forthcoming).

Alexander Lyon Macfie has written widely on the Straits Question, the Eastern Question, the modern history of the Middle East, and other related subjects. His publications include *The Eastern Question*, 2nd ed. (1996), *The Straits Question* (1993), *Atatürk* (1994), *The End of the Ottoman Empire* (1998), *Orientalism: A Reader* (2000), *Orientalism* (2002), *Eastern Influences on Western Philosophy* (2003), and *The Philosophy of History* (2006).

Gregory Mahler is professor of politics and academic dean at Earlham College in Richmond, Indiana. He has written extensively about Israeli and Palestinian politics, and is the author of a long-published comparative politics textbook. Among his most recent publications is *Politics and Government in Israel: The Maturation of a Modern State* (Rowman and Littlefield, 2004).

Martin McCauley, senior lecturer at the University of London and member of Limehouse Group of Analysts, has written over twenty books on Russia and has edited numerous additional volumes. His publications focus on the emergence of the modern Russian state, leadership and succession, the Russian Revolution, Stalinism, Khrushchev, Gorbachev, the Cold War, and East Germany.

Frank Moya Pons, former research director of the City University of New York Dominican Studies Institute, is a well-known columnist and scholar in his home country. His many publications include *The Dominican Republic: A National History* (Markus Wiener, 1998) and *History of the Caribbean: Plantations, Trade and War in the Atlantic World* (Markus Wiener, 2007).

Hank Nelson, professor emeritus, Australian National University, is an expert on Papua New Guinea. First involved with that country when he taught at the University of Papua New Guinea, he has written extensively on both Papua New Guinea and Australia. His publications focus on political history, race relations, and gold mining.

S.C.M. Paine, professor of strategy and policy at the U.S. Naval War College and editor of the present work, is an expert on the relations among Japan, China, and Russia. Other publications include *Imperial Rivals: China, Russia, and Their Disputed Frontier, 1858–1924* (M.E. Sharpe, 1996) and *The Sino-Japanese War of 1894–1895: Perceptions, Power, and Primacy* (Cambridge University Press, 2003).

Philip Robins is a reader in politics, Department of Politics and International Relations at the University of Oxford; fellow of St. Antony's College; and founding head of the Middle East Programme at Chatham House. He is the author of *A History of Jordan* (Cambridge University Press, 2004) as well as numerous other publications on the Middle East.

Dietmar Rothermund is a professor emeritus at the University of Heidelberg. He has published extensively on India, including books on India and the Soviet Union, Indian agrarian relations under British rule, Indian economic history, and a biography of Mahatma Gandhi. His recent publications include *The Routledge Companion to Decolonization* (Routledge, 2006) and *India: The Rise of an Asian Giant* (Yale University Press, 2008).

Warren Sun is a senior lecturer in the Chinese Studies Program at Monash University in Australia. He has published extensively on China, including *The End of the Maoist Era: Chinese Politics during the Twilight of the Cultural Revolution, 1972–1976* (M.E. Sharpe, 2007); *China's Road to Disaster* (M.E. Sharpe, 1999); *The Tragedy of Lin Biao* (Hurst, 1996); and *The Formation of the Maoist Leadership* (Contemporary China Institute, 1994), all co-authored with Fred Teiwes.

Index